W9-BKU-929

Lydia's Impatient Sisters

ALSO BY LUISE SCHOTTROFF
from Westminster John Knox Press

Let the Oppressed Go Free:
Feminist Perspectives on the New Testament
(Gender and the Biblical Tradition)

Lydia's
Impatient Sisters

A Feminist Social History of Early Christianity

LUISE SCHOTTROFF

translated by
Barbara and Martin Rumscheidt

WESTMINSTER JOHN KNOX PRESS
Louisville, Kentucky

Book design by Publishers' WorkGroup
Cover design by Kim Wohlenhaus
Cover illustration: Massacre of the Innocents (*detail*).
Giotto di Bondone. Courtesy of Superstock.

First edition

Published by Westminster John Knox Press
Louisville, Kentucky

This book is printed on acid-free paper that meets the American National Standards Institute Z39.48 standard. ∞

PRINTED IN THE UNITED STATES OF AMERICA

95 96 97 98 99 00 01 02 03 04 — 10 9 8 7 6 5 4 3 2 1

Library of Congress Cataloging-in-Publication Data

Schottroff, Luise.
  [Lydias ungeduldige Schwestern. English]
  Lydia's impatient sisters : a feminist social history of early Christianity / Luise Schottroff. — 1st ed.
      p.   cm.
  Includes bibliographical references.
  ISBN 0-664-22072-X (alk. paper)
  1. Women in Christianity—History—Early church, ca. 30–600. 2. Feminist theology. I. Title.
  BR195.W6S3613 1995
  270.1'082—dc20   95-20339

Contents

II. The Everyday Life of Women

III. The Critique of Patriarchy
and the Power to Become a New Being

IV. Liberating Praxis of Women and Men

Foreword

As Luise Schottroff notes, "enthusiasm for the life-giving power of the Bible" is pretty rare among us, and yet it might be "the most important school for justice." Few scientific books by New Testament scholars are able to spark the enthusiasm created by this book by Luise Schottroff on women in early Christianity.

It is not so easy for me to describe a close friend objectively. Let me begin with a personal reminiscence. Our growing into a feminist theology of liberation has been a long-shared process. Toward the end of the sixties, our thinking on critical issues affecting women began to get us in trouble with the established system of academic theology in the German universities. The deep respect we had held for the great theological teachers started to crumble, and we began to look for new theological methods and a renewed hermeneutics.

About that time, acceptance of the program to combat racism proposed by the World Council of Churches was being discussed by the faculty of the University of Mainz. The male colleagues refused to take this stance against racism. Luise was astounded. When she told me about it, we began to ask ourselves: What exactly do the majority of the Mainz professors think the Bible means? In opposition to them, we could not understand the argument that the money that should be given by the German Protestant church in support of the black liberation movement did not have anything to do with our reading and understanding of the Bible and our political practice. Was it the same Bible that we non-established women and the male university colleagues were reading?

It was in the midst of this conflicted context that Luise Schottroff began to develop what came to be called a "social-historical interpretation of the Bible." *Lydia's Impatient Sisters* marks a new step in both the methodology and the content, but its course was set at this earlier time, before we fully understood words like "liberation theology" and "feminism."

What did it mean for a woman to become Christian in the early days of Christianity? What changes did she go through in her relationships? in her experience of oppression? in her perspective on the future? *Lydia's Impatient Sisters* clearly demonstrates how women decisively shaped the first Christian communities. Christianity replaced the oppressive patriarchal power over women, men, children, and slaves with a struggle for liberation and the building of just relationships within Christian communities. There were setbacks too, but the Jewish tradition of God's creative power, as testified to in the scriptures and proclaimed by Jesus, proved to be a liberating force stronger than the patriarchal powers. Hope for the kingdom of God inspired women and men to translate the Jewish vision of justice into their lives.

In *Lydia's Impatient Sisters,* Luise Schottroff develops a social history of the everyday life of women and relates this history to the central theological topics of the New Testament, such as the revelation of God, the daily life of the church, and eschatology. Schottroff sets common experiences of labor, money, illness, and resistance in the context of the Roman imperial society. After some decades of feminist biblical research, it is now well known that women too exercised leadership roles in early Christianity. But Schottroff's work demonstrates for the first time how these women were embedded in their social world. We can see how they submitted to ancient legal norms and to the economic systems of the Roman Empire.

Schottroff's various descriptions of women's work and income are based on precise research. Reading her contribution gives us a renewed perspective on the New Testament. I did not know, for example, that there were bakeries in antiquity where people could buy bread. I have never asked myself before how the disciples got bread to feed the crowd. Is there any commentary that tells us what a male day laborer who worked for a farmer earned in comparison to the income of a female day laborer?

Let me give another example. Because she is so concerned with the practicalities of everyday life, Schottroff provides a novel interpretation of the parable in which a woman kneads yeast into some bread dough. Schottroff is motivated not only by her interest in real life but even more strongly by her commitment to approach the Bible by way of liberation theology. In her method, we approach the Bible through our own lives. The hands of an average woman kneading dough become a lens through which we see God's work. Traditional theories of parables neglect the everyday images in favor of a theological (and often dogmatically defined) assumption, but Schottroff corrects this. From this point, we can take the second step: we can move from our understanding of the Bible to our own lives. In other words, we can take our biblical knowledge and understand the experiences of today's women who struggle for justice and a different order of world economics, for peace and nonviolent resolution of conflicts, and for the integrity of creation and the conservation of our mother, the earth.

Schottroff makes two more contributions to New Testament scholarship. Her concept of eschatology is another point of difference between her work in this book and traditional interpretations of the New Testament. Leaving the traditional schema of expectation and delay of parousia, Schottroff approaches the traditions of the kingdom of God from a perspective of existentialism and liberation theology. Finally, I'd like to point out Schottroff's renewed understanding of the Jesus movement as a Jewish liberation movement within the Roman Empire. This understanding reveals the multiple anti-Jewish ideologies that have distorted our understanding of New Testament traditions from the beginning of Christianity.

Schottroff's book is not just for theologians and New Testament scholars, however. *Lydia's Impatient Sisters* addresses all laypersons who strive to practice Christian faith today.

DOROTHEE SOELLE

Preface to the
Westminster John Knox Press Edition

Every time I visit North America and am part of discussions among feminist Christian women and feminist women scholars, I am filled with envy of and admiration for the wealth of discourse and relationships. As far as feminist discussion is concerned, the German academic landscape is still in the grip of the stone age of patriarchy. However much we are beset by institutional difficulties, we do exist: German-speaking feminist women exegetes, theologians, Christians. As one voice in our choir, I offer this book and ask that it be received. It shows, among other things, how much we seek to link the German-speaking and the North American discourses.

I owe gratitude to many North American women and men friends who have supported my work for many years. I would like to name some as representatives of them all: Angela Bauer, Bernadette Brooten, Elisabeth Schüssler Fiorenza, William Klassen, Linda Maloney, James M. Robinson, Barbara and Martin Rumscheidt, Fernando Segovia, Cynthia Thompson.

I particularly thank Cynthia Thompson and Stephanie Egnotovich for their competent and engaged attention. I thank Angela Bauer particularly for her support and counsel in relation to questions of feminist-theological terminology in this book; and I thank Barbara and Martin Rumscheidt very much for the great effort of translating this book.

Parts of this book were delivered at Atlantic School of Theology in Halifax, Nova Scotia, as part of the Pollok Lectures of 1991, during which students and colleagues engaged me in inspiring discussions. To all of them, too, I am grateful.

Preface

I write this book at a time in which daily life includes news of earth-threatening catastrophes caused by human beings: wars, sexual assaults, ocean-polluting oil tanker disasters, holes in the ozone layer. Whether human beings will succeed in developing effective measures against the greed of elites for power and money I do not know; nobody knows. And those who do not close their eyes must be afraid.

I perceive in the women's movement, and in the ecological movement widely associated with it, an attempt to labor for peace and justice as an exercise of power from below against the destructive greed of the elites. In the women's movement, as well as in other, related movements, habits of living develop that seek to avoid the destruction of God's creation. One tries to conserve energy and water, to establish just relations with one another, relations that will end the patriarchal subjection of the majority under the power of the rule of men (and a few women). We want to build islands of justice, many little Women-Churches. In Women-Churches, the women and men who meet together have a taste for liberation: liberation from the patriarchal system of coercion that decrees what a woman and a man must be; liberation from the patriarchal system of coercion that constrains human beings to damage creation, for example, just because it is not deemed possible to get children to a medical facility without a car. I know the taste of liberation. It is a liberation that is projected before our very eyes. I call it also the reign of God.

For me, the most important school of justice I know is the biblical tradition. In saying so I do not wish to diminish the value of other traditions of justice, — for example, those of other religions. But in the society and history in which I live, the biblical tradition is a unique treasure. I write this book hoping to enable other women and men to access this treasure more easily. In the course of the years, I have often experienced resignation. Where is strength to be found just to withstand the violent destruction of the earth? Where shall I find the capacity to go against the structural injustice of sexism, racism, economic exploitation, the greed for money and power? I have experienced truly profound blessedness in women's and peace liturgies, when the word of the Bible has begun to speak even before we have to interpret it. It has given us the blessing of experiencing our community and of discerning clear goals, precisely because the injustice has been named. The word of God has transformed people frozen with fear into energetic, attentive, and impatient sisters and brothers.

The impatience of women and men who, today and tomorrow, do not let themselves be driven into resignation by despair and fear will be reinforced by the impatience of Lydia's sisters. Our impatient foresisters have raised up their heads because they have felt the power of God to be near.

I write this book in full accordance with scholarly requirements but also with the intent that it may be used by women and men not versed in academic discipline or who are just beginning their studies. Let me say at the outset that what I mean by scholarship is not what is meant by this term in dominant circles of academic theology. In what follows, I discuss questions of my method and purpose.

I owe gratitude to women without whose voices I would have been left speechless concerning numerous New Testament inspirations; as a representative for many such women I name Christine Schaumberger. I thank Ute Ochtendung, Ruth Habermann, Sigrun Tegtmeier, and Claudia Janssen, who helped me in the preparation and correction of the manuscript. I dedicate this book to the women and men friends who accompany me in the dark valley of illness and on the sun-drenched heights of enthusiasm for the life-giving power of the Bible: Eva Röger, Willy Schottroff, Dorothee Soelle.

I

FEMINIST SOCIAL HISTORY:
HISTORICAL METHOD
AND HERMENEUTICS

1

The Jesus Movement and
Messianic Communities in the
Jewish Diaspora of the First Century C.E.

PRELIMINARY REMARKS

In this initial chapter, I begin with the theoretical position from and with which I approach the history of early Christianity. I shall then examine which structures of oppression are to be assumed in my context and in that of early Christianity. In other words, I shall address basic questions of an analysis of patriarchy. Third, I shall engage the text of the New Testament, and since the New Testament is written throughout in an androcentric language, I must explain in what sense it is the word of God for me. It is indeed the word of God for me, but not in every individual text. It is in this theological context that I discuss the question of historical method. In the final section, I ask about dialogue between the biblical tradition and the women and men of today who hunger for justice.

A. THE JESUS MOVEMENT: A RENEWAL MOVEMENT
WITHIN JUDAISM OR A JEWISH LIBERATION MOVEMENT
WITHIN THE PAX ROMANA?

The Sociological Thesis of Theissen and the "New Consensus"
in Social History of Early Christianity

In 1973, Gerd Theissen published an article titled "The Wandering Radicals,"[1] the central assertions of which prevailed triumphantly in the theological scholarship of the West and still do so today. The crux of his proposal is the distinction between Palestinian itinerant radicalism (the Jesus movement) and early Christian love patriarchalism (Hellenistic urban communities). Behind this thesis is the sociological conception of the distinction between sect and church as institution. The basic sociological assumptions of his proposal have since shaped how early Christianity's social history is discussed in the Western world and in Germany—to the extent that such discussion even exists there.

3

In assessing the triumphant march of these ideas, it matters little whether all material parallels to those assertions were in fact deduced directly from Theissen's publications, or whether a particular social interest of the so-called first world, of the Christian circles that participate in the power of that world, expresses itself in those assertions. Similarly, for the assessment of the success of that perspective on early Christianity, it does not really matter which scholarly traditions Theissen relies on or whom he calls on as his precursors.[2] In 1983, Wayne Meeks spoke with justification of a "new consensus" in this discussion.[3] At the heart of this new consensus he identifies the assumption that Christianity was not a movement "from below" but that it provided a representative cross-section of the population with sufficient social space for the successful spread of Christianity to proceed in a triumphant march "from the top down."[4] The gaze of the interpreters (few of whom are women) is fixed on those who belonged to the upper class or the (higher and lower) middle class and on the role they played in shaping the ways of Christianity. In society, and so in the church, the "poor," the "lowly," either are outsiders or submit to the rich. This was the only way Christianity could survive: "It is Christian love patriarchalism to which we owe the surviving institutions of the church."[5] The thesis of the distinction between itinerant radicalism and love patriarchalism is, among other things, a variation of the late nineteenth-century discussion about the difference between charisma and office.[6]

Theissen's own view of the itinerant radicals as those who "see the world . . . [in the] perspective 'from below' "[7] gets in the way of this consensus only superficially, for according to him itinerant radicals are merely a marginal feature of early Christianity; they remain sectlike, at the fringes of the institutionalized church.[8] They live in voluntary poverty, renouncing home and family; they practice an ethos to which normal people cannot attain:

> The ethical radicalism of the sayings transmitted to us [that is, of the Gospels] is the radicalism of itinerants. It can be practiced and handed on only under extreme living conditions. It is only the persons who have severed their everyday ties with the world—the persons who have left home and possessions, wife and child . . . — who can consistently preach renunciation of a settled home, a family, possessions, the protection of the law, and their own defense.[9]

In such an image of Christianity, these sympathetic and believable itinerant young, radical men enter into discipleship as solitary individuals (e.g., as nuns or monks). To this day, Christians who hold power in the state assert that it is such individuals alone who can live out the peace message of the Sermon on the Mount, whereas normal people are not envisaged in that text.[10]

The age-old splitting of Christian ethics into one for normal human beings and one for a few marginal figures, such as peace-loving nuns or noble, itinerant radicals, blunts the question: What must I do to inherit eternal life? It is this question that the New Testament never fails to raise acutely. According to Theissen and many of his precursors and associates, there are, in principle, two answers: either live as an outsider, sectlike but according to Jesus, or live in the manner of the great tradition (the state or territorial church), essentially in conformity with a hierarchical society and its injustice, violence, and wars. The Jesus-oriented outsiders are the salt in the Christian soup; they call people to repentance.[11]

This new and yet old social-historical theory of early Christianity took shape in the context of the aftereffects of the 1968 student movement in the Western world. The theory reflects a process of radicals moving from margin to mainstream within the patriarchal institutions of the church, university, and society. At the same time, this model of Jesus offers the possibility of distancing oneself nonviolently from the violent leftists of the Federal Republic of Germany[12] and the orthodox Marxist Communists. In Germany at that time, it certainly took some courage to introduce a sociological question at all into established theological scholarship. Subsequent to his initial publications, Theissen responded to charges that had clearly been laid as a result of that action:

> A good deal more could be said, for example, on the consequences of a sociology of the Jesus movement for the quest of the historical Jesus, for christology, ethics, church practice. I hope some time to be able to present my thoughts on fundamental theological questions elsewhere. I must therefore limit myself to a few remarks which I wish were unnecessary. (1) Anyone who thinks that a sociology of the Jesus movement is a rewarding undertaking is not therefore aspiring to a theology of social structures or a sociological theology or a theological sociology or anything of that kind. (2) Anyone who learns from Marxism and finds it stimulating as a result to apply theories of conflicts in society to the interpretation of social and religious processes is not necessarily a Marxist. Remember Ralf Dahrendorf! (3) Anyone who writes about the radicalism of the early Christian wandering charismatics and finds it difficult to deny his sympathies for them is still some way from being a radical.[13]

The word *radical* has undergone a rapid change in meaning in recent years. In 1958, Herbert Braun compiled his research on the Jesus tradition under the title *Late Jewish Heretical and Early Christian Radicalism*. For him, radicalism meant the attenuation of the love for the neighbor into the love of enemy "in an unheard of manner."[14] Because of the social persecution as "radicals" of anarchistic and orthodox leftists in the Federal Republic of Germany after 1970, the word has limited usage, even when it is distinguished from its use by contemporary radicals.

Gerd Theissen's narrative study of Jesus (1986; ET 1987), which, for a theological work, enjoys uncommonly high sales and international dissemination, is based on the same sociological position as his article of 1973, even though he takes account of the critique of Christian anti-Judaism differently than in that earlier study.[15] The coexistence of sect and ecclesiastical institution is of marginal interest because the focus of attention is Jesus and not Christian communities.[16] For this reason, readers of the book who are unfamiliar with its theoretical groundwork will scarcely detect that to follow Jesus, as the book speaks of it, is understood to be an "experiment," an option taken by merely a few persons. Besides this experiment of discipleship, other Christians in society pursue another kind of political activity, acknowledging nonetheless that the "experiment of radical discipleship" remains an option.[17] "Political action cannot use the Sermon on the Mount directly as a criterion."[18] This statement mirrors the debate in Germany concerning the decision of NATO to produce and deploy medium-range nuclear missiles. Christians in the peace movement argued that day-to-day political decisions could not be based on the Sermon on the Mount but that *shalom* for all, as the clear goal of specific actions, could be deduced from it. Christians who supported the decision of NATO argued as Theissen did in the statement just cited.[19]

It is not that Theissen's book on Jesus is situated in an actual discussion that I critique; it is that the paradigm of Christian discipleship as outsider is not stated more explicitly. As a consequence of this lack of clarity, a misunderstanding may arise for readers of the book as it stands.

Gerd Theissen's Historical Analysis of the Social Background of the Jesus Movement

In an article published in 1977, Theissen presented historically his thesis about itinerant radicalism.[20] In his view, Jewish society in Palestine as a whole was in crisis. This was because, under Herod's reign, property was concentrated in the hands of a few wealthy people. Growing progressively poorer, the middle and lower classes defended themselves in the "anomic" actions of "internal Jewish revival movements":[21] the Pharisaic movement, the community of Qumran, the political resistance movement, prophetic movements, and the Jesus movement. These movements have several features in common and others that are profoundly different. The Roman Empire and, since Augustus, the Pax Romana encompassed the conditions of Herodian time. Yet Theissen refers to these factors only in relation to the resistance movements[22] or as a marginal matter.[23] All of these movements failed, except the Pharisaic one. The Jesus movement failed and gained success only outside Palestine and after it had become transformed.[24]

In the Jesus book of 1986, Pax Romana is depicted as a beast. Andreas, the first-person narrator, is a wealthy young merchant from Sepphoris in Galilee who seeks to assume an innocent stance between the Romans and the violent Jewish resistance against them.[25] He does not succeed and is found guilty.[26] His "sorrow"[27] is transformed as a result of the vision of Jesus. Whether he becomes a follower of Jesus is left unresolved.[28]

This image of Jesus contains individual elements reminiscent of aspects of liberation theology: Jesus as the hope of the poor; healing as the empowering of the lowly; Pax Romana as an oppressive beast.[29] The allusions to liberation theology discussion are drawn primarily from the book by Luise Schottroff and

Wolfgang Stegemann (1978),[30] which is not listed, however, in the index of scholarly literature.[31] The most significant change in terms of a liberation-theology social analysis of the time of Jesus is the negative depiction of Pax Romana as a system of exploitation, which plays either no role at all or a merely marginal one in Theissen's older social-historical studies. Such a depiction of Pax Romana represents an exception in the so-called first world; it is found above all in the work of Luise Schottroff and Klaus Wengst.[32] By depicting Jesus as being rigorously against the Zealots, Theissen firmly blocks any connection between the Jesus movement and liberation movements in the sense of those of today's two-thirds world. The "perspective from below" is claimed by Theissen for his own position.[33] He takes seriously the economic and political oppression and the poverty of the Jewish people at the time of Jesus. But since the ramifications for the rich and the poor at the level of praxis are left hanging in balance, the "perspective from below" also remains similarly suspended, and this is intentional.

Liberation Theology and Feminist Critique of Theissen's Position

While dominant theological scholarship criticized Theissen's proposal only in relation to certain details,[34] its very foundations were subject to the critique of liberation and feminist theologians. However, this critique has not resulted in a discussion between the representatives of dominant New Testament social history and their critics. Even the relatively broad reception of Elisabeth Schüssler Fiorenza on the part of many who represent dominant theological scholarship in North America, and also in Germany, has not made known her fundamental critique of Theissen's position.

In 1978, I tried to show that the "itinerant radicalism" of the Jesus movement is to be explained in terms of the actual poverty of the majority of the Jewish population and not in terms of the "renunciation of possessions." For me, this poverty resulted from the economic exploitation of the Jewish people by Rome. The renunciation of possessions on the part of the women and men of Cynic philosophy is not at all an analogy to the Jesus movement, in my view.[35] Nor do I think it appropriate to speak of an "ethos" when it is the liberation struggles of oppressed women and men that are at issue. The word *ethos* is misleading in this context if no distinction is made between the voluntary renunciation of possessions as the ethos of affluent people and the poverty of the poor as an ethos of resistance. The praxis of the Jesus movement is oriented by the encompassing goal of God's reign seeking to reach the whole population; it precisely seeks not to remain the unique ethos of an outsider group. At issue is not the asceticism of individual persons but the conversion of the people. The people and the Jesus movement belong together.

These theses emerged from the critical recognition that the Jesus movement has been portrayed in Western Christian theology from the perspective of a white middle class that participates in the power of the state and which distances the awareness of this from the causal connection between the affluence of the Western world and the poverty of the two-thirds world. What became clear to me was that the New Testament was better understood by the peasants of Solentiname[36] than by the women and men in the first world's biblical scholarship; the peasants of Solentiname lived in a political and economic situation comparable to that of the Jesus movement, and the Gospels would become for them the spiritual bread of life. For Christian women and men of the Western world, the Jesus tradition is the invitation to conversion: the conversion of the rich or the conversion of the poor in a rich land. That alone is how the gospel becomes spiritual bread of life for them.

The historical aspects of my critique of Theissen's position were developed by Wolfgang Stegemann in an article published in 1979.[37] Elisabeth Schüssler Fiorenza has taken up my critique[38] and deepened it by the important addition that Theissen actually takes the Jesus movement to be a men's movement.[39] Her critique is fundamental in relation to the concept of love patriarchalism, which legitimates Christian patriarchalism as something necessary to the survival of Christianity.[40] I would add that Theissen's concept legitimates not only Christian patriarchalism but also the social status quo and its structures of oppression as they relate to the interpreters of the Bible.[41] The difference that Theissen assumes between Christian *love* patriarchalism and *social* patriarchalism is an illusion. Patriarchal rulers, be they women or men, have always claimed to be acting from love and concern for those over whom they rule.[42]

Elisabeth Schüssler Fiorenza adopts Theissen's view that the Jesus movement is to be understood as a renewal movement within Judaism, even though her interest in this concept differs from that of Theissen. She finds the concept suitable to demonstrate that Jesus and his followers were Jewish men and women and that they could take up traditions of liberation from within Judaism.[43] Even though I share this interest, I find the concept "renewal movement" unsuitable because it may suggest that the Jesus movement sought to overcome false and abusive situations within Judaism rather than have at heart the suffering of the Jewish people, which Rome caused by its political and economic oppression. In addition, Elisabeth Schüssler Fiorenza's interpretation of the Jesus movement as a "renewal movement within Judaism" goes with her acceptance of the basic sociological model of the sect[44] and the church as (patriarchal) institution, however much her assessment of the patriarchal institution differs from that of Theissen, Ernst Troeltsch, and the North American representatives of this model. That is why she speaks of "the disinherited and the marginal" in her chapter on feminist historical reconstruction of early Christian origins, that is, she works with concepts that, to say the least, are misleading and do not make plain that the social and political point of departure of Jewish liberation movements was the suffering of the majority of the people.

I see an important point of contact with Elisabeth Schüssler Fiorenza, in contrast to Theissen, in her more differentiated understanding of the extra-Palestinian church. She distinguishes between the Spirit-led early Christian missionary movement—the *ekklēsia* of women—and the patriarchal church.[45] I fully concur with her critique of the historical justification of Christian love patriarchalism.[46] This critique implies the further critique of the theological discussion of the necessary difference between charisma and office. An understanding of office that separates office and charisma, is, as such, hostile to women and justifies a hierarchical institution.[47]

The Jesus Movement as a Jewish Liberation Movement within Pax Romana

The theoretical foundation of my view of early Christianity is, therefore, the distinction between liberation movements and the social oppression of peoples on the part of patriarchal governments and the social strata who profit from such oppression. There is no difference in principle for me between the Jesus movement as a liberation movement within Pax Romana and the early Christian communities outside Palestine. I regard them also as Jewish messianic groups or as messianic groups related to the Jewish religion. To me, the distinction between Jewish Christianity and Gentile Christianity is inappropriate. I understand the Christian communities outside Palestine up to the early second century to be groups within the Jewish diaspora who are either Christian Jews or who have voluntarily embraced Jewish practice. (See below.)

The multiplicity of historical manifestations of liberation movements and oppressive state systems of domination makes it necessary to find out what these structural concepts mean, and to do this in every instance by examining the relevant historical material. With this in mind, I look for the concrete form of oppression and for the praxis of resistance. I search for the organizational forms of liberation work and regard Christian communities, for example (or the Jesus movement), as cooperating subjects of liberation praxis. I inquire about visions and utopias that determine the praxis of liberation. For that reason, both the *ekklēsia,* which for me is the acting community, and the reign of God, that is, eschatology, are essential for my theoretical position.

The social-historical study of early Christian texts may derive its source material from all regions of the Roman Empire. Archaeological findings above all show that Rome's unitary culture quickly pervaded every province under Roman rule, including Palestine.[48] One may therefore, on the one hand, set out from a structural homogeneity of life in the empire and, on the other, inquire in each individual case about the concrete forms, for example, of the praxis of resistance.

The liberation-movement concept is to be applied to the Jesus movement as it is to the manifold other base movements of the Jewish people of the first century: the diverse messianic/apocalyptic movements (such as the one around John the Baptist) and the unarmed or armed prophetic resistance movements.[49] I have found phenomena comparable to this central aspect of first-century C.E. Jewish history in the history of modern religious-political liberation movements, especially in Latin America but also in North America and Europe; what I have not found is a corresponding sociological theory of which to make use.

This Jewish liberation movement that followed Jesus had itinerant female and male prophets (such as Jesus himself) and, presumably right from the beginning, also had "households"[50] who embraced the message of Jesus. How I define the relation of *itinerant female and male prophets, households* or house communities, and *people* and what theological meaning I assign to them are crucially important for the concept of early Christianity. I would like to set another model over against that of sect (the community of itinerant female and male prophets) versus the institution (church) or of the marginalized (itinerant female and male prophets) versus society. My alternate model is that of the liberation movement which is oriented toward the welfare of the whole people; it includes itinerant female and male prophets as well as residential households. Itinerancy may have something to do with the content of the message, but in addition, or simultaneously, it may also have social reasons.[51] The itinerancy of Jesus' group in Galilee is based *also* on the fact that the economic outlook of Galilean villagers at that time looked most bleak.[52]

Of decisive importance for this model is that the praxis of the women and men who followed Jesus (whether itinerant female and male prophets or persons with fixed residence) was not an expression of an elitist special ethics but a work for the future of the people, of the whole creation. The vision discernible in this praxis is that of God's reign "in heaven and on earth" (cf. only Matt. 6:10; 11:25 and par.; 28:18; and Mark 13:27). The praxis and preaching of the women and men who followed Jesus (itinerant or settled) are critical toward patriarchal structures of domination on all levels and are marked by the struggles within those structures. As the Gospels in particular indicate, the central issues are illness, hunger, indebtedness, social exclusion, and (political) violence. In these women and men's praxis and theory (i.e., theology), their analysis of internal social violence among the Jewish people and of violence directed against them (on the part of Rome and those who represent its interests) becomes apparent. In light of this view, one may read the Magnificat, the Beatitudes, or Jesus' "inaugural sermon" in Nazareth (Luke 4:18–21) as a manifesto of this liberation movement. In Luke 1:48, the oppression particular to women and children is named in the language of structural analysis.[53] In the rest of the New Testament, it is named in the language used to describe everyday practice.

It is difficult, historically as well as theologically, to distinguish between the Jesus movement of his lifetime and that following his death, that is, after the resurrection had begun to be preached. It is difficult historically because the Gospels do not make such a distinction and because they view these two historical periods together. It is difficult theologically because praxis and preaching did not change *fundamentally* as a result of the proclamation of the resurrection of the crucified Jesus. The nearness of God (i.e., eschatology) gave shape to the hope and actions of Jesus as it did to the communities, for example, of Paul's time.[54] The understanding of the Messiah changed: the Messiah Jesus who had to suffer became the Messiah who was crucified. The interest in Easter as a firmly fixed date of church history cannot be established from the texts. First Corinthians 15:3–8 is about the appearances of the risen One through which the messengers of God, women and men, are sent on their way anew (as in Rom. 1:3–4, next to 1:5). Those appearances of the risen One are not to be restricted to a specific period of time. The impression that they are time-specific arises only when the church-year sequence (crucifixion, Easter, Ascension, Pentecost) is introduced into one's reflection on the text. The risen One's appearance to Paul, of which Paul speaks and the book of Acts writes and about which we have the most information, does not fit into such a schematization of early Christian history. A schematization associated with a unique significance of the *time* of the resurrection or the beginning of the preaching of the resurrection derives from thinking of church history in terms of epochs of time,[55] which is alien to the New Testament itself.

In the Jesus movement as a movement of liberation, there were at the center women with remarkable independence from patriarchal family relationships and with remarkable autonomy. Mary Magdalene may serve as a representative of this central aspect of early Christian history and demonstrate this historical fact. But the search for the history of women in early Christianity, and for a new perspective on that history, must not restrict itself to these extraordinary features but must put the ordinary ones on center stage: women's day-to-day life, their work, their economic circumstances, and how they functioned within the structures of patriarchy. Feminist liberation historiography makes central the question of women "at the bottom of the barrel,"[56] because without it all historiography remains far from the truth. With this focus, feminist liberation historiography pursues a way of looking that is at the heart of the Jesus tradition itself: it looks at the "last."[57]

B. CHRISTIANITY OF GENTILE WOMEN AND MEN, OR MESSIANIC COMMUNITIES IN THE JEWISH DIASPORA?

Anti-Judaism, Androcentrism, and Eurocentrism within the Concept of Gentile Christianity

Even though distinguishing epochs of time within the early history of Christianity is problematic, it is still necessary to ask whether differentiating Jewish and Gentile Christianity is appropriate.

There already seems to be a *concept of Christianity of Gentile women and men* in the writings of Justin (in his dialogue with the Jew Trypho, sometime after 150 C.E.): "Those [Jewish women and men] who persecuted Christ and still do, and do not repent, shall not inherit anything on the holy mountain, unless they repent. Whereas the Gentiles who believe in Christ and are sorry for their sins shall receive the inheritance . . . even though they neither practice circumcision nor observe the sabbaths or feasts"(26.1). Other than in Paul and in Acts, this recitation of Jewish essentials seems to suggest the *entire Jewish praxis of faith:* Gentile Christians, women and men, "do not observe the law"(10.1). In Paul and in Acts, access to the God of Israel, to the Torah, to salvation, and to the Jewish Messiah Jesus is understood, as I see it, as access to the Jewish praxis of faith; this access is not to be made dependent on circumcision and certain rules of purity governing meals taken in company with persons not of Jewish origin. This means that certain parts of the Jewish praxis of faith are taken to be open to change, but this does not at all question the God of Israel, the Torah as God's teaching, and the legitimacy of Jewish praxis of faith.

For centuries, the notion of Gentile Christianity has governed the historiography of early Christianity. I chose certain current terms of the history of early Christianity in order to analyze in a feminist perspective the implications of this notion. The notion of Gentile Christianity is also connected with thinking in terms of epochs of church history, as, for example, in the question about the *beginnings of the church of the nations.* That the question is inappropriate is shown already by the difficulty of answering it from the texts. If one dates the beginning of the mission to the Gentiles to, for example, the conversion of Cornelius (Acts 10), then the Jewish history of the proselytes and God-fearers,[58] as well as the controversial and multifaceted discussion within Judaism about that history, is kept separate from such "Christian" dates. In other words, the question about the beginning of the church of the nations is related in its substance to the notion of a "Gentile Christianity free of the law." But the notion of such a Christianity is, historically speaking, a fiction for New Testament times and is theologically highly problematic, since it is *the very core of Christian anti-Judaism.* As a rule, the presumption of freedom from the law is affixed to the renunciation of circumcision. The notion of Gentile Christianity (I deliberately do not say, "Christianity of Gentile women and men," because I speak now of the traditional, androcentric model) sees in the refusal of circumcision of men who are not of Jewish origin and who believe in the Messiah Jesus the abrogation of the law as a whole.[59] But this is subject to critique as follows:

1. The refusal of circumcision does not at all mean that the Torah is refused as a whole. According to Paul's thinking, the women and men who follow Jesus adhere to the Torah.[60] To be Jewish without circumcision is spoken of also in the discussion regarding circumcision outside early Christianity.[61]

2. The need to set oneself apart as church from Judaism is projected into the history of Christian origins and allied at the same time with a discriminatory view of "the law"; for the law allegedly makes Jewish people "legalists" and representatives of the sin of seeking to achieve salvation before God on their own. Such an assertion is stereotypical of how Christians set themselves apart from other religions.[62]

3. The notion of "Gentile Christianity free from the law" is *androcentric* because the central issue is said to be the circumcision of men (Jewish or Christian). It is a historical fact that early Christianity was sustained decisively by Jewish women,[63] by women of non-Jewish origin who had already lived Jewish lives before they encountered the message of the Messiah, and by women of non-Jewish origin who accepted the message of the Messiah Jesus. This decisive historical fact is rendered invisible by the notion of Gentile Christianity, and for that reason, this androcentric concept is also hostile to women, as it turns out to be an instrument of their oppression.

In the historiography of early Christianity, the notion of "Gentile Christianity" (the more modern term now is *church of the nations*) frequently occurs to portray the ideal *patriarchal church,* often with a view of the office that is to be neatly balanced, taking the middle road: neither "incipiently Catholic" nor sectarian-Jewish-Christian-charismatic.[64] But what is then sketched is a church with offices, with people ordained to offices, and a church people in a clear hierarchical order. This, however, legitimates the structure of patriarchal society as the ideal structure of the church and accepts the structure of domination of the society in question.[65]

In recent discussion, Elisabeth Schüssler Fiorenza's concept of Christianity of Gentile women and men has been a partial alternative to this notion of Gentile Christianity. She distinguishes between a Spirit-led "early Christian missionary movement" and a patriarchalized church[66] but remains committed to the distinction, which is problematic for me, between the Jesus movement and Christianity of Gentile women and men.

Furthermore, the notion of Gentile Christianity is *Eurocentric.* By *Eurocentrism* I mean the understanding of Europe which, from the perspective of the powerful of that continent, regards Christian Europe as the true culture, whereas other cultures and religions within Europe and elsewhere are, in comparison, of lesser value. Cain Hope Felder has demonstrated that even atlases of the Bible manifest such Eurocentrism when they depict only narrow strips of Africa.[67] In the same vein is the manner in which exegesis deals with the black "Ethiopian" (i.e., Sudanese), a eunuch who is a royal minister to Queen Candace (Acts 8:26ff.). It has not occurred to anyone to hail this man as the first representative of the church of the nations.[68] Instead, the idea of a European church is introduced into the book of Acts when the "jump into Europe"[69] and Lydia as the first European Christian woman[70] are spoken of. The text simply speaks of a jump to Macedonia (Acts 16:9–15), another Roman province among many others. Even though Lydia is often made out to be the first European Christian woman, she is still not spoken of as a representative either of European women or of a European Women-Church but rather as one of the (white) European, affluent, middle-class church.[71]

Messianic Communities in the Jewish Diaspora

I would like to speak of messianic communities within the Jewish diaspora instead of Gentile Christianity or Christianity of Gentile women and men. Obviously, it is difficult to find concepts for the history of early Christianity. Therefore I distinguish among (1) the Jesus movement in Palestine before Jesus' death, (2) the Jesus movement in Palestine after his death, and (3) Jesus communities as part of the history of Jewish diaspora. I regard "Christianity" until far into the second century as one messianic movement next to others within Judaism. At every historical and geographical level of this phenomenon I see the presence of women and men of non-Jewish origin. Like the centurion of Capernaum, they had turned toward Judaism even before their encounter with the person or message of Jesus, or presumably, like the Syrophoenician woman, they met the God of Israel through Jesus.

A church of the nations free of the law is an anti-Judaistic, Eurocentric construct that is hostile to women. Such a construct is foreign to the New Testament. It conceals the substantive continuity between Jesus and the messianic communities in Asia Minor, Greece, Africa, Italy, and elsewhere in the first and second centuries.

Jesus as "Knight in Shining Armor" and
the Hemorrhaging Woman as Female Hero:
When Did the Fall into Patriarchy Take Place?

Writing history in terms of black and white necessitates the construction of the great divide. When did the unimpaired world of early Christianity turn into the not-so-unimpaired world of the church? Unimpaired and impaired may well be defined on the basis of diverse perspectives. One may speak of Jesus as the liberator of women, of such women as the hemorrhaging woman as heroes, and of the church with ordained offices as the oppressor of women. Or Jesus may be seen as a revolutionary and Paul as an oppressor of human beings. Traditional theology often distinguishes between the Pauline church and the church of early Catholicism. The theory of a divide such as this one also allows one to create a canon within the Canon and to relinquish any responsibility whatever for texts that, like 1 Tim. 2:11–16, are no longer palatable to the church. Elisabeth Schüssler Fiorenza is to be credited with clarifying the distinction between the level of New Testament texts, on the one hand, and that of the historical liberation struggles on the part of women in patriarchy at the time of early Christianity, on the other hand.[72]

Equally inappropriate are black-and-white portrayals of the history of liberation struggles of women and men within the history of early Christianity. There never was an unimpaired Women-Church. Nevertheless, from the struggles of early Christian women and men for a Women-Church, there still emanates great strength today. They are a source of inspiration.

It does not do to idealize individual historical circumstances or persons and thereby construct a norm by which Christian faith today may orient itself. For me, the Canon is not a canon; it is an incomplete document of a by no means unique history of the struggle for the realization of the will of the God of Israel. This struggle was situated within a praxis of life lived in community under the conditions of patriarchal society as it existed at that time. (The problem that the selection of the canon was directed by interests that did not necessarily reflect those of the texts themselves will not be pursued any further at this point.) I understand the history of early Christianity as the struggle against injustices and violence. I do not want to measure myself against a Jesus as "knight in shining armor" but against the vulnerable, courageous, and just man Jesus who could allow a woman's critique to touch the very center of his theology. The Syrophoenician woman (Mark 7:24–30 and par.) showed him that his thinking had been too fainthearted and limited when he suggested that the store of God's love sufficed only for the children of Israel.

It is, therefore, inappropriate to inquire when the fall into patriarchy occurred. We should much rather ask where the gospel became confused with the ideology of patriarchy, that is to say, where within the Christian church Christian men and women arose who worked while knowing that what they did oppressed women. Traces of such conscious work of patriarchal oppression are also to be found in the New Testament, for example, in 1 Tim. 2:11–16 (see also below).

Anti-Judaism in the New Testament: A New "Nasty, Big Ditch"?

A social-historical study of the New Testament that does not have for its background a Christianity already separated from Judaism but has rather, an early Christianity as a movement within Judaism of people of Jewish origin faces a new problem of Christian anti-Judaism. When I repeat one of Jesus' threats against Jerusalem as a Christian woman, and especially as a Christian woman of German origin, a Jewish prophetic word turns in *my* mouth into an anti-Judaistic word, which possibly even threatens Jewish people with death. G. E. Lessing once spoke of the nasty, big ditch,[73] referring to the chasm between "accidental truths of history" and "necessary truths of reason." I take up his metaphor. I am separated from the Jewish book, which the New Testament is for me, by two thousand years of Christian anti-Judaism as a nasty, big ditch. I can seek access to this early Christian tradition only after I have acknowledged responsibility for the history of Christian anti-Judaism and German anti-Semitism. Do I still have any right at all to regard as *mine* this tradition that initially was a tradition of chiefly poor women and men who were Jewish or lived Jewish lives?

The New Testament was the book of life for my mother and father; I am deeply attached to its contents, so that my pain over awareness of the nasty, big ditch is deep: the persecution and murder of Jewish people for centuries and then the German concentration camps, the preparation of which was facilitated also by Christian anti-Judaism.

It would be a mistake to assume that the New Testament as a Jewish book will free Christian women and men from the problem of anti-Judaism.[74] I do not regard the New Testament as anti-Judaistic in the sense of a devaluation or condemnation uttered from the outside, from the side of Christians, against the Jewish religion or the Jewish people. Even the so-called anti-Judaism of the Gospel of John can be understood as internal to Judaism from the perspective of social history.[75] The language concerning "the Jews" that is found, for example, in 1 Thess. 2:14, comes from the lips of Paul, the Jew, who attacks the persecutors of the followers of Jesus in Judea. The problem of anti-Judaism does not arise for me from a high Christology, which I view in any case as inappropriate; nor is it caused by the texts of the New Testament taken by themselves. The problem resides for me in post–New Testament history of Christian anti-Judaism, which separates me as a Christian and a German woman from the New Testament.

2

Patriarchy and the
Hope for the Reign of God

A. WHO REALLY IS THE PATRIARCHY?
MY EXPERIENCES WITH PATRIARCHAL OPPRESSION

The experiences of oppression that have opened my eyes to structures of oppression are situated primarily in the context of my professional work, that is to say, in the theological scholarship of the university. My mother was active from her youth in the women's movement. This gave me the privilege of a youth and early education in which I rarely had the impression of being of less worth than my brothers. It has been in the context of academic theology where I have experienced oppression far more massively. I am aware that I trespass against an unwritten rule of patriarchy by speaking of such experiences, but they must be disclosed; for in this way it becomes apparent how the theoretical concept of this book, an analysis of patriarchy, grows out of experience. Because of their corresponding experiences, women, as well as men, will again and again undertake the analysis of patriarchy, even if theoretical discussion of such analysis were to be abandoned or silenced. The sphere of university theology should not be exempted as a special sphere and thereby excused; like the church, the family, the state, and other social structures, it is a locus of patriarchal structures of domination.

It was by a lengthy process of political conscientization that I came to understand that the poverty of the poor in the two-thirds world has something to do with me. It grew on me that unjust prices for raw materials and my function as a consumer in a rich, capitalistic country are interconnected. However, that my theology and my interpretation of the Bible also had something to do with the poor being blocked out of the consciousness of those who profit from their exploitation did not become clear as a result. I first had to witness professors at Protestant faculties of theology, in the mid-seventies, using every means at their disposal to attack the World Council of Churches' antiracism program. It was this experience that led me to comprehend that Christian theology participates in the exploitation and oppression of the poor.

The executive council of the World Council of Churches had decided in 1970, within the framework of the Program to Combat Racism, to establish a special fund (of U.S. $200,000 for nineteen organizations) to be distributed to liberation movements for humanitarian purposes.[76] South Africa and its oppression of its black population received special publicity. The counterarguments heard in the church and from professors of theology, namely, that Communists and murderers were being supported, were untruthful and demagogical. The decision of the executive council touched the heart of the problem and spoke of "the redistribution of power," which gave fundamental significance to the comparatively small sum involved. How was the relation of the rich with the poor to be shaped in terms of the gospel? Was it to be charity or the redistribution of power?

The blatant contradiction between, on the one hand, colleagues' avowal of theological scholarship as objective, neutral, and removed from politics and, on the other, their massive interventions in the discussion and their clear intent of stopping the antiracism program was for me an object lesson in the truest sense of the word. After two decades it is still my view that the analysis and praxis at the heart of this World Council of Churches' program point in the right direction. Beginning to understand then what was at issue for the theology of liberation in Latin America,[77] I came also to see the deep contradiction between the biblical tradition and its Western interpretation. I had once accepted that the gospel of the poor had nothing to do with economic exploitation but that it spoke of voluntary poverty or of humility before God.[78] Now, however, I understood that, even though they are to be found in all scholarly commentaries, such lines of interpretation constitute a collective Western lie. A lie such as this robs the poor of the gospel and renders them invisible in theology. It became apparent to me that the hidden agenda of Western theology is to know the poor at best as recipients of alms, and that this misrepresentation of the poor legitimizes the political status quo of Western societies. This meant that I now had to think contextually[79] about the Magnificat of Mary and the beatitude "Blessed are the poor." I needed to understand them as voices of the prophecy of the poor in Palestine, who preach God's partiality for the "last" (Matt. 20:16 and elsewhere). Given this understanding of the tradition of Jesus, I now had to ask: What about *my* conversion and that of the rich?

A former fellow student, who by then had risen high in the universities and who gave me well-meant paternal advice on how I too might advance in the circles of academe, was shocked by my work. He told me, "You must know what you have done. I can already hear our colleagues speaking contemptuously of you. You won't get anywhere quickly if you publish this. And by the way: those few beggars at the time of Jesus don't matter." The phrase "those few beggars" still rings in my ears today. I did not know then how poor the majority of the people of Palestine were at the time of Jesus, and yet I felt the disavowal: poverty is a problem only of individuals, the fate of a few marginal existences. That was not true of Palestine, and it is not true today when whole peoples starve. "Those few beggars"—the avoidance mechanism is everywhere to be seen.

The reactions of the guild of colleagues in my area of study, which is the New Testament, were indeed radical and far-reaching. I was invited to no further scholarly events, and people ridiculed me in my spouse's presence; I was (and continue to be) excluded from all recognized and informal scholarly associations and networks of men. I experienced that time as one of social death, and it took a lot of energy to find, with a few others, my own way in the theology of Germany.

In those days, I named the structural injustice that I recognized "capitalism." Today I call it "patriarchy" and view capitalism as an essential part of prevailing patriarchal structures of oppression. It took another process of conscientization to discover that the exploitation of the poor and the oppression of women are structurally related. Here, too, personally painful experiences were required to open my eyes. Why, when I spoke of the gospel of the poor, was I a figure of ridicule and scorned in scholarly articles as "silly"?[80] Why did one colleague declare in public, "At least the Schottroffs' marriage seems to be in decent shape," as if the discrediting of marriage were all that was to be expected from us? That colleague understood patriarchy better than I. He sensed the critique of patriarchal marriage in advance and thought that he had to defend patriarchal marriage against my spouse and me. It took me a long time to understand that the gospel of the poor not only is disavowed in Western theology but is refashioned into the categorical imperative of patriarchal marriage.

Indeed, I see bound up in the dominant theology of my context the confusion of the gospel with the ideology of patriarchy. In my context, I experienced and still experience the suppression of the gospel of the poor, as well as the oppression of women in connection with academic theology. In 1969, I presented to the University of Mainz my *Habilitationsschrift* in the area of New Testament. I sensed that my university appointment, contingent upon it, was hanging from a thread. If I also keep in mind that one must go hunting with a magnifying glass to find such academic appointments of women of my generation, I have to make a connection between the oppression of women and of the poor. It is the same persons and structures that perpetrate both.

I find the concept of patriarchy suitable to comprehend this structural connection. For me, the primary meaning of patriarchy is neither the dominance of men nor that of fathers, even though the majority of those who perpetrate this oppression are men and fathers. Here is an actual case in point, which while it exemplifies patriarchal structure in the same area in which my experiences are situated is also highly significant beyond this actual setting. New Testament scholar Klaus Berger, of the University of Heidelberg, published a review of a book by Uta Ranke-Heinemann (in the *Frankfurter Allgemeine Zeitung* of 8 December 1992). His review was brimming with disdain: "Ms. Ranke-

Heinemann was the first woman to be admitted as an academic teacher into a Catholic faculty. However, if she writes books like this, it is grist for the mills of all who do not want this to happen at all." It is not my purpose here to defend Ranke-Heinemann's book; in fact, I make my own critique of it, albeit of a different kind (the substance of which would hardly fill two-thirds of a newspaper page). What I find remarkable is that in this review, what is still being officially contested is remarked on in passing, namely, that in the academies of the nineties there are male theologians who fundamentally oppose women's being admitted to academic teaching positions. The reviewer, in paternalistic condescension, took sides in favor of such admissions but tied it to political considerations. His disdainful review, repeating its contempt monotonously over four columns, suggests that he may expect to be applauded for this act of destruction.

Who, then, is the patriarchy? It is the many men and few women of the elite[81] who directly or indirectly exploit the poor, who make patriarchal marriage the heart of society (and the gospel) and seek specific legislation to bolster it, for example, laws against abortion. They are the many women and the few men who suffer from this system but who participate in sustaining and upholding it.[82] As a rule, those who seek a name in the academies of the Western world either have to be integrated without critical consciousness into the structures of patriarchy or betray what critical consciousness they have. Without bowing to the ideology of patriarchy, there is no scholarly career or no success in social circles.

I have often experienced how men feel personally attacked when I speak of patriarchy. Such a reaction arises from a highly truncated understanding of the concept of patriarchy. Before it has even begun, the analysis of one's own involvement in unjust structures short-circuits. This happens because individual ascriptions or assumptions of guilt subvert the painful process of analyzing patriarchy as embodied, gendered persons.

For further explanation of the response, let me refer to historical experiences on the part of persons who have analyzed Christian anti-Judaism. It was Charlotte Klein[83] who named names here, finding this phenomenon in the work of Martin Noth, Joachim Jeremias, and many others. Her voice was silenced.[84] The perpetrators of Christian anti-Judaism did not let her deter them. She was seen to have done something "unseemly," that is, unscholarly. And yet she wrote the truth. Heard only as pronouncing certain individuals personally guilty, her voice was misunderstood; for she spoke of deep-seated Christian anti-Judaism, which ought not to be construed as an individual problem of certain theologians. The painful process of the critique of Christian anti-Judaism is part of the painful analysis of patriarchy.

I have spoken of an experience related to the critique of anti-Judaism in order to show that more is at stake here than episodic personal injustice. Personal complicity in unjust structures of patriarchy is, indeed, a daily reality in the lives of men and women, including those who are about the analysis of patriarchy.

For example, I go on doing what sustains prevailing injustice: I buy coffee cheaply; I drive a car even though I know that the future of creation is threatened by the family car. The destruction of the environment is a feature of patriarchal structural injustice, so that the automobile industry and I are complicit in a peculiar death pact.

Therefore, who really is the patriarchy? A critical encounter with structures of guilt will have a fruitful outcome only when the analysis of those structures is situated in moments of liberation experienced within communities of human beings. A liberating engagement with the structural sin called patriarchy[85] permits one to admit one's individual entanglements. The naming of patriarchal structures of guilt, as an expression of the corporate nature and scope of the struggle against this oppression, is partially necessary wherever the struggle is to be blocked with such questions as: Are you implying that *I* say anti-Judaistic things, or that *I* am oppressing my wife?

B. PATRIARCHY: A CONCEPT OF FEMINIST ANALYSIS

The term *patriarchy* has been appropriated for a central concept of feminist rhetoric within the new women's movement.[86] Even without any scholarly or historical explanation, it has signaled—and still signals—that there is injustice against women, that partisanship for women is needed, and, finally, that wisdom is required to inform a vision of life without patriarchy. In feminist discussion there are two distinct senses in which the analytical concept of patriarchy occurs. In the first sense, it refers to men's domination of women;[87] in the second, it is the encompassing description of societies that are structured by the "joint forces of racism, classism and sexism,"[88] militarism, the exploitation of nature, and other structural dimensions of violence. From the first days of the women's movement, ecofeminism has cited the structural connection between the oppression of women and that of nature.[89] Another aspect of that same structure of patriarchy is described by Christina Thürmer-Rohr; she speaks of "white nuclear patriarchy":[90] since Auschwitz and the nuclear bombing of Hiroshima and Nagasaki in 1945, patriarchy has entered into a new, no longer reversible dimension of violence. In their own hands, people hold power with which to destroy whole nations and all of life. One must reckon with the renewed use of this violence as long as patriarchy—namely, the many men and a few women for whom mass destruction holds promise for the enforcement of their interests of domination—exists.

As long as the structures of violence of patriarchal domination are analyzed as just a power differential between women and men, only a partial aspect of the prevailing violence comes into view. There will be no liberation of women without the liberation of the trees, the children, and the poor. And the struggle for this liberation cannot be fought without an analysis of this encompassing structure of violence and its historical background. For that reason I hold on to the feminist analytical concept of patriarchy, which explicitly names a system of domination and its long history. By bringing it together with the gospel of the poor, I sharpen the edge of this concept. The analysis of patriarchy must begin with "the last."[91] The gospel of the poor will be vindicated in relation to the liberation of women in poverty.

C. PATRIARCHAL IDEOLOGY OF DOMINATION: THE SELF-PORTRAYAL OF PATRIARCHY AT THE BEGINNING OF CHRISTIANITY (CICERO, *DE RE PUBLICA*)

The Choice of Subject and the Aim of This Section

The word *patriarchy* is no feminist invention. The Latin *patriarcha* (in Greek, *patriarchēs*) is used in the New Testament to describe the fathers of the tribes of Israel and, later, in connection with the office of bishop in the ancient church.[92] This usage expresses no more than what the social teaching of Aristotle and his followers had presented and made reality: the rule of the father in the household, in the state, and in the heavens. Ancient writings on the "economy,"[93] on politics,[94] or *De re publica*[95] regularly describe the structure of patriarchy; it is an encompassing rule of the father (not only over women, which is only one of its aspects). This ancient theory consistently serves not only to authorize the father's rule of the household but also to justify the structures of domination pervading all of society, structures that are construed as analogous to paternal headship over the household.

I find it necessary to begin the analysis of modern patriarchy by exploring this ancient theory of the father's rule, or at least how it functioned within the sphere of influence of Christianity. The theory entered Christian theology through the church fathers, in particular Augustine, and became its predominant content (certainly in the theology of those at the top). The Christian theology of the father's rule has survived the crumbling of Christianity where Western societies have become highly secularized. This may explain the bizarre phenomenon that, where I live, the major churches exert more power in society than their membership would suggest. In its secular form, those churches' theology of paternal domination has become the foundation of the understanding and praxis of domination in the economy and in politics.

Feminist historical analysis has proposed that the various patriarchies need to be differentiated.[96] This can be better facilitated the more the triumphant patriarchal ideology of domination of antiquity is drawn on for comparison. Thus the term *patriarchy* has meaning not merely as a feminist concept of argumentation but also as one of historical analysis. It finds the roots of the theory and praxis of the elites of Western societies in the theory and praxis of paternal domination in antiquity.

Feminist exploration of early Christianity cannot do without the study of this ancient patriarchal theory. But from the outset, the differences between Jewish patriarchal ideas and those of the Greco-Roman theory of society should be kept in mind. In New Testament literature, the Greco-Roman theory of patriarchy is located primarily in the household code tradition. In subsequent history of New Testament interpretation, Rom. 13:1–7 became another text to be interpreted according to that theory; such interpretation, however, must not be confused with the meaning of that text in its original context.[97]

It is with reference to Cicero that I now proceed to elucidate the ancient theory of the father's dominance.

When Christianity was emerging, the Roman Empire was the dominant power wherever Jewish people lived. Jewish patriarchy of that time was the patriarchy of a politically and economically oppressed people who were fighting for the very survival of their culture and religion; as such, one cannot identify it without qualification with the patriarchy of the dominating and oppressive power. Christianity *participates,* as a Jewish liberation movement within Pax Romana (see above, I.1.A), in the patriarchal structures of Judaism and *struggles,* like every other Jewish movement, *for the life* and identity of Jewish and non-Jewish people *under the conditions of Roman patriarchy.* The New Testament (like other contemporary texts of Judaism) must be understood within the context of the social reality of Roman domination and the various steps toward liberation that people took and the defeats they suffered.

I choose Cicero because the way he relates political theory to the state of Rome defines particularly clearly the self-understanding of Rome's dominant class. And I choose him because of the lasting influence of his work on Christianity. Whoever wants to understand how patriarchy functions within current capitalist Christianity will learn more about this Christianity from Cicero than from the New Testament. From the days of the ancient church, and in the dominant theological tradition, the New Testament has been read in terms of a hermeneutics of the imperial rule, the central features of which are found in Cicero but not in the New Testament. For example, the chief purpose of marriage, as it is found in the self-understanding of the two major denominations in Germany, matches that of Cicero but only peripherally that of the New Testament.

My purpose in examining Cicero's portrait of patriarchy is twofold: (1) to analyze the dominant patriarchy under the conditions in which Christianity emerged and to differentiate between Roman and Jewish/Christian patriarchy; and (2) to contribute to the analysis of today's Christian and capitalist patriarchy (and how and where these two overlap) by exploring how they agree with and differ from the patriarchy of Cicero's time.

Cicero's Definition of Patriarchy

Cicero, who was born in 106 B.C.E. and murdered in 43 B.C.E., defined patriarchy in his *De re publica* (written between 54 and 51 B.C.E.). He makes theoretical distinctions among three forms of statehood: monarchy, governance by the aristocracy, and democracy;[98] in his view, a mixture of these three provides for the best state. The positive feature of monarchy—a good that he seeks to find also in the state as he envisages it—is that the state is a patriarchy:

> The name of king is like that of a father to us, since the king provides for the citizens as if they were his own children and is more eager to protect them than . . . his own person. . . . And here the subjects themselves are openly admitting that, lacking in political wisdom, they are best sustained by the care of the one man who is the most virtuous and most eminent. (1.54)

Cicero does not affirm monarchy for his state but rather appropriates its patriarchal structure, which can be maintained in a combination of the three forms of statehood.

Whereas kings often turned into tyrants, Cicero looks on the father as the incorruptible model of direction and guidance. As a king, Romulus had represented such an incorruptible father figure. After his death the people longingly proclaimed his praise: "O Romulus, O Romulus divine, a mighty bulwark of our native land wast thou,—sent down from heaven to our need; O sire, O father, blood from gods derived! Neither 'masters' nor 'lords' did they call those men whom they lawfully obeyed, nay, nor 'kings' either, but 'guardians of the fatherland,' 'fathers,' 'gods' " (1.64).

A clear distinction is made between the rule of the master and that of the father: "But we must distinguish different kinds of domination and subjection. For the mind is said to rule over the body, and also over lust; but it rules over the body as a king governs his subjects or a father his children, whereas it rules over lust as a master rules his slaves, restraining it and breaking its power" (3.37).

Only fatherly rule is legitimate as political rule over free citizens; the rule of masters must be distinguished from it. The rule of masters is legitimate as the rule both of the mind over lust and of the masters over female and male slaves, who are to be seen as analogous to lust. This is a structure of thought that lives on in the racism of our society. All one needs to do is substitute "blacks" for "slaves" in Cicero's statement.

The rule of the fathers is exercised on various levels: that of the gods (over human beings), that of the state (government), that of the household (father), and that of the mind (over the body). At every one of these four levels, rule is based on the natural inequality between the ruling fathers and the ruled children. It is always the rule of *one* man over dependent women, men, and children; only in relation to the state is it better to entrust patriarchal rule to governance by an aristocracy, in order to avoid the danger of tyranny. "But if a free people chooses the men to whom it is to entrust its fortunes . . . then certainly the safety of the state depends upon the wisdom of its best men, especially since Nature has provided not only that those men who are superior in virtue and spirit should rule the weaker, but also that the weaker should be willing to obey the stronger" (1.51).

On all four levels, the rule of the father originates in the father's rule over the household, in his care for the children and in the corresponding obedience. From this primary social unit arises the necessity for a state, the organization of which is administered like the household, albeit by several men. Ruling, however, is always *one man's* task. Cicero speaks of one god in the world of the gods who rules the whole of humankind (1.56; 3.36), even though he distinguishes this one god from the king-god who rules over all the gods on Olympus, because the notion of that god is politically motivated, namely, to legitimate monarchy (1.56).

The Primary Social Unit of Patriarchy

The primary social unit rests on marriage (1.38). Cicero makes this point more explicitly in his *De officiis* than in his *De re publica,* although he applies the same theory in both:

> We may assume that it is naturally common to living things to have the desire to procreate (*libido procreandi*). The first stage of society, then, is in the basic man–wife relationship (*prima societas in ipso coniugo est*); a second stage is in the children of that union; and a third stage is in the single household (*una domus*) where all the members share everything (*communia omnia*). The household is the foundation of the city, what we might call the "seed-bed" of the state. There follows the relationships "brother" and "sister" and then those of "cousin" and "second cousin." When a single house cannot shelter all of them, they migrate to other houses as if they were going out to colonies. Marriages and alliances of families deriving from those marriages follow, and they result in even more relatives. (*De off.* 1.54)[99]

The natural drive to procreate and a father's instinctive love for his children (cf. *De off.* 1.12) are perceived to be the source of the household unit, on which its members depend for economic existence. Here Cicero is thinking, in fact, only of the household of an affluent man. He assumes that the free citizen is engaged in politics, lives on inherited wealth, or at least derives income from large land-holdings or commercial enterprises worthy of a free man. A skilled trade, daily-wage labor, and dirty jobs (*De off.* 1.150–51) are unworthy occupations for a free man. It is the duty of the state to uphold and defend the private property of patriarchs: "[People] founded states and cities primarily on the principle that private property may be retained. Even if [they] first formed groups because of a natural impulse, still, they sought out the protection of cities in the hope of guarding their private possessions" (*De off.* 2.73). Interfering with private property is dangerous for the state, for this touches a vital nerve and smacks of *equalization* of property relations (*De off.* 2.73). The levy of taxes is to be avoided whenever possible and must be undertaken in extreme situations only, and then, if at all possible, with the consent of the affected citizens (i.e., patriarchs; cf. *De off.* 2.74). The natural drives to procreate and to acquire property, as the foundations of the patriarchal household, have a legal and religious status in an orderly state:

> But, as regards the practical conduct of life, this system provides for legal marriage, legitimate children, and the consecration of homes to the Lares and Penates of families, so that all may make use of the common property and of their own personal possessions. It is impossible to live well except in a good commonwealth, and nothing can produce greater happiness than a well constituted state. (*De re pub.* 5.7)

In Cicero's system, women are seen exclusively from the perspective described, namely, as *wives* in the legal and patriarchal sense, with whom legitimate children are fathered as inheritors of property. Whereas the relationship of the patriarch to his children is always referred to as natural *love,* his relationship to the wife is situated at the edges of this love (*De off.* 1.12). As a rule, she is not spoken of: "Our parents are dear, our children are dear, our relatives, our friends, but the fatherland alone embraces all of our deep feelings" (*De off.* 1.57). As part of the household (*domus*), the wife is, of course, cared for and protected with all the others (*De off.* 1.12, 58).

According to Cicero, women are not suited to disposing over a household's possessions. He favors the legislation of Voconius,[100] which, however, he readily admits, "was introduced solely for the advantage of man and is full of injustice toward women" (*De re pub.* 3.17). This legislation is about "women's legacies and inheritances" and prescribes that women may not own any money;[101] a mother may not bequeath anything to her daughter, and only vestal virgins may have a woman as an heir. A wealthy man may leave an inheritance to a daughter if she is his only child (*De re pub.* 3.17). Even though the patriarch's daughters receive his love (cf. *De re pub.* 3.39), they are governed by different rules than are his sons. The "normal case" is that of a father and his son(s) who have the disposition over the patriarchal household and what belongs to it. The careful education of the sons for this purpose is emphasized, and sons are trained from their youth for political leadership (*De re pub.* 1.10, 35).

The central significance of legitimate children prompts Cicero to speak of women several times in relation to *virginity, marital fidelity,* and *sexual assault.* The common denominator is that because women are part of the patriarch's domain of power, sexual assault is perceived as an assault on the sphere of power of the father (in case of a virgin) or on that of the husband (cf. *De re pub.* 2.46—Lucretia—and 2.62—the virginal daughter of Decimus Verginius). As a state cult, the cult of the vestal virgins is of great importance (cf. *De re pub.* 2.26), and the story of the rape of the Sabine women was seen to incorporate a clever move in the politics of conquest and alliance (*De re pub.* 2.12).

When speaking of the primary significance of patriotic love, of modesty in one's way of living, and of marital fidelity, Augustine refers to Cicero (*Epist.* 91.3; cf. *De re pub.* 4.7). In Roman history there once was a king, Ancus Martius, whose mother was the daughter of Numa Pompilius but whose father's identity was unknown. This king is explicitly hailed despite the fact that "the history of Rome is indeed obscure" when "we know who the king's mother was, but are ignorant of his father's name!" (*De re pub.* 2.33). It is quite clear what the woman is there for in patriarchy: she is to be the mother of the children of an unambiguously identifiable father. Cicero cites a Corinthian law, according to which childless men and unmarried women had to make payments to the state for the maintenance of its horses (*De re pub.* 2.36). The reality of women—their situation in the household (*domus*), their productivity, their survival when a patriarchal household did not work out, their situation as members of the population's lower classes—none of these are discussed by Cicero.

There are two texts in which Cicero paints a gloomy picture of what too much freedom and equality in the state might mean; these texts show indirectly, but without uncertainty, that the supervision of women's sexuality and the exclusion of women from power in society are means to an end, namely, the necessary and natural subjugation of women under patriarchal rule. A democracy with too much freedom would mean that

> not only are homes one and all without a master, but the vice and anarchy extends even to the domestic animals, until finally the father fears his son, the son flouts his father, all sense of shame disappears, and all is so absolutely free that there is no distinction between citizen and alien; the school master fears and flatters his pupils, and the pupils despise their master; youths take on the gravity of age, and old men stoop to the games of youth, for fear they may be disliked by their juniors and seem to them too serious. Under such conditions even the slaves come out to behave with unseemly freedom, wives have the same rights as their husbands and in the abundance of liberty even the dogs, the horses and asses are so free in their running about that men must make way for them in the streets. (*De re pub.* 1.67)

The sequence is clear in its descending order: sons, slaves, wives, animals (dogs, horses, asses).

Cicero takes *ad absurdum* the idea that everything should belong to everyone. On the level of economic possessions it is unjust to think of all as equals, but on the level of the family such thinking is even perverse:

> Will wives and children also be owned in common? Will there be no more distinction at all of blood or gender? Will there be no more families, blood relationships, or relationships by marriage? Will all become a mass without order, as in the herds of animals? Will men exercise no self-control and women no modesty? How can there be marital love among two people if there is no definite personal attachment between them? Who will love the father if it cannot be determined who the father is? Who will love the son when he is taken to be a stranger? He[102] even opened the door of the council chamber to women and handed military service and the civil service and their places of authority over to their digression. What misfortune must befall the city in which women take over from men! (*De re pub.* 4.5; cf. Lactantius, *Epit.* 33.38.1–5)

Marital love, which was of little interest to Cicero, is acknowledged only in a portrait of "chaos." Women's sexual liberty leads, in his view, to the even more absurd state of women having a share in the exercise of political power.

Natural Inequality and the Patriarchal Image of Justice

Patriarchal power, the power to guide and direct all aspects of patriarchy (God, state, household, reason), belongs to the few men to whom the many are subjected in obedience. The many are called "the weaker" in relation to "the superior in virtue" (*De re pub.* 1.51), "the lowest" in relation to "the highest" (*De re pub.* 1.53). Cicero relates how Servius Tullius divided the population into classes and names the basic principles that were assigned: "The greatest number of votes belonged, not to the common people, but to the rich and put into effect the principle which ought always be adhered to in the commonwealth, that the greatest number should not have the greatest power" (*De re pub.* 2.39).

The proletarian class may cast votes; to deprive it of suffrage would be "tyrannical" (*De re pub.* 2.40), but the power to decide resides with the few. The *proletarii* who own no real estate are expected by the state to provide *proles,* their progeny (*De re pub.* 2.40). What Cicero does not mention at all is that the progeny are to deliver their labor to the affluent class. In *De officiis* 1.41, he ponders whether it would not be beneficial to put slaves and daily-wage earners on an equal footing, in order to do justice to those of the lower estate (*infimi*): "You should get work out of them, but you must treat them fairly."

This singular thought about justice toward proletarians is not quite as humanitarian as it sounds. Behind Cicero's comment may be the unending *complaint of masters* about the laziness and insolence of slaves and the dictum of certain economics, that daily-wage earners are slaves at their own risk.[103] He speaks of distinctions in the ranking of individual personalities (*De re pub.* 1.43), which necessitates gradations; otherwise equality would in truth be inequality (*De re pub.* 1.43, 53). That I am born into a certain class or have been joined to it by fate may be sheer coincidence, but the distinctions in society are "provided by nature" (*De re pub.* 1.51).

Cicero knows all the counterarguments and recites them accurately, but he does not take them seriously and refutes them only superficially. One such argument declares that the state is unjust (and can be nothing else) and that justice is a concept provided not by nature but by society itself. Justice is what serves those who wield power in the state; justice is what passes for men's advantage, even though it is full of injustice to women (*De re pub.* 3.17, in its context; see also above). The conquest of other peoples, wars, and destruction in the service of expanding Rome's domination may be called wisdom *by people of opposite opinion,* but not justice: "Wisdom urges us to increase our resources, to multiply our wealth, to extend our boundaries; . . . justice, on the other hand, instructs us to spare all human beings, to consider the interests of the whole human race, to give everyone his due, and not to touch sacred or public property, or that which belongs to others" (*De re pub*. 3.24).

Cicero does not counter with a different concept of justice; his is the same as that of his (fictional) opponent. Nor does he distinguish between the wisdom (of conquest) and justice, for to exercise and to expand power in the sense of the politics of Rome's wars and conquests is to administer justice:

> It is just, because servitude may be advantageous to the provincials, and is so when rightly administered—that is to say, when the lawless are prevented from doing harm. And further, as they became worse and worse so long as they were free, they will improve by subjection. . . . Can we not see that the best are fitted by nature to rule over the weak for their very benefit? (*De re pub*. 3.36; referred to, and cited in part, with approval by Augustine, *De civ*. 19.21)

In *De off*. 3.29, Cicero puts the argument on a personal level: "Perhaps someone might say, 'But consider a wise man who is dying of hunger. Will he not take food from another man, a man who is quite useless for anything?' " It would be wrong, were he to take it "for his personal benefit," for the ethical principle is valid: "To deprive another man of something, to increase your own comfort by making another man miserable, is more against nature than death, poverty, pain or any other misfortune" (*De off*. 3.21). "However, if you are the kind of person who can bestow a great benefit on the state and human society by remaining alive, there is no blame if you deprive another man of something to sustain your life" (*De off*. 3.30). The ethical principle becomes ineffectual on account of that distinction between people who are of value to society and those who are quite useless for anything.

The "natural" inequalities that justify the power structure of Cicero's patriarchy are the inequalities between the upper class and the rest of the people, between man and woman, mind and body, God and humanity. Within the same power class there are further hierarchical differentiations, especially within the class of the (upper) patriarchs: old and young, the politically successful and private individuals, and others, all of which are signified by a series of cumbersome rituals (such as described, e.g., in *De re pub*. 1.18). But such hierarchy among patriarchs must not be confused with the hierarchy separating above from below and man from woman. Those who are "below" and women, unlike the patriarchs, have no part in public power. The rituals of subordination of women are quite explicit: women drink no wine (*De re pub*. 4.6), a woman of ill repute is not kissed by a blood relative. Woe to the woman who is unmarried or not monogamous and drinks wine (of course, there was a significant double standard in the upper classes). The domination of women by patriarchs seems not to have been easily achieved, however, for Cicero suggests that "there should be a censor to teach men to rule their wives" (*De re pub*. 4.6).

The Basis for a Historical Differentiation
between Patriarchal Systems

The New Testament paints a picture of patriarchy that, unlike Cicero's account, does not depict a powerful elite's perceptions. Instead, it represents those of the lowly ones of an oppressed people; the perceptions of the majority of that class of people who, according to Cicero, are to have no part at all in the exercise of real power in the state. In fact, there is no language anywhere in the New Testament which belongs, like that of Cicero, to the voice of those who hold the power of the state in their hands; it demands nowhere that Christian patriarchs look after the welfare of the state, nor is there any warning against agitating in opposition to the state. Threats to the social order would have been discussed, more likely, by the "Herodians"[104] and Sadducees in the years before 70 C.E. Political considerations are spoken of at the most in the manner of John 11:48, which names the worry over the survival of the Jewish people and its religious identity in face of Rome's violence. One must ask whether the early Christians' relation to Rome's social order and political organization is really a parallel case to Cicero. Does early Christianity intend, as does Cicero, to arrange the circumstances of the oppressed within patriarchy in such a way that the system will survive? There may have been within Pax Romana circles of people of low estate who had power in the state; clearly, Christianity (and Judaism) did not constitute such circles. I have demonstrated this extensively elsewhere.[105]

And yet the thinking of all New Testament documents is patriarchal. The father–son relationship occupies so central a place that no further evidence is needed. In contrast, a fundamental difference can be found in the function of the family, of the *oikos*. The *oikos* is not the bearer of the patriarchal family's possessions and therefore of its material basis of existence. The majority of Christian families would not be counted by Cicero among those who own property. Neither marriage nor the *oikos* has any ideological significance comparable to that found in his system. We hear about marriage partners working together for the gospel and about divorces occurring because of the gospel. No particular significance attaches to conceiving and giving birth to children (except perhaps in 1 Tim. 2:15). But the *oikos* had an important place in Christianity: it was a private space in which Christians carried out activities identified with the public sphere. Rome's patriarchal system did not infringe on that space; Cicero implies that in the Roman Empire the *oikos* alone could have provided for the formation and expansion of the Christian movement. Organizations were controlled, households were not. The households provided the free space for "strangers" that traveling female and male apostles required, and which, as Cicero makes abundantly plain, was otherwise unavailable to strangers.

What differ fundamentally here are the perception of patriarchal justice and that of the differences between human beings. God's justice is experienced through one's participation in a process in which the lowly are called by God, the dead are raised, and the mighty put down from their thrones. God is the loving and caring father—here the models of the New Testament and Cicero overlap—but God actualizes this fatherly love in that the last become the first, which in Cicero's judgment is tantamount to proclaiming the chaos in which ultimately women and asses will be up in arms. "Father" as an address for Christian officebearers is not found in the texts; indeed, it is specifically rejected in a word of Jesus (Matt. 23:9). The head of the family—the patriarch—has his power taken away by God's patriarchy; the power of the fathers is not divinely legitimated or reinstated by means of religious doctrine.[106] It is precisely the analogy between the human father and God the Father that is repudiated; the *difference* is crucially important ("Father *in the heavens*").

On the one hand, the situation of women is comparable to that in Cicero's patriarchy: women are subordinated to men, at least according to the household codes (and 1 Corinthians 11). On the other hand, they are not spoken of exclusively in terms of being part of the patriarch's sphere of power. There are women without men in the New Testament, and they obviously lack nothing. Not everything revolves around virginity, modesty, and having babies. In my view, then, the portraits of patriarchy found in Cicero and the New Testament have decisive differences: the image of God and the practical significance of *oikos*. At this point, it should be noted that in analyzing modern Western patriarchy, it helps not to let oneself become irritated by the terms *patriarchy* and *the rule of the father;* for the issue is the domination of elites (or of "the establishment") and not the rule of the fathers. Even in Cicero it is the domination by the upper-class patriarchs that is the real issue and not the rule of the fathers in a generic sense. For me, therefore, recourse to Cicero and other ancient depictions of patriarchal ideology is helpful also because dominant interests are so transparent there that they make it easier to see through modern mystifications of those same interests.

D. PATRIARCHY'S INSTRUMENTS OF DOMINATION

In my description of the instruments of domination of patriarchy, I shall continue to rely primarily on materials drawn from the dominant culture of imperial Rome. At the same time, I shall focus on the analysis not only of patriarchal conditions in that culture but also of those in my own context. I shall list instruments of domination that accrue from the ideology of patriarchy itself and others that have become known through socialist and feminist analysis.

Patriarchy's Self-Legitimation as a Harmonious Organism

Enforcing the control by (a few) people over (many) others is often justified in patriarchal ideology of domination in terms of images or metaphors that symbolize a community, tying the community's survival to the necessity of making distinctions among its members. A well-known example of this is Livy's simile

(2.32f.) of the body and its members.[107] It is alleged that with this simile Menenius Agrippa, the emissary of the Senate of Rome, dissuaded the plebeian population from rising up against the patricians (494 B.C.E.):

> The Senate decided to send an emissary to the plebeians, namely Menenius Agrippa, a man of eloquence, whom the plebeians had found acceptable also because he was one of them. He was admitted to their camp and is said to have told them this story, in the archaic and coarse language of the time. "There was a time when not everything in the human body was bound together in unity as it is now; each individual part had its own consciousness and could speak. All the parts of the body became annoyed because by their care, labour and subservience, everything was brought together only for the stomach which sat quietly in the middle and did nothing except enjoy what was offered to it. They made a pact: the hands would no longer lift food to the mouth, the mouth would no longer accept anything even when it was offered, the teeth would not chew things into small pieces. As they, in their anger, sought to tame the stomach by starving it, they themselves and the body as a whole became ever so feeble. It became clear then that even the stomach provided a significant service, that it fed others as it fed itself and that it passed on to all parts of the body the blood, from which we all live and maintain our strength, by sending it in equal measure through the veins, satiated with digested nourishment." And that is how he, comparing the rebellion in the human body to the anger of the plebeians against the patricians, changed their minds.

The plebeians are brought into conformity by a deceptive image; it mystifies the interests of the patricians and implies a mutuality between their goals and those of the plebeians. In ancient state ideologies there are many other instances and contexts in which this simile of the body and its members occurs.[108] It always does so in favor of the interests of the state. Similar meaning is conveyed by images, such as the choir of many voices.[109] The metaphor of the boat is often used in the political rhetoric of today—"We are all in the same boat," for example—when labor unions are told to exercise restraint in their wage demands. When it comes to the mystification of gender in our society, the perennial expression "equal but different" proves to be particularly resistant. Here women are "different," and their equality refers to some inward values or their worth in the eyes of God.[110] The basic anthropological model underlying such a view is that of one man and one woman; it presupposes that dualistic determinations of gender "roles" are the harmony provided by nature.[111] (See also below.) This kind of duplicitous expression justifies the subordination of women by men. Functioning rhetorically, it uses the biological difference between the sexes to legitimate the oppression of women.

It is interesting that Paul, in whose writings the injustice of the oppression of women is articulated and theologically legitimated (see below, III.1), is critical of the ideology of domination as it is found in the similes of the body and its members. He uses the simile himself and presupposes differences in the communities but demands in his simile that there be compensation in honor (*timē*) to the weaker members, those who are less respected (1 Cor. 12:23–24). If "honor" were merely a token word, then his simile would also serve the legitimation of domination (in this case, by those in the community with superior charisma). But I judge such a mendacious procedure highly improbable precisely because Paul's demand for compensatory treatment of the lesser members specifically qualifies the simile. I do not see in 1 Corinthians 12 the patriarchal legitimation of oppression by means of the image of the one body and its members; what I do see is the use of that image to critique domination, in the interest of just relationships within the communities.

The idea of one world and of creation as a body is crucially important in light of today's global structures of human oppression and the poisoning of creation. To be one body should not mean that parts of it must be oppressed so that the rich may profit. Philip Potter of the World Council of Churches created a striking image of one body in connection with the antiracism debate:

> There is a Zulu proverb which says, "When you have a thorn in your toe, the whole body stoops to pull it out." Whether it suits us or not and whether we admit it or not, we all belong to the same body of humanity. If we are not all to be infected by this destructive poison, we must together pull out the thorn of racist and economic oppression. We all require an infusion of attentive and caring love in order to pull this deadly thorn out of the body of the human race. We need to become the body of Christ whose members are dependent one on the other in joy and in sorrow.[112]

Here the image of one body is used not to legitimate oppression but to show how necessary it is to redistribute power downward.

The term *love patriarchalism* is of considerable importance in the patriarchal ideology of domination as described above. It implies that a condescending love from above is bestowed on those below in exchange for the obedience demanded from them.[113] To assume that Christianity survived only on account of its love patriarchalism is a variation of this patriarchal theory of state, elevated to the status of a theory of history. *Condescending love* from above turns readily into *responsibility exercised* by those at the top, a mystification on their part of what privileges them in patriarchy. Both these terms allege that there is a harmonious oneness that rests on hierarchical differentiations. Aelius Aristides speaks of Pax Romana as an ideal society: "Thus, the conditions as they exist are by nature satisfactory and advantageous for both the poor and the rich; there is no other way to live. A unique harmony of social order came into being which embraces everyone; what once obviously could not come together has become united under you: you are capable both to exercise dominion over an empire—a very mighty one at that—and to govern it not without humaneness."[114]

Androcentrism/Kyriocentrism and What Can Be Done against It

Recently, the women's movement has begun to take up the firm struggle against unjust language because such language has been recognized as one of the ways in which the power of the unjust social relations of patriarchy is sustained. Language can make people invisible, turn them into marginal groups, or, by its injustice, inflict other harm. Those who carry out the domination of patriarchy erect linguistic walls in line with their power interests. (Even though I know that there are a few women who participate in patriarchal domination, linguistically I cannot bring myself to use the term *women and men possessing patriarchal power* [*HerrschaftsinhaberInnen*].) The linguistic walls of androcentrism render women and children appendages and invisible. Those walls force the women and men who express themselves in androcentric language to be oblivious of the dominated, to consider them of incidental significance, or even to ridicule them.

Androcentric language focuses on the centers of power. The world becomes the world of the overlords. Women do indeed speak androcentric language; unconsciously or consciously driven by necessity, they render themselves invisible. In a similar linguistic fashion, the productivity of women and men and the enslavement of human beings is denied. I use the term *kyriocentrism*[115] as an extension of the feminist term *androcentrism,* in correspondence with my view of patriarchy. To the androcentrism and kyriocentrism of *language* there correspond those of *historiography* and of *anthropology* (or theology). In what follows, I cite examples from my historical material and the context of my experience of the encompassing phenomenon of patriarchal centering.

The foundation of androcentric language is the fact that, in it, women linguistically represent the exception. In the case of New Testament language, it means that the Christian community of women and men is addressed as "brothers." The androcentrism of this address may mean that women too are envisaged;[116] or it may mean that they are so insignificant in the eyes of those who write or speak these words that they actually have in mind only the men as brothers. Only on being asked whether there are any women in the community would they reply, "Well, of course!" The phrase "men, brothers" (*andres adelphoi*) in Acts 1:16[117] was spoken when the community was discussing tasks of leadership (choosing a successor to the twelfth apostle). Women are assumed to be present (cf. 1:14), and they meet the substance of what is needed in such a successor (1:21f.) except that they belong to the wrong gender (cf. 1:21). May one conclude that "brothers" (1:15) is meant to be "inclusive,"[118] that is, that women are also addressed, or that the expressly male term only makes perfectly clear what is otherwise taken for granted, namely, that women's presence is assumed but that they are *not* being addressed? The phrase "men, brothers" in Acts presumably seeks to guard the designation "brothers" against an inadvertent inclusiveness.[119]

Androcentrism is the handy tool of androcentric historiography, which asserts, for example, that since the Gospels speak only of disciples who are male, Jesus had no *female disciples*. According to such androcentric historiography, women were involved, but only as ordinary members of the community. However, when it comes to persons representative of the interests of patriarchal domination, androcentric language is taken literally.[120] There may have been "sisters," yes, but no women prophets, women disciples, women apostles, women bishops.

When dealing with androcentric language in connection with the biblical tradition, one encounters special problems that do not arise in connection with other historical materials. Aristotle's androcentric language is not recited in the service of worship. I may criticize his language and try myself to develop a just language. But when it comes to the Bible, the androcentrism of its language has profound implications. Either I have to denounce its androcentric language, and that of the liturgy, or I must lay hands on the text. Since the liturgy is not the place for denouncing language, one must lay hands on those biblical texts that normally are read in translation in worship services without qualifying commentary. The "men, brothers" of Acts 1:16 (and elsewhere) must be translated as "sisters and brothers,"[121] even if the text intended to exclude women from those to whom it was addressed. A literal translation without immediate critical qualification results in the exclusion of women, both in the present and in the future, from the Christian community, its administration, and its further formation. To lay hands on a biblical text that speaks in androcentric language by translating it into just language is authorized by history itself; there actually were women disciples, women apostles, women who were "elders," and so forth.[122]

Problems related to translation become more difficult when not only the text but the historical reality itself was more than likely androcentric: the "Twelve," it would appear, were actually twelve men. Even more difficult is the translation of New Testament texts openly hostile to women, such as 1 Tim. 2:11–15 or 1 Thess. 4:3–8. To salvage anything at all here by means of skilled translation, that is, to render the text usable for today's and tomorrow's church, is tantamount to a denial or cover-up of injustice and guilt.[123] It becomes necessary in such cases to criticize openly the text, and even Jesus (in light of Luke 10:38–42, for example), and to make it clear that there are, in the biblical tradition, texts hostile to women, that the history of early Christianity was at least in part a patriarchal history that turned women into second-class human beings.

Kyriocentrism is found wherever the labor (paid or unpaid) of female and male slaves, of free women and men, is rendered invisible, wherever it serves the interests[124] of the overlords or is described as being done by the masters themselves: "A man [i.e., a landowner] planted a vineyard and set a hedge around it" (Mark 12:1 and par.). The actual work on the land was done by female and male slaves or daily-wage earners and not by the owners (cf. below at II.2.B).[125] The invisible hands that, then and now, do the never-ending housework[126] must be made visible in a just language as that of the women and men who work the land. Household labor and the work of educating children, deemed as a rule to be the worthless work of women and not remunerated, provides the infrastructure for the dominance by patriarchal overlords. Furthermore, it is kyriocentrism that is instrumental in keeping women and men unemployed and poor. It assists in making it appear as if people had brought unemployment and poverty on themselves. Such conditions are declared unavoidable; they are rendered invisible through one means or another, or at least minimized in terms of their seriousness. Kyriocentrism opens the door to racism in that it glosses over the brutality of the enslavement of women and men, for example, when *doulē* and *doulos* are translated as "maidservant" and "servant";[127] for such euphemistic translation conceals from all who hear it today the true identity of the *kyrios,* the overlord of women and men slaves, namely, a human being who treated other human beings as subhumans, as things.

When it assumes the theological form of Christocentrism, kyriocentrism is especially painful. A Christocentric interpretation of New Testament texts is, as a rule, anti-Judaistic and hostile to women. Christocentrism depicts Christ's relation to other human beings as one of dominance.[128] The corresponding androcentric anthropology makes for unjust relations among human beings, making them incapable of seeing themselves each as an "I" in community with others.

Androcentrism makes women and children invisible. Kyriocentrism makes the productivity of women, children, and men and their poverty invisible and glosses over the brutality of slavery. The language spoken in patriarchy legitimates violence and militarism;[129] it masks suffering and stigmatizes people as "undesirable." The historiography of androcentrism is that of the winners. Androcentric anthropology and theology shape relationships in the interest of patriarchal domination.

Every action in opposition to androcentrism, kyriocentrism, and others should be guided by this primary question: Who in this history are the "last"? Jesus acted in opposition by beginning with the last and making them visible.[130] Practically speaking, this means we need to take the side of women, children, the exploited, and the aged; it means gynocentrism and Women-Church (to which I shall return).[131] Making visible the "last," *eschatoi*—the Greek word, unfortunately, is also androcentric—requires an analysis of patriarchy that makes the walls of androcentrism and kyriocentrism transparent; it requires a vision of what justice might look like, namely, that justice which no longer oppresses anyone, not even creation.

I would like to elucidate what I have just described by means of two texts of poetry. Bertolt Brecht wonders about the invisible slaves and wage earners:

> Who built seven-gated Thebes?
> The books record the names of kings.
> Did kings haul the blocks of rock?
> The often ruined Babylon—
> who rebuilt it many times?
> The night when the Great Wall of China was done,

where did the masses go? Great Rome
is full of arches; who built them?
Over whom did the Caesars triumph?[132]

The women's movement presupposes such questions and has shown that even
the approach of socialism has laid hold of only a small section of reality.

THE SONG OF THE LACEMAKER-WOMAN

Lacemaker-woman,
Lacemaker-woman,
you teach me to make lace,
I teach you to protest.

Even in her youth
a woman starts believing
that she must be obedient,
like a slave, and not speak.

The sole income of the man
leaves a family in hunger,
but the people go on saying
that she is chasing after men.

Twice as long her working hours,
but smaller her wage,
her child is left alone
and her labor unending.

One master at home,
another at the factory.
She returns to her home
and goes straight to the stove.

Standing at her machine
she produces, like the workmate.
When she gets pregnant
the company lets her go.

And the woman, the widow,
or the one he abandoned,
the mother unmarried,
they have no rights—nothing.

Abandoned woman,
come from the corner, come over here,
and see the rights we have,
and change life for the better.

In women's courage
Jesus put his trust.
He cursed the false distinctions
and gave woman her own worth.[133]

Sexism and Stereotypes of Femininity

The systematic oppression of human beings on account of their sex or sexuality has, since the end of the sixties, been called sexism.[134] In today's world *all women,* both heterosexual and lesbian, and gay men experience sexual oppression. Furthermore, sexism is a feature of racial oppression, for example, in the belief of whites that black men are especially potent and lustful, a belief that was already held in antiquity. Both female and male slaves were sexually exploited in ancient times; they were believed to be especially wanton. This is one more reason for me to look for antecedents of modern racism in the oppression of female and male slaves in antiquity.[135]

The chief instruments of the sexist oppression of women, then and now, are (1) the maintenance of gender stereotypes (what is feminine and what is masculine) and, closely related to it, (2) patriarchal disposition over the body of woman and her reproductive capacity.

The stereotypes of femininity[136] at the time when Christianity came into existence were shaped by three different perceptions. The first was that of what a woman's tasks were in an affluent patriarchal household; it built on the distinction between woman's place, on the one hand, and public political life outside the home (which belonged to the upper-class man who did not need to earn an income), on the other, or between woman's place and a man's labor on the land. The second perception had to do with biology's understanding of procreation, and the third with the mythology of creation and the origin of the world.

Paul draws on ideas and arguments informed by all three perceptions in 1 Corinthians 11. Woman is to submit to the man (1 Cor. 11:3); he is the head of the woman, that is, he rules the *household*. Covering her head during the worship of God, something for which Paul argues vehemently, is to symbolize her submission and to protect her against being sexually molested by angels (1 Cor. 11:10). Woman's long hair (1 Cor. 11:15) is to protect her against being sexually molested (presumably by the lustful leering of men; cf. Matt. 5:28). All this presupposes that the female body as such is the source of seduction and that women's sexuality is sinful and perilous. Women and their bodies are defined in terms of sexuality.

Paul affirms a negative stereotype of femininity that was gaining acceptance in imperial Roman times, namely, that of the seducible seductress. This stereotype was spread particularly by *mythology,* for example, in interpretations of Genesis 2—3 within Judaism and in Gnostic mythology of *sophia* (wisdom).[137] The word *physis* ("nature"; 1 Cor. 11:14) incorporates into the text the perceptions of ancient biology. Paul regards women's long hair as part of their natural female constitution; for him, the contrast between the short hair of men and the long hair of women is a *biological dualism*. Romans 1:26–27 also shows that he presupposes such a dualism and that he relates it centrally to procreation.[138] Female human beings have to submit themselves to a natural use (*physikē chrēsis;*

Rom. 1:26–27) by male human beings. Men are filled with passion in relation to that use and desire women (as Rom. 1:27 implies). It is therefore "natural" biology that predisposes men to be active and women to be passive.

Women who renounce being thus used by men and who make "unnatural" (*para physin*) use of their bodies are ruled by passions that dishonor them, according to Paul. This is a heterosexual definition of femininity as seen from the perspective of patriarchal gender dualism. As the text speaks only of sexual *activity* (*katergazomenoi*), the "unnatural use" of women's bodies most likely refers primarily to avoidance of pregnancy and childbirth and only secondarily to lesbian sexuality (it is quite a different matter in reference to gay relationships; see Rom. 1:27), because lesbian women are seen as women who do not passively submit to *being used by active men* (for purposes of procreation). Use as "the vessel" of men (1 Thess. 4:4) is the female human being's *physikē chrēsis*. A woman who does not submit to this praxis of femininity is in dishonor (Rom. 1:26) or, as 1 Cor. 11:5f. would suggest, in disgrace, comparable to a woman whose head is shaven. The punishment of having the hair shorn off[139] and being pilloried in public deprives woman of her status in the patriarchal household because her femininity, as patriarchal society defines it, has been violently taken from her.

I have elucidated here the subject of stereotypes of femininity at the time when Christianity came into existence, in reference to Paul. As far as I know, the patriarchal construct of womanhood and femininity, as it appears in Paul, has equivalents in all other domains of the period in terms of the definition of woman's place in the household and of being the vessel of men's procreative activity. I would refer to the Mishnah[140] in general and to Aristotle and Cicero[141] as examples where such constructs are to be found within Judaism and Greco-Roman culture respectively. At that time a new sound could be heard in the definition of womanhood, and it spread into every other cultural domain: it was the negative judgment that all women are sinful on account of their sexuality. Philo of Alexandria,[142] but not the Mishnah and the Old Testament, may serve as an example from Judaism; Paul (or 1 Timothy 2), as I have shown, serves as an example from Christianity. This intensification in the oppression of women in the days of imperial Rome will be discussed extensively in chapter II.1.

I have already noted how closely the construct of femininity is connected with patriarchal disposition over the body of woman, her reproductive capacity, and female children. The punishment of women for actual or alleged adultery, even in the form of collective murder by stoning, appears to me to have had the same social significance in the ancient world that abortion legislation has today (e.g., section 218 of the German Criminal Code). Because society has an interest in the disposition of women's reproductive capacity, the right of disposition is not left in the hands of one man alone. (More on this appears later at IV.1, in relation to the story of the adulterous woman in John 8.) The institutionalized stereotypes of femininity enforce violence against women; they are the source of several forms of violence—from the punishment of adultery to sexual assault and battering. Such socialization undoubtedly takes place in everyday relationships.

In this connection, the influence of the education and formation of girls and women must not be underestimated. The materials from antiquity make this quite plain. Xenophon states that the young bridegroom has the task of training the woman for her task as housewife and childbearer:

> When cattle in the pastures . . . are chronically in bad condition, we blame the keeper; when a horse is consistently unruly, we blame the rider. When despite her husband's instruction in the virtues of the housewife, a woman misbehaves, she justly bears the burden of guilt. But if he did not enlighten her in proper behavior and correct disposition toward work, should not the man be justly blamed?[143]

Paul too, in 1 and 2 Timothy, tries to enforce this patriarchal teaching, but Christian women resist this monopoly of formation, which serves only the interests of patriarchal socializing of women.[144] Just how intentionally the representatives of patriarchal hierarchies enforce their interest becomes very clear at this point. Patriarchy understands itself as the socializing agent of women and seeks with every means at its disposal to prevent a formation of women (and men) that is critical of patriarchy.

Does this enforcement of stereotypes of femininity in fact encompass every area of society? The literature on economics (Aristotle, Cicero, etc.) is written from the perspective of the upper-class male who is engaged in politics and who rules over a large household. Whenever work on the land is discussed as men's work, there is the tone of nostalgia: this is how it was in the good old days when life was still simple and ideal.[145] Were those patriarchal definitions, particularly that of womanhood, shared by the men, slaves, and daily-wage earners who actually did the work? Femininity as defined by patriarchal economics relegated women to the home, men to the fields or to public life. In actual fact, women did work in the field.[146] The everyday life of poor people clearly exposes the mendacity of patriarchal constructs of femininity; it gives rise to relations among the genders that elude patriarchal control. All the time, women risked being sexually assaulted while at work on the land;[147] field work continued late into pregnancy and often necessitated giving birth alone, behind the nearest bush.[148] The texts are rare that reveal to us the experiences of women and men who live in poverty and whose working days are never-ending. I regard the New Testament as an important document where such women and men are being heard. In early Christianity one can see the struggle for liberation at the same time as oppression is being carried on.

The silence surrounding women's work in the fields shows the mendacity of these stereotypes of femininity. In other respects as well, surrounding things with silence is a patriarchal instrument of domination: women's struggles and resistance are either not spoken of or simply ridiculed. How precious are the historical sources that break this devastating silence! That is why I love the New Testament and even Paul, for in spite of those texts of his which, unfortunately, are still powerfully effective in oppressing women, he amplified the voices of women and men who were liberating themselves. He passed on a Christian baptismal confession that contradicts the definitions of femininity and resists the disposition over women's bodies: Gal. 3:28. It is a confession that is consciously antisexist; in Christ there is neither "Jew nor Greek, slave nor free, male nor female." Genesis 1:27 is cited here, "male and female God created them." There are two understandings of "male and female" in Gal. 3:28: the first has to do with the procreation of children in patriarchal marriage, a sense that the verse ultimately rejects; the second, with the hierarchy in which men rule over women, as indicated by the parallel to slave and free. "In Christ," which means in lives shared in communities of Christians, the injustice of gender stereotypes is recognized and openly named. People work together to reverse the phenomenon of women's being confined to this prison of male and female.

We must still ask about the intent of Paul's understanding of this baptismal confession. One senses his uncertainty. In his sexist text of 1 Corinthians 11, he remembers that he ought to oppose sexism (1 Cor. 11:11f.), even though there is something half-hearted about the manner in which he makes use of his baptismal confession.[149] Numerous New Testament texts show where the power comes from to overcome oppression and half-heartedness: it comes from common struggle and shared visions.[150] I have titled this general section "Patriarchy and the Hope for the Reign of God" in order to keep before our eyes that patriarchy is not all-powerful.

E. THE FEMINIST VISION AND THE REIGN OF GOD

The word *Women-Church*[151] is a concept of feminist rhetoric and a counter-concept to patriarchy. It refers to a church of the future in which women, men, and children and all of creation live together in just relations, without hierarchies. The concept implies that the churches which actually exist today are dominated by elites of men, in which only occasionally are individual women given a share. For the most part, women do volunteer work, but it is they who hold up the churches, the majority of which are governed by men. Feminist theology is, correspondingly, a theology in opposition to the patriarchal theology that dominates our tradition. In my context, the feminist theology movement has not been able to bring about any real change in that domination. There is no question about what the power relationships are; they are relationships of domination. The struggle for women's liberation is accompanied by the attempts to silence the voices of feminist Christian women.

As a rhetorical concept, Women-Church is effective; its vision, however, is ambiguous. One must always explain that the concept does not exclude men, children, and the rest of creation. And yet the concept of Women-Church as a gynaikocentric[152] concept of argumentation must be retained. It makes plain that overcoming stereotypes of femininity does not mean the creation of sexless, test-tube creatures who are equal to men. Rather, the overcoming of stereotypes strives for women to be women, even though authentic womanhood is still a vision. We are women deformed by patriarchy and are only on the way to becoming women. Truly liberated womanhood in relation to God is seen now "in a mirror dimly"—in the form of a puzzle—"but then we will see face to face. Now I know in part; then I shall understand fully, even as I have been fully understood" (1 Cor. 13:12). In this vision of encounter with God, Paul thinks of the human being, and presumably also of God, as male, and yet I employ it because Paul captured in a classic manner the ancient wisdom that the new human being was one in relationship with God: "face to face."

The feminist vision I have in mind is based on the same three premises that Rosemary Radford Ruether describes in relation to ecological spirituality: the transitoriness of the "I," the living mutual dependency of all things, and the value of the person in community.[153] The biblical tradition offers a rich treasure of visions that, if androcentric, are yet transformable. In spite of their androcentrism, these visions offer radical critiques of domination. Two such images are: the peoples of the earth shall live like birds under the branches of the cosmic tree of God (Mark 4:30–32);[154] the world in its wholeness will comprise the "heaven and the earth," in which God is "all in all."[155] This is not the God of patriarchy; it is a God who is present in every grain of sand and in every corruptible body. The suffering of creation will cease when God gathers the peoples from the ends of the earth and brings them home to God.[156]

The "reign of God" is conceptualized as a counterconcept to that of the Oriental megakingdoms: the mighty are put down from their thrones (Luke 1:52); God alone reigns (*basileuein*). The quality of God's "reigning" is not modeled on the rulers. The presence of God in a man whom the Romans crucified indicates what constitutes God's reigning. I am fully aware that the cross of Jesus, too, has often been interpreted in a dreadful, androcentric-patriarchal manner, that it was and still is used as an instrument to oppress women and to turn others into subjugated people.[157] But this tradition cannot be destroyed by its misappropriation, for we still learn from it that God is not omnipotent but that God is present in the creatures who suffer and shall be "all in all." Early Christianity and the praxis of its life is understood only on the basis of its eschatology.[158] Feminist theology, as a theology critical of patriarchy, derives its power from its vision, irrespective of whether this vision is spoken of as wholeness, matriarchy, or a vision of a just society. The visions of early Christianity are a source of strength for the struggle for justice, including the feminist struggle of women. These visions are also an inheritance of women.

3

The New Testament:
Word of God or Androcentric
Obfuscation of History?

A. IS THE HYMN OF CHRIST IN PHILIPPIANS 2:6–11
CRITICAL OF PATRIARCHY OR NOT?

Sheila Briggs has raised a radical question about the New Testament text from the perspective of a black female liberation theologian in the United States. I want to deal extensively with one of her articles[159] because she goes to the very root of the problem. She identifies three distinct categories of texts in the New Testament. To the first category belong those texts in which the voice of the oppressed may still be heard; those in which the process of the text's transmission and canonization by an increasingly patriarchal church "has not completely erased" (p. 138) these voices. The second category consists of texts that voice "the convictions, values and interests of the dominant social group" (p. 138). In the first three centuries, this group was what Briggs calls "an alienated social elite," since, for members of the elite, becoming Christian meant experiencing social ostracization if they were openly critical of the patriarchal slave household and the imperial government.

The third category consists of those texts that are ambiguous. According to Briggs, "These are texts of which it is not clear whether their *effect*[160] on the original communities and individuals who heard, wrote and read them was conserving of the oppressive social order or produced criticism of and dissatisfaction with it, and even some measure of action towards transformation" (p. 139). Briggs cites motivation and consciousness as factors that complicate a resolution of this ambiguity in the text:

> If the oppressed belonged to the community of producers and performers of the biblical texts, then the issue of "false consciousness" is raised. Yet, false consciousness seems to be more explanatory of historical fact than descriptive of consciousness. For example, since no social revolution succeeded in the Greco-Roman world, it is deduced that the false consciousness of the oppressed was a tragic component in its failure. (p. 139)

With reference to the hermeneutical privilege of the oppressed that is claimed from a liberation perspective, Briggs explains that in dealing with (biblical) tradition, the oppressed have an indirect hermeneutical privilege. "Since the contemporary oppressed know their own relationships of oppression and may seek their own liberation, they are more likely to make the *analogy*[161] between their own experience and similar social relationships reproduced in the biblical texts" (p. 142). Therefore, since one may not approach the past like "the Western development expert [who] claims to know what the needs and desires of a Latin American peasant *qua* human being are" (p. 140), it is necessary to respect the integrity of the oppressed—in the present as in the past. Briggs concludes that analogy, as employed in biblical hermeneutics of liberation, needs to function intuitively, in *two distinct forms:* "the analogy between the elements of contemporary experience uncontrolled through social knowledge and the irrecoverable aspects of past experience, and the analogy between past and present social relationships" (p. 142).

Sheila Briggs examines Phil. 2:6–11 as a text belonging to this third, ambiguous category. She perceives in the pre-Pauline hymn an idealization of the role of slaves; it is found in the obedience of Christ the slave (vv. 7f.) and in the fact that he does nothing to liberate himself and that God saves him (v. 9). And that is how the hymn communicates to the oppressed that resistance is pointless. "Christ's divine priority of worth is seen as confirmed in the paradox of his voluntary renunciation of it. The tension created in the text through the statement that a divine being becomes a slave is relieved through the removal of this christological enslavement from any analogy with an act of human enslavement" (p. 147). Slaves never have a choice. "The text of Phil 2: 6–11, as we have it, is kyriocentric. It does not challenge the interests or beliefs of slave-masters. Yet, there is an irreducible tension in the idea of a god who becomes a slave, which cannot be overcome by depicting Christ as simultaneously the ideal and the atypical slave" (p. 149). A text such as this makes conceivable the inversion of social hierarchies.

In the antebellum South, slaves and their masters often shared the same religion. In Latin America today, the elites and the exploited masses often practice the same form of Catholicism. Here we see "the elements of resistance to oppression in the apparently innocuous religiosity of the oppressed" (p. 151). Something comparable may be assumed in relation to the slaves of the Greco-Roman world. In this way there may be found access to the possibilities for liberation in the subversive reading of texts on the part of the oppressed. A text itself does not provide those possibilities; rather, they are "claimed from it by the oppressed" (p.151).

My understanding of this hymn differs from that of Sheila Briggs in a number of specific nuances. Philippians 2:6–11 is not unique in biblical tradition; it is a text representative of numerous others that present God—or God in Christ—as one who descends to the most wretched and shares their lot. "Jesus Christ, . . . though he was rich, yet for your sakes . . . became poor, so that by his poverty you might become rich" (2 Cor. 8:9). The rich interpret this to be about spiritual and inward values, not about material poverty and wealth.[162] People who are not enslaved declare that Christ's being a slave is a metaphor that expresses nothing about real women and men slaves.[163] Those who have experienced oppression perceive in the voluntary nature of the loss of sovereignty the divinity of the slave Christ, who, *in solidarity, shared the lot of all female and male slaves* and, as a poor Galilean man, shared the poverty of the Jewish people. The characteristically Western distinction between "image" and "meaning" is rarely found in theologies of liberation.[164] The manner in which Western exegetical tradition reinterprets New Testament texts whenever they speak of real oppression (poverty, slaves) tells me, in the first instance, that the text is unambiguous, critical of patriarchy, and not at all kyriocentric. Second, it tells me that the women and men slaves in early Christianity could not have been so completely without voice.

I have tried to read Sheila Briggs's important article as a personal challenge to examine whether I do not wish, after all, to whitewash the New Testament to a large extent, for apologetic purposes. For me, it is unambiguous—and I find myself confirmed therein by dominant exegesis and how it reinterprets texts—that the God of Israel is one who strengthens all who seek God, giving them power to resist, because this God comes among them and begins with the last. God became a slave in Christ, died on the cross, became poor. According to the New Testament conception, God did *not* become a woman. Nevertheless, this does not make me believe that the androcentric circumscription of so many New Testament texts that are critical of patriarchy cancels the critique of patriarchy. As a rule, the oppressed can speak only in the language of the overlords; they have only rudiments of their own language. The critique of patriarchy, begun but not completed in the New Testament, shows me how to go beyond its limits and how to further the critique of the androcentrism and the oppression of women contained within its pages. I think it theologically legitimate, as well as necessary, to extend the hymn of Christ: Christ took the form of a woman (Phil. 2:7).

In my attempts to extend the writing of the biblical tradition, I am conscious of the limits of my language and my ability to see. Which oppression have *I* once again kept from view? But my concern over my blind spots may not preclude my venturing beyond the limits of the text's patriarchal conceptions and androcentric language. Whenever I let the androcentric and patriarchal obfuscation of liberating biblical texts lead me to pronounce that they speak the overlords' language after all, I am depriving people of that time of their own texts. How much shared "blood, sweat, and tears" for and experience of liberation are expressed in Phil. 2:6–11! This text is God's word not because it is *a text;* it is God's word because it is the voice of human beings who, through their relation to God, became strong enough to work together at their liberation. I hear God's word when I hear that voice and when it encourages and empowers me to join with others to work for the future of creation, a future for which there seems to be no hope.

Over against Sheila Briggs's radical question I cite the Western, kyriocentric interpretation of the New Testament. That interpretation obviously contradicts the text. My social-historical rejoinder to her is that the majority of the people who kept early Christianity alive were the lowly, poor women and men, among whom were female and male slaves and owners of slaves. There are traces in the texts that indicate, first, that a Christian female slave was not obedient[165] and, second, that those in the community who owned women and men slaves were people from whom much was expected.[166] At times I wonder whether my hanging onto the majority of New Testament texts or my enthusiasm in working with them comes from Protestant Word-of-God theology. Similarly, I wonder whether the *more emphatic distinction* of the text from the dimly or clearly discernible church of the oppressed or Women-Church behind it is rooted in the faith tradition of Catholicism. Such denominational difference does not mean that I renounce the ecumenical character of Christian and women's movements of liberation. I want only to point to the possibility of denominational differences that exist and should not be neglected. For me, androcentric texts can also be God's word. I am obliged to critique their androcentrism and to point it out once I have recognized it. But even if I believe that Phil. 2:6–11 is primarily the confession of poor women and men and of female and male slaves, the text and its androcentrism are still oppressive of women.

B. SOCIAL-HISTORICAL INTERPRETATION
OF THE BIBLE

The social-historical interpretation of the Bible in which my female and male coworkers and I are engaged grows from a community of people who work for liberation. In other words, it has a place in the *communio sanctarum et sanctorum* of the present and is done in reference to the work of liberation movements. I understand the task of that interpretation as a contribution to liberation theology in the European context.

Such a liberationist understanding of social history is not necessarily implied in the words *social history*. This term may be used for approaches to historical study that are, in fact, different in substance: for example, a social history that paints a traditional intellectual history (or exegesis) with the diverse hues of the time and place in question[167] or that makes a text more vivid by describing what life was like then. Frequently the intention is anything but to contribute to the analysis of oppression or to work for liberation. I make the claim that a social-historical interpretation of the Bible that aligns itself in its contents with dominant Western exegesis in fact pursues the maintenance of the social status quo.

I have argued this in connection with the concepts of "love patriarchalism" and "itinerant radicalism" and the "new consensus" in Western social history.[168] Since dominant Western scholarship shies away from declaring itself in terms of the aims of historical study and its interests, critical analysis is required for those interests to become manifest. Pursuing such analysis reveals that the term *social history* may, indeed, designate substantially different orientations.

When we[169] began to apply this term to our common work, social history as a concept had already become a stumbling block in the West German church and university. It smacked of socialism. We did not object to being understood that way. We had in mind a nonauthoritarian, democratic socialism, a utopia then and now. (The word *utopia* has a positive meaning for me.) We—that is, the majority of the members of the Heidelberg Working Circle, which I will discuss later—did not want to speak of "materialist" interpretation of scripture because the philosophical infrastructure associated with it exceeded our abilities. Besides, this concept was shaped by a tradition of Latin Europe, namely, structuralism, with which we were only marginally concerned.[170] But we did *not* distance ourselves politically from the materialist interpretation of scripture;[171] we worked and still work in our circle together with representatives of this approach. At first, the term *liberation theology* was also one that we did not apply to our work because we believed that this would appropriate what belonged to the base movements of Latin America.

From its beginnings, the Heidelberg Working Circle and its social-historical interpretation of scripture were marked by a commitment to third world solidarity work, as well as by an effort to overcome the split between theory (that is, exegesis) and praxis (that is, Christian conduct of life and liberation work, or—in our context—sermon and meditation on scripture). What this meant concretely was that the circle's female and male scripture scholars had to enter into working relationships with female and male ministers, teachers, and other interested persons engaged in practical work. Together they had to reflect historically and theologically on questions of social justice. A social-historical interpretation of scripture in this sense does not need to be explicitly "translated" into a sermon; it is already supposed to include in its reflection on the biblical tradition a clear perspective on practical life today. Interpretation of this kind mirrors both the social contexts[172] of the people who speak in the Bible and the context of the women and men who interpret them today. The orientation and content of this social-historical interpretation of scripture may be summed up as follows: It is committed to the option of the poor, to *the gospel of the poor,* and tries to be open to the demands of the gospel of the poor in the context of Germany and Western Europe. It is interested in the *abolition of theory and praxis dualisms;* it wants to declare its own interests. It tries not to hide behind the alleged neutrality of the sciences. It understands itself to be taking sides quite openly and, as such, to be critical of an interpretation of scripture aligned with the dominant powers.[173] One aspect of this critique was, from the outset, the critique of the anti-Judaism of Christian theology.

It has been the women's movement of recent years that has taught me the necessity of living and working as a feminist. The history of the oppressed is itself a suppressed history, so much so that the history of women has to be reclaimed often by reading against the sources. The women's movement employs the historical method of a *feminist social history*. Despite their diverse traditions of scholarship, women historians engaged in feminist historiography or interpretation of scripture need to research the history of women as a history with a social context.[174] Feminist historiography will forever remain truncated if it does not search out the oppression of women and their praxis of liberation in terms of the concrete social conditions that have constructed women's economic, political, and social reality. That is why, in a project of feminist social history of early Christianity, I use the concept of patriarchy described earlier.

Social-historical study is arranged according to different aims, depending on whether one's concept is that of the history of women or of feminist historiography. The distinction between these concepts corresponds to that between a social history which does not question domination (as is the case in Theissen) and that which, like mine, seeks to contribute to the work of women's and creation's liberation.

In current interpretation of scripture, one encounters a variety of approaches (such as those of depth psychology, bibliodrama, narrative, and Jewish–Christian dialogue); each presupposes a historically accountable interpretation of scripture. One must ask, in every case, where the historical exegesis comes from that is operative in the given interpretation: Does it come from the dominant Western tradition of interpretation, from a social-historical interpretation that has a liberation theology/feminist orientation, or from elsewhere?

For example, when a feminist bibliodramatic study is based on traditional Western interpretation, it may happen that one can no longer work *with* the text in feminist perspective because it has become an instrument of domination over women. Or it may happen that the underlying interpretation, oriented as it is toward the interests of domination, obstructs or even obliterates feminist interests. It is quite misleading, therefore, to lump together approaches such as bibliodramatic, depth-psychological, and social-historical interpretations,[175] since the first two are more often than not informed by traditional Western "historical criticism." Yet it is also possible for bibliodrama to function quite well on the basis of a social history oriented toward liberation theology.

The dominant biblical scholarship of the Western world usually calls itself "historical criticism." This often incorporates the claim that it proceeds in an objective and neutral manner, producing, accordingly, correct exegesis in contrast to "wild" exegesis[176] or, in more polite terms, to "new approaches to the Bible."[177]

My critique of historical criticism is not that it claims to be critical or that it pursues its work in methodical, reflective steps—I do that myself. If only it were critical: less critical in relation to the texts of scripture and more critical concerning today's institutions of domination and their use of the Bible! My critique of historical criticism is that it does not reflect on its own interests and openly declare them. It sides with existing injustices. It evades all questions critical of it, because the representative men (and a few women) of historical criticism hold power in the institutions concerned.

My relationship to this so-called historical criticism can be elucidated in terms of two examples: the first is the determination of a text's *genre* (*Gattung*) and its *Sitz im Leben*; the second is *literary criticism*.

I agree with the scholarly tradition of historical criticism that, methodologically, it makes good sense to inquire about a text's genre and *Sitz im Leben,* that is, to ask the old question of *Formgeschichte.*[178] What I need to know about those determinants is what is implied by their substance, their theology and social history. Historical criticism, as a rule, understands the "life" (*Leben*) in which the New Testament is situated (has its *Sitz*) to be the Christian community. No further questions are asked concerning the community's situation (*Sitz*) in society or concerning the meaning in that context of gender, class, race, and the political conditions. Without further questions of this kind, establishing the *Sitz im Leben* provides an inconclusive account of the community. This is especially evident where there has been no reflection on the source of the elements that make up the picture of this community.

The example I have chosen in connection with the determination of genre is that of *miracle stories,* in order to elucidate both correspondence with and contradiction to historical criticism. In determining the genre of a text, the scholarly tradition of historical criticism puts the miracle worker Jesus in the center. In the healing miracle, the sick are the objects of Jesus' actions; healing demonstrates the power of the miracle worker Jesus.[179] This permits a fundamentally secular interpretation of Jesus (as a miracle worker of the kind found in ancient religious conceptions of divine men, their powerful deeds, and the miraculous circumstances of their lives). But it also permits a strong interpretation of Jesus as the Christ and the Son of God. Each version of the genre determined is Christocentric in a patriarchal, kyriocentric sense. However, if one approaches the determination of their genre with another perception of Jesus, for example that of feminist Christology, where Christ is understood in terms of his relationship with human beings,[180] one makes a new discovery of the miracle stories. In the exorcisms and healing miracles of the New Testament, the sick are portrayed in the give-and-take of a mutual relationship rather than as objects of Jesus' actions. In addition, the spectators in those stories are not merely onlookers but are equally drawn into the relational event, into the healing. In common turning to and common praise of God, the destruction of human beings is brought to an end. In the praise offered to God by the sick and the others present, I recognize an expression of their experience of God's reign; in other words, I understand this praise eschatologically. It is "the common experience of people that something new has begun in their lives, . . . that passivity becomes activity, . . . as if someone were born anew."[181] They are able to praise God together again, and that is the healing, not a clinical recovery of health in the sense of our medical tradition.[182]

In a schematic way, I want to differentiate my approach from that taken by traditional historical criticism in determining the genre of the healing narratives. Because his theories still influence scholarly tradition, I choose Rudolf Bultmann[183] as representative of historical criticism.

Historical Criticism	*Feminist Social History*

Signs of illness
     length, characteristics, etc.
	Suffering and lack of power
	     as the place to start

The miracle itself
     (the miraculous process is
      not described)
     manipulations
     approach to the sick person
     touching
     the miracle-causing word
     threats against the demons
	The increase of power through the
	     relationship between Jesus and the
	     sick and others present, often
	     against great odds

The success of the miracle
     gradual or sudden
     demonstrations of healing
	The transformation of all participants
	     into agents in the reign of God

The impression of the people
     present
	The praise of the people offered
	     to God
	     God's reign is experienced

I do not critique historical criticism for determining a genre; the problem arises for me when the critical process is itself determined by an unreflected patriarchal kyriocentrism.

Literary criticism is my second example of where analysis of historical criticism is necessary. It looks at texts in terms of the question of how they came into existence. Can one distinguish, for example, between a preliminary literary stage of a text and its redaction? Mark 14:9, the conclusion of the story of Jesus' anointment by an unnamed woman in Bethany, is said by many interpreters to be a Markan redactional addition to an old, pre-Markan story of Jesus. Walter Schmithals comments: "One may well expect such tastelessness from the evangelist's historicizing habit, namely at the climax of the narrative to draw the attention away from Jesus to the woman who had come only for the purpose of serving him."[184] That sentence unwittingly shows that scholarship does have a perspective; it does or does not call attention to something, while it does not, as a rule, declare the perspective within which it works. Focusing on Jesus is said to be the necessary alternative to focusing on the woman; the latter is said to be inappropriate. Yet the text draws attention to both Jesus and the woman (even without v. 9). It is a product of androcentrism, claiming to be Christology, to separate verse 9 in the name of literary criticism.

The example is symptomatic for many other, similar cases. The decision to speak of a break or contradiction in a text and consequently assume an older or more recent written (or even parts of an oral) tradition is based on substantive presuppositions that, as a rule, are not stated or subjected to critique. I do not doubt, of course, that the Gospels do have an antecedent history in oral tradition or even in a written form. A synoptic comparison of the four Gospels manifests certain influences that have led to changes in the texts. But I regard it as fundamental violence to texts to dismantle them and to employ theological judgments in so doing. That is how a text can be made over into an "old" or "genuine" text as one sees fit. It is necessary, instead, to analyze *the existing text as a whole* and to understand it as an expression of life by women and men. That is how one learns much about them in a social-historical sense, as well as about the world in which they lived. That one needs to keep in mind connections to synoptic and other comparable texts does not have to be particularly mentioned. I shall return to this later.

The decisive motivation for social-historical and feminist social-historical work, as I understand it, comes again and again from the biblical tradition itself. There are few books in which the voice of the lowly is heard as it is in the Bible. It is also true that in the Bible voices of women are suppressed, but it is worthwhile to search for them there.

C. THEORY OF THE PARABLES

Jesus' parables in the Gospels are most significant for the methodological approach of feminist social history of early Christianity. Their images are steeped in the world of women and men and provide invaluable information; their message is God's revelation. The theory I rely on in reading the parables impacts directly on how they are understood. I want to present a theory of the parables based on feminist social-historical reflection and compare it, as was done in connection with the miracle narratives, to Rudolf Bultmann's theory (which was itself essentially that of Adolf Jülicher). I shall coordinate with Bultmann's conception those more recent theories that understand the parables as metaphors. For me, the crucial question to be put to the theory is how it assesses the parable's "image" *theologically*. The parables are about the relationship of God to the world, or more precisely, of God to creation.

According to Rudolf Bultmann, the "images" of the parables were neutral: "In my view the difference between the nature of similitudes and parables on the one hand and allegory on the other is most clearly formulated by saying that the former involve the transference of a judgment (derived from some neutral field) from one sphere to another, which is under discussion."[185] In his view, the narratives from everyday life (parables in the stricter sense) and those about interesting, individual events[186] in the world of humans and animals (similitudes) do not seek to communicate anything about everyday life and the world. They seek, instead, to evoke a judgment about God's reign. The images of the parables are, at best, of historical interest; theologically, they are neutral territory. The world of a woman baking bread is an interpretive aid for the reign of God. Nothing is said theologically about her and her activity. God and the world of life stand unrelated, one next to the other.

Newer theories of the parables that, like Paul Ricoeur's,[187] understand parable as metaphor make distinctions between what in the image is of everyday life and what turns this everyday life upside down. That an employer pays a day's wage also to those who worked one hour only contradicts everyday life (Matt. 20:1–16). That is how God's reign finds language. "The scandalous disturbance of the commonplace,"[188] according to this interpretation, does not seek to *illustrate* God's reign; rather, the narrative is to be understood as a speech-event that has a performative character. Even though the attempt is made here to overcome the dualism of image and substance in the theory of Bultmann-Jülicher and to understand image as the speech of revelation, this theory is also worlds apart from the world of the woman baking bread and of children crying. Once again, everyday life is set aside; it is the scandalous disturbance of the commonplace that is the place of revelation. From a feminist social-historical point of view, the old dualism between the world of human beings and the reign of God is still there. The approach which this theory takes actually raises a social-historical question, namely: What is the disturbance of the commonplace? One must establish what is "commonplace." But the "commonplace" or "our conditions"[189] that are disturbed by the revelation of God's reign are *not* identified as the existing *social* reality (e.g., Matt. 20:1–7). The commonplace is separated from social reality and is defined, rather, as a religious idea, such as the Jewish[190] or universal human notion of merit.[191]

A feminist liberation theology (or a social history, as I practice it) has to develop a theory of the parables in which feet once again touch the ground of reality. The parables speak of social reality, including the so-called parables of nature.[192] The parables *describe* and then turn upside down the world of owners of large estates and farms, of the female and male daily-wage earners, tenants, and slaves. It is therefore necessary to make the social-historical exploration of this world the point of departure. What is a drachma worth, and what does it mean when a woman who possesses ten drachmas does not stop searching for the one she has lost?[193] In order to know where in a parable God's reign upends the "commonplace," what I call social reality, I must undertake social-historical research or else I open myself to blunders.[194] Men, too, need to explore the social reality of the parables in terms of the feminist approach critical of patriarchy; otherwise, not only will half of humankind continue in the murkiness of androcentrism but an illusory world will arise as well, in which a daily-wage laborer feeds himself, his spouse, and his children on one denarius. The reality is that in addition to the unpaid labor in the home, the spouse has to do badly paid wage work so that she and the children can live at all.[195]

It is inappropriate to distinguish between *image* and *substance* in the parables, unless these terms are set off by quotation marks to indicate their use as aids for explanation. The parables themselves convey that their language functions on two levels simultaneously: the level of God's reign and the level of human beings (or of plants, etc.). One must ask, therefore, how the relation between the human world (or creation) and God's reign is depicted in the parables or in early Christianity and Judaism of that time. The parables show that creation is the sphere of God's presence and action.[196] God's action is spoken of as goodness or as wrath. The experience of a guest who is bound hand and foot in the royal palace and then thrown out is the experience of a sick world, of creation destroyed, an experience of God's wrath (Matt. 22:11–13). The generous landowner's payment of the full wage to those who worked so little reverses social reality, the reality in which those workers could expect to receive nothing. That payment says something about God's reign and critiques the social reality of the world of work and its brutality. The two levels of the parables—the human world or creation and God's reign—are both spheres of God's action. In the parables the human world and creation are together open to God's action in creation—action in wrath and in mercy. In the parables creation is a window through which God's action can be seen; creation is the place in which God's action may be experienced. The interpretation of parables in subsequent chapters is based on this approach.[197]

The understanding of the church plays a significant part in the tradition of the parables' interpretation. I refer, for example, to interpretations in which the guests in the festive chambers are somehow seen to be the church and those who failed to attend are the nonchurch, those "outside," most often "Judaism," Jewish women and men. Parables that speak of inside and outside I understand *eschatologically*. By "outside" they mean death before God, and by "inside," life before God. It is God alone in the eschatological judgment who decides about being inside or outside. The parables indicate the road to God's judgment; they do not say: Those people there are judged by God. They do say: You now face the task of accepting God's invitation. What the invitation is in the concrete situation of life was made quite plain by the praxis of Jesus and his followers; it is equally plain today after contextual analysis.

I am in accord with much in traditional research which finds that an understanding of the parables necessitates the examination of their metaphors in their historical context. For example, I must examine what is meant by the juxtaposition of fruitful and unfruitful trees in the New Testament and in postbiblical Judaism in order to understand the corresponding New Testament parables. However, in such work on the historical context, a problem often arises: historical research frequently focuses on motifs, and the result is a collection of diverse elements that compose the image. It becomes necessary to remember that every one of those elements of the image already had a certain pictorial and substantive contextual significance. For example, it is quite beside the point in relation to the parable of the sower (Mark 4:3–9 and par.) that pulling things out by their roots is used as an image for God's reign (Sir. 10:15 and elsewhere), since in that parable the issue is not having roots and being unfruitful.

In the next section I develop these considerations into actual working steps.

D. THE HISTORICAL TOOLS

For years I have been trying to develop simple tools for the interpretation of New Testament texts. I shall describe working steps, which are meant not to substitute for the creative act of interpretation but to prepare for it in conformity with the requirements for such interpretation. The following discussion of working steps presupposes aspects I described previously concerning the feminist social-historical approach to early Christianity. These steps are meant to be usable by women and men whether they have theological training or not.

Exegetical Working Steps

In relation to parables

I First text analysis through
—determining the text's basis
—arranging the parts
—assessing linguistic weight and peculiarities
—determining the genre

II Classification in terms of intellectual history and the history of religion (First Testament, postbiblical Judaism, Hellenism)

I First text analysis through
—determining the text's basis
—arranging the parts
—assessing linguistic weight and peculiarities
—determining the genre

II Classification in terms of intellectual history and the history of religion (First Testament, postbiblical Judaism, Hellenism)
—clarification of the metaphorical tradition in which the parable is located (attention particularly to

the First Testament and rabbinic
parables)
—clarification of the relation
between narrative and God's
reign, that is, how the two levels
in the parable are related

III Social-historical analysis in
terms
—of the concept "critique of
patriarchy"
—of details in the text
—of the overall situation of the
Jesus movement or early
Christian communities

III Social-historical analysis in terms

—of the concept "critique of
patriarchy"
—of details in the narrative
("image")
—of the overall situation of the
Jesus movement or early
Christian communities
—of the relation between social
reality and the narrative
("image")

IV The literary context

IV The literary context

V Coordination of the text
with Jesus' message and
praxis or that of his followers
in early Christianity

V Coordination of the text with
Jesus' message and praxis or
that of his followers in
early Christianity

Regarding Step I

Determining the text's basis refers to the feminist social-historical work that
establishes the textual history of the passage under consideration in its Greek
original. For those who work with translations of the New Testament, it is advisable to refer to several translations in order to develop the critical awareness
that texts are not fixed.

Those who cannot refrain from dismantling a text (asking, e.g., "What is secondary?") may *assess linguistic peculiarities* here. But there are more important
questions to be asked: What does the text emphasize and how? What is incidental? What is more fully developed and what is repeated? Where are the verbs,
and what steps and actions are described?[198]

Arranging parts by giving them subheadings is already to interpret the text.
When I begin studying a text, I make as accurate an arrangement of it as possible and then correct it as I proceed in my understanding of the text.

Determining genre presupposes the feminist critique of traditional determinations of genre, as was indicated earlier. In connection with the parables, the old classification of Jülicher[199] (categorizing them as parables in the more restricted sense, similitudes, exemplary narratives, allegories) is of use only insofar as I reflect on why that classification is inappropriate. All parables are based on metaphors that developed over time. When a parable narrated in a Jewish context tells of a king, the people know that God is spoken of. Although not every element of a parable is based on metaphors, when I determine the genre to be that of "parable," I pay attention to the metaphors involved.

Regarding Step II

Traditional scholarship has amassed collections of materials that are excellent for work in intellectual history, the history of religion, and metaphors. When working on a parable (what is the relation between the narrative and God's reign, i.e., between the two levels of the parable?), it is advisable not to be dismayed by the extent of available and complicated studies on the theory of the parables. Their theoretical substance can be established with little trouble and summarized in a few sentences, as I tried to convey earlier. I have already addressed the central theological significance of parabolic narratives (or images).

Regarding Step III

The social-historical analysis that functions, as already indicated, with the feminist critique of patriarchy focuses first on particular details in the text (such as the purchasing power of a drachma) and, second, on the historical situation of the Jesus movement, the early Christian communities, and the Jewish people in the Roman Empire (cf. above at I.1). An additional aspect in connection with the parables is where the narrative locates itself in social reality and where it turns that reality upside down.

Regarding Step IV

I read the whole Gospel or epistle anew when I set out to understand a part of it. Redaction history, structuralist study, rhetorical analysis, and literary criticism are all attempts to understand texts as a whole. What is important is that these crafts do not leave behind the social-historical dimension. In connection with the Gospels, I have to account for how I perceive their formation as texts and their formation in the oral tradition and for how I think of the community as the bearer of oral and written tradition. Attributing the Gospel to a specific writer, named considerably later (Matthew, Mark, Luke, John), is not only historically inaccurate but also misleading: it makes the Gospels appear as *works of individual male authors.* "The redactor" is often pictured as a German professor of theology. The truth is that the Gospels contain words and narratives by and about Jesus that women and men told and retold and finally wrote down, because for them they were words of life. Therefore, I need to inquire about the community of women and men that expresses itself in these texts. The Paul of the Pauline epistles, too, must not be perceived as an "author" in the sense of a theology professor. With his epistles he is situated in a living context of communities—alive with very self-aware women (and men).[200]

Regarding Step V

It is often difficult to identify the new praxis in the Jesus movement and in the communities. This is because Western tradition has almost always suppressed the questions about actions that accord with God's reign and the praxis of faith. Jesus' message is inseparably connected with his praxis. The more people ask about that praxis, the more it will emerge from the debris of that history of interpretation which is held captive in the interests of domination.

As has been shown here, feminist critique of traditional Western history of New Testament interpretation is an essential component in every one of these working steps. The tools of patriarchal oppression are manifested in that history which, when analyzed in terms of the feminist critique, also contains traces of the history of Christian women. The feminist analysis of aspects of that history of interpretation always informs my material in working with texts of the New Testament (beginning in Part II). The implicit or explicit claim of Western biblical scholarship to being objective, neutral, and scientific requires unambiguous rebuttal. The interests of that scholarship are obvious as soon as they are critically examined. Bertolt Brecht has designed a helpful tool for such critical examination (which may also be used in critical questioning of the New Testament); it could be read as if it were feminist: "Who benefits from this statement? Whose benefit does it claim to serve? What does it call for? What praxis follows from it? What other statements does it lead to? What statements support it? In what situation is it uttered? By whom?"[201]

4

"From Life to Scripture— From Scripture to Life"*

A. THE READING OF SCRIPTURE AND THE WOMEN'S MOVEMENT

I situate my work with biblical texts within the context of the women's movement.[203] I have learned much there and want to contribute with my historical and theological work to the further development of feminist theology. In the *women's movement related to the churches,* a significant role was—and still is being—played by an independent *new reading* of biblical texts: in anger at biblical traditions that were and are instruments of the oppression of women, and in enthusiasm at the discovery of traditions of liberation.[204] Irrespective of differences, the reading of scripture in this part of the women's movement is a conscious act of disempowering the male oppressor: we are taking away his instruments of oppression and fighting for what is ours in the tradition; we are fighting for our female heritage. We are better able to interpret these traditions than the gentlemen exegetes who, often knowingly, prevent a liberating reading of scripture with their formal claim to being scientific. I understand my work, being feminist history and feminist theology, as something that assists in a reading of the Bible independent of the institutions of domination. The reading of scripture in the women's movement, in the peace and justice movements, as well as in the movement of bibliodrama are all examples of independent reading. I want to assist in the rediscovery of early Christianity's legacy of women and of justice.

In their liberating reading of scripture, there are two theoretical approaches which might be used by communities that are engaged in feminist liberation theology and praxis in the context of Western Europe. I want to introduce and discuss them now: first, the reading of scripture as it is done in the base communities of Latin America and, second, feminist, experience-based research. It should be noted that hardly any theoretical positions for the reading of scripture have been developed in the feminist theology movement, even though reading the scriptures is highly relevant for that movement in the German-speaking world.[205] It is nevertheless these two approaches that women seem to have appropriated.

*I am using the title of Mesters's 1983 book.

It is astounding that the secular women's movement has not taken much notice of the feminist theology movement. (It is quite different the other way around.) But the reason is plain: many of the women who make up the women's movement have definitely turned their backs in anger on the church and cannot imagine that liberating potential for woman can be found—of all places—in the Bible. They may believe and be able to understand that feminist Christians still read the Bible for the sake of maintaining "legitimacy" in the eyes of ecclesiastical employers. Such an interpretation nevertheless assumes that there is no meaningful content in the biblical tradition. Besides, what is involved here is really a question of power. As it turned out, I generally knew the New Testament better than those in the church and in theology who had set out to obstruct my work and make it invisible. Any legitimacy derived from such knowledge just made no difference. Communities that work for liberation from capitalist patriarchy need not bother reading or knowing the Bible, much less in a feminist social-historical perspective, if it is institutional legitimacy that they seek. Where the Bible is experienced as relevant in the women's movement, it is read because women have sought and found treasures, regardless of critique.

B. THE READING OF SCRIPTURE IN LIBERATION-THEOLOGY BASE COMMUNITIES

My example of a liberation-theological reading of scripture comes from Brazil; it is one from which I have learned much. This in no way means that I view similar readings in other contexts as less valuable.[206] Access to the reading of scripture is found in the work of Carlos Mesters,[207] Milton Schwantes,[208] Regene Lamb,[209] Ivoni Richter Reimer,[210] and Ivone Gebara and Maria C. Lucchetti Bingemer.[211] Dorothee Soelle, among others, has introduced the approach of liberation theology into the Western context. Many other midwives of this approach to reading scripture need to be named; it is not my intention here to be exhaustive. What I do want to make plain is that such names do not refer to lone female and male heroes of the spirit but to human beings who, in the context of liberation movements, expended their energies and became allied with the many others whom I do not name here.

"The communities are places of new learning. In the Bible groups people move quickly and easily from the biblical text to their experience and back to the text."[212] This process may also be described as a sequence of working steps. The first step is to start with life as the first word of God; the second is to read the Bible, and the third is to discover "the message of God's word for us today."[213] The first step, that is, setting out from one's own experiences, is about acknowledging conflicts and contradictions "from a particular place, namely that of the weak."[214] This is where "the economic, social, political, and religious situation of the people is analyzed."[215] For feminist Christian women, the fate of those with whom libera-

tion theology is concerned is decided in the liberation of women: "We have become more and more sensitive to the suffering and the struggle of the women
of this continent, particularly of the poorest among them, namely those who,
according to the brutal classification of our class system, are people of the third
and the fourth classes. They are not all holy or pure, but they are women who
give life and keep it going in the midst of garbage."[216] "We can speak of the
gospel as good news for women only when we place the experience of poor
women in the center, for they have been deprived most of all of the right to
be human."[217]

It is to androcentrism in the understanding of experience as found in the
older positions of liberation theology that such feminist Christian women point.
Like the androcentric approach in liberation theology, this approach also presupposes social analysis as part of naming one's own experiences. The instruments of this analytical reflection are fashioned in the school of Karl Marx and
oriented by the view from below, because that is the only way to see what is real.
Those same analytical instruments[218] are usually employed in the second step,
the interpretation of a text, as well. The social situation of the women and men
who narrated the biblical text is also taken into consideration.

The third step—the sequence is not fixed—is the attempt to translate God's
word into a new praxis. "The poor translate their reading of scripture into action: they respect the text, for they listen carefully to what God has to say. And
if God calls for it, the people are ready to make changes."[219]

At the end of the seventies, Dorothee Soelle wrote a short guideline for
groups doing liberation theology in a Western context; it is a text that, in my
view, continues to be relevant and applicable.

Dorothee Soelle: "How can we do liberation theology? A proposal for a
process in four steps."[220]

> How are we to do theology in a meaningful—that is, life-changing—way? My pro-
> posal is grounded in different liberation theologies and moves in a four-step pro-
> gram. I call them praxis, analysis, meditation and renewed praxis. . . .
>
>   Whereas traditional theology starts with the text (the Word of God, the gospel),
> liberation theology starts with the context of our lives, our experiences, our hopes
> and fears, our "praxis." This is not to deny the power of the text and its spiritual
> quality, but to make room for it.
>
>   In order to understand our own praxis, we have to listen and to see and to feel.
> None of it is given. The descriptive has to touch the depth of our feelings. The first
> question to ask about our praxis is: "Who is victimized?" The literary form will be
> the narrative or the descriptive. Our concern, our worrying becomes visible in the
> process. We have to expose ourselves personally and increase our vulnerability. The
> goal of the first step is to make us see the Cross.
>
>   When we listen to the cry that comes out of praxis we develop a need for the
> best available analysis. The second step is to understand, to identify the causes, to
> name the Beast. The analytical question then becomes: "Who profits?" The liter-

ary form is the socioeconomic analysis. We move from the personal experience to the institutional analysis. We make use of other materials and broaden our experiential understanding, but by asking all the whys we ground our understanding in the depth of the historical process. The goal of the second step is to recognize the Principalities and Powers.

The narrative and the analytical together constitute the context. We should withstand the temptation to leap too early into the text, which then would be a "leaning on the everlasting arms" without foundation in the historical and institutional realities. In order to dialogue with the Word of God, the praxis of the prophets and Jesus, we need the clearest understanding of our own praxis. When we delve deep enough into our own situation, we will reach a point where theological reflection becomes necessary. We then have to "theologize" the given situation. We read the context (steps 1 and 2) until it cries out for theology. The only way to reach this point at which we become aware of our need for prayer, for hope, for stories of people who have been liberated, is to go deeply enough into our sociohistorical context. The theologian will discover the inner necessity of theology in a given situation and its potential for unfolding theological meaning. We have to reach this point of no return where we will know anew that we do need God. This is the basis of doing theology, but the only way to come to this point is worldly analysis of our situation.

The third step is meditation. The verb is "to remember." We read the Bible out of our thirst for justice. We search in scripture and tradition for help. In what sense does the tradition help us? If we don't find an answer, we look for those parts of the tradition which at least speak to our despair. The literary form now is exegesis and the goal is to "remember" ourselves; to remember that we are members and children of Life and not of Death. We remember the resurrection.

The fourth step is a renewed praxis. What the theologian should learn here is to dream and to hope. Our imagination has been freed from original sinful bondages, and we are empowered to imagine alternative institutions. We become agents of change. Prayer and action become our doing. The literary form is now the creative envisioning. We find new language. Only this last step discloses the text and makes us not only into readers but into "writers" of the Bible. We say to each other "take up your bed and walk," which is a necessary step in any liberation theology.

These four steps from praxis to analysis to meditation to renewed praxis have an irreversible dynamic. In this sense the Spirit who moves in all these phases transcends where we are and who we are.

C. THE FEMINIST UNDERSTANDING OF EXPERIENCE-BASED RESEARCH AND FEMINIST READING OF SCRIPTURE

There has been considerable development in Western feminist social sciences of the theoretical clarification of the first step in liberation theology. Maria Mies distinguishes between event and experience:

Experience is often equated with event, with the mood a woman is in or the feelings she has in a particular situation. But in my view, experience means to begin
with real life, both in its subjective concreteness and in its social web.[221] . . . As I
understand it, experience comprises more than the specific, momentary, and individual state people find themselves in; it comprises the sum total of the processes
that individuals or collectives have gone through in the production of their lives,
their reality, their history.[222]

Christine Schaumberger sums up the history of feminist theology to date: this
orientation toward experience "has led feminist theology to unfold as a broad
movement of women who give theological expression to the diverse contexts
from which they come, the situations of their life and work, the groups they belong to, and their ways of knowing."[223] Feminist women theologians set out
"from their own experiences of oppression, struggle, and liberation and relate
them to those of other women."[224] Feminist analysis, cooperation in the fight
for liberation, and one's own experience, including the experience of the body,
are the bases of a process that is "critical, self-critical, and done in solidarity."[225]

I believe that there is a historical development taking place also in my context. At the beginning of this experience-based research process, there was always the realization that what we had taken to be our private problems were, in
fact, social structures. The commonality of women's experiences was discovered.
After that, especially when women from other social contexts joined the discussion, the diversity in women's experiences was understood. Because of its orientation toward experience, feminist research contains within itself the reciprocal relation of research and liberating praxis/women's movement.

Feminist reading of scripture is a special area of such feminist research; here
the word *research* is intentionally distanced from the sphere of academic elitism,
whose competence to research all of reality is disputed. Unfortunately, there is
no extensive documentation of feminist readings of scripture from base communities. Therefore I can refer only to publications whose interpretations of
scripture reflect, indirectly, research in feminist reading similar to my own.[226]

On account of its experience-based approach, feminist bibliodrama too belongs as a movement within the domain of feminist research and reading of
scripture.[227] However, as far as I can see, it does not work with an understanding of experience and social analysis that is as consistent in its methodical reflection as that of feminist research and its discussion of method.

Elisabeth Schüssler Fiorenza has developed an extensive framework for a feminist-theological reading of scripture. It arose in the North American context but
has also proven to be practical and an appropriate variable for other contexts. I
want to describe it briefly and relate it to the other liberation theology frame-
works spoken of earlier. She distinguishes four interrelated hermeneutical steps
in a feminist-theological discussion of biblical tradition. They are the hermeneutics of suspicion, remembrance, proclamation, and creative actualization.[228]

The hermeneutics of *suspicion* submits the consistently androcentric text of the Bible to a critique of ideology. It does so assuming the Bible to be a text that may be oppressive and serve the interest of patriarchy.[229] The critique of ideology focuses also on both the scholarly and popular traditions of interpretation and their theoretical foundations. The critical instruments Elisabeth Schüssler Fiorenza relies on in this fundamental hermeneutical step are feminist analysis of androcentric language and the feminist analysis of patriarchy, which is integral to her approach.[230]

The *remembrance* of the suffering and the hope of women who struggled in patriarchal structures is something one can also reconstruct in patriarchal texts. Such reconstruction of women's struggles for liberation also unearths the original "nonpatriarchal ethos" of the Jesus movement as a "discipleship of equals." In her use of "memory" as dangerous, subversive memory, Elisabeth Schüssler Fiorenza relies on Johann Baptist Metz.[231]

The *proclamation* which grows from that remembrance is addressed to today's community of believers. It removes oppressive texts of scripture from use in the community and draws on those "texts which transcend their patriarchal context"[232] or that allow the discernment of women's struggles in spite of their patriarchal functions. The text is not treated in this proclamation as if it were conveying historical facts.

Creative actualization presupposes an active engagement for women's liberation; it is primarily situated in artistic expression, in narratives and rituals.

This hermeneutical model is based in liberation theology and traditional discussion of hermeneutics. Just like the praxis orientation of liberation theology hermeneutics (particularly in its fourth but also in its second step), this model connects with the hermeneutics of "doubt"[233] or suspicion about the false consciousness of society that Marx, Nietzsche, and Freud spoke of. Schüssler Fiorenza distinguishes, as does the existential interpretation of Rudolf Bultmann, between proclamation and historical report in scripture and submits oppressive texts to a "substantive critique" (*Sachkritik*).[234] She adopts existing hermeneutical principles on the basis of her own understanding of patriarchy on the one hand and her perception of an *ekklēsia* of women, "a feminist movement of self-identified women and men identified with women's struggles," on the other hand. This women's liberation movement between the "already" and the "not yet"[235] is a democratic countermovement against patriarchy.

In view of the liberation theology models discussed above, I deem it necessary to elucidate critically Schüssler Fiorenza's model at several points. The hermeneutics of *suspicion* about scripture presupposes as its first step the hermeneutics of suspicion about one's own social context: that is, the first step in Soelle's model or the first step in that of Mesters or the analysis of women's experience in the model of Mies and Schaumberger. In fact, Elisabeth Schüssler Fiorenza too presupposes an analysis of patriarchy that is experience-oriented and focused on one's own social context. My concern here is that the process of understanding move "from life to the Bible," and that the interpretation of scripture not take place in isolation from the social context and the social-political feminist praxis. An isolated application of her four hermeneutical steps could create the impression of such unrelatedness. Something comparable may also occur in relation to the final step. *Creative appropriation* must be related to a social feminist praxis intent on liberation. Nevertheless, I believe that, compared to the hermeneutical models of liberation theology, the model of Elisabeth Schüssler Fiorenza should be affirmed in its contention that the suspicion of being oppressive must be applied *also* to the biblical tradition and to the traditions of interpretation of the scriptures.

It is my view that the entire range of the historical method employed by feminist social history must be built into the reconstruction of history, that is, into the hermeneutics of remembrance. Here, too, I see no need for a fundamental critique but only for clarification. Such clarification is needed also in Dorothee Soelle's third step.

In their practical use of scripture, groups of women or groups of women and men doing feminist liberation theology may well adopt a combination of Soelle's, Schüssler Fiorenza's, and my model. The original process that Dorothee Soelle describes is quite amenable to Schüssler Fiorenza's concept of feminist analysis (analysis of patriarchy, critique of the androcentrism of language) and also to my feminist social-historical praxis of interpretation, in which one's own social context *and* that of the people who speak in the Bible are taken seriously. Feminist analysis of patriarchy or feminist social history critical of patriarchy cannot be understood without the Marx-inspired analysis practiced in liberation theology. Historically speaking, the way of liberation theology has led from the option for the poor to the option for women. The option for the poor is, indeed, decided in the option for women. That is why feminist liberation theology asks of every species of men's theology: Does the gospel open your eyes or not?

At the close of this section, I can refer only to the research for which a feminist and liberation-theological reading of scripture still calls. The rich material of new insights into the contents of the biblical tradition and their significance for today is a nearly hidden treasure. For readings of scripture based in feminist theology, feminist liberation theology and liberation theology have been a living source of faith in many contexts of the world. Real life is acknowledged here and shaped through common labor into something new.

In the chapters that follow on the exploration of method and hermeneutics, I shall try to frame a feminist social history of early Christianity in terms of two basic questions: What did everyday life of women look like? What did it mean for women to become Christians? In the *second part* I begin from the texts of the New Testament because they are a unique source for important aspects of *women's everyday life,* for the ever-present oppression of women, and for their resistance. Social-historical study must include the question of women's work and the control of money. In every instance I distinguish between the situation of women in the large cities of the empire and that of women in the rural provinces; however, in relation to the situation of the majority of the people in the Roman Empire, that distinction is often of no relevance. I am aware that such a claim is in stark contrast to many a presentation of early Christian social history. The actual study of texts to follow will substantiate the claim.

In the *third part* ("The Critique of Patriarchy and the Power to Become a New Being"), I will explore the (chiefly androcentric) critique of patriarchy of early Christianity's theory and praxis and their renewing strength—in spite of their androcentric limitations. This will be done in relation to three theologically central foci: the call of God, the gospel of the poor, and eschatology.

Finally, the *fourth part* addresses core aspects of liberation praxis: the elevation of debased women and the new formation of society—in marriage, family, and community of believers.

All chapters, beginning from individual texts, seek to comprehend structures. The sections dealing with individual subjects are organized in the same way: section A deals with questions related to the texts discussed, B with social-historical issues, C with feminist observations on the history of interpretation, and D with additional feminist perspectives on the further use of the materials and texts discussed.

II

THE EVERYDAY LIFE
OF WOMEN

1

Oppression of Women and Hatred of Women's Liberation (1 Tim. 2:9–15)

A. THE TEXT

I begin with my own translation of the text.

9   Similarly, [I want] women to adorn themselves in dignified attire[1] with modesty and decency and not with braids and gold or pearls or costly apparel,

10   but with what befits women who profess to revere God, namely, good deeds.

11   Women should learn in conformity[2] and all submissiveness.

12   I do not permit woman to give instruction to or to exercise power over man; she is to live in conformity.

13   For Adam was formed first, then Eve.

14   And Adam was not seduced, but the woman was seduced and fell into transgression.

15   She will be saved through bearing children if they [women] continue in faith, love, and holiness, with decency.

This text speaks intentionally in the language of the overlords' laws and decrees:[3] "I want," "I do not permit." It pronounces a law to govern all women. Seeking to direct Christian communities, presumably around the beginning of the second century, with the borrowed authority of Paul,[4] the authoritarian laws are addressed to Christian women. The text is marked by the notion that by nature[5] all women are the same and that there is, for all of them, only *one* correct way to live. It is often said, on account of the law concerning men's prayers in verse 8, that this text has to do with instructions to Christian women on how they are to dispose themselves in *services of worship*. Not only is this interpretation untenable for reasons of language,[6] but to interpret this text as being about women's demeanor in worship also serves to defuse the text for apologetic reasons: "When they attend worship, Christian women should forgo artful hairdos, ostentatious jewelry of gold or pearls, and costly fashionable attire. . . . The positive ideal [is] of the Christian woman poised . . . in dignified, composed silence."[7] Indeed, the text is out to enforce an encompassing law for women to which they are to pay attention in everyday life (and in worship).

B. SOCIAL-HISTORICAL QUESTIONS

Laws for Women

Extra-Christian texts of the time show that representatives of what is called "conservative"[8] regulation of women thought it quite necessary to have special laws prohibiting women from striving for their liberation. Tacitus reports in his *Annals* (completed ca. 120 C.E.) on a political debate in Rome in the year 21 C.E.; the question was whether Roman civil servants should take their wives with them to the provinces. Severus Caecina speaks against it, basing his argument on the natural essence of women:

> The female gender is weak and unable to deal with strain; when the reins are loosened, it is brutal, ambitious, and power-hungry; women enter the ranks of soldiers and make centurions do a handyman's work. . . . Once they were reined in by the Oppian Laws[9] and other regulations; now, let loose, they give orders in private households, the law courts, and even in the armed forces.[10]

His opponent, arguing *for* women's being taken to the provinces, also insists on men ruling over women. If women were not to be taken along, "the gender that is weak by nature is being abandoned and left to its inclination to excess and to the covetousness of others. . . . The burden of guilt rests on the man when the woman transgresses the restrictions imposed on her."[11]

Almost one hundred years before Tacitus, Valerius Maximus produced an anthology of historical vignettes for the use of orators.[12] In the section on "the love of luxury and sensual desire," he refers to the Oppian Laws for women:

> The conclusion of the Second Punic War and the defeat of Philip, king of Macedonia, encouraged a libertine way of life in our city. At that time women dared to besiege the estate of the Bruti, who were opposed to the abrogation of the *lex Oppia*, which the women sought to bring about. That legislation permitted women neither to wear multicolored clothes, nor to adorn themselves with more than one half-ounce of gold, nor to approach the city in horse-drawn carriages and come closer than one thousand double steps, unless they came to offer sacrifice. And they even succeeded in repealing the law, which had been in effect for twenty years. The men at the time did not surmise to what excesses the stubborn pressures of the unusual alliance [of women] would lead and where their boldness would end, which had defeated those laws.[13]

Valerius Maximus shares the notion Tacitus had cited, namely, that women are weak by nature;[14] but contrary to his own belief, he depicts them as stubborn and ungovernable, kept in rein only by strict laws and the supervision of their men. For him, it was the fault of men that they gave in to the women's collective resistance and allowed the abrogation of the Oppian Laws. A husband's rigorous, decisive action against an insubordinate woman is necessary in order to discipline *all* women with such a deterrent. It is appropriate, according to Valerius Maximus, that a man club his wife to death because she drank wine: "The deed found no one to lay charges, no one even criticized him, because everyone knew that she was punished in order to provide an effective example against breaking the rules of sobriety. For every woman who immoderately partakes of the bottle bolts the door to every positive virtue and opens it to every vice."[15] He supports such exemplary punishment of women and the corresponding legislation.[16] Tacitus, too, essentially shares this point of view. He is critical, however, of Augustus's legislation governing sexuality because it declared adultery to be a religious offense and lèse-majesté.[17] His critique is that the upper classes will experience spying and denunciation, caused by that legislation, as a discomfort.[18] And yet Tacitus tells dispassionately of numerous cases in which women were charged with and punished for adultery, for preparing poisonous concoctions, and for religious practices hostile to the state.[19]

The first epistle to Timothy belongs to the history of this specific form of women's oppression. Women must be disciplined by coercive measures because without them they will not know their place as defined by patriarchal society, which speaks the order given by nature. These texts (1 Timothy, Valerius Maximus, Tacitus)[20] not only propagate a patriarchal order but also seek to enforce a patriarchal order *against the resistance of women;* for women had indeed succeeded in gaining spaces of independence. Their efforts to obtain freedom are depicted with hatred and distortion, and attempts are made to enforce coercive measures against women.

It is appropriate to classify the pastoral epistles in the history of ancient economics,[21] for that helps make the connections between ancient theories of patriarchy and state, on the one hand, and the praxis of antiquity, on the other. But more is required still; for this is not a conscious description of patriarchy, as Cicero[22] had offered it, in which women stay at home, obey, and have babies. Another sound is heard here: the sound of hatred for women's liberation struggles.

Dangerous Women

Lists of malicious accusations, polemics, and distortions against and about women are to be found in many literary documents of this time. When women are not subjected to discipline, they become excessive, promiscuous, seductive and seducible, bossy toward men, lazy, and loquacious; they become inclined to sorcery, to concocting poisons. They are to blame for the bad state of the world. The first epistle to Timothy contains a number of such malicious polemics: women who adorn themselves with gold are lewd and, consequently, potentially seductive and adulterous (1 Tim. 2:9). One needs to listen also to the implicit charge of excessiveness against women who wear jewels, because of its importance[23] in the widespread polemics against women's finery.[24] First Timothy 5:11f. assumes that young Christian widows do not keep the previously made commitment not to remarry because they want to live "away from Christ in abundant and wanton ways." The word[25] used here hovers between an addiction to the "good life" and uncontrolled sensuality.

Such polemics against women are often self-contradictory: women are weak by nature but uncontrollable unless constrained (cf. above at the discussion of Valerius Maximus). Their jewelry signals sexual availability, while men are open to that signal and afraid of it at the same time. Valerius Maximus waxes eloquent about the good old days of Rome:

> In order to soften what made their virtuousness burdensome and unpleasant, and to make themselves more attractive without transgressing against decency, women, having received their men's permission, adorned themselves with much gold and in purple clothing; they carefully dyed their hair with red ashes so that it would look prettier. But in those days one needed not to worry about possible adulterous glances.[26]

Another patriarchal self-contradiction has a place in 1 Timothy. It heralds the ideal of the *univira,* the woman who does not remarry after the death of her husband. And yet the epistle decrees that young widows in the community of believers be forced to remarry because they are quite incapable of remaining celibate (1 Tim. 5:14, 11). Where, then, does the idea come from that a real widow should be over sixty years old and married only once (1 Tim. 5:9)? When it comes to men, the patriarchal sexual morality of that time is equally self-contradictory. It admires the men who enter into marriage only once in their life;[27] it also admires the wife who both tolerates her husband's adultery and covers it up.[28] The first epistle to Timothy thinks of men who were the husbands of only one wife, lifelong,[29] as being well suited to be bishops or deacons.[30]

Traditional polemics against insubordinate women are also used in 1 Tim. 5:13. Women who do not confine themselves to their prescribed role in the household are labeled lazy, talkative, inquisitive, and involved in sorcery.[31] Talking outside the home, not to mention what they talk about—something the author of the epistle repudiates outright—is something a virtuous woman just does not do.[32]

That the theology of creation is used as the argument for women's subjugation to men is this epistle's most portentous discrimination against women. Woman was created second, and she alone was seduced by Satan (1 Tim. 2:14). It is presupposed that Satan, as a serpent, had sexual intercourse with Eve.[33]

Therefore, the only road to salvation for women is to bear children.[34] This text demonstrates that polemics against women construct women's nature as seducible seductress, unchaste, and so on. The list of misogynist imputations of 1 Timothy must be completed by adding the following: old "wives" believe and spread silly myths, tales (4:7). This attack on old women is not a harmless aside[35] in a society that persecutes old women in hateful pictures and words.[36]

The aim of 1 Timothy's misogynist polemic is to subjugate women to men. This polemic is spelled out particularly in 2:11f. "In every respect, in all," women are to obey and live in "quietness," that is, in conformity.[37] The opposite of this would be a woman who exercises power over a man:[38] a nightmare scenario for patriarchal men that pervades, for example, the *Annals* of Tacitus.[39]

The History of Women's Liberation

Like many other literary documents that contain comparable polemics against women, the first epistle to Timothy also documents women's liberating struggles in an unwitting but interesting manner. Reading the traditional motifs of misogynist polemics with critical eyes shows, in 5:11–14, that young Christian widows did not want to be forced either to remain unmarried or to remarry but that they wanted to choose for themselves how to live. They insist on the freedom of widows to decide, the freedom known from Paul's Christian praxis (1 Cor. 7:8–9, 39–40). Even though Paul deems celibacy to be the better way, he does not curtail widows' freedom to decide. First Timothy 5:11–14 and 2:11f. show as well that women claimed for themselves the right to learn[40] and to teach[41] outside the home and in public, and that men were among their pupils.[42] What this means is that Christian women were precisely the ones who shook the main pillars and buttresses of the oppression of women. They did not seek their freedom in the niches to which patriarchal order assigned them (cf., e.g., Titus 2:3–5); they spoke in public and refused to be relegated to the role of the dutiful domestic bearer of children or of the *univira*, the ascetic widow. They also adopted independent positions in the faith of the church. First Timothy was to bring to an end this history of women's liberation, to discredit it and render it invisible. In this respect the epistle is no different from Valerius Maximus's misogynist work. In Valerius's polemics also dimensions of that history can be discerned, once his polemics are analyzed in terms of the critique of patriarchy.[43]

C. FEMINIST OBSERVATIONS ON THE HISTORY OF INTERPRETATION, PARTICULARLY THE PRESENT

The very presence in the Christian canon of such a spiteful document from the history of women's subjugation to men has led to various apologetic patterns of interpretation. Elisabeth Schüssler Fiorenza has cataloged them in connection with the New Testament household codes.[44] These apologetic interpretations attempt in diverse ways to explain and excuse the embarrassment related to 1 Timothy. Schüssler Fiorenza has worked out three types of interpretation: (1) The household codes reflect the church's conformation to Greco-Roman patriarchal society. (2) They express the worldliness of faith, a faith that remains in the given order of the world and does not seek to flee from the world by emigrating from the given order. (This view is chiefly that of Lutheranism.) (3) This type is a variation of type 2 and states that in adopting social structures, Christian faith shows its subversive power.[45]

The first type, according to Schüssler Fiorenza, is divided into two subcategories. Interpretation 1a speaks of conformity negatively; the (negatively valued) household codes are set over against the (positively valued) person of Jesus or Paul. Contrary to this interpretation is the positive assessment of the conforming process: conformity was a historical necessity for the church's very survival (type 1b). Elisabeth Schüssler Fiorenza counters all three types with her "feminist evaluative hermeneutics of the Bible," which "derives its canon from the struggle of women and other oppressed peoples."[46] Seen in this perspective, the household codes are to be judged "a setback" insofar as they do "not strengthen Roman cultural tendencies to equality and mutuality between women and men."[47] The negative evaluation of "setback" applies also when the household codes are interpreted as a way of humanizing or Christianizing even more rigid prescriptions of subjugation,[48] or when one realizes that the church in the empire was under massive political pressure to conform. The political apologetic of the first epistle of Peter, for example, "gradually introduced the patriarchal societal ethos of the time into the church."[49]

"The Pastoral Epistles advocate the patriarchal order of submission for more than apologetic reasons."[50] The church's patronage system comes into ascendancy here, usurping previous and current democratic structures of community; it cements "the social exploitation of slave-women and men" and restricts the leadership functions of wealthy women.[51] In her assessment of the household codes and the pastoral epistles, Elisabeth Schüssler Fiorenza follows the first of her types of interpretation; she views the conforming process negatively. However, her evaluative criterion is not, as in type 1a, the canon within the Canon but the liberation struggles of women and men (see above), which, in the Jesus house churches, had resulted in egalitarian structures. It is important to keep in view the history of what those texts have wrought,[52] because type 1a declares them to be no longer valid today, which overlooks their perduring effects.

Except for a different social-historical assessment of the role wealthy women played in the house churches,[53] my views on the types of interpretation of the household codes and on the pastoral epistles match those described. I want to examine the hermeneutical treatment of 1 Timothy in dominant biblical scholarship *after* the emergence of feminist theology. I focus on 1 Timothy because its undisguised hatred of women, as a part of the Christian canon, is a clearer challenge than the household codes of Ephesians, Colossians, and 1 Peter, whose formulations offer more scope to excuse the texts. With insight heightened by the study of 1 Timothy and its interpretation, we shall return to the historical Paul and the household codes.

In his volume on 1 Timothy in the series Evangelisch-Katholischer Kommentar, Jürgen Roloff[54] has some critical words to say, particularly to 1 Tim. 2:14–15 ("for the contemporary reader they are extraordinarily alienating," p. 140) and 5:13 ("a grossly caricaturizing distortion" of the image of young widows, p. 297). And yet this critical distance is sporadic. He maintains it especially in relation to the biblical reasons stated in 1 Tim. 2:14f., which he understands to be the result of Jewish influences (pp. 137, 140). The idea of verse 15, "saved through the bearing of children," is theologically justified (p. 142), as is the compulsory silence of women in church and their subordination to men (p. 138). For him, the reasons stated in 2:14f. are problematic, but not the author's reasons for using them: first, to defend against Gnostic heresy that devalues the bearing of children (pp. 142, 147), and second, to attract non-Christian worshipers with the rubric of women being submissive in the service of worship. His are types 1b and 2 of Elisabeth Schüssler Fiorenza's classification (necessary conformity and worldliness of Christian existence).

Roloff critiques only the adoption of a Jewish interpretation of Gen. 2:3 in 1 Tim. 2:14f. He exonerates the Christian document by denouncing Jewish interpretation; his denunciation is not informed by any search for extra-Jewish sources with comparable contents. This creates an impression that there is a specific connection between scorn for the liberation of women and Judaism (see below, in connection with Max Küchler). Roloff even links anti-Judaism with an implicit critique of feminist theology: to critique the contents of the biblical reasons stated in 1 Tim. 2:14f., "one has to begin with the New Testament witness as a whole rather than with the social ideas of the day" (e.g., type 1a of interpretation) (p. 147). "This text shows the danger in which all interpreters to this day find themselves, which is to squeeze from biblical texts those views and arguments which they find necessary to support their own convictions" (p. 147). In the church, a popular argument against feminist theology is the charge that it is oriented by certain prevailing social ideas and that it uses the Bible to support its own convictions. Jewish and feminist interpretations of scripture are held up as a negative foil in defense of one's Christian scholarly interpretation, which knows itself to be far superior to current conceptual trends.

Max Küchler's extensive analysis of 1 Tim. 2:9–15[55] also must be criticized from a feminist perspective, despite its splendid collection of material and its critical attention to the contempt for humanity manifest in the oppression of women. To Jewish interpretations of Gen. 2:3 that are hostile to women, he responds by holding up against such readings the Old Testament as a whole, as a positive inspiration. In light of that inspiration, he rewrites 1 Tim. 2:8–15: "I desire that . . . women be adorned in dignified and tasteful attire, not with braids, gold, pearls, and costly apparel" (p. 493). But there is no change here: women as women are still told (by whom?) what to do. Küchler demonstrates well that the misogynist interpretation of Gen. 2:3 was "modern exegesis in those days" (p. 492). But since he does not make any critical connection between that contemporary Jewish exegesis and the extensive propaganda in first-century C.E. Rome opposing women's liberation, even the construction of his book unwittingly occasions anti-Judaism. The interpretation of Gen. 2:3 which is in contempt of women asserts that from creation, woman was of less worth than man, and that she was a sexually seducible seductress. The same notion, albeit in different form, is found in Valerius Maximus. The *conditio naturae* of woman, the way nature has fashioned her, is inferior to that of man (8.3; 3.2.15; cf. 4.6.5; 6.1.1; and elsewhere). Woman is a seducible (4.5) seductress (9.5.3). This is one voice among many in a war of words fought against women's liberation during the first century C.E.[56] The Jewish exegesis that Küchler describes belongs to that context; that does not excuse it, but it should no longer be viewed as a specifically Jewish problem. This hate-filled propaganda against women's liberation was spread by Greek and Roman authors just as it was by Jewish, Christian, and Gnostic religious literature.

Despite my critique of Küchler, I value positively his clear and unfettered stance in opposition to texts hostile to women, such as 1 Tim. 2:9–15, since he has the courage to leave behind him the apologetic Christian tradition of interpretation.

Klaus Thraede believes that his studies are friendly to women but that, contrary to those of feminist women exegetes whose studies are only friendly to women, his are both "closely related to the text and friendly to women."[57] In 1977, he judged that in spite of their authoritarian character, there was in the pastoral epistles no break yet with the gospel.[58] Ten years later, he notes the contrast between the pastorals and Paul but justifies the development from Paul to the pastoral epistles as a consequence of the church's conforming to the structures of the cities in the empire.[59] (He follows the first type of interpretation mentioned above.) His article on the household codes, published in 1980, received much attention; in it, he alleges that the household codes are love patriarchalism, which he justifies as the middle way between emancipation and rigid conservatism.[60] "The problem of woman" (Thraede 1987, passim) cannot be solved in terms of love patriarchalism, and love patriarchalism cannot be justified because it is just that: patriarchalism.

In the so-called expert opinion of the *Tübinger Gutachten* of 1990, the writer of the relevant section, Peter Stuhlmacher, asserts that New Testament statements hostile to women were judgments found to be expedient in the climate of the time. Indeed, they were understandable in defending against Gnostic heresy (1 Tim. 2:11–14).[61] In Stuhlmacher's judgment, those statements must be criticized in light of "the main affirmations of the gospel" (type of interpretation 1a). What was at that time a defense against Gnostic heresy (which held much attraction for women) becomes the historical precursor of the defense against feminist theology perceived to be necessary today.[62]

These four examples of interpretation are drawn from the German-speaking world, but they are texts known and accepted elsewhere, for example, in North America. They manifest the currency of the types of interpretation that Elisabeth Schüssler Fiorenza has described and critiqued. One exception to this pattern is the book of Max Küchler, where the contempt of women's liberation in 1 Timothy is not glossed over.

D. FEMINIST PERSPECTIVES

Elisabeth Schüssler Fiorenza's "feminist evaluative hermeneutics of the Bible" cannot be given up. To establish *grades*[63] of hatred regarding women's liberation or discrimination against women in the historical Paul (1 Cor. 11:2–16; possibly 1 Cor. 14:33–36); in the household codes of Ephesians, Colossians, and 1 Peter; and in the pastoral epistles *offers no basis for a solution of the problem.* The submission of women to men is demanded in all those texts and can in no way be justified. Similarly, to speak of different degrees of intensity in the discrimination against women, for example, in Musonius and Valerius Maximus, offers no grounds on which to justify a patriarchal society. (Musonius, too, prescribes the submission of women.)[64] In the first century C.E., misogynist propaganda prevailed in every dimension of imperial Rome's dominant culture, as it did in dominated cultures, for example, Judaism and Christianity. I have no doubt that this is a more contemptible phenomenon than the consciously patriarchal proposals for the household and state (such as those of Cicero). There can be no distinctions and gradations to justify "milder" forms of patriarchy. Within the New Testament there is no canon within the canon that is not patriarchal or hierarchical, uncontaminated by notions of patriarchal order. But there are traces within the patriarchal systems of violence of a history of liberation, and there are texts in the New Testament in which we can hear voices of women and men who are working at liberation. First Timothy shows traces of a history of women's liberation, albeit most unwittingly and entirely contrary to its declared intentions.

The analysis of how interpretations justify the New Testament's discrimination against women requires considerable feminist investigation, that is, detailed critique of misogynist exegesis. To cite just one example: 1 Tim. 5:14f. The authoritarian decree that young Christian widows must remarry, bear children, and look after the household[65] is said to have a political apologetic purpose: "to give an enemy no opportunity to revile" (as it is most frequently translated)[66] or "on account of bad-mouthing";[67] "for some have already fallen away and followed Satan." Some commentators describe the implied process as follows: some young widows have become disloyal and have become followers of Satan (i.e., heretics; v. 16), others have spurned marriage and now live lives "dependent on others' generosity, lazy and indolent,"[68] which causes "the opponent," someone opposed to the community of Christians, to bad-mouth the community (v. 14). Given the positioning of "opponent" in v. 14 and "Satan" in v. 15 and the use of *charin* ("because of" the reviling), it seems less far-fetched to suggest a different process: young widows refuse to remarry, for which reason the community is being bad-mouthed; bad-mouthing gives the opponent, that is, Satan, the opportunity to lure Christians away from the community and become Satan worshipers (cf., e.g., Mark 4:17).

Why are young widows so readily blamed for Satan worship? And why does no one say that the discrediting involved is, in fact, misogynist and discriminatory slander against women? The linguistically more obvious interpretation is not discussed because negative judgment on the young women is appropriated and applied beyond the text.

It is not enough to describe types of interpretation and to reach hermeneutical clarity; in addition, a critical feminist analysis of biblical details and interpretation is necessary. What is essential is to provide commentary that goes against the flood of the centuries' and current patriarchal commentaries of scripture.

The text of 1 Tim. 5:14 also provides the opportunity to deal with the fundamental problem of the *political apologetic* of Christian communities at the expense of women and female and male slaves in the New Testament. The social and political pressure on Christian communities was considerable. The oppression of women was a function of demonstrating the loyalty that the state demanded of its citizens.[69] There surely is a difference between Valerius Maximus's propagating the oppression of women and 1 Timothy's doing so in a document of a community that, socially and politically, belongs to the minority. But an observation such as this does not excuse the oppression of women.

New Testament texts that, like the first epistle to Timothy, engage in the oppression of women and of female and male slaves and that spread hatred and discrimination are part of the Christian canon. Although it is not enough to subject such texts to critique, it would be a mistake to remove them from the canon or to conceal them. A new understanding of the canon is needed: it is a document of a history of contempt for human beings, of a history burdened with guilt. And yet, at one and the same time, it is the gospel. The life-giving gospel will surely not suffer damage when Christian women and men face up to the history of Christianity, tainted as it is with contempt for women, colonialism, persecution of Jews and Judaism, and its traffic with patriarchy.

2

From Women's Hands: The Work of Women in the New Testament (Matt. 13:33; Luke 13:20f.)

A. THE TEXT

The brief parable of the leaven appears in almost identical form in the Gospels according to Matthew and Luke, for which reason it is assigned to the Sayings Source.[70] In both narratives, the opening sentence connects this parable with the parable of the mustard seed, which in both Gospels precedes the parable of the leaven. Being thus linked has come to mean that the parable of the leaven is understood as a women's parable next to the men's parable[71] of the mustard seed, an understanding that applies to the Sayings Source as well as to "Matthew" and "Luke."[72] The wording of the parable of the leaven is identical[73] in both versions except for their opening sentences; God's reign is to be compared to "leaven that a woman took and hid in three *sat* [a Hebrew measure of cereal] of flour until all the meal was leavened."

B. SOCIAL-HISTORICAL QUESTIONS

A Closer Look at Bread Making

Many interpreters of this text have not seen a baking trough or even looked into a cookbook. This is evident in the tradition of this text's interpretation, especially in connection with two questions. The first one is much discussed: Is *hiding* the leaven in the meal not an inappropriate term for the procedure involved for making leavened bread? Two solutions are proposed: the first is that "to hide" actually means "to mix into"; the second is that the verb *to hide* is used as a metaphor for the hiddenness of God's reign, which means that the parable has abandoned its image.[74] Both solutions offered are superfluous, since the "hiding" involved here is a normal step in preparing leavened bread.

My mother's and grandmother's cookbook (written for a rural household in Germany at the beginning of the twentieth century) outlines the bread-making procedure as follows: "The bread is leavened on the evening before baking. Use one-third of the sifted flour." The recipe calls for thirty kilograms (sixty-six pounds) of rye flour. "The sourdough and yeast are completely dissolved in 15 liters [nearly four gallons] of lukewarm water. Pour this over the flour and stir into a thick paste. Throw three handfuls of flour over the mixture, cover it, and leave to rise till the morning. Then knead the remaining flour into the leavened batter with your hands."[75] The parable recounts the procedure in abbreviated form, centering on the time in the process when the dough is mixed and covered to rise. In the theological tradition of interpretation, as well as in the tradition of social studies[76] and of the history of technology[77] relating to baking bread, it would appear that details of preparing dough were unknown to the men of these scholarly disciplines. The studies of Adolf Jülicher and Joachim Jeremias are an exception here.[78]

The second exegetical question arises from a similar ignorance of an everyday phenomenon; it asks whether the amount of flour cited is not out of touch with reality. "No housewife would make use of such a huge amount of flour"; what is spoken of here are "realities of God."[79] The text speaks of three *sat*, that is, of 39.4 liters of flour. The cookbook cited a moment ago calls for thirty kilograms of flour. Unlike unleavened flat bread, sourdough or leavened bread is not baked every day. According to my own recollections of rural conditions in the Mark Brandenburg region of Germany up until 1947, leavened bread, baked on the farm, was not always prepared for *one* family only; a number of people were involved, because not every family had a suitable oven.

It is possible to calculate the equivalent of three *sat*, or 39.4 liters of flour, to be just about one-third of the total amount of flour the recipe mentioned above calls for. The reference to the huge amount of flour in the parable is in relation to the word *holon*, "all," at the conclusion. The yeast is able to leaven so large an amount! The proportionality of "little leaven" and "so much flour" is of no significance. That the leaven is small is not mentioned in the text and consequently is of no importance. It is from the parable of the mustard seed or from 1 Cor. 5:6 or Gal. 5:9[80] that this small/large contrast has moved into the parable of the leaven, in the history of how it has been interpreted.

The reference to the recipe has shown that the parable seeks to direct attention to a specific time in the bread-making process: the dough has been covered and the woman baker waits for the large amount of flour to be fully leavened.

Women's Work

A woman's work of baking bread becomes a picture for God's reign. *The hands of the woman become visible:* "she took," "she hid." In patriarchal perception, women's work and that of women and men slaves, such as baking bread, is effectively invisible. What is visible are the hands of the overlord. The following text illustrates my point: "The Master commanded that I [i.e., the guest] be escorted into the house; he led me with his own hands to the dining hall and, after the table had been prepared, commanded many dishes to be served."[81] The hands of the women and of the female and male slaves that had prepared the table, the dishes, and that then served the meal remain invisible. But the master's hands are spoken of. Manual work of men also is often rendered invisible in patriarchal perception, but in a different manner. It is spoken of as the overlord's work: "A man [that is, the owner of the large estate] planted a vineyard and set a hedge around it, dug a pit . . . , and built a tower" (Mark 12:1). The owner linguistically appropriates the work of slaves and peasants as his own.[82] A division of labor based on the hierarchy of gender is apparent as well, namely, in the absence of any reference to the hands of women and women slaves who perform menial tasks. Nowhere would we read, "A man [that is, the owner of the large estate] cooked a meal, prepared the table, and served the food," when in fact the work had been done by women or women and men slaves.

What is remarkable is that here, as elsewhere in the Sayings Source (but also in the Gospels according to Matthew and Luke), *women's work is paired with that of men.* A man sowed a mustard seed, a woman prepared sourdough bread. Men work in the field, women spin (Matt. 6:28; Luke 12:27);[83] men toil on the land (or they sleep there), women grind at the mill.[84] On the one hand, such pairing reflects gender hierarchy, based on division of labor; "the man goes out into hostile life"[85] while the woman stays at home. On the other hand, the Gospel texts referred to equate women's work *as work* with men's work, which is most unusual in relation to the perception of women's work in antiquity. It is in reference to married couples of manual laborers that the woman's work is spoken of in the same vocational designation as that used for the man;[86] what is hard to determine is whether the gender hierarchy is not present once again in the division of labor between husband and wife.[87] There is an altar at a grave in Este, dating from the first century C.E., which appears to present a parallel to the pairing of women's and men's work. The narrow right side depicts a wool basket, a spindle, and two other utensils; the narrow left side depicts an anvil, tongs, and one other such tool.[88] The woman's housework, represented by *lanificium*, her work with wool,[89] stands parallel, *and without denigration*,[90] to the man's work as a smith. As a rule, women's work with wool was seen at the time as a symbol of women's subordination and decorousness and not, as seems to be the case here, as *work* that is of equal value to the man's. A spindle is often used as a symbol for the deceased woman, together with jewelry, combs, mirrors, and other toiletries,[91] to indicate that she was decorous, industrious, beautiful, and well-groomed.

The parable of the leaven makes the work of a woman a picture of God's reign and confers on her work a significance of which I shall speak later. At issue now is the problem of the perception of women's work. How women's work is theologically contextualized, the visibility which that work receives, and how it is paired with men's work provide together a foundation for a just perception of women's work. What the text does not question is the gender-specific *division* of labor (the woman inside, the man outside), which in the reality and ideology of patriarchy is also a gender hierarchy. Patriarchal injustice toward women's work is committed without awareness of the problem. But such self-contradiction is no coincidence; it is a structural characteristic of these texts. The context (i.e., the Sayings Source, Matthew, and Luke) that provides foundations for justice also includes rigid patriarchalism and blindness to women's world of work. By rigid patriarchalism I mean such things as the dispossession of women's work by the father of the household or by God, who gives the son bread (or an egg) and fish (Matt. 7:9f.; Luke 11:11f.), which as a rule are prepared by women. By blindness to the reality of women's world of work I mean the fact that it is only women's housework that is mentioned, but not their work outside the house, on the land, in trade, in textile production, in the sex trade. Patriarchal ideology, according to which women do not work on the land but only in the household, disregards the fact that work on the land, for example, occupied much of women's time.[92]

I want to present this contradictory picture of the Sayings Source, Matthew, and Luke in a schematic survey of how women's work was perceived in the New Testament. I shall list my findings and pursue further the question of the visibility and invisibility of women's work.

References to Women's Work (Work in the Household
and Paid Work in the New Testament)

Matt. 6:28; Luke 12:27	spinning
Matt. 13:33; Luke 13:20f.	baking bread
Matt. 24:41; Luke 17:35	grinding at the mill
Matt. 21:31f.	working in the sex trade
Luke 7:36–50	working in the sex trade[93]
Luke 15:30	working in the sex trade
Luke 2:21–22 and par.	mending
Luke 15:8	sweeping the house
Mark 14:66, 69 and par.	working as a woman slave
Luke 12:45	working as a woman slave
John 4:7	drawing and carrying water[94]
Acts 9:39	sewing, weaving[95]
Acts 16:14	dyeing, selling purple goods[96]
Acts 12:13	working as a woman slave (?)[97]
Acts 16:16	making money for the owners as a woman slave soothsayer[98]
Acts 18:3	making tents
Titus 2:5	doing housework (*oikourgos*)[99]

In addition to women's work in the household and their paid work, one should also list the references to women's work in the Christian community, such as learning, teaching, prophesying, serving, working hard (*kopian;* Rom. 16:6, 12), and others. The focus here, however, is on working in the patriarchal household and on paid work.

The reference to the *diakonia* of women in Mark 1:31 and par.; Luke 10:40; John 12:2; and Mark 15:40 and par. must be discussed in connection with the early Christian understanding of "to serve" (*diakonein*).[100] In relation to Luke 10:40 and John 12:2, one must ask whether those statements have not already departed from the new Christian understanding of "to serve" and speak again of women waiting on people, work that a free man would never do.[101]

When the New Testament makes it *visible*, women's work—in the majority of cases—is the *unpaid work of waiting on people* within the patriarchal household (spinning, baking bread, grinding at the mill, serving, sweeping, drawing and carrying water, sewing and mending clothes, doing housework). When it speaks of women's *paid work*, it is work derived from the range of women's activities in the home; it is work of the household but done "outside": in the sex trade and in textile production (Acts 16:14). Prisca, the tentmaker, more than likely produced tents of leather;[102] she was engaged, in other words, in a skilled trade and paid a daily wage,[103] which indicates that women were engaged in work beyond the range of activities related to the household.

The work of *women slaves* was unpaid. The high priest's woman slave in the courtyard of his palace (Mark 14:66, 69 and par.) is certainly not just standing around; she is there to keep the fire going and to open the gate (John 18:16). In Luke 12:45, the women slaves live in a large household in either the country or the city. I tend to think that it is in the country, since the text speaks of the overlord being away for several days,[104] leaving the supervision of the male and female slaves to the manager (Luke 12:42–48). In Acts 16:16, the female slave earns money for her owners by soothsaying.

What remains invisible in the New Testament is women's work on the land,[105] as well as the work that is normally depicted as men's work (except for Prisca's). We hear about fishermen but not of fisherwomen, of men collecting taxes but not of women who do that, and so forth. I want to use the example of fisherwomen to show that women's work in the sphere of men's work is even more invisible than women's work in the household, or derived from the range of activities related to the household.

That there were fisherwomen is confirmed by an inscription, *CIL* 6.9801: "Aurelia Nais, a freedwoman, fisherwoman from the warehouses of Galba. C. Aurelius Phileros her master. L. Valerius Secundus, freedman."[106] The fisherwoman is also seller of the fish she has caught.[107] The New Testament and many other sources of antiquity allow for a relatively good perception of the hard life of fishermen and the poverty that marked that life;[108] they say very little about fisherwomen.

I choose fisherwomen as an example of women's work in the sphere of men's work to make it absolutely clear that one must assume the presence of women and of women's work even when both language and (ancient or modern) conceptuality leave the impression of an exclusively male context. In her translation into German of Elisabeth Schüssler Fiorenza's *In Memory of Her,* Christine Schaumberger chooses terms that indicate the presence of women whenever it could not be *demonstrated* that *only* men were involved. In her translation she speaks of *ZöllnerInnen, PharisäerInnen,* and so forth—of women and men tax collectors, women and men Pharisees, and others. She reaped criticism for doing so.[109] My example here is intended to show that it is necessary to assume the presence of women until it has been proven that women were, in fact, *not* present. The "burden of proof" cannot be laid on the women and men critics of androcentric language but must be assumed by those women and men who defend it. It is plain that there were women tax collectors and women Pharisees, even if the evidence for that is meager.[110] For millennia, women have borne the major burden of agrarian production in patriarchal societies; and yet there are those who, even today, pronounce that women did not work on the land. Therefore, the presence of women must be assumed even where patriarchal consciousness rules they do not belong.

The belief is widespread that Jesus' first and most important disciples were fishermen at the Sea of Galilee. When I put together Mark 15:40f. and Mark 1:16–20,[111] I have a picture of a large group of women who followed Jesus in Galilee right from the beginning—and of four fishermen who were also present. Peter, Andrew, John, and James came from the same milieu of small fishing communities at the northern end of the Sea of Galilee as Mary Magdalene and, presumably, the Mary of James the Lesser, the Mary of Joses, Salome, and the many other women spoken of in Mark 15:41. We hear nothing of the work of those women. It should be assumed that they were just as engaged in the work of fishing and fish processing[112] as were the four men disciples. But their work is not mentioned because in patriarchal consciousness, women are not defined in terms of their work, as is normally the case for men. To the contrary, women are defined in terms of their relation to a member of the patriarchal household or, if they do not belong to a patriarchal family,[113] in terms of their place of origin—for example, Mary of Magdala.

The invisibility of women created by androcentric language leaves the impression that the productive labor of farmers, fishers, and skilled workers is primarily men's work, whereas the work of women is in the home. The New Testament, too, creates such an impression. And that perpetuates the illusion that the economic foundation of women's life was men's income. That this is not true for New Testament times and for the social class from which it derives will be discussed again in II.3.B, where the question of wages paid for women's work is addressed.

The Symbolic Dispossession of Women's Work

The evening meal serves a central function in the patriarchal household. One aspect, of course, is that it provides nourishment; another is that it actualizes social hierarchy and gives it presence through religious symbolism. The beginning prayer offered by the paterfamilias at table is part of Roman mealtime ritual.[114] Feasts and rituals in Jewish society, too, begin with symbolic and ritual acts performed (as a rule) by the paterfamilias. They include breaking the bread and distributing it, speaking words of blessing.[115] This patriarchal custom is reflected in the New Testament in the image of God and in Christ's Last Supper. God gives to those who ask, as the father of the house gives food, and not a stone or a serpent (scorpion), to the son who asks for bread or fish (or an egg), as Matt. 7:7–11 and par. report it. The paterfamilias is the giver of nourishment, and correspondingly, God is the paterfamilias in heaven who fulfills petitions and who gives bread (the "Our Father"; Matt. 6:11 and par.).

The symbolic dispossession of women's work of baking bread—of all work women do in connection with food—by the role of the paterfamilias during the main meal plays a significant part in patriarchal societies of every historical kind. Today, remnants of such dispossession appear, in secularized form, for example, in the custom of men paying in a restaurant. Therefore, when God appears in the "Our Father" and in Matt. 7:7–11 and par. as the heavenly reflection of the paterfamilias and the provider of bread, the symbolic dispossession of work that women do in connection with food becomes an aspect of the image of God.

In the Last Supper, Jesus has the role of the paterfamilias who takes the bread, blesses, breaks, and gives it (Mark 14:22 and par.; 1 Cor. 11:24). It follows that the symbolic dispossession of women's work in providing bread has become part of the most solemn rite throughout the history of the church. Only the participation of women clergy in the distribution of the bread and wine has brought change to the Protestant celebration of the Last Supper. And yet that change is only superficial, inasmuch as the women clergy are constrained to repeat without critique a patriarchal rite which, for that reason, retains its power.

The Woman Baking Bread and God's Reign

Let us return to the parable of the leaven. It reflects the ideology of patriarchy: the woman is shown to be in the house. It breaks through that ideology in making her work visible, placing it on the level of men's work and in making a woman baking bread a parable for *God's reign*. Her hands, which knead the bread dough, become transparent for God's actions. The women and men who hear this parable *see* the work of a woman symbolizing that human beings have food to eat while, at the same time, they *see* God's life-giving power. Bread and God, the hands of a woman baking bread and the hands of God, are brought into relation.

Women's work in baking bread has another symbolic meaning beyond its reference to everyday reality. "Give us this day our daily bread" (Matt. 6:11; Luke 11:3) is the prayer to be able to have the basic staple food for one day. Bread is life; it is elementary stuff of life, like water. In Roman Palestine, bread was also baked in bakeries.[116] There even were machines for kneading large amounts of dough.[117] If the parable were only about the rising process, it would have been quite sufficient to speak of leaven and a kneading machine. But the parable tells of the hard work of a woman who kneads away at a huge amount of dough, the dough for the very bread without which people cannot live. The poverty of the population in first-century C.E. Palestine is the life context in which the symbolic meaning of this parable belongs. "The narrative describes a common activity, a task that until the most recent past determined the rhythm of daily life of practically every housewife and still does so for women in two-thirds of the world. . . . For the poor, the product of mixing flour and leaven is the raw material of life itself."[118]

C. FEMINIST OBSERVATIONS ON THE HISTORY OF INTERPRETATION, PARTICULARLY THE PRESENT

In the foregoing brief interpretation of the parable of the leaven, I speak of how, at the level of their images, the narrated events are transparent to God's reign. God is not the woman baking bread, the bread is not holy, but what God's actions mean becomes visible in the work a woman does to keep life going. Her action is transparent for God's action. Bread is the symbol for being able to live.

Such an interpretation presupposes a theory of the parables that is fundamentally different from the theory predominant in the Western world's New Testament scholarship. According to the theories of traditional theology, no theological significance accrues to the reality described in the parable's image (see above at I.3.C). The world that appears in the parables' images, insofar as that world reflects everyday life and turns it upside down, is not related to the content of the revelation of which the parable is said to be speaking. So it becomes a matter of method to declare that the everyday world of the parables is incidental and that the key to their meaning is the metaphorical leap that may be found in the image. "The scene is common enough. Anyone who has observed bread made, here or in the Near East, recognizes the scene for what it is: a piece of everydayness. Well then, have we any clues *beyond an undifferentiated common picture of a woman*[119] kneading dough for bread?"[120] In light of the theoretical approach to the parables taken here, the everyday life image is incidental, of no significance. The attention of this interpreter, Robert W. Funk, is focused on those features of the image that, in his view, do not fit into everyday life (e.g., "she hid"; cf. above on this point).

"The image of the leaven is taken from the kitchen. . . . The formulation *hid* is surprising."[121] In the interpretation of Ulrich Luz also, the image "from the kitchen" is irrelevant for the interpretation. According to Adolf Jülicher's theory of the parables, the image plane must not be broken by metaphorical leaps. But he himself breaks that rule by resting his interpretation on the (unsubstantiated)[122] contrast of small/big. "And so it is that this pair of parables [mustard seed and leaven] with combined effort seeks to make it plausible for us from experiences of everyday life that a glorious outcome in the kingdom of heaven can come from unpretentious beginnings."[123] In spite of elaborate discussion about the theory of the parables, the everyday world of the parables remains, in the Western tradition of interpretation, without any significance for the revelation they announce.

Carlos Mesters interprets parables in terms of liberation theology. He rediscovers the parables' image world and *everyday reality as a source of revelation.* "Anyone who does not know, for example, what leaven is will not be able to understand the sentence that 'God's reign is like a leaven.' . . . When we come together to reflect on scripture we first think on the things of life before we think on the reign of God."[124] Even though I share his basic approach to the theory of the parables, I must criticize Mesters for his androcentrism: the parable speaks of "the leaven that a woman took," that is to say, of a woman's work with leaven, the very work of people's nourishment.

This touches on the second aspect of a feminist critique of the history of interpretation. As a consequence of that history, the woman baking the bread is often left invisible—other than in the parable itself. Women become invisible as the consequence of two factors: first, in theological thinking as we know it, women are invisible *as women,* and second, women's work is not an object of theological reflection.[125] To illustrate the point: commenting on the version of the parable of the leaven in the *Gospel of Thomas,* Hans Weder writes that "*the parable of the leaven* has been altered to the point that *the bearer of the action is no longer* the yeast but the woman."[126] Jesus' parable, as recorded in the canonical Gospels, is interpreted on the basis of something that takes place, namely, the dough rises. "A beginning has been made, the glorious future is assured, and so the present, too, is in motion."[127] Such is the interpretation of the parable in the context of the Sayings Source. In the *Gospel of Thomas,* the text is as follows: "Jesus [said], the Father's reign is like a woman. She took a small amount of leaven; she [hid] it in flour. She made it into big loaves" (*Gospel of Thomas* 96).[128] Compared to the canonical version, only the ending is changed; an additional verb describes the woman's action. But in the canonical version she is the bearer of the action just as much as in the *Gospel of Thomas,* as the two verbs (she took, she hid) demonstrate. Interpretations that pass over the woman as the bearer of the action pass by the text altogether.

Joachim Jeremias acknowledges the woman and her work;[129] still, he too finds the woman baking the bread insignificant for the theological content of the parable. This results from his theory of the parables.

When one looks at what the New Testament has to say about women's work in terms of how it has been interpreted historically, one can measure the extent of the invisibility of women's work in the world of theological tradition, for which "work" (men's work, to all intents and purposes) is itself a marginal issue of social ethics.[130] Lydia the seller of purple goods and Prisca the tentmaker (Acts 16:14 and 18:3) occupy a pivotal position in the discernment of women's work in the history of interpretation. That is because those texts speak explicitly of women's paid work. Patriarchal consciousness does not consider other materials to be about women's work: prostitution is a moral problem, and women's housework derives from their "role that nature provided."[131] And it would seem that the existence of female slaves has merited neither historical nor theological reflection in the history of interpretation.[132]

There are two versions of Acts 18:3 in the handwritten manuscripts. One version, relevant to this discussion, says that Prisca, Aquila, and Paul worked in the trade of tentmaking ("he stayed with them and they worked"). The other version uses the singular—"and he [Paul] worked"—creating the impression that Paul is living with people of the same trade and, on that basis, pursues his work. What I judge to be the more reliable and older version leaves the impression that Aquila, Prisca, and Paul live together and, for that reason, also work together. The change to the singular, which makes no mention of Prisca working, belongs to the recognizable intention of one part of the handwritten communication of Acts, which was to push Prisca into the background. Even Adolf von Harnack, who had clearly brought this matter to attention and had commented extensively on Prisca, devotes to her work the singular notice that she and her husband made tents.[133] In more recent commentaries, I find either that Aquila and Prisca were a well-to-do couple who owned a tentmaking business and that Paul was employed by them or that Aquila and Prisca were tentmakers. Reference to Prisca's work is missing even where the vocation of tentmaking is discussed as the vocation of Aquila and Paul or of Aquila and Prisca.[134] The conditions under which women live are no subject matter for traditional interpretation even when the text, as in this case, speaks about them directly. Extensive analysis of and theological reflection on women's work in the New Testament can be found particularly in the work of Ivoni Richter Reimer, a woman scholar of feminist liberation theology.[135]

In every commentary of traditional theology I know except one, Lydia, the seller of purple goods (Acts 16:14), is said to be a well-to-do woman.[136] Not one explores the reality of her work, even though there is plenty of information regarding her vocation.

The tradition of interpretation is marked by patriarchy. This is the conclusion of feminist critiques of the traditional interpretation of the parable of the leaven and of New Testament texts that speak of women's work. The parables' everyday reality is not included in *theological* reflection (in the theory of the parables); women's work is not noticed even where it is mentioned in the texts. In place of a woman who works there is one who is well off.[137] Housework is a task that nature has conferred on women and is not regarded as work. To this day, Christian theology congratulates itself on holding work in high esteem, which, for example, the upper classes in antiquity did not. Christian theologians may not speak with the disdain of a Cicero about working people. But the perspective that pervades the tradition of interpretation is, like Cicero's, that of the upper class and of the men who wield power.

D. FEMINIST PERSPECTIVES

The scholarly discussion of the theory of the parables traditionally separates everyday life from the event of revelation. The task is to recover a perspective in which the experiences of everyday life depicted in Jesus' parables are once again transparent for God's revelation. The parable of the leaven directs attention to the hands of women baking bread: "she took," "she hid." The conclusion signals that she waited "until it was all leavened." The parable interprets eschatologically the here and now of those who follow Jesus: the dough is covered, we wait with calm. The parable brings the here and now into relation with the powerful process of God's reign; that powerful process[138] is experienced when people look at the hands of a woman baking bread. The Misereor Lenten Veil of 1989 from India placed the bread-baking woman at the center and thereby at the center of the gospel. This Lenten veil is an interpretation of our text of lasting significance, because it tells of the connection between the woman's action and God's reign.[139]

One must guard against two possible misunderstandings. First, does not a feminist interpretation, in which the hands of a bread-baking woman manifest God's hands, undermine the feminist interest in the liberation of women? Are women not once again assigned a "feminine" role not of their choice, to work in the house and keep life going? It should be obvious that this cannot be the intention of feminists who deal with this text. Their interest is rather that theology take seriously the story of women baking bread, a story that had been made invisible.

A second misunderstanding relates to women's work of hope, which always seeks to secure the future but which functions all too often as the support system to be called on in humanly created catastrophes.[140] It would be a mistake, given the eschatological frame of interpretation, to conclude that this is what is being expressed here. Women labored under the radioactive clouds of Chernobyl to find uncontaminated food. Their struggle served life and unwittingly played into the hands of those who wanted to keep on with nuclear energy. For what future do women who bake bread work? The future envisaged by the parable is the life of creation made anew; it is the reign of God and not the prolongation of the status quo.

The parable directs attention to a woman's hands at the moment when they are at rest. This has often caused the tradition of interpretation to declare that humans could do nothing for God's future; nor should they try, since it is God alone who acts. God's reign comes "of itself."[141] But the parable sets neither human action and trust in God, on the one hand, nor the action of human beings and of God, on the other, over against each other. To act and to trust in God, to work for life and to be able to wait, belong together here. The failure of the New Testament to acknowledge women's work is something that can be dealt with through critical work. But it is much more difficult to deal with that same failure in the dominant tradition of Christian interpretation. That is because this tradition, through its patriarchal hermeneutics, stubbornly skews biblical texts that speak of women's work. It is a task of Christian theology to discern God's revelation in the midst of human life and to inquire for that reason about everyday life, about what the economic conditions of people's lives were and about their and our own experiences. When it comes to women's work, Christian theology has a blind spot.

3

The Lost Coin: Women's Daily Struggle[142] for Money and Bread (Luke 15:8–10)

A. THE TEXT

In the Gospel according to Luke, the parable of the lost drachma, a woman's parable, is combined with the men's parable of the lost sheep (Luke 15:4–7), forming a parable pair (v. 8 is related to v. 4; both parables have the same narrative form). Comparing the two parables shows that each has its own distinctive accent. The shepherd and the woman both diligently search for something lost. The woman's search is linguistically more developed than that of the shepherd. She lights a lamp in her windowless house, sweeps the room, or the one-room house, and carefully checks the sweepings for the coin. Both woman and shepherd act under pressure. The latter cannot afford to report the loss of a sheep to the owner of the flock; the former urgently needs the money in order to live. In both cases, these are everyday experiences of poor people, a shepherd in the position of dependency[143] and a woman for whom *one* of ten drachmas represents a significant portion of her means of support. A wealthy owner of the flock would quite likely go to far less trouble than the shepherd for *one* of one hundred sheep. And a well-to-do woman could easily suffer the loss of one drachma.[144]

These are not romantic pictures. The image of the woman searching for her money cannot be turned into an image of intimate love, as the image of the shepherd is again and again.[145] Instead, another question should be asked. Given that in Luke the parables of the lost sheep and the lost coin are combined in a narrative unit with the parable of the lost son (Luke 15:11–32), in what perspective does the patriarchal father–son relationship appear? The father is a loving father (cf. Luke 15:20), but his love parallels the poor woman's search for her money and a shepherd's search for a sheep. The father needs his son/sons for his livelihood; it is not only that they need him. He needs his sons not only for his heart's delight but also for his farm and his old age. I note in passing that Luke 15:11–32 places a father and his sons in the center of things without any critique of the structure of domination in patriarchy.[146]

91

Like the men's parable (Luke 15:4–7), the women's parable (Luke 15:8–10) begins in the interrogative: "What man among you . . . ?" (Luke 15:4); "What woman, having . . . ?" (Luke 15:8), and not "What woman among you . . . ?" An interesting surmise surfaces in the history of interpretation:[147] Does this difference imply that the crowd being addressed consisted only of men? The question can hardly be answered because the difference may simply serve stylistic reasons. The speculation needs to be pushed, however. It is to be assumed that women were in the crowd.[148] The tenuous phrasing of the question in Luke 15:8 may indicate that women were presumed to be present but are nevertheless *not spoken to.* That would make Luke 15:8 yet another example of androcentric language.

B. SOCIAL-HISTORICAL QUESTIONS

A Woman Has Ten Drachmas

A drachma has the same value as a silver denarius.[149] Matthew 20:1–16 provides important information about the latter: it is the wage paid to a man who has worked all day in the fields. We also learn from that text (and from other sources)[150] that this daily-wage worker must have expected to be without employment for days or even months.

Arye Ben-David has calculated the average yearly income of a daily-wage worker on the land to be about two hundred denarii. For a family of six, he continues, this income would yield about fourteen hundred calories (from bread) per family member per day.[151] Such a level of nutrition cannot sustain a person's ability to work, he notes, even in relation to the destitute. He surmises therefore that those proletarian land laborers would work a small plot of land on the side to help out with the low income.[152] How women and children participate in creating income is not stated in Ben-David's calculations. One has to ask, therefore: Who works that additional land? What is known about the (extra) income of women and children? Is the yearly income (of a man) of two hundred denarii in fact the minimum income of a family?

According to the Tosephta, "A laborer should not work for himself during the night and then hire himself out to others during the day, because he will only deprive his employer [on account of low productivity] in the work given him to do."[153] One may conclude from such legal regulations that as well as daily-wage work, men did have additional work; that they came under pressure from their employers; and that they faced excessive physical demands. It stands to reason, therefore, that when an additional plot of land or other extra work was attended to, the labor could not have been done exclusively by the able-bodied men (during the night or in periods of unemployment) but that women and children, the aged women and men too, would have been involved.[154] As Acts 4:34, 37 and

5:1 (cf. Acts 2:45) make clear, the small plot of land, the additional source of income of peasants growing increasingly poorer, often had to be sold.

The sources do indicate, however, that the economic survival of families depended on the *additional paid labor of women*. Anna, the wife of Tobit, goes to work when her husband is no longer able to work; her employment is that of *eritheuein*, a paid woman laborer in the women's quarters, and she delivers what she produces to the owners (*kyrioi*).[155] She is paid for that and, in addition, she is given a kid. But her husband thinks that she has stolen the kid and creates an awful scene. She insists that the kid was given to her as a present in addition to her wages. It could well be that this "gift" is part of the "wages," not unlike the "board" that women wage earners are to receive according to the edict of Diocletian (see note 175, below).

The Mishnah (*Ketub.* 5:5–9) distinguishes between the work a woman has to do for her husband (grinding, baking, washing, cooking, feeding the baby, making the bed, working with wool; 5:5) and her work in producing handicrafts (5:9 twice; 6:1; 6:4 indirectly). The income of that latter work normally goes to the husband in payment for her keep, even though she earns more than her keep (5:4 refers to this "surplus"). This economic productivity of a married woman, which, according to the Mishnah, is to be regarded as a *regular* feature for the majority of the poor population, does not appear in Ben-David's calculations. It is not possible, therefore, to declare that two hundred denarii are the necessary minimum of a family's income. It is rather the necessary income level for one person. For that reason, the *ketubbah*[156] of a virgin is also two hundred denarii,[157] assuring the woman's livelihood for the first year after her husband's death or divorce. For a widow the *ketubbah* was only one hundred denarii.[158] The rules governing the *ketubbah* presuppose that after a set transition period, women will engage in paid work to secure their livelihood.

According to the Babylonian Talmud, it is taken for granted that children will work from age six onward.[159] What they earn belongs to the father; this is already stated in the Mishnah in relation to daughters.[160]

We should generally assume, therefore, that the poverty-stricken majority of the population in the period under discussion (i.e., the first and second centuries C.E.) had to work for its own livelihood from the age of six. When it comes to paid labor, the conditions for women and girls differ from those for men: they have no right to dispose of money and they earn less than men (more about this later). Jewish as well as Hellenistic-Roman sources describe those conditions,[161] as will be shown in the following.

The sources consistently show that the levels of payment for women's work are such that, as a rule, the income earned by women and girls could not support an independent economic existence. Women worked in the rural economy and, most often, in textile production. Their wages at times matched only what they had to spend on food.

Are you not worried about poverty, woman? It burdens you heavily with much
want and inflicts on you the thorn of toil. There was a time when you could spin
one skein of wool a day, your older daughter even one and a third, and the little
girl spun one half. And now, all three of you can weigh out only one skein a day
and it pays just for your food.[162]

This little exercise in arithmetic from the *Anthologia graeca* assumes that spin-
ner-women are paid according to the weight of wool they process. In good days
the woman and her two daughters earned two and a half plus one-third skeins;
the same women together now spin one skein and their income pays "just for
your food." This poem is interested in arithmetical calculation, and we learn
only incidentally something about payment for women's work. Lucian also presupposes that a woman working in textiles cannot support herself and her
daughter adequately on the income of her work alone.[163] After the death of her
husband, who had been a coppersmith, "I found myself forced to sell the tongs,
the anvil, and the hammer for two minae. We lived on the proceeds as long as
they lasted; since they are gone, I have enough trouble barely to eke out a living for you and me by weaving, warping, and spinning." She hopes that her
daughter can earn more now in prostitution. Terence also speaks of the harsh-
ness of the work of a weaver-woman, who leaves it for the sex trade.[164]

Unfortunately, the literature I have consulted in relation to women's work in
antiquity says little about the issue of wages. In the absence of further evidence,
I rely on Diocletian's edict[165] that speaks about the wages paid a female weaver.
A woman whose work is weaving (silk? *gerdia, textrix*) is paid twelve denarii a
day and board (20.12). (A denarius was worth considerably less at that time
[301 C.E.] than it was in the first century C.E.) A daily-wage earner working the
land earns twenty-five denarii a day (7.1), which would correspond in value to
the one denarius spoken of in Matt. 20:1–16. Just like the woman weaver, the
daily-wage earner working the land receives board in addition. The woman
earns, in other words, barely half of what the man earns. She is paid sixteen
denarii when she works with especially valuable fabrics. Comparisons with corresponding men's work are difficult to make since the weaver's products listed
in Diocletian's edict are paid for by the weight of wool or by the piece.[166] Perhaps one may compare the male weaver of silk mentioned in 20.9 with the
woman weaver in 20.12; he earns twenty-five denarii a day plus board, just like
the wage earner on the land. These wage rates permit one to conclude that male
wage earners can survive on their income as long as they can find work. The wage
paid the woman weaver, however, does not suffice for her to live independently,
since it amounts to barely one-half of a man's wage and his poverty is itself beyond dispute. The board provided in the employer's house is clearly a significant
part of the wages.

I have cited material about wages paid in connection with women who work
in weaving because that job seems typical to me for women who must try to sur-

vive by income-producing work. The parable of the laborers in the vineyard (Matt. 20:1–16) seems in its substance to be the counterpart to the parable of the lost coin (Luke 15:8–10). In the former, the male daily-wage earners are on the edge of bare existence; in the latter, a woman is searching for a drachma, which it takes her twice as long to earn as it does the men.

The wages for women's paid work are a little more than what one person re-quires for food and clothing; they amount to somewhat less than half the yearly income of two hundred denarii which a daily-wage worker on the land earns. This is supported by *m. Ketub.* 5 (cf. above on the question of whether two hun-dred denarii is the minimum income for a family or for one person). A woman's minimum costs for food and out-of-pocket expenses are thirty-one denarii a year, according to *m. Ketub.* 5:8f., in Ben-David's calculations (p. 307, Table 14). At least fifty denarii for clothing need to be added to that, as *m. Ketub.* 5:8 stipulates. The man's expenses for those items are covered by the woman's in-come, which belongs to him, leaving him with a "surplus." That surplus allows a family of six to survive, on condition that the man can earn an annual income of two hundred denarii (see above). A woman who receives a *ketubbah* of one hundred denarii after the death of her husband or after their divorce has to find full employment in order to reach the annual subsistence level. The text from the Mishnah cited earlier—and Luke 15:8–10—presuppose women's work for money and natural goods, but this raises little more than what one person re-quires for food and clothing and hardly permits a woman to have an indepen-dent existence. The patriarchal myth and its notion of the "normal" woman who is cared for in her husband's household have little in common with women's re-ality, as the Mishnah text makes particularly evident. The workshop in the base-ment of the burnt house in Jerusalem[167] provides an archaeological picture of women's workplaces.

In the parable's image, the one drachma the woman searches for represents one two-hundredth of the annual amount required for one person to subsist at the poverty level. One drachma pays for barely two days of provisions and other needs (five hundred grams—17.5 ounces—of bread cost one-twelfth of a denar-ius.)[168] What that one drachma clearly symbolizes, like the one denarius in Matt. 20:1–16, is this: *the money for the daily bread.*

Housekeeping Money, Dowry, or a Woman's Wages?

The parable's image is that of a woman for whom one drachma is utterly indis-pensable. The sources discussed thus far take it for granted that girls and women, even within the context of an "intact" patriarchal household, have to provide for themselves; this lets one see how normal it is for the parable to make such a strong connection between the woman and the coin. In face of this material, it will not do to idealize the woman's existence as that of a housewife with house-keeping money, living in pleasant rural ambience. If the woman in Luke

15:8–10 were meant to be understood as a farmer's wife, her search for one drachma would make little sense. A woman in a rural household that produces enough grain and other foodstuff itself does not depend that way on one drachma. The text presupposes conditions such as are depicted in Matt. 20:1–16, of human beings who own no more land and who must buy their daily food. The urgency to raise the money (or to find it) is great and ever-present. This is exactly what the parable presupposes, and it patently wants to tell of a typical situation that is known to the hearers. But why is that situation associated with a woman? Why is a woman's concentration on a lost coin, of all situations, taken to be so typical? Should it not be the daily-wage earner (in the sense of Matt. 20:1–16) who is associated with the search for money? Does his wife not merely bake the bread from the wheat for which he has provided the money? Such an idea, however, fails to do justice to the parable, which presupposes that women have to earn and spend money themselves.

The image of women who do not have to earn money and, when they do spend it, use that of their husbands is connected with another patriarchal image, namely, that of the woman's "role" in the home. This patriarchal myth did not correspond with reality then—as the parable itself indicates—and it does not correspond with reality today either. Therefore, an interpretation of this parable according to which the woman searches for the housekeeping money her husband had earned is not warranted in the text; it is patriarchal mythologizing.

Joachim Jeremias gave rise to the widely held interpretation[169] that the money in Luke 15:8–10 is the woman's dowry: a particular headdress composed of coins. But this misses the text. A dowry of ten drachma is no endowment, no "treasure," but at best a minimal emergency fund for a few weeks' survival.[170] This reading, as dowry, arises from the readiness of the patriarchal perspective to connect women with jewelry rather than with the means of survival, even when it does not fit the text.

The parable depicts how women had to deal with financial survival in their everyday life and how much pressure this put on them. Social-historical research substantiates this again and again.

Going Shopping

The situation of a woman searching for a drachma may also be illustrated from another perspective, namely, from that of the merchandise she buys with that money. Poor people's food consists primarily of wheat products. A famine means that wheat, more than anything else, increases in price:[171] "A whole day's wage [a denarius] for a quart of flour; a whole day's wage for three quarts of barley meal; but spare the olive and the vine" (Rev. 6:6). The latter two do not go up in price. Bread—the chief foodstuff—was baked then by women in the household or else produced and sold in bakeries. The Mishnah presupposes an apposition of "the master's bread" (i.e., the bread baked by a woman in the home) and "the baker's bread" (*m. Baba Meṣ.* 2:1, 2); one finds it also in the New Testament. Women grind at the mill (Matt. 24:41 and par.) and bake leavened bread (Matt. 13:33 and par.);[172] but there are also mills driven by donkeys (Luke 17:2; Matt. 18:6; and elsewhere), which grind larger amounts of grain and which are associated with commercial bakeries.[173]

What commercial bakeries meant for the rural population in New Testament times can be seen in the feeding miracles. Mark 6:36 and par. presupposes that one could purchase foodstuffs in the small and larger villages of Galilee. It is not likely that the texts think of unusual circumstances (such as sales to travelers) or of purchases from private homes. Rather, they take it for granted that it was possible to buy food without having to rely on special favors. The same is true in relation to Samaria (John 4:8, 31). Only in the desert could one not buy anything (Mark 8:3–4 and par.). It is easier to explain why commercial baking played a significant part in the larger cities. Rome's tenement houses made no provision for home baking.[174] According to Dio Chrysostom,[175] poor people in the rural towns of Asia Minor had to buy everything they needed, from fuel to provisions. Since bread is more expensive than grain,[176] possibilities for baking bread at home must have been such that women were forced to buy bread instead of baking it themselves. In relation to Palestine, the prevailing constraint would most likely have been lack of time, because the women were engaged in paid work. In all cases, the presence of bakeries indicates that a part of the population is landless and no longer produces any foodstuffs. To lose the possibility of providing for oneself and others by one's homegrown products would bring to women a massive loss of self-determination. When a woman searches for a drachma, like the woman in Luke 15:8–10, she certainly has no farm, not even a tiny one, to fall back on. She is constrained to provide for herself—and her children—by her own paid work or to supplement with her income her husband's insufficient wages.

Acts 2:45; 4:34, 37; and 5:1f. presuppose that money had to be raised in order to provide for all members of the original congregation in Jerusalem.[177] The money derived from the sale of fields or houses. Had those fields been large enough that, by its own labor, the congregation could have grown sufficient food to make up for its lack, there would have been no reason to sell them. Acts 2:45 and the other verses reflect an economic situation comparable to that of Matt. 20:1–16 or Luke 15:8–10; either there are no more landholdings or the land owned is too small to supply the needs of people. What land remains must be sold so that provisions can be bought. And this means that the condition of grinding poverty escalates, becoming ever more the rule.

Women's Neighborhoods

After the woman finds her coin, she shares her joy with her women friends and neighbors. At that time, their neighborhoods were of great importance in women's everyday lives; women prepared dough and cooked meals together, they would borrow and lend utensils,[178] and, as this text indicates, they shared their joys and sorrows. However brief this parable, it is an important source for women's history, and it is a source that takes the side of women (see below at II.3.D for the theological importance of the image).

C. FEMINIST OBSERVATIONS ON THE
HISTORY OF INTERPRETATION,
PARTICULARLY THE PRESENT

The tradition of interpretation rarely, if ever, discusses the question of *what sort of money* the woman has. The most widely held view is that she is a poor woman[179] and that the money is her dowry (see above). Just as paltry are the answers to the question of *whether the woman is ever recognized as a woman in the description of the parable's image.*[180] Jülicher (1910) made the most interesting comments that I have found:[181]

> According to Plumm [*sic*],[182] the most notable difference between this parable and the one before it is the *hen apolesa* ("which she lost") in contrast to the *to apololos* ("which had gotten lost," in Luke 15:6). The woman herself is responsible for the loss; she had been careless. —J. T. Beck blames her even more harshly: "negligence, pilfering and cunning," whereas the sheep had merely wandered off.

Jülicher defends the woman with good arguments. One often senses the smile that comes to his face as he reads his contemporary or older colleagues' commentaries.

The image of this parable is associated at times with Prov. 2:4.[183] Such a comparison is insightful, however, when one contrasts rather than parallels the texts. Searching for silver and hidden treasures is the action of *pleonexia* (covetousness), of the wish "to possess even more." But the woman searches for *one* drachma only. There is a rabbinic commentary on Prov. 2:4 that shows how little comparison there is between this text and Luke 15:8–10:

> R. Pinehas b. Jair [ca. 200] began his address by quoting Prov. 2:4. . . . Like a man who, having lost a sela . . . in his house, lights many lights and lamps until he has found it. Behold the inference from something lesser to something greater. If someone lights many lights and lamps for the sake of things which belong to the life of this world's fleeting hours until he finds and recovers them again, how much more must you search as for a hidden treasure for the words of the Torah which concern life in this world and in the world to come.[184]

The image of the rabbi's parable does not conform to that of Prov. 2:4— hidden treasures—but tells of a man who searches for a *sela;* he searches for a coin that corresponds in value to four silver denarii or four drachmas. This man too searches for the money for his subsistence and not for riches. A world is spoken of other than that of Prov. 2:4, in which an upper-class man hunts for a hidden treasure. The rabbi's parable of the *sela* and Luke 15:8–10 depict comparable experiences.

When it comes to *the theological interpretation of the parable,* the woman is of no significance for recent interpretation. The theory of the parables is one reason for this (see above at I.3.C and II.2.C). Hans Weder justly comments that, in relation to the image, "it is important that the woman be seen consistently as the acting *subject*." But he then proceeds, in line with his theory of the parables, to interpret the image without any connection between the woman and God: "In this parable God is spoken of as one who searches for the human being and is exceedingly joyful when the human being has been found."[185] Hardly anyone ever asks *whether the parable has its own particular value as a women's parable next to that of the lost sheep.* For many years I have been influenced by this tradition of interpretation and took the parable of the lost coin to be a relatively insignificant analogy to that of the lost sheep.[186] The parable stands in the shadow of the shepherd's parable, just as the parable of the leaven stands in the shadow of that of the mustard seed. But there are interpreters who refer at least to the pairing of these parables (well-to-do shepherd and poor housewife,[187] or "that is how people think and act, be they men or women"[188]). The parable of the lost coin has played a marginal role in recent history of interpretation.

D. FEMINIST PERSPECTIVES

Greek and Latin writers of the time called it a barbaric habit[189] when women had to do hard work on the land to earn money or, if they did not want to lose their income, even gave birth while on the fields:

> Poseidonius[190] reports that his host Charmoleus, a man from Marseilles, told him in Liguria that he once hired men and women together to dig his fields. One of the women, overtaken by labor pains, went away a piece and, after having given birth, returned immediately to work lest she lose her wages. Charmoleus noticed that she was in pain but did not know why at first. He found out only later, whereupon he sent her away and paid her the wages. She took the baby to a brook, washed it, and wrapped it with whatever she had at hand and took it home hale and hearty.

The same story is told by Diodorus Siculus (4.20.3). He says that the foreman had tried to get the woman to stop working, but she refused to be sent home; he finally took pity on her, gave her the wages, and dismissed her. Strabo tells the story as an illustration of exotic customs; Diodorus Siculus says people are forced to do this on account of the rocky and unproductive soil of Liguria. One could still encounter people at that time who cultivated the land by hoeing while others already used plows. It is to be assumed that women worked very hard on the land in every region of the Roman Empire, and not only in those faraway provinces where hoeing was still the custom.[191] Only the unreal perspective of patriarchy finds women's hard labor on the land to be an exotic custom.

Both versions[192] of the story indicate that women would lose their daily wages if they were to stop working early. Late in the process the foreman is moved by her pain to pay her the wages,[193] or he only afterward comes to know what had caused her pain. In both accounts she works long hours in spite of her pain in order not to lose her wages. Both times the story is presented as if reporting an unusual event, whereas it reflects actual reality. The usual event of giving birth would have forced women daily-wage earners to interrupt their work for a certain length of time. The pressure on women to earn money was no exotic phenomenon but an everyday necessity for the majority of the population. Luke 15:8–10 depicts women's day-to-day dependency on money; the parable speaks of it in the perspective of solidarity.

Luke 15:8–10 is a parable of God's searching for lost human beings and of the joy of God's angels when a lost human being has been found by God. The very struggle for survival of women, who have to work twice as long as men to earn one drachma, is a parable for the struggle of God, the One searching for lost human beings who repent.

The solidarity of a group of women neighbors becomes a parable for the angels' joy.[194] Image and meaning (or substance) are not to be taken as two separate entities; rather, in such parables the reality of life is made transparent for the activity of God. The solidarity of women's neighborhoods is, indeed, not identical with the angels' joy. The jubilant laughter of the group of women at the end of this parable is not associated with women's gossip[195] but with the angels' happiness in heaven. The little parable truly deserves to be taken more seriously than hitherto. It is a surprising document of justice in the midst of an androcentric and patriarchal context—irrespective of whether it is older than the Gospel according to Luke or came into being only when that Gospel was being written.[196]

4

The Stubborn Widow
and the Resistance of Women
(Luke 18:1–8)

A. THE TEXT

In the parable of the stubborn widow, a little story is told of women's resistance against injustice, a story in which the stubborn widow is held up as an example of believers' behavior toward God and human beings.

The *injustice* done to this widow is on two levels. She is the victim of a man who undermined the economic foundation of her life;[197] she attempts to defend herself against this man with the help of a judge. She lays charges against the one whom the parable calls her "adversary." In addition, she is a victim of an unjust judgment, one that ignores her rights. The parable says that several times the judge refused to see her. The double injustice done to her is the subject of the perennial complaint of the Hebrew Bible against the perpetrators of injustice and against the people in whose midst it is done. Both the Old Testament material and the parable allow the conclusion that this double injustice done to widows is *structural* injustice. By sheer repetition of this complaint, the Hebrew scripture texts signal that this is injustice of a structural kind. The New Testament parable does the same by portraying the distress as a typical case.[198] This text shows, in other words, that there was in early Christianity, as in the Jewish tradition and elsewhere, an awareness about patriarchal society's structural injustice, against which God proceeds.[199] The parable says that the judge did not fear God (vv. 2, 4); it also documents his deficient fear of God in his behavior toward the widow, inasmuch as the God of the Hebrew Bible demanded justice for widows.

The *judge* represents the unjust ruler who thinks of himself as all-powerful, according to biblical tradition (cf. Ezek. 28:2 and Isa. 14:13f.), and who in his arrogance tramples on the rights of the poor. The biblical tradition speaks about such arrogant rulers, from whom the people of Israel had much to suffer in their history, from the perspective of a people who know God to be on their side: God pushes the mighty off their thrones (Luke 1:52). This tradition is found both in the judge's own words (Luke 18:4) and in how he is described (Luke 18:2): "neither feared God nor regarded human beings."

The *resistance* of the widow against this double injustice that she and many other widows suffered consists, first, in her going to court on account of the damages, and second, in her not being deterred by the unjust judge's refusals. She keeps coming back so often, in fact, that she becomes a real nuisance. The judge complains and admits to being annoyed (v. 5). He vindicates her in order to be troubled no longer by her stubbornness.

Interpreters have long had trouble with the *application of the parable* to the relationship of believers to God in verses 1 and 6–8. As a rule, there is an inference from the lesser to the greater: if an unjust judge vindicates a widow, how much more will God[200] vindicate those who ask. The difficulty here is the *comparison* of God with an unjust judge. I see a *contrast* between them, as is described in Sir. 35:12–22. It is not appropriate to make the judge's or God's action the focal point of the parable. The text's center of gravity is the behavior of the believers (Luke 18:8), of the elect (v. 7) or the women and men disciples of Jesus addressed in v. 1; they are to behave toward God like this stubborn widow, to pray without ceasing and not to despair[201] (v. 1), to cry to God day and night for their rights (v. 7), and to have faith (v. 8). Their whole existence is to be like that of the widow in relation to the unjust judge. Since praying and crying to God refers to their entire existence—as does having faith—one should not think of prayer in a narrower sense, such as the prayer offered in early Christianity during Jewish times of prayer.[202] Praying and crying to God against injustices describes the whole life of believers: their efforts, their protests against injustice. It describes also their trust in God, for they know that God acts very differently than the unjust judge. Romans 8:15 and 26 also refer to this prayer as the behavior of believers; they cry out like women in childbirth and do not give up,[203] holding fast to that patient power of resistance (*hypomonē*) which comes from the hope in God's nearness.[204]

The parable concentrates the attention on this resisting behavior of believers, for which a stubborn widow provides the example. But this kind of prayer and stubborn hope is not limited to the isolated relation of individuals to God, as it is in the views about prayer in modern dualism. Rather, this kind of prayer also characterizes the acting and praying of the community in its surroundings and constitutes its strength and persistence in its dealings with human beings. The community is filled with the hope that God's judgment will bring justice.[205]

B. SOCIAL-HISTORICAL QUESTIONS

Resistance at court is a much-discussed topic in antiquity; many texts speak of it. An ancient Egyptian text tells of an "eloquent farmer"[206] who returns nine times to a judge even though his efforts failed; once he is even whipped by the judge's servants.[207] In his speeches at court, he holds the judge to his solemn duty to give justice to the powerless. "People trusted you," the man says; "now you have become a villain. You were put here as a dam for the wretched, to prevent them from drowning. And now, behold, you have become the very sea."[208] Again and again he accuses the judge of having become a thief: "The one supposed to guide people to the law gives orders to steal." He invokes evil on the wicked judge and on his livestock; in offering resistance, he sees himself as the representative of justice who will not keep silent anymore. "The one you made to speak will not keep silent; he whom you have awakened will sleep no more. . . . No more ignorance where you have planted knowledge. For such are they who drive away wickedness."[209]

In 2 Samuel 14, we read of a "wise woman" who, disguised as a widow in mourning, asks King David for protection for her only remaining son; he killed his brother and now the blood avengers are after him. By means of her disguise and the fictive incident, she wants to move David to show mercy to Absalom—David's own son—who had taken his brother's life. The woman's steadfast resolve, her staying power, is well described in the text: in appearance a widow pleading for her own and her son's safety but in reality someone seeking, by means of a made-up story, to have David render a judgment that he will end up having to apply to himself. Four times she lays out the case, directly, indirectly, because David's assurances are not good enough for her. The story assumes quite simply that widows have to take legal action and that the king does not think it unusual that a widow keeps after him so stubbornly.

One of the Oxyrhynchus Papyri from the early first century C.E.[210] describes the deposition by a "weak widow" who already made an earlier deposition against her son-in-law concerning a crime against her. The offending party, the text states, "had succeeded in getting the petition blocked so that no action could be taken against him." But the widow would not let herself be deterred by this; she renewed her pleas against an old injustice and also petitioned the court in relation to the new injustice.

An Egyptian priest named Appian,[211] condemned to death by Emperor Commodus, calls the emperor a perpetrator of injustice and a tyrant.

These four examples of resistance against the court's rulings allow us to see the widow's behavior in Luke 18:1–8 in a new light. Over and over she went back to the unjust judge and *demanded that she be vindicated* (v. 3); *she reproached him and reminded him of his solemn duty,* just like the eloquent farmer and the widow in disguise. Verses 1 and 6–8 of the chapter,[212] which frame the parable, so to speak, imply that the widow spoke out or even cried aloud, without ceasing.[213] One may safely assume this, given that the outcry of women is often found in descriptions of their resistance.[214] The widow of Jesus' parable knows that her judge is unjust, and yet, by her stubborn and resistant behavior and language, she gets him to render *justice.* How many experiences of unjust judgments, particularly toward widows, cry out in this text and in the parallel cases cited? This widow belongs to a recognizable tradition of resistance.

Often the persistence that marks the struggle for justice in these texts is associated with transgression against socially assigned roles. The "eloquent farmer" becomes himself the guardian of justice and resembles a prophet; the woman disguised as a widow turns out to be the king's counsel. Beyond doubt, Luke 18:1–8 depicts transgression against socially assigned roles: no widow—and presumably, no woman—is allowed to behave that way. This transgression against roles is the cause of what is referred to so often in commentaries on this text as the judge's "sarcasm";[215] he says to himself: I'd better vindicate her "so she won't come to me at the end and slap me in the face." The Greek word *hypōpiazein* means a violent blow to the face under the eyes with the fist and has no symbolic meaning.[216] Because several translators and interpreters found it odd that a widow should resort to striking someone, they have provided a weakened translation, such as "otherwise she could blacken my face."[217] This kind of attenuation is inappropriate. The judge's "sarcasm" is the sexist sarcasm about a woman who does not behave as a woman is supposed to; he surmises that she is now capable of anything, even violence. I know of modern parallels: the press reports of 1984 on the resistance activities of women against the stationing of nuclear cruise missiles. The women's symbolic actions are dismissed as "aggression" and "violence."[218] The sarcasm of the judge in Luke 18:1–8 is an expression of sexism and a cynical reversal of that reality in which the people seeking justice, rather than the judges, are beaten up by the servants of order.

Women's Resistance in Early Christianity

By *women's resistance* I mean actions and behavioral patterns of women in which they individually or collectively defend themselves against oppression. Their resistance may be in relation to the so-called private sphere, that is, the home, or to the social, public domain. Women's resistance is directed against their oppression and against other aspects of patriarchal subjugation that often go hand in hand with it. Traditional Christian history shows quite clearly that women were among the persecuted of Rome just as often as men, if not even more often.[219] What it rarely shows is that their tortures and punishments were frequently more brutal than those of men.[220] No one asked why women took part in this manner in the Christian resistance[221] against the injustices of Rome and what their resistance has to do with experiences of oppression of women. There is no study of New Testament material from this perspective.

In the section on "Oppression of Women and Hatred of Women's Liberation" (cf. at II.1 above), I demonstrated that a Christian text such as 1 Tim. 2:9–15 is part of the history of Rome's extensive oppression of women, the weapon against women's resistance. The anthology of Valerius Maximus cited earlier is a document rife with the oppression that must be reinforced against the resistance of women. It is therefore essential to relate the history of early Christian women's resistance to its larger context, namely, women's resistance in the

Roman Empire. The women who demonstrated against the Oppian Laws in Rome are of a kind with the Galilean women who stood beneath Jesus' cross and with those Christian women who in post–New Testament times resisted patriarchal violence, in private or in public.

I became aware of such connections only through social-historical analysis of that action of the Galilean women. They stand under the cross "at some distance,"[222] risking—the distance notwithstanding—being identified with the followers of a crucified person and being punished, possibly even tortured and executed, for that.[223] Peter had serious reasons for denying Jesus, it would seem.[224]

A Christian novel of the end of the second century C.E., the *Acts of Thecla,* sensitized me to the traditions of women's resistance in the New Testament. Speaking in terms of method: it is necessary to study New Testament texts also from the perspective of the ancient church's traditions, that is to say, to understand them in the context of early Christian history. It is especially helpful in relation to the question about Christian *praxis,* which the dominant tradition of interpretation rarely, if ever, puts to the New Testament, to seek an understanding of what is earlier on the basis of what is later. Of course, in each case one must assure that actual connections can be made. I begin by presenting the *Acts of Thecla* and its description of women's resistance.

The *Acts of Thecla*[225] is a significant document of women's resistance in early Christianity. Although it may be read as a novel-like story (like many other apocryphal acts of apostles) and should not be treated as a historical report, it is not to be underestimated in its relevance for reconstructing historical reality. When this work speaks, for example, of women resisting in the arena in Antioch (it is most likely the Antioch in Syria), one should not conclude that this actually happened in first-century Antioch as written. Clearly, however, the women's public resistance was discussed in second-century Christian communities, was women's praxis, and had become the subject of theological reflection.[226] Similarly, Thecla's self-baptism[227] shows that women fought to be baptized as the men were, that they could and even did administer baptism.[228]

Repeatedly, the *Acts of Thecla* speaks of women's resistance. Thecla herself, (Queen) Tryphaena, the women of Antioch and of Iconium, and even a lioness struggle against injustice and bondage. Thecla—so the story goes—is a beautiful virgin from an upper-class family in Iconium. She is engaged to Thamris. From a house next door, she hears Paul preaching on abstinence and the resurrection, a message that spoke particularly to women.[229] Even though she had not met Paul face to face, her response tells her mother and her fiancé quite plainly that she believes Paul and his message and that she will not marry Thamris. On account of his impact on women, Paul is put in prison. Thecla visits him there and, together with him, is brought before the governor. In the eyes of the governor, her crime—the refusal to marry—is greater than that of Paul. She is sentenced to die at the stake; he is flogged and chased out of town (21).

The crowd (15) as well as the governor (20) and her mother (20) fear that her refusal will signal to *all* women to do the same. The mother shouts: "Burn the lawless woman! Burn the bride of wretchedness in the arena so that all women who let this Paul persuade them become afraid!" (20). Her execution is to act as a deterrent to all women in the city. The refusal to marry is a breach of "the Iconian's law" (20). It may be that this refers especially to the honoring of Thecla's marriage contract;[230] what is clear in the text itself is that the refusal to marry challenges public order and is seen to be a political offense.[231] At issue are the rights of all men to have women[232] and their progeny. A heretical teacher had opposed Paul's teaching by saying that resurrection had already taken place "in the children" (14), thus accusing Paul of failing to regard new generations as humanity's hope and future.

Thecla's "no" to marriage, like the refusal to marry of other Christian women in the ancient church, is seen by non-Christian society as a threat to the stability of public order. In contrast, women experience virginity as liberation and power.[233] Although the Christian message on abstinence is addressed to both sexes, more women than men were drawn to it, and consequently, more women were persecuted than men. Later, in Antioch, Thecla also fights at court for her virginity (27). Her course is forever threatened by the likelihood of sexual assault. One of the conclusions[234] of the Thecla legend tells of her many healing miracles in Seleucia; the doctors of the city fear for their business and hire thugs to rape her so that she will lose her powers of healing.

Women's refusal to marry is taken to be an attack on the social order of patriarchy. The basic unit of the state is marriage, Cicero declared.[235] The domination of women by men is a pivotal aspect of the social order of dominance. Sexual abstinence offers women the possibility of escaping direct submission to men and of developing their own counterculture.

The rulers of the Medes and Persians in the book of Esther also looked on a woman's refusal to be obedient as a signal for a general female rebellion against male domination. When Queen Vashti refuses to follow the king's command, during a royal carousal, to "show the people and the princes her beauty," the king orders her to be degraded. "When the decree made by the king [to punish her] is proclaimed throughout all his kingdom, vast as it is, all women will give honor to their husbands, high and low" (Esth. 1:20).[236]

Thecla survives the attempted fiery execution through a divine miracle. She follows Paul to Antioch, where she experiences something like what had happened to her at Iconium. A powerful man, Alexander, falls madly in love with her. First he tries to buy her from Paul, who tells him that she does not belong to him (26). Thereupon Alexander tries to rape her in the street. Thecla defends herself with loud cries, tears up his garments, and rips the wreath off his head, causing him to be ridiculed. On account of this, the governor sentences her to death by mortal combat with wild beasts in the arena (27). Her defense of her virginity is once again the cause for her death sentence. It is an intentional analogy to the crucifixion of Jesus when the story tells that her crime was written down, as it had been on the inscription of Jesus' cross (Mark 15:26): "Her crime was recorded on the inscription: she has desecrated the temple" (*Acts of Paul and Thecla* 28, 32). The word *hierosylos* describes, in its general sense, a person who has committed sacrilege against a sacred place. That Alexander, against whom she defended herself, was a priest is not mentioned in the text and is quite unlikely.[237] It is more likely that her public self-defense, in which she bases her sexual self-determination on religious grounds, is interpreted to be a trespass against the rights of the city's gods. She judges herself by the law of another God.

In the arena Thecla refuses to be the victim; she prays with her hands outstretched (34). During the attempted execution in Iconium, she made the "figure of the cross" with her body (22).[238] She makes it very clear to all that she has been condemned to death *as a Christian woman*. Her self-baptism in Antioch also transforms her role as a victim of wild beasts into that of a believing and courageous woman who, in the hour of her death, uses the pond full of crocodiles as a baptismal font.

She clearly defends her virginity against all attempts to force her into the patriarchal role of women; in the process, she establishes not only her *religious* identity but also her new identity as a *woman*. This explains why she has been a role model for many Christian women. She must defend this self-chosen identity even against Paul. He refuses to baptize her, saying that she is beautiful and for that reason seducible (25). In addition, when Alexander tries to assault her sexually in the street, Paul abandons her (26).[239] This means that twice Paul, in his own way, forces Thecla against her will into the role of women in patriarchy, despite the fact that her virginity had become her road to emancipation through his preaching.

A description of the resistant behavior of a *group of women* is found in the context of Thecla's fight with the wild beasts in Antioch. The women had been present in court when the verdict was read. They criticize the verdict: "The women became alarmed and shouted before the judge's seat, 'What terrible judgment! What godless judgment!'" (27). The women are part of the crowd, which also plays a role in other apocryphal acts of apostles.[240] But here the crowd takes on a very special configuration because of the women who initiate one action after another. In the crowd are people who want to stop the women because Thecla's death is what they have come to see (32). But the protesting women are in the foreground of both story and event. During the procession that precedes the fight in the arena, Thecla is tied to a lioness. Again "the women with their children" protest against the judgment (28). When the fight begins, they cry, "May the city perish for this outrage; kill us all, governor! What bitter game! What foul judgment!" (32). All through the fight their lament is heard.

After Thecla has baptized herself, they throw green branches, nard, cinnamon, and amomum into the arena. They anoint the woman martyr who has been bathed in baptism and symbolically tend to her violated body.[241] The governor releases Thecla; on account of Thecla's suffering, Queen Tryphaena fainted and was thought dead. After Thecla's rescue, the women again "cried with a loud voice and praised God as if with one voice, saying, 'It is the One God who saved Thecla!' " Now they believe in her God—as does Queen Tryphaena and, after Thecla's instruction, the majority of her female servants (38f.). The women were not yet Christians at the beginning of the event. As women of the city, they enter into solidarity with Thecla on account of the judgment against her and become Christians only as a result of their experiences with her.

Even though it reads like a novel, it is clear that this text presupposes these or similar events. It invites others to emulate Thecla's behavior and that of the women in Antioch. Their behavior suggests that when they appeared in court to protest procedures hostile to women, they were not acting as a group for the first time. From Josephus we know of a similar solidarity and organizing capacity among women in Damascus[242]—in this case, the Jewish minority of the city. Elsewhere there are reports of women's groups acting independently.[243] It is legitimate therefore to assume that politically active women's groups in fact existed in some places, groups in which women developed consciousness about women's oppression, as did the women of Antioch.

Tryphaena, a widow from a powerful Roman family (36), gave Thecla shelter between her trial and her fight in the arena. This way she protects Thecla from sexual assault. On the morning of the fight, Alexander appears, the upperclass man whom Thecla had refused in public (and who finances the animal fight), to escort her to her execution. "But Tryphaena cried out so that he fled" (30). Subsequently, the governor sent soldiers. "But Tryphaena did not stand aside, but took Thecla by the hand and escorted her" (31). Again she saved Thecla from sexual assault; in the arena, God covers Thecla's nakedness in miraculous fashion.

The *Acts of Thecla* is in many respects a unique document[244] of women's history. My focus here is on the special aspect of women's history of resistance. The text itself is clearly concerned with women's resistance. Even a lioness defends Thecla and loses her life in the process (33; cf. 28). According to this text, women's resistance grew from women refusing the role forced on them over and over by agents of the patriarchal order. Not only men acted as such agents; so did women. Thecla's mother was her daughter's harshest judge. The group of women who publicly denounced the court in fact broke away from the role assigned to women. In the Roman Empire and in parts of early Christianity, for women to speak as women in public was considered inappropriate[245] and politically subversive. The pressure on those loudly protesting women in Antioch was, without doubt, considerable.

It would be inappropriate to interpret this resistance of women as resistance of women against men per se. The *Acts of Thecla* does not see it that way either.[246] It is rather the resistance of women against the patriarchal system that, through the enforcement of women's roles, plunges them into unfreedom. The suppression of women through women's roles is experienced by them from their "private," day-to-day human relationships to the domain of their public role. The description of Thecla's sentencing in the *Acts* shows that women's oppression is also understood in its political dimensions and that a beginning is being made of the analysis of patriarchy in the sense of feminist liberation theology.[247] The concept of patriarchy here denotes a complete social system of organized structures of domination, in which domination of women—but also of men who do not comply with the role assigned to them—is forced on the poor and on strangers with subtle or blatant violence. The *Acts of Thecla* also acknowledges militarism to be a part of the patriarchal system of domination: soldiers (31) saw to it that the fights with animals functioned as a public demonstration of the people's collaboration—however coerced—with the violent structures of patriarchy. Those who did not attend voluntarily were compelled to be present at the fights.[248] The resistance of women in the Antiochene *arena* occurs precisely at the place where the violence of Roman patriarchy celebrates its triumphs and exposes the connections between animal fights, the military, government administration, and oppression of women.

The sources about women's history and particularly about the history of women's resistance are few in number. As was stated above, it is methodologically responsible to interpret texts by acquiring eyes for women's history through studying texts such as the *Acts of Thecla* and then to analyze other, similar texts with those new eyes. Since the New Testament says much too little about the praxis of early Christian communities and even less about women's resistance, one should consider whether the *Acts of Thecla* could assist in the reading of the New Testament. It helps in reading the anointing at Bethany (Mark 14:3–9 and par.),[249] which becomes understandable as a—public—act of solidarity with Jesus, who is moving toward crucifixion by Rome.

It also helps focus the reading of Lydia's story (Acts 16:11–15, 40). The synagogue beyond the city gates is a place of women, a place, surely, where women could be attentive to injustices to women and men. The tension-filled relationship of Paul and Thecla throws light on the texts of the historical Paul but also on the relationship of Paul and Lydia. He wins Lydia over for the message of the Messiah Jesus; she is baptized and wants to invite Paul and his companions to her house. The men decline, but "she prevailed upon us." With an eye on the politically dangerous situation facing traveling Jewish itinerant preachers in

Philippi, Lydia offers them hospitality, as had the disciples from Emmaus to the itinerant Jesus whom they did not recognize (Luke 24:29).[250] Luke 24:29 shows that Jesus does not seek the protection of the house, while the disciples deem it necessary; at the same time, their invitation shows that *they* seek the protection of the one they want to protect.

The situation of Acts 16:15 is somewhat different and may be compared in part to that of Luke. "The expressions used in the text hint at a turbulent situation."[251] Lydia "besought" them; she argued on the basis of the rights bestowed in her baptism and "prevailed upon" the men. The issue here is not only temporary hospitality but also the establishment of the first Christian community in Philippi (cf. 16:40).[252] With eyes acquired through the study of Thecla, one may conclude that the situation in Acts 16:15 differs markedly from that in Luke 24:29 in that Lydia is a woman and her "house" is inhabited by women; certainly, no adult, free man lives there, otherwise he would be the paterfamilias.

Paul's refusal and that of his companions do not reflect the modesty of folk who are reluctant to accept hospitality; rather, they are the refusals of Christian men to grant to women, whose baptism they have just authorized or performed, those baptismal rights that concern their role as women. Lydia argued, implicitly or explicitly, on the basis of the Christian baptismal confession, which we know from Gal. 3:28; the Paul of the Acts of the Apostles behaved similarly to the Paul of the *Acts of Thecla:* because you are a woman, you are seducible and a seductress and therefore dangerous as a hostess or a leader of the Christian community. Lydia offers hospitality and, consequently, political protection,[253] but Paul refuses it because he regards women as untrustworthy (i.e., not to be "faithful" in the sense of v. 15), even though baptism has just sealed this faithfulness.[254] Lydia addresses this contradiction and she prevails. The power to offer political resistance is manifested in this case by her offer of hospitality. But that power is undermined by the role of women in society. She has to fight for both together, which is what Paul does not grasp. It is clear that only the critique of women's role, made possible by Christian baptism, permits women to engage in political resistance; it is also clear that men, who do not participate in that critique, undermine women's resistance. The only thing that helps is women's and men's critique of patriarchy (in an all-embracing sense of the term). Resistance to economic and political oppression that shies away from including gender roles will not lead to real liberation.[255] Lydia's story shows as well that women's groups and communities of resistance, like the early Christian house churches, were the foundations on which resistance rested.

In an aside, Paul says that Prisca and Aquila "risked their necks" for his life (Rom. 16:4). Paul uses a figure of speech that at the time referred concretely to substitutionary execution.[256] The brief sentence permits more extensive reflections than the mere comment that Prisca and Aquila had risked their lives in order to save Paul's. The formulation makes me think of someone pledging his or her neck[257] or of serving a sentence on someone's behalf, as in *1 Clement* 55:

> We know many among ourselves *who have given themselves up to bonds, in order that they might ransom others.*[258] Many, too, have surrendered themselves to slavery, that with the price which they received for themselves they might provide food for others. Many women also, being strengthened by the grace of God, have performed numerous manly exploits [*andreia*]. The blessed Judith, when her city was besieged, asked the elders' permission to go forth into the camp of the strangers; and exposing herself to danger, she went out for the love which she bore to her country and people then besieged; and the Lord delivered Holofernes into the hands of a woman. Esther also, being perfect in faith, exposed herself to no less danger.

Christian women and men sought prisoners' freedom and served prison terms on behalf of others.[259] Such praxis is put on a level with Judith and Esther, women who risked danger for the lives of people. This action of Prisca and Aquila, as that of the Christian women and men of whom *1 Clement* speaks, is seen within the Jewish people's tradition of martyrdom; one's own life is put at risk for the benefit of other persons or the people. What is striking in the reports concerning solidarity with Christian prisoners,[260] such as that in *1 Clement*, is that women are at the forefront of engaged Christian praxis. The "manly deeds" for which they are praised in *1 Clement* 55 are deeds in the tradition of Judith and Esther; these are acts of resistance done by women whose "manliness" is recorded not because the women did men's deeds but because they did not deport themselves according to gender norms envisaged by patriarchy: passively and obediently.

Not recorded are the many small acts of resistance by women, acting against men who want to manage them as women and have them act in prescribed manner. Tradition reports particularly women's resistance in the larger contexts of politics, martyrdom, or resistance against Rome's legislation governing women.

In one of the legends told about Beruriah, a learned Jewish woman of the tannaitic period,[261] there is a small incident that depicts the invisible resistance of women in everyday life. "Rabbi Jose, the Galilean, was walking on the road and when he met Beruriah, he asked her: 'Which road does one take to go to Lud?' She replied: 'Dumb Galilean! Wise men have said that one does not speak much with a woman. You should just say: To Lud?' "[262]

According to this legend, Beruriah cites rabbinic tradition[263] and in her repartee critiques the entire tradition of learned contempt of women.[264] She exposes how remote that tradition is from life and emerges as the truly wise teacher. The legend belongs to a small collection of similar legends in the Babylonian Talmud in which some people (a woman, a boy, and a girl) "defeat"—as the text puts it—a rabbi who naturally felt superior to them. One may object that this legend should not be confused with the real, historical Beruriah and that she was not really a learned woman,[265] even though that is what the Babylonian Talmud says.[266] From the point of view of social history, such objections are negligible. The legend shows that within the purview of Judaism, to which the Babylonian Talmud belongs, Beruriah is regarded as a wise woman[267] and a hero in criticizing an erudition that excludes women and is hostile to them. That is why she is respected by women but also by some men.[268] Such critique of contempt for women is not limited to the Babylonian Talmud.[269] There is no doubt that the legends of Beruriah are legends, but as such, they are part of a tradition of women's resistance within Judaism.

The Androcentrism of the Sermon on the Mount

To unearth traditions of early Christian resistance by women leads one necessarily to ask how the praxis of resistance depicted in the Sermon on the Mount is related to the history of women's resistance.

The Sermon on the Mount—like the whole New Testament—is an androcentric text, the language and perception of which are governed by the perspective of men. Women are mentioned only in the context of male behavior (as the objects of lust, marriage, and divorce; Matt. 5:28, 32). The situations presented as examples are taken from the daily life of men. I name two: the quarrel among brothers (5:22) and the building of a house (7:24, 26).[270] Presumably, the fifth and sixth of the so-called antitheses[271] on the renunciation of violence and the love of enemy are also based in male experience. Accordingly, one must ask (1) whether such an assumption is correct, (2) whether the socially prescribed gender roles of men are significant for the behavior described, and (3) whether that behavior is at all applicable to women or what it would look like for them.

My interpretation of Matt. 5:38–48 proceeds from the understanding that the text is a set of directions for a *praxis* of peace and not directions for accepting passivity or for private life or for dealing with a hostile neighbor.[272]

I have chosen a work by Walter Wink[273] as an example of the interpretation of the Sermon on the Mount as a direction for a praxis of peace. He pictures the following situation for Matt. 5:38–48: evil is not to be repaid with evil (v. 39). The person in the subordinate position is struck in an insulting manner. By turning the other cheek, he robs the oppressor of the possibility of humiliating him (v. 39). The creditor who is awarded the undergarment in court is embarrassed when the debtor voluntarily hands over the coat as well. The debtor leaves the court naked, and his friends and neighbors gather around him. The love of enemy "can free both the oppressed from docility and the oppressor from sin."[274] But when a woman is struck by her husband (or by any man, for that matter) with the back of his hand and she turns the other cheek, it is most likely that he thinks she has learned her lesson and that female subservience dictates that action. Turning the other cheek as a praxis of attack is effective only when, under normal conditions, the one who strikes expects to be struck in return. Walter Wink is aware of this problem: "How many a battered wife has been counseled, on the strength of a legalistic reading of this passage, to 'turn the other cheek'?"[275] He accordingly calls for a change of Jesus' thoroughly concrete directions to fit the given context and that they not be turned into laws.

The male outlook on nonviolence is even more evident in the cases of the creditor and the soldier who exacts compulsory service. If a woman had removed her undergarment publicly in court, it would have been an invitation to rape—certainly in the ancient world. Women sentenced to fighting wild animals were raped before being chased naked out into the arena. Before her fight in the arena, Perpetua had a vision that she would be spared that ghastly exposure by God's intervention: "There came . . . handsome young men to help and protect me; I was disrobed and was a man."[276]

In the case of the soldier: had he exacted service from a woman and made her carry his bags, her willingness to go farther with him than the legal distance would have been taken as an invitation to be raped. In other words, the three model situations in Matt. 5:39–41 presume that normal victims would strike back, that there would be argument in court about garments, and that compulsory service would be given unwillingly right from the start. The three models presuppose the *accepted roles of men in society,* according to which injustice is repaid with the same means and self-defense can be a matter of violence; it is assumed that "proper" social behavior for men is to meet force with force.[277] The model's effectiveness depends on men giving up their *right to use violence* and to seek retribution.

The stubborn widow does the exact opposite of what is asked of Christians in Matt. 5:40. She fights in court for her rights; she does not give up seeking retribution. The parable of the stubborn widow, which finds her behavior exemplary, demonstrates anew that Matt. 5:40 thinks of men's behavior and that in the tradition of Jesus there is an awareness that women's resistance has *a form of its own.*

It is not enough to situate a story and praxis of women's resistance next to the androcentric Sermon on the Mount and its androcentric interpretation, even when the latter is conceived in terms of a praxis of peace. Both the sermon and its interpretation, in their androcentricity, need to be submitted to a critique of patriarchy, since otherwise they would carry on women's oppression anew into the work of peace, usually without knowing it. In the androcentric interpretation of the Sermon on the Mount—to which I subscribed in my earlier years—the alternative to the armed revolutionary is the unarmed resistance fighter who is exempt from all critical examination concerning his patriarchal role and how, in its own way, it gives renewed legitimation to existing domination. Historically, women who are deployed as "equals" in the initial resistance of revolutionary struggles later experience being told by their men to go back to their women's role. It is no different when it comes to nonviolent resistance in the androcentric perception and praxis of patriarchy. Until sexist oppression and resistance against it become a serious focus for nonviolent resistance, the androcentric perception and patriarchal praxis of pacifism will continue to undergird sexist injustice.

What If Women Hit Back?

For the patriarchal consciousness of patriarchal societies, it is axiomatic that women may be hit by husbands and men but that they themselves do not hit. In antiquity, furthermore, female and male slaves could be beaten by the women and men who owned them but could not hit back. Corporal punishment and the right to hit someone are attributes of hierarchical structures. This feature of patriarchal everyday life becomes very apparent in discussions on how a good paterfamilias and a good king give up their right to use force in order to secure their dominance even more.[278] The parable of the stubborn widow shows that it is typical of sexism to slander women by accusing them of being violent. I would like to cite another example that is relevant for the history of women in early Christianity. After that, I shall explore what it means when women actually do hit back.

Samuel Krauss wrote about Beruriah that "she contemptuously kicked one of her husband's students";[279] "a rather brutal action, done in those days even by women." This is how Krauss generalizes what had been said about her.[280] His remark is based on the following Beruriah legend from the Babylonian Talmud: "One day, Beruriah noticed a student studying silently. She kicked him and said: it is written *'ordered in all things and secure'*; if [the teaching] has been ordered in all of your two hundred and forty-eight members, it has been made secure also, but if not, it has not been made secure for you" (*b. 'Erub.* 54a).[281]

Beruriah is depicted as a teacher of Torah who disciplines a male student for studying silently instead of speaking out loud, which is the custom in Jewish learning.[282] She cites scripture in support of holistic learning.[283] Kicking was within the range of a teacher's physical punishments[284] that were held to be unavoidable. Whether the verb used by the Talmud actually means to kick with the foot or refers to a verbal rebuke is still an open question.[285] There is no question that Krauss belongs to the tradition that deprecates Beruriah;[286] in another context, however, he interprets the story in a way more friendly to Beruriah, thereby contradicting himself.[287] The woman who hits back is a cliché hostile to women, to which Krauss registers no critical sensibility. I say this with deep regret because Samuel Krauss's work is of inestimable value for women's history in talmudic times and has been of benefit to me again and again.

The comment concerning the hostile cliché—women who hit people are particularly contemptible—is not meant to assert that women never hit. One must examine carefully what it means when a woman does hit back and when her action is not to be interpreted in terms of the patriarchal cliché of "bad" violent women and "good" nonviolent women.

From today's perspective, the Christian legend of Xanthippe the martyr is especially revealing. Without any rebuke of violence, this legend tells the following story. Xanthippe, a noblewoman, had become Christian. One evening, in a dark corner on the staircase of her house, she encounters a demon who wants to frighten and torment her. The demon has made himself look like an actor whom she knows because he regularly performs when she gives feasts in her home. She angrily says (to him or to herself) that she has often told him that she is no longer interested in games and that he despises her because she is a woman. She reaches for an iron lampstand and hurls it at his face, disfiguring his features. He cries out: "Violence! Violence! Even women have been given the power by that destroyer [God or Christ] to hit us [demons]."[288]

The story has many layers. It depicts Xanthippe as a model for Christian women and shows that (like Jesus) women drive out demons.[289] From the perspective of Xanthippe, however, it is a story against misogyny and against the actor's intention to rape her. Both layers in the legend take it for granted that her violence is legitimate. Christian women may indeed hit a demon with a lampstand, and a potential rapist. It is interesting from today's perspective how this women's legend connects fear of rapists with fear of demons. Ancient fear of demons is, here and in general, a portent of real threats that menace the common life of humans far more than death. In the end, Xanthippe does not triumph over the defeated demon but is deeply frightened. The legend is told from the point of view of women; indeed, there are numerous details in the *Acts of Xanthippe and Polyxena* that suggest a woman's perspective. Xanthippe's deed, which the demon calls "violence," is, from the narrator's point of view, an act of desperation that ends not in victory but in fear.

C. FEMINIST OBSERVATIONS ON THE
HISTORY OF INTERPRETATION,
PARTICULARLY THE PRESENT

We have seen that the parable of the stubborn widow is useful for the clarification of androcentrism in the Sermon on the Mount. I want to extend the critical discussion of Luke 18:1–8 in the history of interpretation by examining the question of nonviolence in the sense of the Sermon on the Mount. How are nonviolence and (women's) resistance connected in current interpretations of Luke 18:1–8 and Matt. 5:38–48? As a rule, the resistance aspect is noted in neither text. The parable is often titled "the parable of the pleading widow."[290] That is how the parable loses its context of insubordination and the woman once again fits neatly into the patriarchal model, according to which widows plead rather than "trouble" people by stubbornly crying out for their rights (Luke 18:5). Matthew 5:39 is also interpreted, as a rule, to be a renunciation of all resistance; resistance is identified with counterviolence and rejected.[291] Exceptions to this pattern are interpretations such as that of Walter Wink, used above, which regard resistance and counterviolence as two completely different forms of behavior. This closely resembles my own approach.[292]

The dominant tradition of interpretation culminates in a picture where Jesus as the unconditionally nonviolent man is set apart from the violence-prone terrorist.[293] What is kept out of the discussion is patriarchal society's structure of violence, its militarism as well as its structural violence against women, children, the poor, minorities, and stubborn disturbers of the status quo. In patriarchal society, the Christian church with such a picture of Jesus becomes a nonviolent "woman" who concedes to "the men" the power, dominion, and the right to use force. That picture of Jesus shows also that gender dualism plays its part in the church–state relationship. It is necessary to make a feminist analysis of ecclesiologies, to examine and critique their images of mother church. The nonviolent Jesus (as described here) and women who accommodate themselves to their nonviolent role in patriarchy, strengthen the perpetrators and are cogs in the transmission of complicity.[294] It is illusory, then, to posit the innocence of a nonviolent Jesus.

D. FEMINIST PERSPECTIVES

The parable of the stubborn widow provides a cameo model and an example in which faith is pictured as the patient labor of resistance in everyday life, a crying for justice. The parable speaks of a widow because, within the context of biblical tradition, talk of widows conjures up the structural violence of patriarchy and God's partiality for its victims. What we see in the parable is not a victim to be pitied but a woman who fights tenaciously and whom a sexist judge denounces as potentially violent. It is worth considering whether the stubborn widow does not hold up a better model for Christian women—and men—than the model of an innocent, nonviolent Jesus.

From a feminist perspective, declarations of unconditional nonviolence are nothing but ideology. In face of women's experiences such as those of Xanthippe on her dark staircase, the substance of such norms evaporates into thin air.[295] However, the violent destruction of real or imaginary enemies is a daily actuality but not the only alternative to nonviolence. The third way[296] is resistant, stubborn pacifism that takes the offensive and orients itself by God's reign. Such pacifism always includes critical examination of one's gender role.

"Every woman who refuses to 'know her place' offers resistance against sexism."[297] Every man who refuses to "be a man" offers resistance against sexism. In neither case does this mean that women take on the role of men and men that of women, as in the model of the innocent Jesus. Resistance to sexism has to be seen as part of the resistance to violence in all its forms. Pacifism without resistance to sexism leaves untouched the roots of violence and complicity. Pacifism without resistance to sexism also ignores the heart of class exploitation: the poverty of women and children in the two-thirds world. I propose that peace research integrate the feminist critique of patriarchy; for only then will it become apparent that nonviolent resistance and pacifism cannot be individual actions in certain political situations but must be a feature of everyday life. It may then be possible to exist in the context of military threats and the specter of ecological catastrophe. I think of real life as one that allows visions of a healed creation and that focuses all energy on protecting and passing on life.

In the Sermon on the Mount, Jesus describes the love of enemy as the way of the women and men who follow him. It is the labor that seeks the conversion, the turning back of God's enemies, of the perpetrators of violence and their accomplices. Such labor for conversion includes labor for one's own turning back. In the pictures that the Gospels paint of him, Jesus, too, does not stand in a place apart from the patriarchal structures of violence, in a place of innocence. Only later Christologies have put him there. The Sermon on the Mount has an eloquent picture of this illusory place of innocence: it is a man who wants to pull a splinter from a brother's eye without knowing that he has a log in his own eye (Matt. 7:3 and par.).

I want to use another legend of Beruriah in interpreting Matt. 5:39 as a portrait of a self-critical and resisting Jesus:

> In Rabbi Meir's neighborhood there lived some ruffians who caused him much torment. He prayed that they might die. His wife Beruriah said to him: "You rely on the scriptural verse: *may sins be taken.* But it does not say *sinners,* it says *sins.* Note also the end of the verse: *and the evildoers will be there no more.* When the sins have been destroyed the evildoers will, too, be gone. Pray then for mercy for them and that they will repent." He prayed that they might receive mercy and they repented.[298]

Beruriah made an argument that was emphatic and relied on her own exegesis. According to the legend, her husband gives in right away. He quickly grasps the contradiction between counterviolence and God's reign. The stubborn widow faces harsher conditions, but her strength comes from the same hope that also nourishes Beruriah.

Women's resistance is resistance in everyday life and may remind men that men's resistance also belongs there. "We want to break the spell of powerlessness and oppression and act responsibly toward ourselves and others by beginning to assume, where feasible, full responsibility and power."[299] Today that means defying the gender roles that collaborate to support the violent structures of our world. Resisting in everyday life also means taking the seemingly unimportant small steps toward liberation: recognizing violence in language and learning and teaching different speech, avoiding pointless consumption and reducing garbage, boycotting goods and manufacturers connected with arms production. In the Christian tradition, this lifelong resistance in everyday life is called "conversion."

III

THE CRITIQUE OF PATRIARCHY
AND THE POWER TO BECOME
A NEW BEING

1

Do Not Remain in the State in Which You Were Called . . . : The Calling of God and Social "Status" in Patriarchy (1 Cor. 7:15–24)

A. THE TEXT

The allegedly Pauline statement "Everyone should remain in the state in which he was called" is found as the translation of 1 Cor. 7:20 in numerous versions of the Bible used in churches and in scholarship.[1] The statement is associated with the further notion that Paul had taught that Christian living in no way meant changing the status quo, the "state" in patriarchal society. Female and male slaves should remain slaves without opposition,[2] women should accept their role in patriarchy, circumcised Jews or uncircumcised men should not artificially change their status (1 Cor. 7:18). The text of 1 Cor. 7:17–24 has a central place in the articulation and substantiation of Christian status quo theologies, whether they be supported[3] or rejected.[4] I know well from my experience of myself that this interpretation of Paul is anchored so firmly in people's heads that it is most difficult to read those verses in a different way.

But there are reasons why it is necessary to read that text differently. First, in 1 Cor. 7:20, the word *klēsis* does not mean "state" but (God's) "calling," as it does everywhere else in the New Testament—contrary information in Walter Bauer's dictionary of the New Testament notwithstanding.[5] Second, from the perspective of feminist liberation theology, it is necessary to determine historically where Paul stands: Is he an ally or a theological opponent? Third, and connected with the second reason, the point theologically is not to devise a biblicistic argument that seeks possibly to settle Paul in feminist theology—or to keep him out of it; the point is to clarify theologically how the reality of the "status" is related to God's calling. Do we do feminist theology in such a way that it may be integrated into patriarchy and its interest in maintaining the patriarchal status quo, or is our Christian praxis and our theological scholarship committed to a new "paradigm"[6] that fundamentally criticizes and rejects a status quo theology?

121

I will provide a translation of 1 Cor. 7:17–24, adding the two preceding verses, since it becomes clear then that verses 17–24 are an excursus on the topic of "calling" and that the point of the excursus is to raise several individual questions about marriage and sexuality on a more profound level. The text of 1 Cor. 7:17–24, both at its beginning and its end, is so firmly tied to its context that one can lift it out of its context only for technical reasons. What Paul attempts to show, in particular, is that from the Christian point of view it is legitimate to divorce a mixed marriage. It is this situation that evokes the excursus on "calling." On account of Jesus' words about divorce and the consequent praxis[7] of Christian congregations, it is plain that this situation needs clarification.

The Translation of 1 Corinthians 7

15   If the unbelieving wife or the unbelieving husband divorces, let it be her or him who divorces! The [Christian] brother or sister in such a case is not bound. For God has called you [to life] in the peace [of God].[8]

16   For how do you know, wife, whether you will save your husband? Or you, husband, whether you will save your wife?

17   But whatever the case may be:[9] all[10] [believers] are to conduct their lives in accordance with the portion [of the Spirit][11] that God[12] has given them and in accordance with the fact that God has called them. That is what I teach[13] in all [our] communities.

18   When a man was circumcised when he was called, he should not seek to have his circumcision reversed [by an operation]. A man who was not circumcised when he was called should not seek circumcision.

19   For it does not depend on circumcision or on the foreskin but on keeping God's commandments.

20   All are to remain in the calling [of God] to which[14] they have been called.

21   If you were a female slave or a male slave when you were called, do not be troubled. But if you can gain your freedom, avail yourself the more [of God's calling].

22   The women and men slaves called in Christ[15] are freedwomen and freedmen; likewise, they who at their calling had been born free are Christ's female and male slaves.

23   You were bought with a price: do not become women and men enslaved to human beings.

24   Sisters, brothers, all are to continue to live before God in accordance with the calling to which[16] they have been called.

What concrete life situations are shown in this text?

Being someone's slave would have meant (vv. 23, 15) maintaining *a marriage against the wishes* of the non-Christian partner in order to secure his or her possible conversion (v. 15). This would most likely have applied more frequently to Christian women with non-Christian partners than the other way around.[17] The woman who remained faithful to her calling would have the freedom to leave her marriage in order to lead a life according to God's command-ments (v. 19) and in the peace of God (v. 15). If the non-Christian partner wished to stay in the marriage, it would, in Paul's opinion, be possible to lead a life within the marriage (v. 13) in accordance with the calling. Lead-ing one's life according to God's commandments would be abandoned if a Christian woman or man (coerced by the community) were to put pressure on the partner and force the marriage to be maintained in order to secure the part-ner's conversion. (An inhuman situation indeed! I understand the phrase in v. 15, *ou dedoulotai* [not to be in nonfreedom or slavery], to mean that Christ-ian people are exerting pressure, which Paul rejects because it is people enslav-ing people).

A slave, female or male, is concerned with whether it is possible, being in slav-ery, to conduct one's life in accordance with the calling. Paul says that this con-cern is quite justified (v. 21) but that it should not torment such a person; for being freed in Christ, after all, provides the possibility to live life in accordance with God's will and not as people enslaved by other human beings. They both are and are not slaves. True, those who have been set free have greater oppor-tunity to conduct their lives in accordance with their calling.

Whoever was not Jewish at the time of God's calling has no reason to seek circumcision (cf. Gal. 5:1–6; 6:15). A Jew whom God has called also has no rea-son to alter his Jewishness in terms of his circumcision.

The position of Jewish and non-Jewish women before God is no different from that of circumcised Jewish men.[18]

The orientation of our lives does not depend on the marital status of the gen-ders or on social-legal status (subject to someone else's or to one's own laws);[19] it is not determined by belonging or not belonging to the Jewish religion. The orientation of our lives is the calling of God. This means keeping the com-mandments and living in the peace of God (vv. 15, 19). For that reason, Paul repeats his basic assertion several times: conduct yourselves in accordance with your calling (v. 17), remain in your calling (vv. 20, 24).

The "states"[20] of patriarchy of which Paul speaks here (as in Gal. 3:28) are not all alike. It is another's decision whether I am a slave. When people are be-ing freed from slavery, they can play an indirect part in the process[21] but they cannot refuse release for any reason, even if being freed means subjugation un-der forms of exploitation and dependency other than those of slavery. The de-cision whether to divorce, to remain celibate, or to remarry is much more within the power of those affected, including women.[22] Some Gentile men who had become Christian concluded that, as a result of their conversion, they should be circumcised; Paul was opposed to the idea, as we saw above. A circumcised Jew, possibly under political pressure,[23] might try to have his circumcision reversed surgically, but only at the price of losing his identity.

Paul puts together questions that would be asked by people from completely different "states." His own ordering principle is that of a free, patriarchal Jewish male who defines himself in contradistinction to women, non-Jews, and slaves.[24] In this text he does not address economic and other class differences, but he very clearly does so in 1 Cor. 1:26–31 (see below at III.2).

The text is concerned with degrees of self-determination, which differ widely according to the social "state" to which one belongs. One ought not, therefore, proceed with abstract concerns (to remain in one's "state" or not) but rather ask concretely: What does it mean for a female slave to be Christian?[25] What does it mean for a Jewish male to be Christian? What does it mean for a Jewish or non-Jewish woman to be Christian? and so forth. It is clear that, for Paul, the orientation of our lives is in terms of God's calling; it may well be, therefore, that a female Christian slave comes into conflict because of her slave status, or that a Jewish man finds himself in profound conflict with his Jewishness and the Jewish food laws on account of the pivotal place of common meals in the community of Christians.[26] The conflicts encountered by Christian free women and men on account of their gender roles within patriarchy are the reason why Paul raises the subject of calling at all in 1 Corinthians 7.[27] God's calling is primary; it takes precedence over the constraints of slave existence, gender roles in patriarchy, or one's original religion. To live that calling's priority, people need assertiveness, a self-assertiveness that, quite obviously, even female slaves had gained from the Christian faith.

A theological position is stated in 1 Cor. 7:17–24 (or 15–24) which declares that it is utterly appropriate for Christian life to cross over the boundaries that patriarchy puts between human beings. This is because it is God's calling that gives orientation to our lives and not society's prior definitions of what a woman, a man, or a slave, or any other is. First Corinthians 7 and the household codes are fundamentally opposed. But the traditions of interpretation and translation have turned the text of 1 Cor. 7:17–24 into its very opposite. We must explore later how to understand the Paul who showed both support for and massive opposition to women's crossing over those boundaries.

B. SOCIAL-HISTORICAL QUESTIONS

Living a Christian Life as a Female Slave

"If you were a female slave when you were called, do not be troubled." Paul's androcentric language indicates a perspective focused only on male slaves, but we can assume that he "meant as well"[28] female slaves. But it is necessary to interpret 1 Cor. 7:21 on the basis of the question: What did it mean then to be a

Christian female slave? I would like to reflect on that question first in light of New Testament materials and then in light of those from the ancient church.

A slave woman by the name of Rhoda (Acts 12:12ff.) belonged to the community of Mary, the mother of John Mark, in Jerusalem. She recognizes Peter by his voice, that is to say, she had been integrated for some time into the context of the early Jerusalemite community's Christian life. Ivoni Richter Reimer has shown that there is no warrant in the text for regarding Mary to be Rhoda's owner or that Rhoda's job was necessarily that of the doorkeeper.[29] There is no warrant either for thinking of a large, affluent house.[30] The text pictures a situation where Rhoda is not standing at the door but is taking part in the early community's assembly. She is one of those who, in the sense of Acts 2:42ff., were devoting themselves to praying together, eating, and praising God together. When there is a knock at the door during the night, she goes to the gatehouse to open the door. She hears and recognizes the voice of Peter, the man whom she and the others knew to be in prison. She understands the miracle that has taken place. In her joy she does not open the door but runs back to the assembly room. She tells the gathered community that Peter is at the gatehouse. Her Christian sisters and brothers cannot believe that Peter would really be there. But she persists strenuously[31] so that the community will believe Peter has been freed from prison. But they tell her, "You are mad," and, "What you heard was Peter's angel but not Peter." In the meantime, Peter keeps knocking. They all go to open the door and are overjoyed at the miracle.

Ivoni Richter Reimer has demonstrated that in this narrative the structures of domination, as they apply to women and men slaves and their female and male owners, play no role at all. The community's refusal to believe her has nothing to do with her being a female slave. Just like the women in Luke 24, she trusts instead in God's power and fights so that the others will also believe the miracle of liberation. The community's disbelief in Acts 12:12–17 is analogous in substance to the disbelief of the men disciples in Luke 24:11, 22–23, 41. Just as the female disciples of Jesus cling to their belief in Jesus' resurrection in face of the male disciples' disbelief, so Rhoda, the female slave, clings to her belief in God's power in face of the community's disbelief. "A slave woman stands her ground in the house of Mary. This fact testifies that she has the space to do so."[32] This narrative shows us how to picture the praxis of the community of Gal. 3:28. The slave woman's self-assertiveness in the midst of the gathered community and her exemplary trust in God's power are at the core of the legend.

The owner (female or male) of this slave woman had granted her leave to take part in the community's gatherings rather than be available to her or him during those many hours. There were groups of Christian women and men slaves whose owners were not Christians, for example, some of the slaves whom Aristobulus and Narcissus owned (Rom. 16:10–11).[33] It is natural to regard those groups as women and men slaves from a larger city household; it would have been exceptional for those on farms or in industry to attend Christian assemblies. Like Rhoda, these groups had free time after work, at the end of the day, and during the night.

Living in accordance with God's calling would have been decidedly more difficult for female slaves, unless they were aged, than for male slaves. To be a female slave meant to be sexually available: as the owner's sex object or that of the men to whom he rented her for sexual purposes[34] or as a nurse.[35] How would Christian preaching on purity have sounded to a normal slave woman, whose slave status meant sexual exploitation? Society accepted without legal or moral second thoughts that female slaves had to be available for their owner's sexual purposes. A female slave who was part of a Christian (or Jewish) religious community must have felt inferior religiously and morally in spite of every assurance of the equality of all, unless there were enough thoughtful people in that community who affirmed her calling even though she was forced into adultery and prostitution. "If you were a female slave when you were called, do not be troubled"—the important thing is that you live your calling. Female slaves would have been among the women named in the list of people to be greeted (Romans 16).[36] Perhaps we may assume that the woman slave in Philippi, the soothsayer, was taken in by the community as their own[37] after Paul had made her useless to the owners,[38] obliging him to make restitution to them. How astonishing that the same Christian document, the Acts of the Apostles, which narrates with sensitivity the story of the slave woman Rhoda lacks the sensitivity to ask what it meant to the slave woman in Philippi to lose her powers of soothsaying.[39]

It would have been somewhat simpler for female slaves who became Christian together with their owners, such as those who belonged to the "house" of Lydia.[40] First Corinthians 16:15f. implies that Christian women and men who owned slaves were prepared to entrust leadership tasks to and subordinate themselves under slaves, female and male[41] (and free women).[42] Such female slaves would, without doubt, have experienced control over their own bodies as a huge liberation. A Christian owner, female or male, would hardly have been able to prevent them from living in sexual abstinence, in marital fidelity, or in divorce.

What the ancient church has to say about Christian female slaves matches this picture. When they belonged to a Christian owner, they could expect to be granted free time and sexual independence. Female slaves also expected to be set free[43] but found no support from Christian authorities.[44] The story of the slave woman Sabina tells of a community who—at the risk of acting illegally[45]—protected a female slave who had been tormented because she was a Christian. She had been prevented from living a Christian life by her non-Christian female owner. Sabina's fate demonstrates the life circumstances of female slaves who were in no position to live in accordance with their calling. Her non-Christian owner, a woman named Politta, sought to turn Sabina away from her Christian faith and "banned her, bound hand and foot, to the hillside." How the Christian community managed in that situation to support and protect her materially and spiritually is not mentioned;[46] we are simply told that they did so. Presumably, there were Christian communities who were even prepared to send delegations to visit and support members who lived at a great distance.

One notices how, in the martyrology of women slaves, their power and sovereign demeanor take center stage in the legends. At court, Sabina laughs publicly when the mocking and menacing of her fellow martyr Pionius reach their climax:

> During that exchange, some saw Sabina laughing and said to her, menacingly and in a loud voice: "You laugh?" She replied: "I laugh when God wills; we are Christians." Whereupon they said to her: "You will have to suffer what you do not want. Those who refuse to offer sacrifice must serve in houses of prostitution and keep company of women of easy virtue or satisfy the lust of pimps." She replied: "As God wills it."[47]

According to Eusebius, Potamiaena is threatened with a similar fate; "but on being asked, after she had reflected a little, what her decision was, gave such a reply as, according to their opinion, contained something profane."[48] The legend of the martyrdom of Blandina, a female slave, also places her power at the center. "Things . . . which appear mean and obscure and contemptible [in human eyes] with God are deemed worthy of great glory."[49] "Although small and weak and greatly despised, she had put on the great and invincible athlete Christ, and in many contests had overcome the adversary."[50] The legend of Blandina, like other legends about the martyrdom of slave women,[51] holds up the power and courage of a female slave as an example of the power that faith gives to the weak. The legends are meant to give courage not only to the enslaved but also to the free.[52]

It is regrettable that only in the context of martyrdom do we hear legends of female slaves, for it creates the impression that women received their power only to die *in maiorem dei gloria,* to die for the greater glory of God rather than to live their calling. The slave woman Rhoda of the first Jerusalemite community, a Christian woman of notable assertiveness and trust in God, must represent the many female slaves who received power and a strong sense of self from faith and could also live their calling. Without a clear perception of such ways of living, one only misunderstands the slave women's ways of dying.[53]

Early Christianity did not question or oppose slavery in a fundamental and generalized way, that is, as a social institution. One cannot determine whether the New Testament regarded slavery as a given of nature.[54] Ending the oppression of female and male slaves is not discussed in terms of the origin and social significance of slavery; ending slavery is discussed as a praxis of Christian communities and an eschatological orientation.[55] The early Christians were well aware that the liberating praxis of their communities and what it led to had a broad social and political dimension. Both the eschatological-cosmic dimensions of Christian hope and the conflicts, polemics, and persecutions to which the praxis of faith had led confirmed this awareness. Christians were told that theirs was a contemptible religion for women and men slaves and for people with a slavish mentality.[56] At the same moment, they were accused of disturbing the patriarchal order and of giving women and children a place in their communities that, in the eyes of their social environment, they did not deserve.[57]

The consciousness of many Christian women and men became divided; this is illustrated when one holds together the legend of Rhoda (Acts 12:12ff.) and that of the soothsaying slave woman in Philippi (Acts 16:16ff.), which is so insensitive to her fate. Liberating crossings over patriarchal boundaries are described next to massive attempts to repress such liberation, for example by demands such as those of the "household" codes.[58] These contradictory orientations do not belong to separate groups and discrete approaches; often it is one and the same Christian person who has limited ability to perceive the injustice of patriarchal boundaries.

The Divided Consciousness: Paul

Paul is no representative of patriarchal theory of marriage. He gives precedence to the refusal of marriage and to sexual abstinence over marriage (1 Cor. 7:7); he considers divorce more in accordance with God and more conducive to peace than a marriage against one partner's will. In matters of marriage, one must credit Paul with a consciousness critical of patriarchy and a public praxis that corresponds to it. But this does not suggest that there is even a trace of critical consciousness in him about men's domination of women and its praxis. He grounds that domination in a theology of creation, even though it lands him in a self-contradiction.[59] He understands women refusing to cover their heads or veil themselves when they prophesy and pray (1 Cor. 11:2–16) to be an act of liberation on their part against their subordination to men—a correct understanding, in all likelihood—and then he rejects it.[60] Refusing to marry is a good thing; women throwing off the veil is not. He undergirds both judgments with massive theological arguments. It is apparent that his (theological) judgments are related to his own praxis in the communities, just as he said in 1 Cor. 7:17. To have a critical consciousness about marriage, despite its potential for the critique of patriarchy, does not mean that one has grasped the injustice of the hierarchical domination that men exercise over women. Paul's divided consciousness explains how the same person can hold up Gal. 3:28 as fundamental to Christian existence and also write a text such as 1 Cor. 11:2–16, perhaps also 1 Cor. 14:34–36. "In Christ there is no 'male and female,' " but the man, not the woman, is the image of God (1 Cor. 11:7), and the man is head of the woman (1 Cor. 11:3); women are not to question the order of domination.

Paul's divided consciousness makes itself known also in his different responses to the oppression of slaves and of women. He describes the dominion of sin over humankind in a metaphor which indicates that he is quite aware of how unjust Rome's imperial rule and the subjugation of slaves are (he thinks only of male slaves).[61] Sin dominates human beings as a slave master dominates slaves. The dominated is wholly subjugated, a *sōma* (body) that becomes the instrument of the overlord (cf. Rom. 6:12). Human beings are sold under sin (Rom. 7:14). Sin rules as an imperial ruler and as a slave owner. Paul is attentive to this contempt-filled oppression and sees it as one who is in solidarity with the oppressed, and yet his perception remains androcentric. For him, women's oppression is God's good order, even though, on the basis of his patriarchal categories, he speaks of women's oppression as a parallel to that of slaves in Gal. 3:28, if not also in the related verses of 1 Cor. 12:13 and Col. 3:11.[62] In light of the whole Pauline corpus and of his view on women's role in the communities, one may wonder whether Paul meant Gal. 3:28 to declare not that the rule of men over women had been brought to an end but only that liberation from the slavery of marriage had come. First Corinthians 11:2–16 leads to the conclusion that women in Corinth understood the Christian baptismal confession of Gal. 3:28 differently than Paul did; along with their veils, they threw off men's subjugation of women.

Legends from later times about Paul and his star pupil Thecla also reflect Paul's divided consciousness in relation to patriarchal oppression. Paul's preaching on the blessing of virginal life wins Thecla for the gospel of Christ and causes her to break her engagement (7f.).[63] Both are persecuted for this preaching and praxis of virginity; her punishment is far harsher: she is to be burned, he beaten and expelled from the city (21). In her anguish, she searches for Paul "as a lamb in the desert for its shepherd" (21). But Paul offers prayers for her only from far off (24); instead of Paul, Christ appears to her in the form of Paul. In terms of the overall direction of the legend, this vision of Christ in the form of Paul signals a cautious critique of Paul.[64] He had withheld solidarity, and Christ covers for him.

Paul's demeanor toward Thecla is consistently degrading. He refuses her baptism on the ground that she is beautiful (25). She baptizes herself (34) while being martyred. She wishes to follow him as an itinerant woman preacher (25), but he does not wish it. At the end, she declares her intention: "I shall go to Iconium." Finally he agrees, belatedly: "Go, and teach God's word." The sharpest critique, however, is the description of his failure to do anything when an upper-class man attempts to assault Thecla on the streets in Antioch. The powerful man first wants to buy Thecla, only to be told by Paul, "I do not know the woman . . . she does not belong to me" (26), whereupon Alexander attempts to rape her right there and then. "But she does not keep still and looks around for Paul." She screams loudly and defends herself successfully, for which she is condemned to death. Where Paul had disappeared to is not told in the text; it does tell implicitly that he had betrayed her once again. The legend of Thecla is testimony of much anger on the part of women against Christian men who preach virginity but, cowardly, allow violence against women or even condone it without critique. Thecla keeps searching for Paul in spite of all those experiences. The divided consciousness of the historical Paul toward patriarchal structures of domination is reflected in the two faces he has in the eyes of Thecla and of many women in the early church. The *Acts of Thecla* is the document of a woman's history in early Christianity, a document that, however cautiously, criticizes the great apostle.

Another outcome of his divided consciousness is that, from early times onward, he is claimed as the authority both against as well as for the liberation of women. In the years 198–200 C.E., Tertullian wrote:

> But the woman of pertness, who has usurped the power to teach, will of course not give birth for herself likewise to a right of baptizing. . . . But if the writings which wrongly go under Paul's name claim Thecla's example as a license for women's teaching and baptizing, let them know that, in Asia, the presbyter who composed that writing, as if he were augmenting Paul's fame from his own store, after being convicted and confessing that he had done it from the love of Paul, was removed from his office. For how credible would it seem, that he who has not permitted a *woman* even to *learn* [or teach][65] with overboldness, should give a *female* the power of *teaching* and *baptizing*! "Let them be silent," he says, "and at home consult their husbands."[66]

The text makes plain that a Christian woman at the time of Tertullian appealed to the writings of Paul and to the example of one of his pupils, Thecla, for the right to teach and baptize. Tertullian contests the authenticity of those writings of Paul. Some presbyter (or priest) in the province of Asia Minor had composed them from his love for Paul. This man was dismissed, ostensibly not because he had composed a work in the name or to the honor of Paul (many admirers of Paul had done so at that time) but because women relied on his writing to support their case and legitimate their action in Paul's name. Men like Tertullian who deny women the right to baptize and teach also cite Paul and appeal to 1 Cor. 14:34f. and 1 Tim. 2:11–15. The latter passage comes from a text composed in the name of, but not written by, Paul. Tertullian's text gives evidence of a heated conflict in the politics of the church concerning the rights of Christian women. Can women take upon themselves, without restriction, the same public functions in worship and leadership as those maintained by the women and the presbyter in Asia, or are they to keep silent in public and be taught at home by their husbands? Both sides appeal to Paul; both sides can appeal to pseudepigraphal Pauline writings, or to writings with a Pauline orientation (such as the *Acts of Thecla* or 1 Timothy), or to the "genuine" Paul himself.

In asking what it meant for a slave woman to live according to God's calling, I asked a question that Paul did not ask and that lay beyond the range of his perception. Nevertheless, the Pauline text of 1 Cor. 7:15–24 has the potential to challenge the boundaries dictated by patriarchy and to legitimate their being crossed over as an act in following the divine calling.

C. FEMINIST OBSERVATIONS ON THE HISTORY OF INTERPRETATION, PARTICULARLY THE PRESENT

The apologetic moves of Christian interpreters in dealing with misogynist New Testament texts were described earlier (II.1.C). I now ask how recent interpretation has dealt with 1 Cor. 7:(15), 17–24, a text the content of which is relevant on account of its potential to undermine patriarchal structures and that is not exceptional within Paul's corpus (see, e.g., Gal. 3:28).

As I see it, there are two tracks of interpretation that declare it to be the pivotal text of a status quo theology. An eschatological interpretation states that this text expresses Paul's expectation of the imminent return of Christ. Here Pauline status quo theologies are seen as a critique of every form of belief in progress and, to a lesser extent and more superficially, as a demonstration of how irrelevant social realities are for theology. A second form of interpretation uses this text to legitimate a conservative[67] view of Christianity. It claims that adherence to the Christian faith signifies that one should not question patriarchy and should respect the differences and boundaries of class. As a rule, such a "conservative" reading of Paul supplements 1 Cor. 7:21 with "slavery" as a state, making the case that a slave should renounce the opportunity to obtain freedom on account of his faith. S. Scott Bartchy has prepared a survey of ancient and modern representatives of this interpretation. I will not deal further with this interpretive track but will focus on diverse variations of the eschatological interpretation.

Albert Schweitzer's views on the expectation of Christ's imminent return continue to influence interpretation to the very present. His name is associated with arguments which assert that at Paul's time Christians did not think about a more lasting Christian praxis; they expected God's reign to begin soon and had no interest in the here and now. I have encountered such views not only in the contexts of church and theological scholarship[68] but also among people who have nothing to do with Christianity (anymore). Derived from Schweitzer, this perception of eschatology serves the dualistic separation of social reality and Christian faith, a separation that was alien to Schweitzer himself. Since the beginning of this century, he and others have said that early Christians were mistaken in their expectation of Christ's imminent coming; to this day, that view is influential.

Schweitzer puts the case vividly:

> [The believer] is like a house sold for breaking up, all repairs to which become irrational. If in spite of this he begins to make alterations in his natural condition of existence, he is ignoring the fact that his being is henceforth conditioned by the being-in-Christ, and not by anything else connected with his natural existence. His

natural condition of existence has therefore become of no importance, not in the general sense that it does not matter what is done to it, but in the special sense that henceforth nothing must be done to it. The contract relating to the house which has been sold specifies that it has been sold only with a view to breaking up, and that consequently nothing must be done to keep it in habitable repair, not to speak of alterations designed to make it more commodious![69]

This view of Paul's eschatology and "interim ethics"[70] arose within the critique of a reign-of-God theology that sought to materialize religious-social progress in the here and now. From his understanding of Jesus and Paul, Schweitzer had derived a humanistic ethics contrary to his own emphasis, and to that of others who also taught this "consistent eschatology," on how *unknown* the historical Jesus was, and to a certain extent also Paul. Schweitzer's ethics did not suffer from the hostility to the flesh which marks that eschatology.

Representatives of consistent eschatology stress how alien Jesus and Paul's expectation of the imminent coming of God's reign really is, leading them to criticize Paul: "It is to be seen everywhere how frightfully situation-bound" Paul's view is.[71] He could well have chosen to adopt instead the revolutionary praxis of life found among the enthusiasts in his communities or those of the Essenes.[72] This ignores the question of whether the interpretation of Paul that people's concrete lives are like a house ready for breaking up is applicable. The conception of the enthusiasts in Paul's communities, to which Siegfried Schulz refers, can be found also in Ernst Käsemann: Paul's opponents want gender equality this very instant; for them, eschatology, hope, and the expectation of an imminent coming have all become meaningless.[73] Here Käsemann speaks of Paul's status quo theology as a critique of those enthusiasts; Käsemann speaks of but does not question that theology.[74]

Other interpreters reject this eschatological reading of Paul because, they say, it introduces a historicizing falsification of Jesus and Paul. These interpreters categorically deny that there is eschatological thinking; they interpret christologically instead: in Christ the enslaved are just as free as those who were born free, who are the slaves of Christ.[75] Here the "state" of the believer is relativized: irrespective of the state in which you were called, live out the service of Christ. This Christology has no revolutionary consequences; at best, the common life of the diverse "states" *within* the Christian congregation is to be based on equality.[76] Such christological relativizing of the states, whose given actuality is not questioned, allows one to supplement 1 Cor. 7:21 as follows: "If you have the chance to obtain liberty make all the more use *of freedom*," even if this yields no revolutionary follow-up such as a fundamental critique of slavery. It is true, current exegesis of 1 Cor. 7:20f. in the Western world differs in where Paul's status quo theology is to be situated in Christian dogmatics, but there is never a doubt that it is theology of the status quo.

The interpretation of 1 Cor. 7:17–24 is fundamentally affected by the dissertation of Scott Bartchy (written in 1971 under Krister Stendahl's supervision); its exegetical, philological, and social-historical argumentation is solid. Bartchy has shown that *klēsis* in 1 Cor. 7:20 means divine calling and that Paul seeks to make it clear in the whole passage that we are to live out God's calling in the actually existing conditions of our life, holistically and bodily. He understands Paul's theology of calling as a critique of a position defended by enthusiasts in Corinth; it follows from our faith, they said, that our bodily existence is irrelevant (p. 142), so that we are not to be fools any longer but "wise"—in a spiritual and religious sense (p. 142). Paul wants to bring the exalted Corinthians down to earth, which means that he rejects flight from the world and regards status in society as irrelevant. One may keep or change status; it has nothing to do whatever with living according to one's calling (pp. 140, 152, 154).

I believe that Bartchy's perspective on 1 Cor. 7:17–24 leads to a different conclusion, namely, that living according to one's calling does impinge on the everyday life of female and male slaves, as well as freeborn women and men. They continue to be men, women, slaves, but they change the praxis of life as a woman, a man, someone enslaved. For me, Bartchy's conclusion that Paul relativizes the social state is a retrograde step—very formally conceptualized—behind his own exegesis of 1 Cor. 7:17–24, an exegesis that I hold to be a rare high point in recent history of Pauline studies.

There is yet another matter in Bartchy's work that I want to criticize. He pictures the Corinthian enthusiasts as a homogeneous group, seeing the revolutionary women who throw off their veils on the same level as the men who insist that their faith permits them to buy sex since, after all, the body and bodiliness are irrelevant. The people in Corinth also need to be seen as concretely as possible. Among the women who, when they prayed and prophesied, no longer wanted to wear veils as a sign of their subordination there may well have been women working in the sex trade who no longer wanted to accept the daily experience of being subjugated by men.

Bartchy's important work is barely discussed in New Testament scholarship, where it has found little attention.[77]

I contrast my own interpretation once again with the interpretations above. According to Paul, God's calling is lived out in social reality and impinges on every concrete condition of social life. That calling means, for example, that as a Jew or female slave, one crosses over the boundaries imposed by one's "state" whenever keeping the commandments or the peace of God leads one to do so. Faith has a dimension that encompasses our bodies and, in its intention, all of creation: the common life of humanity and the future of the world. For free women, it meant throwing off their veils. For female slaves, it meant living their faith in equality with self-consciousness and determination. The conduct of the slave woman Rhoda in Jerusalem is connected with an eschatological hope in which her courage is a bridgehead of a just world.

From a feminist perspective, it is not enough to supplement 1 Cor. 7:21 with "freedom" or to translate "state" in the verse preceding as "calling." It is essential to grasp the bodily consequences of this calling and its eschatological dimension. A feminist interpretation of Paul that, in concert with prevailing exegesis, attributes to him a theology of the status quo,[78] only to critique or reject Paul thereupon, ignores with what power the theology of the status quo is enforced (in Paul's name) in the Western world. It leaves unexamined the social interests of that image of Paul. The history of the Christian women in Corinth loses nothing of its radiance and power if Paul is not the archvillain of this bright history but its tarnished hero.

D. FEMINIST PERSPECTIVES

First Corinthians 7:20, or 7:17–24, serves an essential function in the understanding of freedom in traditional Western theology. The false translation of 1 Cor. 7:20 lays the groundwork for a problematic understanding of 1 Cor. 7:17–24, of Paul himself, and of Christian theology in general. For this understanding, existing boundaries within patriarchal society are theologically legitimate or irrelevant. Both alternatives are hostile to women, racist, and unjust to all who live in economic and social misery. "Everyone remain in the state in which he [*sic*] was called"—this sentence inscribes oppression and injustice in society even where the Christian community is portrayed as a place of equality. Many of the authoritative versions of the Bible that are in official use have a false translation of 1 Cor. 7:20. The tradition of translation following Luther is no alternative when it translates *state* as *vocation,* since it gives vocation substantially the same meaning. The revised (German) version of 1984 reads: "Everyone remain in the vocation in which he [*sic*] was called." This no longer says: remain in the profession (= state) in which you were when you became a Christian, but the relative clause turns the word *vocation* into the description of the social status at the time of one's becoming a believer.

The one exception I have found in this flood of invocations of the status quo through false translations of the scriptures is the (indeed androcentric) translation of Fridolin Stier:[79] "Everyone remain in the vocation just as he [*sic*] was called"; this makes it clear that vocation is a matter of God's action and not one of social status. This text shows that we need a new translation of the Bible, which is what feminists have been saying. Their demand fundamentally questions the theological paradigm of the traditions of translation and thereby the theology of the church and scholarship behind it.

The divided consciousness of Paul shows once again how important is Elisabeth Schüssler Fiorenza's hermeneutical insight that neither the canon nor the text itself can be the criterion for discerning what is Christian substance. That criterion can only be the history of the struggle of women and other oppressed peoples for their liberation[80] and that of creation. Paul's divided consciousness, however, also shows that we may not presume of ourselves that we have the cor-

rect, undivided consciousness. Rather, my observations of how his consciousness is divided prompt me to look for those invisible and visible boundaries that
I myself honor, even though they enforce injustice. The title of this chapter is
intended to problematize with the notion of conversion the traditional translation and interpretation of 1 Cor. 7:20. Of course, the title is not meant to become the new translation of that verse, for God's calling also gives people
courage to cross over the boundaries of patriarchy where it is not within their
power to rid the world of the "state" of poverty and oppression.

This chapter (III.1) is not primarily about the history of Christian women in
Corinth but about the feminist discussion of the stature and limitations of Paul.
Other aspects of that history are dealt with in III.2.

2

The Gospel of the Poor
and the Option for Women
(Luke 6:20ff. and par.; Matt. 11:25 and par.)

A. THE TEXTS

In this section I bring together several texts about the gospel of the poor as the message and praxis of Jesus and the early Christian communities. The gospel of the poor is found, for example, in the Beatitudes, which are part of the oldest tradition of the words of Jesus (Luke 6:20ff. and par.). It is found as well in the Magnificat of Mary (Luke 1:46–55), in a prayer of Jesus (Matt. 11:25 and par.), and in Paul (1 Cor. 1:26–31). It is quite apparent and well known that, from the perspective of intellectual history, these and many other texts are rooted in the same soil. The gospel of the poor has its spiritual roots in Third Isaiah (Isaiah 61), for example, and in the Song of Hannah (1 Sam. 2:1–10). It was the prophets' message of justice that again and again powerfully evoked in Jewish history the hopes and liberating struggles of a suffering and oppressed people. Two women stand out as prophets of the gospel of the poor: Hannah and Mary. With them are bound up many generations of women, whose own prophetic voices repeated those of Hannah and Mary.

In early Christianity the gospel of the poor was both preaching and praxis. What did this praxis mean for women and men, for poor and rich? The injustice of patriarchal domination functions in many forms of oppression. The connection between economic exploitation and sexism is manifest in women's and children's experiences of violence and excessive demands. The gospel of the poor offered Jewish and Christian people a language with which to critique patriarchy and be about their liberation at the same time.

The beatitude of the poor (Luke 6:20f.) is addressed in both versions[81] to the *ptōchoi*, the utterly destitute. It is repeatedly assumed that the beatitude of the poor in spirit (*ptōchoi tō pneumati;* Matt. 5:3) is a spiritualized version of a macarism addressed originally to the poor in an economic sense. Depending on people's theological interests, the spiritualized version has been praised or condemned.[82] Yet the assumption that Matthew's Gospel presents a spiritualized version is based in a false conception that itself presupposes a dualistic distinction

136

between bodiliness/material existence on the one hand and spiritual poverty on the other. Such a distinction fails to do justice to the language of the Hebrew Bible and the New Testament. In the context of the theological tradition of Judaism, *poverty* is in every instance a theological and holistic term. Whoever is poor in the material sense cannot praise God; whoever experiences hunger also experiences the destruction of the relationship with God. That is why poverty is a scandal before God and humankind, a transgression against the likeness of God. "Poor in spirit"[83] says explicitly what Luke 6:20 says implicitly: the poor are poor right down to the marrow of their bones; even their very *pneuma,* their capacity for the dignity and power God bestows, is threatened.

The prophet Jesus promises the reign of God to the poor who are hungry and who weep (Luke 6:21f.). In the context of apocalyptic and early Christian eschatology (cf. at III.3), this is no consoling promise of some future St. Never-Never Day; it is a promise from which comes liberating praxis here and now. Poor women, like the hemorrhaging woman (Mark 5:27 and par.), found the self-respect to step out of invisibility. Hungry people shared their meager resources. The shared meals of the women and men disciples of Jesus[84] expressed visibly their community of mutual support and the present reality of a beginning of God's reign.

The "woe" to the rich (Luke 6:24–26), found in the context with the beatitude of the poor only in Luke, perhaps does not belong to the oldest tradition of Jesus, as that beatitude does. But from the point of view of intellectual history, that woe is an appropriate supplement to the beatitude of the poor. At its innermost core, the gospel of the poor always meant that God is on the side of the poor and dethrones the rulers who defend their affluence with violence (cf. only Luke 1:46–54 or the eschatological saying "The first shall be last," Mark 10:31 and elsewhere). "The tables are being turned"[85]—a perception that to modern Western Christianity appeared primitive, revengeful, or "Jewish."[86] And yet this perception pervades all of early Christianity and is being stated here. The message of impending judgment being announced to the rich, whose affluence derives from injustice, and the powerful, whose rule is unjust, has a broad Jewish and early Christian tradition (cf. Mark 10:42–45 and par.).

Jesus' prayer of praise (Matt. 11:25 and par.) belongs also to the oldest tradition of Jesus; it is certainly part of the Sayings Source.[87] Jesus praises God that God has chosen to grant revelation to "those not of age" (*nēpioi*) and to withhold it from the "wise and understanding," thereby confronting them with God's judgment. Jesus interprets his own work and that of those who follow him to be the beginning of an eschatological division. Those not of age are right with God, the rich are not. Those not of age are the poor who cannot talk well and have no formal education. There were hardly any chances for girls of the poverty-stricken majority of Palestine's population to become educated; nor is there yet much chance for girls in the two-thirds world. The notion of "those of tender age"[88] is especially suited to explain the option for women, which is what the gospel of the poor is about. In the opinion of many rich men—but also of many poor ones—an education for girls is superfluous, if not dangerous. Such men despise the uneducated as people "not of age." The gospel of the poor describes social reality, using concepts that embody the language of the upper classes, for whom the despised poor—but above all, poor women—are just that: "not of age." The gospel of the poor picks up that contempt-filled language and fills it with new meaning: "the tables are being turned." Only those not of age receive God's revelation;[89] they come of age, but in a new, different sense and not that of the upper classes.

Paul's statements about the Corinthian community's social composition (1 Cor. 1:26–31) are situated in a presentation of his Christology of the cross and wisdom Christology. For him, there is a substantive connection between God's electing action in Corinth and the veneration of the crucified Jesus as God's wisdom.

The text indicates that, in its majority, the Corinthian community consisted of people without formal education, of the infirm, and of those of common birth (in other words, people who were in slavery or had been freed from it).[90] There were also the isolated "wise," "powerful," and "of noble birth," the formally educated members of the urban upper classes who were born free and participated in the exercise of power.[91] Those who have formal education despise those who do not (cf. v. 28). The latter are "what is foolish in the world" and are not only despised by the world but also part of the world hostile to God.[92] When God chose them they were the godforsaken, the "nobodies." And here, too, the contempt of the upper classes for the "nobodies" down there,[93] for the "last,"[94] is picked up and turned around: the despised and godforsaken are God's chosen; they live out God's calling. God's calling transforms them and draws them into a process (cf. above at III.1). The uneducated women in Corinth open their mouths and prophesy in public (1 Cor. 11:5). The despised "nobodies" no longer[95] put up with the few upper-class people who want to claim privileges (1 Cor. 11:17–22) and who humiliate the poor (1 Cor. 11:22) even in community assemblies and eucharistic celebrations, which are also their shared meals.

Paul's proposed solution of the Corinthian conflict surrounding the Eucharist and its attendant circumstances contradicts the election of God as described in 1 Cor. 1:26–31. Paul proposes a separation of private and public,[96] but that turns the community's assembly into a place of injustice. The affluent do not share with the poor; they can go on despising them, except that they may not show it when the community gathers to celebrate "the meal of the Lord." A "solution" such as that violates the gospel of the poor, which Paul himself finds so important. The Acts of the Apostles[97] provides a different understanding of Christian table fellowship and the readiness to share. The narrative of the rich young man[98] shows quite plainly what God's calling means for the rich. What these texts declare is that Christian communities clearly expected the rich to renounce their wealth voluntarily for the benefit of the poor.[99] Despite the profound importance that the gospel of the poor had for him, Paul allowed himself to be corrupted by the rich in the Corinthian community.[100] To be indignant about Paul today in the context of the "first" world presupposes that one reflects with care on one's own susceptibility to the corruption of affluence.

In 1 Cor. 1:26–31, Paul says, in accord with the gospel of the poor, that the community of the poor and uneducated Corinthians is a sign to the wise of God's judgment.[101] And that surely means that he wishes to confront the rich who desire to be part of that community with the necessity of their inward and active conversion. For the majority of the community, namely, those without formal education, the gospel of the poor meant, among other things, that they learned to contend with the rich when the rich wanted to enforce their privileges. God's calling did not transform them into the wise in the sense of the upper classes, nor did it make them upwardly mobile;[102] their calling did, however, change them into a group of lower-class people who could appeal to solidarity, support one another materially, and name explicitly the injustice of economic exploitation.

B. SOCIAL-HISTORICAL QUESTIONS

Paul's Corinthian correspondence permits only a fragmentary grasp of what God's calling meant for the majority of that community, namely, women without formal education, female slaves, and freedwomen. We are told that they pray and prophesy in the assembly (1 Cor. 11:5). They contend for the rights they claim are theirs from the gospel of the poor (1 Cor. 11:16, 18). They no longer want to exhibit women's subjugation under men, not symbolically (1 Cor. 11:10) or in their conduct in the community gatherings; they want to speak and learn publicly (1 Cor. 14:34–35).[103] What women prophets had to say in their charismatic utterances was connected with their struggle for the right to speak in public and against women's submission to men. In early Christianity there was a broad charismatic movement, particularly of women. I still agree with Leopold Zscharnack's 1902 analysis:[104] "These women were primarily women 'of the people.' Yet the nameless ones were always in the majority compared with the noble and the wise, whose names history and tradition record. The nameless ones alone would allow us to comprehend fully the significance of the female gender in those movements."[105] The women whom the mainstream Christian church of the first centuries C.E. still knew as prophets were domesticated in retrospect. This is what Hippolytus had to say about the evangelist Philip's four daughters who, according to Acts 21:8f., were prophets in Caesarea in the days of Paul: "But they did not rise up against the men and stayed within the boundaries set for them."[106]

I do not intend now to write the history of Christian and Jewish women prophets[107] but to inquire about the *content* of women's prophecy. Here I encounter difficulties that are commonly known, because women's speech is silenced in the New Testament and, increasingly, in the ancient church—in real life as in the texts. Luke tells of an eighty-four-year-old woman who lived in the Temple; at the hour of Simeon's proclamation that the child Jesus was the Messiah, she announced the redemption to come. "She came up and gave thanks to God and spoke of him[108] to all who were looking for the redemption of Jerusalem" (Luke 2:38). Her announcement is to be understood in a Lukan sense like that of Mary's Magnificat (Luke 1:46–54), namely, that Israel's liberation means that the hungry shall be satisfied and that the unjust tyrants shall be toppled from their thrones. The messianic liberator has arrived. He is a child. In Luke 4:18ff. the grown-up Messiah-prophet proclaims his messianic message himself; it is the gospel of the poor according to the words of Isaiah 61.

By means of two totally different sources, I want to show that women prophets are to be seen in a unique connection with the gospel of the poor.

The *Targum Jonathan*[109] has rendered the Song of Hannah in 1 Sam. 2:1–10 as a complete prophetic text that heralds the liberation of the Jewish people from its political oppression. Hannah's prophecy traces the people's liberation history:

1   And Hannah prayed in a spirit of prophecy and said: "Now Samuel my son is to be a prophet on behalf of Israel. In his days they will be saved from the hand of the Philistines, and by his hands signs and mighty deeds will be done for them. Therefore my heart is strong in the portion that the Lord has given to me. And also Heman, the son of Joel, the son of my son who is to arise—he and his fourteen sons are to be speaking in song by means of lyres and lutes with their brothers the Levites to give praise in the house of the sanctuary. Therefore my horn is exalted in the gift that the Lord has anointed for me. And also concerning the marvelous revenge that will be against the Philistines who are to bring back the ark on a new cart, and with it the guilt offering. Therefore the assembly of Israel will say: 'Let my mouth be open to speak great things against my enemies, for I rejoice in your saving power.' "

2   Concerning Sennacherib the king of Assyria—she prophesied and said that he and all his armies would come up against Jerusalem, and a great sign would be worked on him; there the corpses of his camp would fall. Therefore all the nations, peoples, and language groups will confess and say: "There is not one who is holy except the Lord, for there is no one apart from you"; and your people will say: "There is no one who is strong except our God."

3   Concerning Nebuchadnezzar the king of Babylon—she prophesied and said: "You Chaldeans and all the peoples who are to rule in Israel, do not say many boastful things. Let not blasphemies go forth from your mouth, for the all-knowing God is the Lord and upon all his works he fixes judgment. And also to you he is to repay the revenge of your sins."

4   Concerning the kingdoms of Greece—she prophesied and said: "The bows of the Greek warriors will be broken; and those of the house of the Hasmonean who were weak—mighty deeds will be done for them."

5　Concerning the sons of Haman—she prophesied and said: "Those who were filled up on bread and growing in wealth and abounding in money have become poor; they have returned to working as laborers for bread, the food of their mouth. Mordecai and Esther who were needy became rich and forgot their poverty; they returned to being free persons. So Jerusalem, which was like a barren woman, is to be filled with her exiled people. And Rome, which was filled with great numbers of people—her armies will cease to be; she will be desolate and destroyed."

6　All these are the mighty works of the Lord, who is powerful in the world. He puts to death and speaks so as to make alive; he brings down to Sheol, and he is also ready to bring up in eternal life.

7　The Lord makes poor and makes rich; he humbles, also he exalts.

8　He raises up the poor from the dust, from the dunghill he exalts the needy one, to make them dwell with the righteous ones, the chiefs of the world; and he bequeaths to them thrones of glory, for before the Lord the deeds of the sons of men are revealed. He has established Gehennah below for the wicked ones. And the just ones—those doing his good pleasure, he has established the world for them.

9　He will keep away from Gehennah the bodies of his servants, the righteous ones. And the wicked ones will walk about in Gehennah in the darkness, to make it known that there is no one in whom there is strength having claim for the day of judgment.

10　The Lord will shatter the enemies who rise up to do harm to his people. The Lord blasts down upon them from the heavens with a loud voice. He will exact just revenge from Gog and the army of the violent nations who come with him from the ends of the earth. And he will give power to his king and will magnify the kingdom of his anointed one.

The text is androcentric throughout, but it is not by accident that it combines the hoped-for messianic liberation with the preaching of a woman prophet. Jewish tradition also regards the activities of Judith and Esther as actions for the people's liberation. It is not by the military that the people are set free but "by a woman's hand"[110] and by the power of the prophetic word that proclaims the demise of the world's overlords. At the time when this Targum was written, people longed for the end of Roman rule, just as the people in New Testament times did; "and Rome, which was filled with great numbers of people—her armies will cease to be; she will be desolate and destroyed" is how Hannah put it, according to the Targum. In the context of the Christian communities of the time, Mary's prophecy about the mighty who are toppled from their seats of power (Luke 1:52) has to be understood as an announcement concerning the demise of Rome. Just like the Magnificat, the gospel of the poor as proclaimed in Hannah's song promises that the poor shall have food to eat, the poor shall share in the exercise of power, and the rich will again have to work for the bread they eat. As in Mary's Magnificat, the message of justice contained in the gospel of the poor develops concrete hopes for just human relationships, the end of hunger and of affluence at the expense of others.

A woman's prophecy with very similar content can be found in the *Kerygmata Petrou*, a source of very different genre.[111] This source disqualifies women's prophecy as inferior and this-worldly; but the text may be read against the grain, so to speak, and used in women's history. In the manner of a great variety of philosophers and theologians of the time, the text speaks, on the one hand, about unpopular women prophets and, on the other, about Eve as the cause of the world's misery.[112] The cause of the world's misery is named: it is Eve, the first woman prophet. Contemporary women prophets are in continuity with her.

> 22.1 Along with the true prophet there has been created as a companion a female being who is as far inferior to him as *metousia* is to *ousia*, as the moon is to the sun, as fire is to light. 2 As a female she rules over the present world, which is like to her, and counts as the first prophetess; she proclaims her prophecy with all *amongst those born of woman*. . . .
>
> 23.1 There are two kinds of prophecy, the one is male . . . 2 The other is found amongst those who are born of woman. Proclaiming what pertains to the present world, female prophecy desires to be considered male. 3 On this account she steals the seed of the male, envelops them with her own seed of the flesh and lets them— that is, her words—come forth as her own creations. 4 She promises to give earthly riches gratuitously in the present world and wishes to exchange <the slow> for the swift, the small for the greater.
>
> 24.1 She not only ventures to speak and hear of many gods, but she also believes that she herself will be deified; and because she hopes to become something that contradicts her nature, she destroys what she has. Pretending to make sacrifice, she stains herself with blood at the times of her menses and thus pollutes those who touch her. 2 When she conceives, she gives birth to temporary kings and brings about wars in which much blood is shed. 3 Those who desire to get to know the truth from her, are led by many opposing and varied statements and hints to seek it perpetually without finding it, even unto death.

The women prophets who are disqualified in this text claim to be of equal rank with men ("desires to be considered male," 23.2; "because she hopes to become something that contradicts her nature, she destroys what she has," 24.1). These women speak as autonomous prophets (23.2) and thereby allegedly steal from men. They do not accept unified teaching (24.3) and are not prepared to set themselves apart from other religions, presumably the local religion of origin. They practice a sacrificial rite with menstrual blood (would that be a nightmare scenario of the author?). That they give birth to kings and wars is a probable weapon of the defamatory arsenal of this negative mythology of Eve. Women's prophecies speak of an eschatological reversal ("exchange

. . . the small for the greater," 23.4; and they want "to give earthly riches gratuitously in the present world," 23.4). They promise the poor an economic improvement of their lives in the community. In spite of the polemical tone of the text, women's prophecy, proclamation, and praxis of the gospel of the poor are quite apparently connected in terms of material existence and the liberation of women.

The Syrian *Didaskalia,* a document from approximately the same time (the beginning of the third century C.E.) and region (northern Syria),[113] paints a vivid picture of the conflicts between a church of women and laypeople[114] on the one hand and a centralized, hierarchically structured church on the other. It supports the image of women's prophecy painted by the *Kerygmata Petrou.* Extremely hostile to women, this is another text that, because of its documentation of misogyny, can be valuable for the history of women. That the women, who are to be disciplined in the terms of male hierarchy, are prophets is presumably not something the text means to convey.[115] But it tells clearly that the women have a calling from God and that they have received the gift of God's Spirit. Women in general,[116] but particularly widows in the congregations, are to be disciplined. Although the author's defamation of the church of women and laypeople makes it very difficult to glean any historical substance from his text, the following may be said.

The women and laypeople seek to have their offerings distributed in a decentralized and public manner, whereas the author wants the bishop to receive them all, the donors to remain anonymous, and those who receive assistance to refrain from telling other Christians.[117] Offerings are very important because the women are destitute.[118] The author does not want those women to make independent contacts that would allow them to eat elsewhere or to find resources on their own. Because women's poverty is so prevalent, the charges against widows that they are greedy, out for profit, and that they lend money with interest[119] are hardly realistic.

Another sphere of conflict is *doctrine.* The author wants only the leading men to provide information about the substance of Christian doctrine: "Our Lord compared the word of his gospel with the mustard seed; if this mustard is not expertly prepared, it becomes bitter and sharp."[120] Women ought not to teach and baptize. We see, in other words, that there was a living church of women and laypeople in which women baptized and taught and refused to be disciplined. Obviously, the disciplinary goal of the bishop's church, which here cannot be attained, is that of confining widows, or women, to the home. Women go about in public; they distribute the offerings, win people for Christ, and criticize the church of the bishops. They refuse to submit to the men. The author of this text interprets this phenomenon to mean, "You want not only to be wiser and more understanding than the men, but also than presbyters and bishops."[121] The women even join women who have been excluded from the bishop's church, thereby undermining that church's means of exercising power.[122]

This is an important document for the history of Christian women; it seeks to restrict women's praying to the home. At the same time, it shows that, at the beginning of the third century C.E. in a particular part of Syria, there was a lively and contentious church of women and laypeople who still lived in the spirit of Acts 2:17, namely, that all whom God has called share equally in the Spirit and the power: "Your sons and daughters shall prophesy." Despite the polemics of the Syrian text, the content of that Spirit-animated prophecy is clearly discernible as mutual support, feeding the hungry, equalizing women, disclosing the community's affairs, and discussing in public the form of the church. One may conclude from the portrayal of women's prophecy in the *Kerygmata Petrou* that as the substance of women's (and laypeople's) prophecy, the gospel of the poor had a long history and was valiantly defended by women, in spite of the many difficulties that beset it from the beginning.

I have inquired about the substance of women's prophecy. According to 1 Cor. 1:26–31, the overwhelming number of the Corinthian community came from the poor majority of the population. The women prophets of that community, who become visible briefly in 1 Cor. 11:2–16, belong to the harbor city's poor. With the help of the material cited in II.2, 3 and III.1.B above, I can picture their everyday lives. There are women who must earn money but whose income does not provide them with an independent living. There are slave women and freedwomen, whose economic dependency often involves sexual services to men. There are female street vendors, textile and sex-trade workers. It may be that among the Christian women in Corinth there were individual upper-class women; nevertheless, the substance of Corinthian women's prophecy must be examined with a view to the predominantly poor women. The gospel of the poor occupies a central place in every sphere of early Christianity and is related in 1 Cor. 1:26–31 to the social reality of the congregation in Corinth. It was the gospel that spoke to these women and gave them courage; it was the same gospel that they passed on to others. We are assisted in our understanding of this by what Luke had to say about women's prophecy, by the Jewish tradition concerning Hannah, and by a brief examination of women's prophecy and churches in Syria at the onset of the third century C.E. The message of women prophets in the early Christian church surely has other dimensions as well. I do not address them here,[123] where what is to be clarified is the relevance of the gospel of the poor for those Christian women who prophesied the justice that God demands.

In this sense, Mary's Magnificat (Luke 1: 46–54) represents also the women of Corinth and other communities in the early church.

The early Christian praxis, which was to achieve, on a voluntary basis, the material equality of the members of the community and among communities in all regions,[124] must not be seen as an idealization of the original Jerusalem community according to Acts. The praxis of sharing is integral to the gospel of the poor and to the liberation of women, as the texts from the early third century C.E. still show.

C. FEMINIST OBSERVATIONS ON THE HISTORY OF INTERPRETATION: THE "STIGMA" OF CHRISTIANITY'S INFERIOR SOCIAL STATUS

In dominant theology, one powerful interest still governs—almost exclusively and to the smallest detail—the history of interpretation of the whole New Testament. That interest is that Christianity must be rid of the liability of being a church of the poor; it must be portrayed as a religion that offers middle-class and rich people scope to create identity and to occupy their positions of power. In describing how the New Testament speaks of women's work (see II.2.B and C), it became clear that in the history of interpretation Prisca and Lydia were made out to be well-to-do women, a portrayal that distorts the perception of the hard work of badly paid women in the early church and, concomitantly, of women in church and society today.

To describe how the church of the poor and the option for women are denied, I make reference first to Origen's *Contra Celsum*. This work is of fundamental importance for our task; it is the star witness in dominant social history of early Christianity. After that, I will discuss several examples from recent Western discussions that seek, with much effort, to demonstrate that the church was a church of the middle class and well-to-do. I have personally experienced[125] the opposition against every historical and theological attempt to call attention to the church of the poor and the Christian option for women. The issue of the social historical question impinges directly on the way of the church now and in the future. But how easy it is to dismiss those who call for justice as being "ideologues"! My criticism of the obscuring of the church of the poor from Western Christianity's sight derives from two sources. The first is my conviction that front and center before God must be the lives of those who hunger, are overworked, and whose children have no future. The second is the New Testament itself: it informs my resistance against obscuring from view the church of the poor and the option for women. The New Testament preaches the gospel of the poor, as was shown above. New Testament texts cannot be interpreted as one sees fit. Those texts remain strong and unambiguous enough to move Western Christian women and men toward conversion despite their domestication in interpretations oriented toward domination.

Origen's Contra Celsum:
A Christian Betrayal of the Church of Women
and the Church of the Poor

Origen's defense of Christianity against Celsus's charges[126] provides much historical information about early Christianity and Christianity between ca. 180 and ca. 248 C.E. It must, however, be read critically. Both Origen and Celsus fight for the intelligentsia of Roman society. Celsus wants to demonstrate that Christianity is throughout a religion of the inferior classes and that no educated man in his right mind would become a Christian (3.73, 50). In contrast, Origen understands his life's work to be the task of making Christianity attractive for educated men (3.52, 57 and elsewhere). Both are, in fact, concerned with educated *males*.[127] Celsus's clear interest is to prove that Christianity is, at its roots, a religion exclusively for lower-class people. He argues accordingly that the church is open to members of the lower classes *only* (3.44), the uneducated, slaves, women, and children. It is Origen's interest to assert clearly that even though the majority of church people are of the lower classes, it has a growing number of educated and rich people, an elite minority (3.9; 1.19; and elsewhere). By means of allegorical interpretation of the words of Jesus, they discover his true wisdom, which the mass of believers do not (3.46); this deeper truth is kept from simple folk (3.52).

Despite the clearly discernible interests of both men, much of the social-historical information they provide may be taken seriously[128] because in a number of instances common assertions occur, despite their contrary interests, and because other historical sources substantiate some of what they say. On that basis, the following picture emerges.

The Christian mission work at the time of Celsus and Origen may be compared to that of Judaism and Cynic philosophy. Poor itinerant preachers, female and male,[129] move from town to town and speak to people in the marketplace (3.50), in workplaces such as cobblers' and fullers' workshops, or in women's quarters (*gynaikonitis*) (3.55). These places also offer an opportunity to elude the control of educated men and fathers (which Origen does not deny in substance; 3.56f.). There is documentation showing that similar methods were used in the mission work of Judaism and Cynic philosophy.[130] Christianity's social composition is mixed; a small minority of upper-class people lives alongside an overwhelming majority of poor people, and even Celsus has to admit this, contrary to his primary interest (1.27). Origen maintains that the number of upper-class people corresponds to the percentage of educated persons in the mass of the uneducated. Historians of antiquity calculate the ratio of upper- to lower-class population in Rome as 1 percent to 99 percent,[131] which allows one to gauge the ratio of which Origen speaks. Even if one considers that there were also, for example, educated lower-class Jews, the kind of education Origen has in mind—education in Greek philosophy—is primarily an upper-class privilege. Even the terminology used to describe the majority of the uneducated and the minority of the educated clearly reflects the class distinction of antiquity, seeing that Celsus and Origen drew on concepts customarily used to depict "social types."[132]

There seem to have been frictions between the Christians of different classes, for Origen concedes that there are communities which "defend their own ignorance" (3.44; cf. 5.16); nor do they want to admit people of the upper classes. He believes that this is contrary to the teachings of Jesus. The church Origen has in mind is one that is guided by the leading elite, which seeks to instruct and improve the lower-class people (3.49, 51, 59). "We keep women from unchastity and marital infidelity and seek to convert them from all morbid passion for theater and dancing and heresy" (3.56). Criminals are invited so that they may be healed; their wounds are bandaged with the teachings of Jesus, and "the feverish heat of the soul aflame with sin is [soothed] with the medicine faith supplies" (3.61). Jesus is the physician for sinners *and* the teacher of wisdom for the pure (3.62). In Origen the church appears as a great rehabilitation center for women, children, criminals, workers, the uneducated, and the poor, all under the leadership of an upper-class elite. Origen's contempt for women and the lower classes is congruent with that of his own class—the upper class—*and* that of Celsus.

The New Testament church is for Origen the mirror image of his own church. He cites 1 Cor. 1:26ff. and reads that text, in his sense, as an offer to the lower classes for rehabilitation (3.48f.). At the same time, it requires a bold interpretation to fit Jesus into such a picture. It is true, Jesus was the child of poor people and, read superficially, his words are in language for the uneducated; the wise, however, using allegorical interpretation, have access to Jesus the teacher of more profound wisdom (1.29; 3.46; and elsewhere). The disciples and Paul do not fit Origen's picture either: the disciples were at first uneducated, and some were even criminals (1.62, 63); gradual rehabilitation and the gift of divine power turned them into persuasive speakers. But they were not speakers in the sense of the Greek arts of dialectic and rhetoric (1.62). It is apparent that Origen's conception of a Christian doctrine of wisdom lacks any point of contact with the New Testament except for the allegorical interpretation of the Jesus tradition (Jesus was a teacher of wisdom); that interpretation, however, is itself alien to the texts of the New Testament.

In Celsus's picture of early Christianity, the contempt for the lower classes is very plain. It climaxes in his contempt for women, for example, in his description of the social origin of Mary, the mother of Jesus. She was a poor country-woman who had to earn her living as a *chernētis,* a woman doing needlework or spinning for pay. Celsus refers explicitly to this work of women in order to underscore how inferior and contemptible her social condition was.

Celsus is undoubtedly mistaken when he asserts that *no* educated person becomes Christian. Nonetheless, his description of earliest Christianity grasps much more correctly than Origen's the partiality of the Christian message. His interpretation of Mark 2:17 (3.59) is true to the text: "The kingdom of God will admit those who are sinners, . . . without understanding, not of age, in a word, those who are wretched." Origen's interpretation, in contrast, is not true to the text, because for him a certain circle of people require particular rehabilitation before they can be worthy of wisdom (3.59). Something quite similar may be said in relation to 1 Cor. 1:27, the partiality of which Celsus quickly perceives (3.44). Origen, however, angrily cites that verse in characterizing the lower-class church and what is, in his view, its primitive expectation of judgment (5.16); he does not know what to do with the text's partiality. He relates the verse solely to Greek philosophers who are mistaken about the true worship of God; they cannot boast in the presence of God for that reason (6.5). What Paul had spoken of was the utter reversal of the upper and lower social class relationship. Origen consequently reinterprets the gospel of the poor by spiritualizing it (6.16; 7.18, 23). Regardless of whether Celsus is citing Christian groups or is using his own words, he expresses in classic form what partiality means: "Those people [the uneducated] *are worthy of their God* after having made a confession of their faith, *without further ado*" (3.44).

Origen and Celsus have no quarrel about the social composition of the church at its beginning and in their time; they are at odds about the implications. Origen, the Christian, wants a church with social diversity but which reflects the class differences both in organization and theology; Celsus points to the church's praxis of partiality that excludes the upper class or at least is not governed by it. It is historically false that the church from the beginning excluded the upper class; it was a church of the uneducated and the poor, of women and children, who formed the church themselves without the control of the predominant.[133] In that sense Celsus, the enemy of Christians, came closer to historical reality than did Origen, who had difficulty in basing his perceptions in the New Testament.

Both enemy and defender of Christianity are at one in their outlook as educated upper-class males, in their contempt for women, and in their belief that poor people are not of age. Both are representatives of a reinforcement of patriarchy against a church of women, which is also a church of the poor. Unwittingly, both reflect what power that church of women and the poor had in their day. Origen's work is an invaluable document for the history of church of the poor and of women; it is also a sad document of Christian betrayal of that church. Paul had shied away from the concrete implications of the gospel of the poor—in his conflict with the rich about sharing in the eucharistic meal. Origen, however, replaces the gospel of the poor with an all-encompassing ideology oriented toward patriarchal domination.

The Repudiation of the "Stigma" of Christianity's Inferior Social Status

I have chosen an article by Joseph Vogt, "The Reproach of Early Christianity's Inferior Social Status," published in 1975,[134] to illustrate how dominant theology writes the social history of early Christianity. I chose it because it refers to the same material I have just discussed—Origen's work against Celsus—but also because Vogt's arguments are representative throughout of a social history from the perspective of dominant theology. In his view, Celsus paints a "distorted picture" (p. 402) of Christianity because he wants to attach the "stigma" (p. 401) of social inferiority to it. "In his aggressiveness," Celsus "oversimplified his opponents' actuality by erasing the educated from the picture of Christians" (p. 403). The distorted view of Christianity as the scum of the earth—"the uneducated people, scraped from the very bottom of the barrel, the credulous women, who in the complaisance of their gender stray off everywhere"[135]—took firm hold and was refurbished in the nineteenth century by Friedrich Engels (p. 405). The truth, however, is that "from the beginning, Christian mission found its way into the urban middle classes and then into the highest social class" (p. 405). First Corinthians 1:26ff. testifies to that, and it is only one source among others (p. 407).

The membership of educated men in a community of believers is a deciding factor for Joseph Vogt in determining the value of Christianity. He does not even find it necessary to ask *what role* educated men play in such a community. His article implies that he takes it for granted—like Origen—that they exercise leadership. The issue between Origen and Celsus was not *whether* educated men belonged to the communities but *what place* they had there. First Corinthians 1:26ff. says that few educated men and many uneducated women (and men) belonged to the Corinthian community. Paul says nothing about a leadership role of the educated. Rather, he talks about God's judgment on the rich, powerful, and educated. The "distorted picture" painted by Celsus and deplored by Vogt is indeed polemical and indeed a distorted image, not because it disputes the presence of educated men in the communities but because it depicts the church of the poor and women as credulous and dissolute scum.

Joseph Vogt's depiction belongs to the dominant social history of the New Testament. One may see it already in Origen; since the rise of socialism in the nineteenth century, this view has gained a substantial place in New Testament scholarship. Studies with an orientation like that of Joseph Vogt seek to demonstrate that the socialist picture of the first Christian communities' "love communism" and of the earliest church as a church of slaves and the *Lumpenproletariat* is inaccurate.

The presentations of early Christian social history by Friedrich Engels,[136] Karl Kautsky,[137] and Rosa Luxemburg[138] are not affected at all by such counterarguments. That is because all three subject Christianity to a fundamental critique and do not want to elevate it to the status of precursor of socialism in their understanding. If early Christianity and the socialist movement have anything in common, according to Engels, it is primarily their empty cash boxes and the proliferation of sects.[139] Not one of the three regards early Christianity as a revolutionary movement in their sense. I rather see in their depiction of early Christianity as a movement of "the lowest strata of the people"[140] the intent to hold up a critical mirror to the church of their own time and its utter separation from the working class.

The portrayal of early Christianity from an antisocialist perspective often does not even discuss the views of those classic socialist writers. Instead, such presentations project onto an alleged opponent assumptions about their views. "If you believe in class struggle, the best thing to do is to take a group of Galilean farmers, add the community of goods, speak of Paul 'who works with his own hands' and who said that in Corinth there were 'not many wise . . . not many powerful and not many of noble birth,' and that is how a protest movement of the working classes comes into being."[141] Such historiography and its antisocialist orientation may count other presentations within dominant theology among its own: those of Troeltsch[142] and, following him, Theissen[143] and numerous authors in the United States.[144] At the center of attention are Paul, an upper-class man,[145] women of the upper class, and educated men.

My critique is not directed against the assumption that rich women and educated men were part of the Christian communities but against the fact that, on account of them, the majority of the uneducated, poor, and weak (in the sense of 1 Cor. 1:26ff.) becomes invisible and the gospel of the poor and the option for women disappears. Contentious women prophets, who at one time had to live their lives without education and with excessive demands made on them, nevertheless gain a new space in the community and self-respect in groups of solidarity. Interpretive traditions such as those cited here turn them into squabbling hags against whom Paul quite properly defends himself[146] or into status seekers.[147] The repudiation of the "stigma" of social inferiority exacts a high price above all from women, who make up the majority of the uneducated and poor and who become the dummies of history or simply invisible. But in early Christianity they are the active subjects of an inspiring story, which even their Christian and non-Christian enemies concede.

D. FEMINIST PERSPECTIVES: BITTER MUSTARD

Because there is not enough money on which to survive, a woman must earn additional income, for example, as a street vendor. Work is not a means to self-realization as it might be for women with advanced education; rather, it is a sheer necessity. A woman has to work for pay, even though she does not want to. She must, in order to survive. Even if he is active in peoples' movements, the man has no idea that both must work in the home.

That is how Elsa Tamez[148] described the point of departure of a contextual feminist liberation theology in Latin America. The option for women is taken up first by women themselves. "In the past decades, women have become very actively engaged in processes of liberation and in the struggle for life on many, diverse levels."[149] A vision of all-embracing justice nourishes the option for women.[150] Every child's life is valuable; therefore, justice work has to create new options for street children in metropolitan Latin America. It seeks to abolish megatechnologies such as nuclear power stations that even now threaten children's lives. Every woman's life is valuable; therefore, it is a scandal before God that the majority of women in every nation on earth are forced into badly paid work and their lives are marked by the fight for survival. In the context of the so-called first world (which it still must be called, even after the demise of Eastern bloc socialism), a feminist theology of liberation can develop. It begins where women no longer allow themselves to be invisible objects of the machinations of dominant power but name injustice and together build community.

It is the experience of women's movements that women's communities of solidarity are the matrix of justice. That experience has a long history. Early Christianity already shows that justice was conceived in women's communities. For me, the contentious prophets, like Hannah and Mary, awakened the inspiration for a praxis of what we call today the option for the poor and for women. The gospel of the poor is decided in the option for women. The misogynist Syrian *Didaskalia* said that the mustard seed of the gospel becomes bitter and sharp[151] if it is not expertly prepared by men in leadership positions who function from a sense of dominance. This sharp and bitter mustard of women's prophecy tastes of justice and liberation—as it did yesterday, so it does today.

3

Impenitent Patriarchy and the
Nearness of God (Matt. 24:37–39;
Luke 17:26–27, 30; and Mark 13:28–33):
The Eschatology of Early Christianity

A. THE TEXTS

This chapter addresses the eschatology[152] of early Christianity and its power in the critique of patriarchy, which is also a source of hope. My examples of representative texts are a word of judgment and a parable of hope.

The word of judgment[153] is found in Matt. 24:37–39 and Luke 17:26–27, 30; it is already contained in the Sayings Source of the Gospels. Both versions of this announcement of God's judgment on the final generation after the Flood are identical except for some inconsequential details. The word begins with an eschatological typology of history: the generation preceding the coming of the Human One for judgment corresponds to the generation of the Flood in the days of Noah (Matt. 24:37; Luke 17:26). Then the analogy is filled in: the generation before the Flood ate[154] and drank, married[155] (Luke 17:30) or gave daughters in marriage (Matt. 24:38), until the day Noah entered the ark and the Flood came and swept everything away. The conclusion of the word comprises the announcement of judgment: as was the day of the Flood, so will be the day (Luke 17:30) or the arrival (Matt. 24:39) of the Human One. The central idea remains unexpressed, but it is implicitly quite apparent: the generation now also eats and drinks, marries, and goes on as usual[156] until the judgment of the Human One comes upon and judges those people.

The parable of hope about the fig tree and the eschatological sayings that follow it (Mark 13:28–33) make a connection between the seasons of the year and the expectations of God's reign.

There has been much reflection on what the pre-Markan tradition of this parable and the eschatological sayings may have been. But the attempts to determine pre-Markan substance have remained speculations; it is more reliable to understand the text from its existing literary context. This allows one to establish in particular what those intentionally mysterious formulations mean: "when you see *these things* taking place" (v. 29) and "this generation will not pass away before *all these things* take place" (v. 30). The apocalyptic prophecy in Mark 13 and elsewhere in Jewish and Christian apocalyptic distinguishes the actual "end" ("all these things," v. 30) from the portents of approaching end, its "birth pangs" (Mark 13:7, 8, 13, 24–27; "these things," v. 29).

The portents of the end are the actual and expected catastrophes, which cause people to be fearful (13:7f.). But these catastrophes do not culminate in the catastrophes of the end of the world; apocalyptic thinking has often been misinterpreted this way, so that the word *apocalyptic* has this negative meaning even in everyday language. Apocalyptic prophecies such as this one in Mark 13:28ff. (or 13:3ff.) are *texts of hope*. The horrors of the present and of the near future are understood as the passing birth pangs, at the end of which comes the birth of the new heaven and the new earth. God desires salvation, seeking to gather the scattered people together again through the Human One (13:27). In this context the word *end* is a word of hope: at last the end of misery is at hand.

The parable of the sprouting fig tree (13:28–29) takes up people's illusory certainty about the course of nature and the security they derive from the cycle of the seasons. If it is April and the fig tree has leaves, summer must be near. On God's seasonal calendar it is April now, and you may be certain that the Human One is near (v. 29 must be put together with v. 27), for you see the signs of the end.

This parable has often been interpreted as an announcement of God's final and all-encompassing judgment. But this prevents the understanding of apocalyptic language as a language of hope. In the face of catastrophic wars, earthquakes, and famines in Palestine, the people said that those were portents of the nearness of God, who through the Human One gathers and saves the people. The good end is at hand. The tree in springtime is a picture of hope (cf. Joel 2:22; Song of Songs 2:10–13). Pictures like this may also be used to announce the judgment (cf. Luke 12:54–56; Amos 8:1f.). Even the word *harvest* is used to identify God's judgment (cf. Matt. 13:30); at other times, *harvest* speaks of hope: God will gather together (cf. Matt. 9:37). There is no doubt that in the Jesus tradition the expectation of God's salvation cannot be separated from the expectation of God's judgment; but in Mark 13:28f., the conclusion of the apocalyptic speech that begins at 13:5, the judgment to come is not the heart of the matter. It is rather the hope of the women and men who follow Jesus and who live in fear; it is *they* who are addressed in this text. Luke 21:28 describes quite clearly what will happen to those addressed when the events occur of which this parable speaks: "When these things [namely, the portents of the end] begin to take place, arise and lift up your heads, because your redemption is drawing near."

The eschatological sayings following the parable assure those addressed that God's intervention for humanity's salvation is close at hand.

Mark 13:30 declares that the coming of the Human One will occur during the lifetime of the current generation.

Verse 31 (cf. Isa. 51:6) asserts that Jesus' prophecies will remain when (the old) heaven and (the old) earth pass away, and as one could add with Rev. 21:1ff., a new heaven and a new earth will be the dwelling place of God and humanity. When I bring the idea of an old and a new creation, of a new heaven and a new earth, into my own time and context, I face the problem that we, the children of a throwaway culture, may hear these word pictures in such a way that we may pollute and exhaust our old earth, our old heaven, and our old ocean without any concern. Of course, those biblical pictures have a different meaning: God wants to put an end to humanity's suffering and to give people a new space, a new, unspoiled creation.

Verses 32 and 33 say that no one but God knows the time of salvation, its day and hour. These statements are often understood—mistakenly, in my view—as indications of delayed Parousia.[157] They are, rather, genuine aspects of apocalyptic expectation of a near end (cf., e.g., Zech. 14:7; *Pss. Sol.* 17:23), which precisely does not want people to calculate the time that remains[158] and just rest their hands in their laps. These verses immediately go on to say that people should open their eyes instead and be watchful, wait joyfully for God, and live in sober attentiveness to the catastrophes that people cause, which are the signs both of their guilt and of the horrors yet to come. Hopeful alertness marks those who follow Jesus; in the face of the coming end, of God's nearness, they do not rest their hands in their laps but begin now to gather those who are dispersed, to heal and upbuild them, just as the Human One will at the end of days. In early Christianity the expectation of the imminent end did not lead to a relativizing of everyday conduct; it led to the doing of Christ's deeds (Matt. 11:2 and par.) here and now. The women and men who followed Jesus like him gathered the dispersed, healed the sick, and brought people together so that in their festive meals they could have a foretaste of the bread of God's new creation. They did Christ's work "in patience" (Mark 13:13),[159] which in the language of the New Testament means tenacity, perseverance, and power of resistance.

Matthew 24:37–39 and Luke 17:26–27, 30 criticize the impenitent ignorance of patriarchy's persistence in actions and thoughts that see the future in a linear way, as the natural continuation of what already is. Mark 13:28–33 brings together acting and thinking based in hope with a cyclical image of time, on the one hand, and the notion of the imminent end of the world and the beginning of the new, on the other.

B. SOCIAL-HISTORICAL QUESTIONS ABOUT MATT. 24:37–39 AND LUKE 17:26–27, 30

The Patriarchal Household

Even though women could be proactive agents in their own marriage,[160] and even though their actions in the contracting of marriage find linguistic expression in the New Testament (Mark 10:12; 1 Cor. 7:28b, 34; 1 Tim. 5:11, 14), these two versions of Jesus' saying make invisible the actuality of women being of age. In the Matthean version, the father (or guardian)[161] and the grown-up son are the actors. In the Lukan version, the couple is spoken of: he marries, she is being married and is once again the object of men's actions. The androcentrism of the Sayings Source is more rigid than reality.

It is difficult to decide whether to favor Matthew or Luke in relation to Q. Luke's description of the patriarchal household (Luke 14:20 and 26; 18:29) depicts the woman in the house (albeit not as someone who acts independently) more frequently than do the parallel passages in Matthew. In contrast, Matthew is more interested than the Lukan texts in describing the patriarchal household as a father-and-son domain (Matt. 10:34–36, 37). In its substance, the difference is insignificant, for the perspective of both is that of the male actors in a patriarchal household. Matthew 24:38 makes no mention of the mother of the sons who marry or the daughters who are being married (cf. Luke 15:11–32; Matt. 21:28–32). In light of these observations, one may ask why Luke 14:26 and 18:29 speak of wives. Is it because he, unlike Mark and Matthew (and the Sayings Source), does envisage a Christian praxis of men renouncing their marriages?[162] Or is he interested rather in describing the renunciation of the whole household on the part of the paterfamilias and therefore has to refer to the woman as an item of the household? Matthew 10:37 does not need to mention the wife, not because she is not being left behind but because a patriarchal household can be described without referring to the mother of the children. It was Christian praxis that women and men renounced marriage (women more often than men) for the sake of the gospel or that couples both embraced the gospel.[163]

There are descriptions in Luke of the patriarchal household that take up these thoughts from the Sayings Source and develop them (Luke 17:28 and 14:18–20). In the first of those texts, the household is described in terms of its economic activity: buying, selling, planting, building; in the second, we hear about purchasing a field, buying five yoke of oxen, and marrying a woman. Luke thinks of such activities as being typical and important in the patriarchal household of the master of a large farm;[164] obviously, they prevent him from accepting an invitation to (God's) feast. Attention is focused, here as in Luke 17:27, on the "boss" of the household, the father or the adult son who has been given procuration, like the lost son to whom the father has handed the signet ring (Luke 15:22).[165] The description given of the patriarchal household in the Sayings Source (Matt. 24:38; Luke 17:27) is terser: eating, drinking, marrying, giving in marriage or being married; it might be that it generally presupposes, as do Matthew and Mark, that poverty is the "normal" situation of people's lives, whereas Luke directs attention again and again to the upper-class households.[166] Of course, buying and selling happens also in poor households, but Luke's listing of activities in 17:28 manifests a good deal of patriarchal consciousness,[167] which is not so blatant in Matt. 24:38 and Luke 17:27.

In every instance referred to, the text's critique of patriarchy focuses on the behavior of the men who rule over the household. It is their entirely "normal" conduct that is blameworthy. What does not meet with reproach in this business-as-usual scenario of patriarchal dominance is the oppression and exploitation that this normalcy afflicts on women, children, and the enslaved; rather, the critique is focused on the fact that people conform to this rule *even though* God demands that God's will be done and that the women and men who teach God's will be listened to, in other words, that people break with business as usual, let go of it, and live different lives. Matthew 22:30 and Luke 20:35 incorporate from Mark 12:25 that in God's reign people do not marry and are not being married. What is the perspective from which Mark 12:25 and par. and Matt. 24:37–39 speak about marriage? Is it that of sexuality in general or that of the patriarchal interest in the production of legitimate progeny?[168] Whenever women refuse marriage,[169] patriarchal marriage is referred to as a relationship in which love and sexuality play a part. Sexuality was not a normal dimension of the patriarchal household as its male actors saw it.[170] Even the discussion of levirate marriage (Mark 12:18–27 and par.) does not focus on sexual needs but on patriarchal concerns with assuring progeny. In Matt. 24:38 and Luke 17:27, it is the business-as-usual behavior of the patriarchal household—eating, drinking, producing children, as if nothing had happened—that is found guilty.

In this context, eating and drinking in a patriarchal house do not look like the elementary human necessity to survive but much more like activities that occupy energies and interests which should be channeled toward doing God's will. Attention is directed on supper as the chief meal and primary *social focus* of the house. The text does not name the alternative, but it seeks to raise questions about it: for those who listen to the voice of God's messengers, the place for the evening meal is *no longer* to be sought in the patriarchal home but in the company of women and men who follow Jesus. The text's acerbic and radical but also androcentric critique of impenitent patriarchy reduces the existence of women in the patriarchal household to that of wives, that is to say, to birthgivers. That eating and drinking are, as a rule, the product of women's labor has escaped notice.

The work of women is placed in an eschatological context in Matt. 24:41 and Luke 17:35. But the context of those verses is different from that of Matt. 24:38 and Luke 17:27. The two women grinding at the mill are separated by God's judgment: one is accepted by God but not the other ("she did not want to listen to the voice of God's messenger" is how one might continue that sentence); Matt. 24:38 and Luke 17:27 are about impenitently persisting as usual; Matt. 24:41 and Luke 17:35 speak of the separation of two people who were only inches apart.

Apocalyptic Conceptions of Time

On the basis of my observations (above) on Matt. 24:37–39; Luke 17:26–27, 30; and Mark 13:28–33, I now want to examine the Synoptic Gospels' conception of time in texts that are eschatological—in the more rigorous sense of that word.[171] Because the interpretive tradition of these texts is governed by the notion of linear time (more on that in the next section), it is necessary to relinquish that view in order to see these texts in a new way. If I look at statements about the "nearness" of God's reign in the sense of linear time that goes on into infinity, God's reign will indeed appear as an exotic, obsolete notion that counts on time coming to an end, even within a foreseeable period ("expectation of the imminent end"). If I relinquish that view, it will be possible to see that the eschatological texts of the Synoptic Gospels contain very different conceptions of time. They speak of the time of watching and waiting in the night, the time of joy at a marriage feast, the time of a woman's labor pains, the time of alarm over losing one's security, the time of growing and ripening—of trees, seed, bread dough rising. These eschatological texts, like those of the entire Jewish apocalyptic, are *announcements of what time it is now*.[172] They tell of jubilation and of being able to wait, of stubbornness and of getting up, of waking and of giving birth. They speak of the rhythm of life between day and night, of the rhythm of the seasons. And they speak of the sudden terror that puts an end to patriarchal management of the time that keeps on as usual.

I gather textual examples from four different sources.

The Time of Alarm over Losing One's Security

Matt. 24:37–39; Luke 17:26–27, 30 (see above; Sayings Source; Matthew; Luke)
> The present generation lives, like the generation of the Flood, in ignorant security, believing that in the patriarchal house marrying (producing children), eating, and drinking will go on as always. The arrival of the Human One will come on them as the Flood engulfed that earlier generation.

1 Thess. 5:2f. (Paul)
> When people proclaim "peace and security" (cf. Jer. 6:14), destruction comes on them suddenly, like a thief in the night or like labor pains to a pregnant woman.

Luke 12:16–21 (a parable unique to Lukan tradition)
> The rich farmer hoards wheat in order to push up its price. He sees himself heading for good times and many years of affluence. "This very night" God will call him to account. The fright over the farmer's sudden death is a parable for the rude fall from security of those who believe that their material future is well in hand.

Luke 13:6–9 (unique to Lukan tradition)
> For three years the owner has waited in vain for the fig tree to bear fruit. He intends to have the tree cut down. But because the vinedresser who

looks after the tree begs him to give it more time, he grants the request. The reprieve is limited, but God waits with the judgment.

Matt. 3:10; Luke 3:9 (Sayings Source; Matthew; Luke)
"The ax is laid even now to the root of the tree" is a word of John the Baptist, the meaning of which is not different from what Jesus said about expecting the judgment to come.

Matt. 22:1–14; Luke 14:15–24 (Sayings Source; Matthew; Luke)
The invited guests deem their business interests (or their commerce and marriage) to be more important than the feast and do not want to know that they irretrievably forfeit their salvation. In the parable there is a plea to hear God's invitation and to act accordingly.

Other texts are Matt. 25:31–46; 13:24–30; 11:20–24; Luke 10:12–15; Matt. 10:15; Luke 6:24–26. They all picture the sudden end of security: the confrontation with God's judgment. The structure of security depicted is that of political domination (1 Thess. 5:2f.) or of the patriarchal household and its economic organization. Patriarchal security is characterized as an impenitent refusal to listen. The texts give a sense of how thin the ice is under the feet of those who think that their future is materially secured by the patriarchal support system.

Now is the time before the catastrophe; there is still time to turn back. Texts such as these are not spoken from the perspective of rich, patriarchal men. They are spoken with the critical outlook of those who are alarmed over the impenitent obstinacy of rich, patriarchal men who carry on as they always have. The perspective is critical of patriarchy but androcentric; the voices we hear are those of women and men whose everyday lives are not marked by affluence and patriarchal order and whose vantage points are external to that affluence and order.

The Time of Growing and Ripening

Mark 13:28–33 and par. (see above; Mark; Matthew; Luke)
The sight of a fig tree's sprouting leaves and the succulence of its branches in springtime fills people with confident hope for the summer and the ripe fruits it brings.

In spite of the current suffering inflicted by war and persecution (Mark 13:7–13 and par.), those who trust in God see signs of hope in the present: summer is near, the Human One—the liberator of creation—is near. This nearness transforms those who despair into springtime people, into people of hope. The knowledge that summer is near is faith's primary experience. One destroys the meaning of this nearness when one forces it into the Procrustean bed of a linear conception of time. The nearness of the Human One or of God transforms the present into springtime; it has nothing to do with a timetable ("the Human One will arrive in a few years at the latest").

Matt. 13:33/Luke 13:20f. (Sayings Source; Matthew; Luke)
The parable of the leaven (see above, II. 2) directs attention to the moment
when fermentation sets in. The woman has mixed flour and leaven together
and covered the dough. Now she waits for the leaven to finish its work.

Mark 4:26–29 (unique to Mark)
The parable of the seed that grows—no one knows how—calls up the won-
derful experience that seed grows without human beings doing anything
to help. They sow and harvest, but God causes growth (cf. 1 Cor. 3:6).[173]

In a very particular way, this parable has given rise to the idea that human beings
contribute nothing to the coming of God's reign, and provides support for the
separation of faith and works.[174] This theological axiom is grafted onto a number
of other texts as well, such as the parable of the leaven. The parable of the seed
that grows while the women and men who work the fields run their course in the
rhythm of day and night has no intention of declaring that people cannot and
should not try to work for God's reign. Rather, the parable wants to give people
the confidence that God's wondrous action accompanies all who work for God's
reign. Growing wheat fields tell of God's wondrous action to liberate people for
God's reign, for genuine life. The equanimity that characterizes people who know
that God lets life grow—in the fields and among human beings—is not passivity.
Such people will do their work for God's reign, without fanfare of self-importance
and hyperactivity, precisely because they are not alone in that work. I imagine such
equanimity when I think of parents who are confident that their children will not
only be the "products" of their educational successes and failures but will also
grow in the warmth of God's love, which goes with them.

Mark 4:30–32 (Sayings Source; Mark; Matthew; Luke)
The parable of the mustard seed[175] interprets the present moment of those
who follow Jesus in terms of the dynamic power of a little seed and in terms
of the future of a worldwide commonwealth of divine peace, in which human domination over humans is past. God's reign has already begun; now
is the moment of the mustard seed.

Other texts in this category are, for example, Matt. 9:37–38; Luke 10:2 (Sayings Source; Matthew; Luke) (cf. above at III.3.A); Mark 4:3–9 and par. (Mark;
Matthew; Luke).

These eschatological texts express an experience of time and people who think
in pastoral and theological categories. Their perception of time[176] incorporates
their dependence on plants for nourishment. For that reason summer is eagerly
anticipated, but it is also the reason for cutting down a tree that bears no fruit. To
look upon fruit-bearing trees, growing wheat fields, and sprouting mustard seeds
is to look upon God's present and wondrous activities in creation; they open a
window on God's action on behalf of humankind and human life now and in the

coming reign of God. To discuss the nature parables of the Jesus tradition in terms of the contrast-*or*-growth schema is to miss the texts altogether. The parable of the mustard seed, for example, is about the contrast and elevation of the lowly, but the plant's growth naturally also plays a role.[177] The idea of growth was theologically suspect to those generations of Christians who saw it in conjunction with God's reign as the outcome of moral progress.[178] But the experience of the people in the Gospels' parables of growth, people who think in agricultural categories, is not the experience of time associated with the conceptuality of progress. Instead, it is the experience of the believing equanimity and hope of those who see God's nearness to humanity in the rhythm of days and seasons.

The Time of Watching in the Night

Slaves guarding the gate by night may not sleep when the master of the house is absent (Mark 13:34–36; cf. Matt. 24:42). They must await his return even when they do not know the time of his arrival. The owner of a house, fearing that a thief might break in during the night, will not go to sleep but will be very watchful (1 Thess. 5:2, 4; Matt. 24:43; Luke 12:39–40). Staying awake, ready to take flight (Luke 21:36), prepared to move at any time of the night with lamp lit (Luke 12:35) or fully prepared (Matt. 25:1–13)—these images make most concrete the admonitions to be watchful (cf. above on Mark 13:32, 33 at III.3.A).

A slave entrusted with the care of other slaves in the absence of the overlord must reckon with the owner's return at any time, even when there is a delay (*chronizein*); so declares the parable of the good and the bad slave in the Sayings Source (Matt. 24:45–51; Luke 12:41–46). The parable is not about the *delay* of the Parousia, even though it speaks (like Matt. 25:5) about a delay in the expected arrival. It is the watchfulness of those who do not know when they are to be present that the parable speaks of, and not the delay of the Parousia. The time of watching in the night is explained in terms of experiences of fear: slaves must fear their owners if they do not stay awake or act as they had been told; waiting for a thief in the night or taking flight is a tense and fear-filled time. The ten virgins are in a situation of female slaves as well, who are punished if they do not complete their assigned task (Matt. 25:1–13). Here God's nearness is described as that of an angry God who sits in judgment. And people need to fear this angry God's nearness as slaves fear their owners when they fail in their duties. This does not legitimate slavery at all;[179] the experience that all slaves, female and male, know so well becomes a parable for the tense waiting for the coming of the Human One or for God's judgment on humankind. The strain of slaves watching through the night is a parable for the watchful expectation of God's judgment.

The Time of Festive Rejoicing

Jesus' presence is experienced as a feast by those who see and understand it as the presence of the people's messianic liberator; we are guests at a marriage, they say, seated at a festive table, eating (Mark 2:19 and par.). "Blessed your eyes because they see; blessed your ears because they hear" (Matt. 13:16; cf. Luke 10:23). Jesus' messianic deeds tell those who see and hear that they no longer need to wait for the liberator: he has come (Matt. 11:2–6 and par.). "He has done all things well" (Mark 7:37). Elijah, the messianic messenger, has been here (Matt. 11:27; Luke 10:22). The jubilation (Acts 2:46) of the festive joy celebrates the presence of God's reign in the healing that Jesus and his followers bring, in the community of the poor who no longer need to go hungry. Supper shared together becomes the celebration of remembering Jesus' death and the occasion to rejoice in the presence of salvation. Acts 2:46 refers to the dimension of joy during the meal that often unjustly disappears in traditional Christian appropriation of the New Testament tradition of the Last Supper (Mark 14:22–25 and par.; 1 Cor. 11:23–26). The Christian Eucharist derives its order and festive form from traditions of festive meals in Jerusalem. The eschatological context to which this feast belongs is alluded to in the jubilation referred to in Acts 2:46, but also in the expectant waiting for the arrival of the *kyrios* (1 Cor. 11:26).

Eschatological texts of the New Testament speak of experiences of time on the basis of diverse levels of tradition; those experiences see the present in relation to God. God is near: it is the time for growing and ripening, of being roused from the slumber of patriarchy's confidence in its structures of alleged security; it is the time of the ominous strain of watching slaves and the time of festive rejoicing.

These examples show that the texts of Paul and the Synoptic Gospels, on every discernible level of tradition, interpret the present in relation to God's nearness and do so in terms of identical content. Only when these experiences of time are assessed in terms of linear time does there arise a contradiction between the festive joy about the Messiah's presence and, for example, the fear-filled watch of slaves. Seen in the perspective of linear time, Mark 2:19 and par. (to cite an example) speaks in terms of a present eschatology, while other texts may be read as functioning with a shorter or longer expectation of the future. But precisely this linear view of time is quite alien to the texts. People who follow Jesus experience festive joy as well as the challenge to meet God's judgment. They work for God's coming reign; they also rest their hands in equanimity.

These experiences of time are rooted in the everyday experience of Jesus' followers. They are dismayed about the confidence of patriarchal overlords that everything will go on as before. Other everyday experiences are those of agricultural workers who perceive nature as the provider of food, the fear of slaves of the accounting that will be demanded of them when the owner returns home, and the blessedness of shared meals that feed the hungry and create communities of solidarity.

The Synoptic Gospels, which reflect a longer process of tradition, show that it was quite possible for generations to live with the sense of God's nearness without ever wondering whether God should not have established the kingdom long ago. Believers hear that question only from the lips of their despisers (2 Peter 3:4f.; *1 Clem.* 23:3); the question of the delayed Parousia does not occur to believers. The expectation of God's imminent coming is part of faith. Those who believe do expect strength and justice from God's nearness.

"Woe to Those with Child . . . ": The Social-Historical Context of Apocalyptic Experiences of Suffering and Hope

From the point of view of social history, the expectation of judgment and salvation manifest in (Jewish and) Christian apocalyptic is really the political and religious medium of a people, or peoples, whose suffering in oppression makes them long for "the end." However much war and rumors of war and other terrible political events are experiences of suffering, whenever they are seen as signs of an imminent good end (Mark 13:7 and par.), people are convinced: it cannot and will not go on forever, for God's sake. And yet, in the same town, there are houses where people live as if things would in fact go on forever as before. The Gospels name in the apocalyptic speeches of Jesus the following experiences and foreboding of suffering: the destruction of the Temple in Jerusalem (Mark 13:2 and par.) after its desecration (Mark 13:14 and par.) by the Romans (they alone could be the perpetrators of such action at that time); wars (Mark 13:7 and par.); earthquakes and famine (Mark 13:8 and par.) and the plague (Luke 21:11). By then, the Christian community also knew persecution by Roman authorities;[180] there had been executions (Mark 13:12 and par.).

Such apocalyptic hopes for an end that will bring God's judgment and a reign of godly peace on earth and in heaven are to be found in every dimension of the early Christian tradition. This indicates that both Jewish fisherfolk at the Sea of Galilee and non-Jewish people at the time of Paul, for example, in Thessalonica, shared in apocalyptic thinking. This kind of apocalyptic thinking resists being classified as Jewish or Hellenistic thinking, related to an urban or rural context, or belonging to the time of the historical Jesus or the end of the first century C.E. Christian communities believe themselves to be suffering oppression, persecution, and poverty, waiting for God's reign. But in the same town live those who are embodied by the rich wheat farmer or the patriarchal paterfamilias who does not want to hear the message of Jesus; it is the upper class of the Jewish people in the Hellenistic and Roman cities who collaborate with Rome. It is their hope that the present will go on ad infinitum, while their victims hope for the end of suffering and for a new creation.

Sociological functionalism attempts to interpret apocalyptic thinking by relating it to the conflicts between sects and majorities, "in-groups" and "out-groups"; what they do not consider is the political and economic situation of the people, in this instance, the people during the Pax Romana.[181] However, that reality is crucially important in determining the social-historical location of the expectation of God's reign within early Christianity. In addition, all New Testament texts urge one to take seriously, in all its dreadful dimensions, the re-
of oppression that the majority of the population experienced at the time

of Rome's heralded peace, the Pax Romana.[182] Every page speaks of it, from Matthew 1 to Revelation 22. The issue is not to stabilize a minority group by means of threatening the majority with judgment but to find strength for resisting and living in the midst of the painful burden of the Pax Romana.

Only *one* New Testament text refers explicitly to what suffering will afflict women in those catastrophes of their present time that apocalyptic thinking interprets as the portents of the coming end. That text is Mark 13:17 and par.: "Woe to those who are with child and to those who nurse a child in those days." The Judean population is in flight into the hill country before the approaching army of Rome. In this prophecy of doom, pregnant and nursing women are identified as the first casualties of flight. Why are they the first victims? The text is not even thinking of the gruesome actions of victorious armies—in this instance, those of Rome—who cut open the bellies of pregnant women and smash infant children.[183] Pregnant and nursing women are the first victims even while fleeing before the victors give vent to their brutality.

Josephus recounts a flight that may explain why these women are the first victims. The location is the town of Gishala during the Jewish–Roman war of 66–70 C.E. Confronted by the superior power of the Roman commander, Titus by name, and his one thousand horsemen, the Jewish commander John, son of Levi, flees (Josephus, *Bell. Jud.* 4.2.4). He takes his fighting men with him, but also noncombatants and their families. He finds it difficult to keep everyone together in retreat, and after a little more than two miles, he abandons the women and children. "Many also of them missed their ways; and the earnestness of such as aimed to outgo the rest threw down many of them. And indeed there was a miserable destruction made of the women and children; while some of them took courage to call their husbands and kinsmen back and to beseech them, with the bitterest lamentations, to stay for them" (4.2.4).[184] As the military leader, John of Gishala orders the men to leave women and children behind. They are pushed off the road. Every man runs as fast as he can (4.2.4). According to military logic, the first victims during flight are one's own women and children. Not named explicitly are the aged, but they too are among the casualties; elsewhere they are named with women and children. Mark 13:17 makes plain the logic of military thinking in which women and children, not to mention pregnant and nursing women, are only a hindrance during flight. Wars are not conducted for their protection or for their freedom. They are fought for the freedom of the freeborn men. During the flight from Gishala, women protest in vain to the men who follow the orders of John.

The social-historical background of apocalyptic thinking at that time is named in the texts themselves: it is, above all, war, rumors of impending war, and famine. Mark 13 and the apocalypse of John (esp. Rev. 6:1–8) describe those hardships from an androcentric perspective. Therefore, one must really hunt if one wishes to find out anything about the fate of women, children, the aged, and the sick in times of war and famine.

Revelation 6:5f. says the following about famine: "Behold, a black horse, and its rider had a balance in his hand. And I heard what seemed to be a voice in the midst of the four living creatures, saying: 'A measure [*choinix*] of wheat for a denarius and three measures of barley meal for a denarius, but spare the olive and the vine.'"

According to this text, famine means that one day's pay of a male wage earner in the fields, one denarius (Matt. 20:1–16), covers the cost of one person's daily requirement of wheat. One *choinix* is the measure of wheat paid to a soldier per day.[185] As I showed above (II.3.B), in normal times women earned barely half per day what male daily-wage earners were paid. Even in normal times, the yearly income of that earner was not enough for one family. A famine was no rare occurrence;[186] when it struck, the price of grain went up to such a degree that, according to Rev. 6:5, a male daily-wage earner just managed to survive. But there is more to basic human needs than grain for the day: clothing, shelter, and so forth. And what happens to women and children?

Josephus's depiction of the famine in besieged Jerusalem before its capture by the Romans in 70 C.E. is an important source for answering this question. Jewish soldiers in the city (having made Rome's perspective his own, Josephus refers to them as "the seditious") plunder houses and torture the inhabitants so that they will reveal where they have hidden food. Wheat is a rich people's staple; they too are affected by such hardships. Barley was much more a poor people's foodstuff (Josephus, *Bell. Jud.* 5.10.2).

> It was now a miserable case, and a sight that would justly bring tears into our eyes, how men stood as to their food, while the more powerful had more than enough, and the weaker were lamenting [for want of it]. But the famine was too hard for all other passions, and it is destructive to nothing so much as to modesty; for what was otherwise worthy of reverence, was in this case despised; insomuch that children pulled the very morsels that their fathers were eating, out of their very mouths, and what was still more to be pitied, so did the mothers do as to their infants. (5.10.3)

The text continues the description of how these "seditious" violently plundered their own citizens. Their victims are the aged, women, and small children (5.10.3). This text and others[187] identify the aged, women, and children as the first victims of famine; they also picture the reversal of patriarchal order: women take food from children.

The famine in Rev. 6:6 is only a "regular" famine measured against the hunger suffered in the besieged Jerusalem; there the war caused death from starvation. In a "regular" famine, people like the rich wheat farmer, who exercise power, are not interested in population control by means of starvation but in maximizing profit from their scarce grain. The price of grain climbs to the point where men and animals become unable to work: one measure (*choinix*) of wheat for one denarius and three measures of barley for one denarius, for the animals must not die; the three measures of barley are identified as the animals' feed.[188] In a war, by contrast, starvation is a means of population extermination. In a "regular" famine, the first victims are women, children, and the aged, but not all of them will die. In starvation caused by war, they are the first to perish, and only after them do the conquered soldiers die.

In a legend, Josephus describes how war and famine upset the order of patriarchy. I want to speak of it as a document of patriarchal historiography of women. A mother kills her child. I do not intend to disclaim that women are capable of slaughtering their children; what I am saying is that it is a patriarchal perspective from which Josephus describes the horrors of dying from starvation.

He tells of Mary, daughter of Eleazar (*Bell. Jud.* 6.3.4), who before the war fled from the village of Perea to Jerusalem. Every day, like every other home of the civilian population, her lodging is searched for food by their own soldiers. She tries to make the soldiers kill her, by frequent reproaches and imprecations. For Josephus, her extreme desperation depicts the height of the wretchedness of the Jewish people. Threatened with death by starvation by her own people's soldiers or by enslavement by the Romans, she kills her child, a boy whom she is still nursing. She sees no future for him anymore: "O thou miserable infant! for whom shall I preserve thee in this war, this famine, and this sedition?" She roasts the slain child. "Come on; be thou my food, and be thou a fury to these seditious varlets and a byword to the world, which is all that is now wanting to complete the calamities of us Jews" (6.3.4). Immediately the plunderers return, drawn by the smell of the roast. In horror they draw back from the food, but it does not help them because the mother has eaten in their place. She calls the killing a sacrifice (*thysia*) and demands that the Jewish men eat of it.

The story belongs to the tradition of narratives about the hardships of starvation inflicted on besieged cities when the population is to be eliminated.[189] The abyss of horror has come when, from sheer starvation, parents eat their children.[190] Mothers eating their own children is seen, as it is here, as a destruction of human order that cannot get any worse. There are texts which suggest that fathers are even more susceptible to cannibalism than mothers.[191] Given Josephus's motives, one may be tempted to judge this story of Mary, daughter of Eleazar, to be his literary invention to convey how dreadful was the Jewish population's misery. However, contradictions within the text invite a more careful analysis, even if not every word describes historical facts. There is contradiction in that the mother does not kill her child for her own survival, even though she eats the child. She wants to die herself and kills the child because he has no future. She speaks of sacrifice and that the child is to be an avenging spirit against the plundering Jewish soldiers. Josephus may well want to portray Jews fighting against Rome as criminals and destroyers of their own people, but the confrontation between Mary and the Jewish soldiers does not quite match the tenor of that intent. Mary at first tries to get the soldiers to kill her. Then, against their wills, she involves them in the eating of the child. In her eyes, it is they who, through their horrendous plundering, have brought the greater guilt on themselves. One may ask whether Mary makes her sacrifice of the child in the tradition of child sacrifice by besieged royalty,[192] who sought to assuage the divinity so that an enemy would become defeatable. But the legend of Mary does not fit into this tradition. Indeed, she understands the killing as a sacrifice not for the liberation of Jerusalem but as a judgment on the Jewish soldiers, that is to say, those able-bodied men of her own people who could have acted on other options.

There is another contradiction in how Josephus describes the political consequences of that event (6.3.5); it throws light on the conflict between Mary and the Jewish soldiers. The killing of the child feeds the Romans' anti-Jewishness, "who were hereby induced to a more bitter hatred than ordinary." The emperor Titus blames the Jewish soldiers and uses the killing of a child as the reason for razing Jerusalem, a city "wherein mothers are thus fed." Josephus comments: "Such food be fitter for the fathers than for the mothers to eat of, since it is they that continue still in a state of war against us, after they have undergone such miseries as these." In Josephus's eyes, the Jewish soldiers were seditious against Rome and should have surrendered earlier. In Mary's eyes, they were active participants in destroying her own future and that of the child. Josephus interprets the deed as an abomination to which a woman is driven by hunger; for him, she is a woman dehumanized. Contrary to the intention of Josephus, Mary is a woman who knows that she and her child are being driven to death by able-bodied *men of her own people*. Unlike Josephus, she judges the Romans negatively. All she can expect from Rome is slavery, whereas he stresses again and again, as he does here, that Caesar "had proposed peace and liberty to the Jews" (6.3.5). Mary's political discernment is more realistic, and consequently, her critique of the Jewish men differs from his. She despairs about the conduct of able-bodied Jewish men toward children, women, and the aged.

Even though hunger in wartime is described in this legend from a patriarchal perspective, we still get a glimpse of women's experiences in political catastrophes and of their critique of men's conduct. If we read this legend together with Rev. 6:6, we will have to ask whether women did not have to reckon with men keeping their measure (*choinix*) of wheat for themselves, regarding it *as their right* as men to survive longer than women, children, and the aged.

That the first victims are pregnant and nursing women, to be followed by other women, children, and the aged, is not just the logic of an enemy's military. It is the logic as well of the actions of the men of one's own people. They take it for granted that in war and emergencies they, as men, must survive longer, even at the expense of women, children, and the aged.

When I first read the story of Mary, daughter of Eleazar, I was touched that it let a woman speak so explicitly. I came to understand only gradually, as I analyzed the text, that Mary goes against a patriarchal emergency rule, according to which able-bodied men *are permitted* to take food from women and children. Mary fought desperately against it, and with desperate means. Today, the first victims of environmental destruction in the interest of profit and industry are pregnant and nursing women. The legend of Mary in Josephus opened my eyes to the fact that, in my context also, able-bodied men take it to be their *right* to rob vulnerable people of the air and the water they need to live.

Mark 13:17 and par. give visibility to this fundamental patriarchal injustice: "Woe to the pregnant . . . " In spite of their androcentrism, these apocalyptic texts are sensitive to victims of catastrophes made by human beings. They are in the tradition of Jewish prophecy, which looks first to the victims. We owe it to his rootedness in Jewish tradition that even Josephus is—despite his patriarchal perspective—a very useful source of insight for the fate of women and children in wartime. In Lamentations, Jeremiah provides his orientation in describing war; reading Caesar's book on the Gallic Wars, I find he has room for victims only in passing.

Women's experience with enemy soldiers is rape, which victors also claim as their *right*. Other such experiences are enslavement, torture, murder, cutting open pregnant women, and smashing infant children. Inhuman acts of this kind are seen to be normal, albeit sad. Only when a mother slaughters her baby does she stand "human" order, that is, the order of patriarchy, on its head. For descriptions of the fate of women in times of war, I refer readers primarily to the portrayals of war in the Lamentations of Jeremiah, Josephus, and 2 Esd. 10:21–22.

The story of Mary, daughter of Eleazar, provides a certain insight into the perspective of women on the men of their own people during wartime; I know of no text from antiquity where one can learn from the perspective of women about women's experience of enemy soldiers in wartime. I remember from my own experiences of World War II the custom of women who, when the victorious armies were approaching, made themselves look as ugly as possible so as to deter rapists.

Jewish and early Christian apocalyptic was the medium of women and men who at that time had to expect and endure the age-old hardships of war and hunger inflicted on them by their Roman oppressor.[193] They were able to make sense of their suffering by means of apocalyptic prophecies and at the same time cling to the power of God, who would soon bring suffering to an end and who desires that there be peace also on earth: now is the time of war, but the summer of God is near.

C. FEMINIST CRITIQUE
OF THE HISTORY OF RECENT
INTERPRETATION OF EARLY CHRISTIANITY'S
ESCHATOLOGICAL TEXTS

Using recent Western interpretations of Matt. 24:37–39 and Luke 17:26–27, 30, I want to elucidate the injustice of a patriarchal perception of time intent on having current conditions (of domination) continue as before. Following on this, I will submit to a feminist critique a representative example of a general description of New Testament eschatology and pay particular attention to the role of the linear view of time.

"Instinctive Preoccupations"

Traditional scholarly interpretation of Matt. 24:37–39 and Luke 17:26–27, 30 is unaware that the text wants to typify the patriarchal household. In addition, the majority of interpretations do not notice that the guilt and impenitence of patriarchal life are at issue. Here are some examples of interpretation.

According to Bultmann, this saying threateningly "warns of the surprising suddenness of the parousia."[194] Siegfried Schulz develops this thought:

> The accent rests clearly on people not being prepared. There is no reference to any especially terrible sins of the people who are subject to perdition. Their only sin is that they believe themselves to be completely secure; for judgment breaks suddenly and unexpectedly precisely into the altogether too everyday carelessness of their instinctive preoccupations.[195]

The text wants to admonish people to be watchful, according to Schulz. But he makes no substantive connection between "eating, drinking, marrying or being married" and insufficient watchfulness. People may well go on with their "instinctive preoccupations," but they ought to be watchful. A number of interpretations follow this line.[196]

Other interpretations do make a substantive connection between insufficient watchfulness and the activities that are mentioned but continue to be seen as "instinctive preoccupations," as nourishment and sexuality. "Careless unpreparedness marks a generation that is absorbed in satisfying elementary needs. *Gamein* and *gamizesthai* are euphemisms for sexual intercourse" (Wolfgang Wiefel).[197] This assumes that there is a right and a wrong way to satisfy elementary needs. It is wrong, in the sense of the text, when human beings (men?) are "absorbed" in their elementary needs. Other interpreters say at this point that the generation of the Flood is "steeped in earthly business" and "absorbed" in satisfying elementary needs.[198] "Eating, drinking, marrying and being married, in themselves ethically unreproachable, are expressions of a false nonchalance."[199] "The reproach is obviously not directed against the activities of Noah's contemporaries as such but against their being captive to these functions; people forgot to pay attention to the signs of the times" (H. E. Tödt).[200]

Both types of interpretation confuse the (androcentric) description of patriarchy with the description of everyday human elementary needs. Even the interpreters who do make the substantive connection between everyday preoccupations and insufficient watchfulness argue for a changed way of satisfying elementary needs but not for the renunciation of the patriarchal household's privileges, an idea that should readily come to mind from Matt. 10:37 and Luke 14:26. What is not seen is that texts such as these criticize the manipulation of the future so that present privileges may continue. This is how the affluent and powerful imagine the shape of the future; to concede finiteness would rob them of their comforts.

Eschatological Christology

I have already responded critically to constructions of New Testament eschatology that conclude from their understanding of early Christian expectations of the imminent coming of God that social status has no bearing in this context (*interim ethics;* cf. III.1.C). The idea of the *delayed Parousia*—God's reign did not begin when expected—is associated with this construction of early Christian eschatology. In the perspective of this construction, the expectation of the imminent end must now be regarded as a "mistake." The notion of "enthusiasm" also belongs here, an eschatology that, misusing the expectation of an imminent return of Christ, wants complete and utter freedom even now. All these aspects of the construction of early Christian eschatology must be submitted to feminist critique. The claim that the "delayed Parousia" became a problem in many areas of early Christianity misinterprets the conceptions of time found in early Christian eschatology, as was shown in the foregoing section.[201] The victors of history, who take it for granted that things will go on as they have, pronounce the verdict of "mistake." The women of Corinth in particular have long been disqualified as "enthusiasts."[202] To disqualify Corinthian women as enthusiasts or "opponents of Paul," implicitly or explicitly, assists modern interpreters of Paul to disqualify the emancipatory striving of women in any and all actual historical situations.

The construction of New Testament exegesis in terms of the conceptions of an expected imminent return and the delay of the Parousia always went hand in hand with contrasting New Testament eschatology and Jewish apocalyptic, with the latter being judged negatively in an anti-Judaistic fashion. Jewish apocalyptic, it has often been said, was intent on determining the span of time left until the end.[203]

I want to address a recent general presentation of New Testament eschatology that seeks to overcome the construction of that eschatology which has shaped discussions since the introduction of A. Schweitzer and his followers' concept of "consistent eschatology." I have intentionally chosen an encyclopedic article that, as such (and overtly), claims to represent a research consensus. In actual fact, the article describes a Western world approach to New Testament eschatology, namely, one that interprets eschatological texts on the basis of New Testament Christology. In his 1982 article, published in *TRE*,[204] Günter Klein attributes the expectation of the imminent coming of God's reign to the historical Jesus only and not (or hardly at all) to post-Easter Christianity.

"It is beyond doubt that a dimension of futurity, in the sense of linear time, is appropriately attached to God's reign" (p. 272). That dimension is "different from that of earliest Christian eschatology" (p. 274), but "the superiority of the future over the present, experienced even now, implies *also* that, in the sense of this world's time, the future will relieve the present" (p. 274). As I understand that sentence, it seeks to form a bridge between Jesus' expectation of the imminent end that relativizes one's own present (it has a "transitory character"; p. 274), on the one hand, and, on the other, subsequent early Christian eschatology. It does so because Jesus, besides expecting God's reign to be near, reckoned implicitly with a "future in terms of the world's time," that is, with a time proceeding in linear manner.

According to Klein, earliest Christian eschatology after Easter, in all its diverse variations, is of one mind "in the decisive aspect, namely, in its orientation on the salvation that has already come in Christ and is permanently present" (p. 295). Post-Easter eschatology originates wholly from the presence of salvation on account of the Christ event, yet it never "submerges the unchanging futurity of salvation in its presence here and now" (p. 295). Thus it is accomplished that "eternal salvation and temporal welfare remain distinct for God's sake" (p. 297). According to Klein, one must distinguish between "the future that 'has been given, within limits, into human hands and that which God has reserved to himself'" (quoting Gerhard Ebeling approvingly). Therefore, "every project for the welfare of this world is eminently subject to the ideological critique" of the eschatological proviso (p. 297).

From the social-historical perspective, the historical truth is the exact opposite of the last sentence; for it is precisely those movements which take the eschatological proviso seriously that both seek and work for welfare *on this earth*. They expect the future from God and derive from that expectation the power needed for their creative action. This is as valid for twentieth-century theologies of liberation[205] as it was for early Christianity.

In Günter Klein's opinion, there was never a doubt in early Christianity that the "world's time" would go on as it always had (cf. p. 296). Christ is not the end of history but its wholesome crisis (p. 286); he does not liberate from the world's *time* but from its *power* (p. 286). Christ questions every other conception of time, particularly that of Judaism (p. 282).[206] But this christological crisis of history occurs "within the world's time" and "under the conditions of temporality" (p. 296).

The transition from Jesus' expectation of the imminence of God's reign, in the sense of a linear future time, to this christological "eschatology of presence" or "permanent preparedness" (e.g., p. 296) occurred quite incidentally, according to Klein. At first, Paul did expect God's future to come in his own lifetime; yet he taught a Christology in terms of an "eschatology of presence" right from the start (as early as 1 Thessalonians; pp. 280f.). The problem of the delayed Parousia is raised relatively early but is of secondary concern next to the importance of Christology (p. 296).

Such a construction of early Christian eschatology neither submits to a radical critique nor alters the traditional schema: expectation of an imminent end (judged to be a mistake)—the delayed Parousia; abandonment of the expectation of Christ's return; and incorporation of faith into linear time that is taken for granted. Only the historical moment when Christianity outgrew its expectation of God's imminent coming is determined for a very early time: the beginnings of Christology. Whatever alienation may have existed between earliest Christian eschatology and the theology of a twentieth-century church has disappeared. Jesus alone is left in the contextuality of the imminence expectation; he had, after all, no Christology in a post-Easter sense. But his thought is compatible with the fact of a future "in the sense of the world's time" (cf. above).

When this article appeared in 1982, there already was a broad public debate about the threats to future life on this planet from nuclear technology and other global destruction of the environment. When Rudolf Bultmann's program of demythologizing appeared in 1941,[207] the Second World War raged on, and the "final solution of the Jewish problem" by Germany's National Socialists could at least be surmised (by 1938, the latest). Günter Klein lives in a theological tradition the representatives of which assiduously partition themselves off from people who experience their time as the last chance to act before God's judgment and as the time of hope in God's nearness.

D. FEMINIST PERSPECTIVES

The analysis of patriarchy offered in Matt. 24:37–39 and Luke 17:26–27, 30 is solidly androcentric and in need of critique for that reason; it also offers an important point of contact for feminist critique of patriarchy, namely, the critique of the patriarchal understanding of time. This saying of Jesus critiques patriarchy for seeing life in linear time, a concept in which it is assumed that life will go on as it always has. The understanding of time under critique is described in very carefully chosen language. The generation after the Flood figures that its future cannot be any different from its present and so *blinds* itself to the sufferings of the present moment.

The blindness of "business as usual" is confronted with the coming of the Human One, with a vision and a revelation. Faced with the vision of the Human One's coming in judgment, those who have eyes to see suddenly experience the present differently. It is the time of the birth pangs of the last hour;[208] the horrors and guilt of the present can still be dealt with. The hour of conversion is right now. Thinking in terms of linear time is equated with blindness. Apocalyptic ideas of revelation draw for their vision on the perception of suffering through injustice. *Those* are the tears that God will wipe away (Rev. 21:1ff.). God will sit in judgment on the injustice that is done now.

Philosophers have critiqued the linear conception of time and its business-as-usual blinkers; they see "progress" for what it is: a catastrophe. "The notion of progress has to be grounded in the idea of catastrophe. The catastrophe is that things 'go on as they do.' It is not what is yet to be that is the catastrophe; it is what is now. Strindberg said: 'Hell is nothing that lies ahead of us—it is life here' " (Walter Benjamin).[209] Apocalyptic[210] visions are not about future catastrophes; they cast a blinding light on the catastrophes of everyday life. Jürgen Ebach's interpretation of apocalyptic, written in 1985, has worked out this thought admirably.

Rosemary Radford Ruether's feminist critique of Christian linear eschatology, liberal conceptions of the evolutionary process, and Marxist views of the future as the product of revolution corresponds in substance to the critique of this saying in Matt. 24:37–39 and Luke 17:26–27, 30, of the impenitence and blindness of the patriarchal paterfamilias. She opposes thinking in terms of linear time ("endless flight into an unrealized future") with "a different model of hope and change based on conversion or *metanoia.*"[211,212] She might well appeal to Jewish and early Christian apocalyptic thinking as well as to this saying.

The power and tenacity of patriarchy's conception of time can be seen in the tradition of interpretation discussed above. It is a branch of a larger tradition in which interpreters portray the innocence of that everyday life, which might as well keep on as it always has. Rudolf Bultmann rejected apocalyptic thinking with the following argument: "Mythical eschatology is finished basically by the simple fact that Christ's parousia did not take place immediately as the New Testament expected it to, but that world history continues and—as every competent judge is convinced—will continue."[213] The interpretation of Matt. 24:37–39 and Luke 17:26–27, 30 makes plain that Bultmann's premise still meets with broad agreement, at least in Western Christianity—despite Auschwitz, Hiroshima, and ecological catastrophes.

Christina Thürmer-Rohr's feminist analysis of women's situation in patriarchy has shown that women contribute in a particular way to things' continuing as they always have and that the "competent judge" of whom Bultmann spoke may safely hope for progress:

> Women's system of order is their system of hope. Their sympathizing, empathizing, thinking ahead, accompanying, limiting, figuring, directing, producing, understanding, disapproving, controlling, judging, prejudging, is all in the interest of producing, out of a small and easily disrupted collection of people . . . a stable

unity, hopefully safe for the future, a unity which no one is allowed to break away from. . . . And all on the basis of a wide-eyed trust in everything that happens outside our own field of vision.

Women create "the helpful climate of hope for the good." "Whenever hope and illusion become the source of the will to live, all knowledge of reality becomes highly threatening." "We should learn to live in the *present*."[214]

Apocalyptic thinking lacked the ability to engage in such a feminist analysis, in spite of its critique of patriarchal everyday life and patriarchal conceptions of time. How women perceived their present, if they could see their *own* present as women at all, is not told in those texts. And yet it is possible to probe texts as to what perceptions by women such an androcentric perspective might convey.

Early Christian eschatology and its critique of patriarchy and language of hope may be a source of inspiration for feminist theology. Western theology's inability theologically to take seriously the expectation of the imminent end on the part of Jesus and early Christianity is because the experiences of those who do theology are those of the winners of history; such people cannot comprehend that those who suffer yearn for the end. Those who today want to open their eyes and see the dying people in the regions of nuclear contamination or even the dying trees in their gardens will feel what power the nearness of God gives to human beings who, in the midst of wars and rumors of wars, feel that spring is here and so believe in the approach of God's summer.

IV

LIBERATING PRAXIS OF
WOMEN AND MEN

1

The Exaltation
of Debased Women
(John 7:53–8:11 and Luke 1:48)

A PRELIMINARY REMARK ON
THE CONNECTION OF THESE TEXTS

When the hemorrhaging woman (Mark 5:25–34 and par.) comes through the crowd, approaches Jesus from behind, and draws power from him, she does what her Jewish foremothers and sisters have taught her: she fights against her misery, in her case, an illness with dire social consequences.[1] She acts from the discernible consciousness that her misery is also of human origin and that God is on her side. She knows that those shunning hemorrhaging women, whom patriarchy find "abnormal" and of no use, do not have God on their side. She acts like Hannah,[2] Tamar,[3] or the Samaritan woman.[4]

When Jesus confirms that God is on her side, he also does what his Jewish forefathers and brothers have taught him: openly and in an act of solidarity, he stands with a nonwoman, a debased and socially outcast woman. He acts like Elkanah (1 Samuel 1 and 2), Boaz in the book of Ruth, Rabbi Aqiba (*BQ* 3.6), or Daniel in the legend of Susanna.

There is a broad Jewish narrative tradition that tells of the liberation of debased women as the exaltation of the lowly. The following is a list of some (not all) of these narratives:

	Debasing of Women	*Helping Herself*	*Help of Men*	*Liberation*	*Is Patriarchal Order Sustained?*
John 7:53–8:11	Stoning on account of adultery	?	Jesus takes sides, accusers depart	Acquittal and return home	No
1 Samuel 1—2	Barrenness and provocation	Prayer and promise	Elkanah's love, Eli's support, God's intervention[5]	Birth of son, praise of God	Yes (liberation through birth of son) and no (critique of patriarchy)

	Debasing of Women	*Helping Herself*	*Help of Men*	*Liberation*	*Is Patriarchal Order Sustained?*
Luke 7:36–50	Distress of despised prostitute	Weeping and anointing	Assurance of God's forgiveness by Jesus and valuation of prostitute as one who loves (v. 47)[6]	Return home in peace of God	No
John 4	Exploitation through forced marriage,[7] labor	Question and petition for water of life, denial of husband, leaving jar behind	Jesus affirms denial of husband (vv. 17–18)	Liberation from husband and from hauling water, messenger in Samaria	No
Luke 1 (Elizabeth)	Barrenness, "shame"	Meeting with Mary	Conception with God's help	Birth of son, praise of God, prophesying	Yes (liberation through birth of son) and no (meeting with Mary; prophetic utterance)
Luke 1—2 (Mary)	Poor woman without power, oppressed like all her people	Trust in divine future	God and the Messiah of people God,	Woman prophet's praise of prophesying	No
Matthew 1 (Mary)	Illegitimate pregnancy	?[8]	God and, through God's intervention, Joseph	Birth of Jesus	Yes (because of Joseph's role) and no (because of child's father-lessness)
Mark 5:25–34 and par.	Chronic disease of woman, loss of function, impurity	Her own initiative to get healing from Jesus	Jesus affirms her action	Return home	No

	Debasing of Women	Helping Herself	Help of Men	Liberation	Is Patriarchal Order Sustained?
Luke 13:10–17	Chronic bone condition, spirit of infirmity, demon possession		Healing by Jesus, even on Sabbath	Praise of God	No
Ruth (Ruth and Naomi)	Widow, poverty, childlessness	Solidarity between Ruth and Naomi	Boaz redeems field of Elimelech, fulfills obligation of levirate marriage with Ruth	Liberation through marriage or birth of son (cf. Ruth 1:9), Ruth finds home in man's house (cf. 4:14), Naomi gains kin	Yes and no
BQ 8.6	Humiliation through exposure of hair, poverty	Charges against perpetrator in court	Rabbi Aqiba rules in her favor	"Noble sons" of God, vindication before the court	No
Susanna (sequel to Daniel)	Defamation of adulterous woman, threat of execution	Plea of innocence	Daniel's protest and just judgment	Rescue from defamation and danger	Yes and no; calamity shows potential of the injustice of women's oppression
2 Esdras 9–10	Son's death outside bride chamber (no grandchildren)	Cries of travail	God's intervention	Glory of Zion, resurrection	No
Genesis 38 (Tamar)	Childlessness, refusal of levirate marriage, threat of execution because of incest	Pregnancy by "trickery," achieves justice for herself	Reluctant compliance by Judah	Sons	Yes and no; calamity shows patriarchal injustice

From the point of view of method, the list is a selection from the history of a specific theme. A selection like this may help in discerning the commonalities and differences among individual narratives. But above all, it may be probed for social-historical information. In those numerous narratives, the women and men who express themselves repeat one pattern of activity: the struggle for justice for women in a patriarchal society that inflicts gross injustice on women. In its content this narrative tradition is closely related to narratives of women's resistance (cf. above at I.4); it has its own form as well, in that it raises consciousness of patriarchal debasing of women and offers women and men options for action. This tradition is an important help in understanding Jesus' actions and those of his followers.

From this narrative tradition I have chosen the stories of the rescue of the adulterous woman (John 7:53–8:11) and of Mary's pregnancy (Matthew 1; Luke 1 and 2—Luke 1:48 being the central thought). For centuries in Jewish theology, the narrative tradition of focusing on a specific theme had played a very significant part; it will help us in determining what the structural injustice of patriarchy is and how it has been actively opposed. This was the pattern in biblical times; how that tradition is seen today is another question.

A. THE TEXTS

Not until the third century C.E. did the story of a woman rescued from being stoned for committing adultery find its way into the canonical tradition.[9] After that, the pericope suffered a varied fate in that it was often deleted from tradition, even though evidence of its existence comes from a very early time (Papias, ca. 125 C.E.).[10] "The ancient church was suspicious about the pericope of the adulterous woman not only for reasons of textual criticism; it opposed and suppressed it also for its content. Jesus' forgiving words to such a woman were at odds with the church's penitential discipline."[11] Augustine also speculates about the fear by men that the text could "make their women immune to punishment for their sins."[12]

I shall proceed from the assumption that this story is, like other parts of the Synoptic Gospels, an equally believable piece of ancient tradition of Jesus[13] and that the only difference is its late and disputed incorporation into the canon. In terms of language and narrative type, the text fits better into the Synoptic Gospels than into John. The fact that this story had difficulty being accepted into the canon is, from a feminist perspective, an indication that the story could not be harmonized with the interests of a church oriented toward dominance.

Luke 1:48 is part of Mary's Magnificat: "For [God] is concerned with the debasing [*tapeinōsis*] of his slave woman. For behold, from now on all generations shall call me blessed." It is not only the *substance* of women's prophecy that manifests the connection between women's prophecy and the gospel of the poor (as was shown in III.2); it is manifest also in *narratives of God taking sides with debased women who then become prophets.* Luke 1:48 describes Mary's fate as that of a woman's degradation and her subsequent exaltation by God. Elizabeth's fate is understood similarly as a lifting of her "shame" (Luke 1:25; *oneidos*). Both stories are to be read in their formal and substantive connection and in relation to Matthew 1. What was Mary's debasement and exaltation? Certainly, Joseph at first believed her to have been adulterous (Matt. 1:19).

B. SOCIAL-HISTORICAL QUESTIONS

Adulterous Woman

There is no doubt expressed in John 8:1–11 that the unnamed woman is adulterous and that her adultery should be called "sin" (8:11). However, the text depicts a situation rife with injustice toward the woman, even though the text itself manifests no consciousness of that injustice. The woman was caught "in adultery" (8:3), says the narrator, who does not separate himself from the Pharisees' and scribes' declaration: "This woman has been caught in the act of adultery" (8:4). Since we must presume that such a declaration required at least two witnesses (Deut. 19:15; cf. Num. 5:13), we must conclude that the woman was trapped, a procedure that has been used for ages to convict women of adultery.[14] In addition, the adulterous man is not present in the text, even though he too should have been apprehended and punished. That he had already been stoned *before* the woman is a surmise[15] that does no justice to the text, because it does not explain the text's silence about this man. Instead, we must assume that the text reflects a social praxis of getting rid of women by means of accusing them of adultery, in other words, that patriarchal law[16] is being used against women and is being *mis*used. The text assumes that witnesses were procured and that the woman was isolated as the sole perpetrator; it does not call those actions a misuse of the law.

One may well ask whether Jesus' assessment of the situation prompts the complaint about misusing the law: "Whoever among you is without sin should throw the first stone at her" (8:7). According to the text, sin is noncompliance with the concrete biblical instruction. Verse 11 envisages the woman's sin in the sense of Lev. 20:10 and Deut. 22:22, that is, as adultery. The scribes and Pharisees would be accused of having broken God's commandments by serving as planted witnesses or accomplices in the action for any number of reasons (e.g., for financial gain). In terms of H. F. von Campenhausen's categories, such an interpretation would be classified as "banal." In his eyes, the attempts of bygone years to interpret John 8:7 as referring to concrete (sexual) sins of the scribes and Pharisees were banal.[17] But the description of an Iranian woman's stoning in 1990[18] allows one to regard this praxis of destroying individual women with

the help of patriarchal marriage laws as a frequent occurrence in which participants commit injustice (*including* in terms of patriarchal law) and then silence
their guilty conscience through mass hysteria and group coercion. "The scribes
and Pharisees" (8:3) who act as the agents of the prescribed stoning are not representative of *all* scribes and Pharisees; in the perspective of the text, they are
men who stand for all agents of this form of killing women. The plural use of
the article, the scribes and the Pharisees, does not deny such an interpretation;
for this generalizing terminology is also used in the New Testament when clearly
a group of people in a concretely defined situation is being depicted.[19]

According to the patriarchal marriage legislation of Jewish tradition, adultery
is an injury to the husband's right of possession of his wife's sexuality.[20] Punishment is prescribed for the woman and the adulterous man. In Roman law,
women's legal position is worse because it allows for the immediate murder of
the alleged adulterous woman by her father, husband, or even a third party,[21]
that is, it allows for arbitrariness. Every legal system of antiquity threatens
women, whose sexuality is the possession of a man (father or husband), with se-
vere punishment or death in case of adultery or premarital intercourse. This
threat must have had a profound impact on every individual woman from her
childhood onward. Even the slightest suspicion and the faintest of whispers
amounted to a deadly threat. The *sotah* procedure of Jewish law and corresponding procedures in other legal systems[22] permit a husband to submit his
wife, whom he suspects of adultery, to an ordeal. For the woman involved, this
procedure—if she survived at all—was an experience of degradation and horror
that would mark her for the rest of her life. The sources with which I am familiar say nothing about those women's experiences. My own recollection of the
far more "harmless" rumors with which women were persecuted when I was
young (e.g., "she's an easy one to lay") is enough to inform an initial picture of
the horror experienced by those women.

Stoning

Stoning is an execution carried out by a group or community that feels threatened by a certain deed.[23] It is to be done by the men of the community involved.[24] The succession in which the rocks are hurled at the victim is significant; it may be arranged, for example, according to the rank of the people who
were (or alleged to be) injured. The witnesses throw the first rock, according to
Deut. 17:2–7; the person whom the guilty party tried to seduce into idolatry,
according to Deut. 13:8f. During the stoning of the Iranian woman referred to
above, the father of the allegedly adulterous woman condemned her to death
and threw the first rock. He was followed by her husband, then the imam, rep-
resenting God and the sons. They also pronounced the death sentence in the
same order of succession:

The mayor came out, then Sheikh Hassan and, leaning on a cane, a bent-over man, of small build and a wrinkled face that was framed by an unkempt white beard. Ebrahim and Hassan descended the steps and turned reverently toward the old man. With a shaky voice he uttered the word "Mahkum!" An enormous cry went up, followed by a salvo of gunfire. Frightened by all that noise, dogs began to bark. The men applauded, enthusiastically waving their arms. "Guilty! She is found guilty!" The shrieking got even louder when the old man, with difficulty, climbed up the stairs that separated him from the Mullah and the mayor. They hastened to his aid and the crowd moved aside. Morteza had just pronounced the sentence on his own daughter. Quiet returned. A fourth man had appeared in the doorway; it was Ghorban-Ali. Deliberately, he raised his right hand and waited until all were silent. In a calm and serious voice he said, "Sang sar!" Hysteria swept through the crowd, insults were shouted, and people began to dance. As if infected by this collective rage, Ghorban-Ali kept shouting, "Sang sar, sang sar!" He had condemned his wife to death by stoning. Radiant with joy, he slowly descended the three steps to the crowd. Some men patted him on the shoulder with rough affection, others embraced him, children clung to his clothing. Strong arms took hold of him and lifted him up high. The festivity could begin, the ritual carried out. The other men who came out of the red brick house received hardly any attention. They were Ghorban-Ali's two oldest sons, two tough boys of sixteen and eighteen years of age, and the mayor's two deputies; with them was a blind man who was guided with care through the seething crowd. They all shouted their judgment, "Sang sar, sang sar, sang sar!"

. . . The mayor reached for a rock and handed it to Morteza. "The honor of throwing the first rock belongs to you, Mr. Ramazani . . . Please . . . "The old man laid down his cane and took the rock. He gave God thanks, extended his arm to its full length, and threw the rock in the direction of his daughter, yelling: "Ya Allah! That's for you, you whore!"

. . . Now, it was Ghorban-Ali's turn. He had rolled up his sleeves and laid out four rocks. He waited for a sign from the mayor. "Your turn, my boy," Ebrahim said lovingly. "May God guide your arm." The "cheated" husband straightened his arm and snapped it forward.

. . . Now the two sons took their rocks and hurled them at the same moment.

. . . Sheikh Hassan's turn was next. He put the Qur'an into his left hand and with his right lifted up a big rock. Before he threw it, he turned to the crowd and said in an unctious voice: "It is not I who throws this rock. It is God who guides my arm. He gives me his orders and I avenge our imam for the heinous crime which this woman has committed."[25]

Every one of the men involved is plaintiff, judge, and executioner in one.[26] The alleged injury to their honor has an order of rank and is also an injury and threat to the community, whose honor and integrity are reinstated by the stoning. The order of succession in the stoning, which looms in John 8, is reflected in the sequence in which the accusers leave the scene (v. 9).

People in antiquity were fully aware of how cruel this execution is. The Mishnah recommends that the adulterous woman not be stoned but be strangled to death (*Sanh.* 11:1, 6). But Acts 7 and John 8 show that collective stoning was still practiced for idolatry and adultery.[27]

It follows from the collective character of both apprehension and punishment that Jesus is called on in this text (v. 5) to condemn the woman and to *take part in the stoning.* He is to join the men's collectivity as a judge and the execution-ers' collectivity as an executioner. Whatever the gesture of writing in the sand signifies,[28] it takes the place of the sentence demanded of him and of his partic-ipation in the execution. Jesus refuses the role of a Jewish male[29] who restores the honor of a people injured by a woman's adultery. Jesus' conduct and the success of his initially wordless and then explicit critique of the men, who want to stone the woman according to the law and as agents responsible to the peo-ple, shows that stoning was still a practice of the day but was also seen as a prob-lem.[30]

The situation described in the text is not about the theoretical discussion on the cruelty of stoning; the dramatic moment comes when the woman is put "in the middle" (v. 3; cf. v. 8). In the Iranian village where Soraya Man-outcheri was stoned, she was buried in a hole up to her shoulders; a deputy of the mayor then drew a circle with chalk around the hole, "the middle of which was Soraya's head."[31] When Stephen was entrenched he was allowed to kneel down (Acts 7:60); presumably no hole had been dug. Placing the woman in the middle (John 8:3) is, in view of the Iranian scenario, the beginning of the ston-ing. The role of Jesus is, accordingly, that of a Jewish male whose responsibility to God, to the scriptures, and to the people is being evoked, at a moment when the woman already stares death in the face. Jesus opposes the stoning with an act of civil courage. He resists the pressure of the group and of the presumably hysterical atmosphere of the stoning and refuses for himself to condemn and stone the woman. It is not very likely that, in so doing, Jesus repudiates the scrip-tures, which call for the execution of adulterous women; after all, Jesus' hermeneutics often present him as an independent Jewish *interpreter* of the scriptural tradition and not as someone who rejects that tradition.[32] We do not learn in this instance what the biblical grounds for his action were; it would be in line with his argumentation had he cited the Decalogue against stoning, us-ing scripture against scripture and, in particular, against a certain practice of in-terpretation (cf., e.g., Mark 2:25–26 and par.). The text gives evidence that the group of executioners puts heavy pressure on Jesus: "They kept on asking him" (v. 7).

I do not believe that Rome's representatives, especially the prefect in Cae-sarea, would have regarded a woman's execution by stoning as a trespass against Rome's sole jurisdiction over capital punishment (John 18:31), even though some interpreters of John 8:6 suggest this.[33] The killing of adulterous women was in Rome's interest and did not impugn the power and law of Rome—no more than did the killing of an allegedly adulterous woman by her husband or any other self-styled avenger of the people's honor.[34]

By an act of civil courage, Jesus prevents a woman from being stoned. With theological reasons he fundamentally pulls the rug out from under the legitimacy of this practice of execution: "Whoever among you is without sin throw the first stone" (v. 7). In so doing, Jesus puts adultery on the level of all other trespasses against God's will. The "sin" of this woman is alike to the trespasses of those men, be it defamation, incest, theft, adultery, or any other offense. And Jesus disputes the particular status of adultery (shared with idolatry) as a capital crime.[35] What this recognizes and critiques is the brutality that the patriarchal order brings into every woman's life through its power to regulate women's sexuality and the particular punishment meted out to women who have, or are alleged to have, committed adultery. In terms of the text, Jesus, the messenger of God, takes sides with an afflicted and debased woman. He and those who told this story do think of adultery as a "sin," but no longer as a capital crime. And that challenges patriarchal order at one of its crucial points, namely, its power over women's sexuality. In terms of its social function, I consider Germany's current legislation concerning abortion, section 218 of the criminal code, comparable to laws that, for adultery, sentence women to death by stoning; in both instances, the social order enforces control over women's bodies in the interest of patriarchy.

Debased Women: Childlessness and Other "Disgraces" of Women

What the adulterous woman in John 8 had to suffer is in line with the suffering of debased women, whose side God takes; women who themselves struggle against degradation and at whose side is a man as God's representative. The long list above of Jewish stories of God's solidarity with debased women is what I want to examine now in terms of the social history of women's experiences of degradation.

Hannah

First Samuel 1 and 2—Hannah's degradation (*tapeinōsis*, 1 Sam. 1:11, LXX) is her *childlessness*. In the Hebrew text, Hannah's humiliation is aggravated by her husband's other wife, Peninnah, who provokes her because of her barrenness (1:6–7). Here the biblical text projects patriarchal guilt in relation to Hannah onto another woman. This aspect is missing in the Septuagint. Postbiblical retelling of the Hannah story often expands on this aspect.[36] In the hymn[37] known as the Song of Hannah, the reference to Hannah's "enemies" is made in the context of her humiliation (1 Sam. 2:1). In spite of her husband's love for her, as a childless woman Hannah is in abject misery. In the eyes of patriarchal societies in antiquity, a barren woman was someone who had failed in what creation had destined her to be.

The Babylonian Talmud (*Ber.* 31b) has some very moving words for Hannah's degradation:

And Hannah spoke in her heart. In the name of R. Jose b. Zimra R. Eleazar said: concerning the matter of her heart. Hannah said in his presence: Lord of the world, nothing of what you have created for a woman is without its purpose. Eyes are for seeing, ears for hearing, a nose for smelling, a mouth for speaking, hands are for working, feet for walking, breasts for suckling. Did you give me the breasts at my heart that they should not be suckled? Then give me a child that I may use my breasts and suckle it.[38]

Even though Old Testament and Jewish tradition believe that it is God who opens the womb when God wills it, nowhere in this context have I found that barrenness is God's punishment of an individual woman.[39] The Hannah legend, as told in the pseudo-Philonic *Antiquitates biblicae*, has an astonishing twist: Peninnah's boasting of having the heir is criticized (50.2). "But I know that she is not rich who has many sons, nor poor who has few; she is rich who overflows in her submission to God's will" (50.5). But here, too, Hannah's childlessness is her misery; it is lifted when God causes her to have a son.

The legend of Hannah (or the narratives of Sarah and Rachel) also influenced other legends or myths in which an important son comes from a one-time barren mother (such as John the Baptist; Luke 1).[40]

The childless woman's "disgrace" (Gen. 30:23; *herpah* in Hebrew, *oneidos* in Greek—LXX Gen. 30:22 and Luke 1:25) is her worthlessness in human eyes. Her "misery" (1 Sam. 1:11, *ani* in Hebrew, *tapeinōsis* in Greek; taken up in Luke 1:48—cf. below) is parallel to that of the poor; it is seen as powerlessness and social devaluation (cf. 1 Sam. 2:4–8), but also as a mockery. Both terms presuppose a social system of value and power in which a woman's value is defined in terms of children (sons) and in which poor women and men are of no value. It is a patriarchal order that stamps childless women and the poor as nonpersons.

The debasing of the barren woman means that, in her own eyes and those of others, she has failed in the destiny creation had bestowed on her, a destiny equated with the values of patriarchy. Hannah's laments and tears show (1 Sam. 1:7ff.) what injuries the value system of a patriarchal society inflicts on a childless woman. She suffers misfortune like the poor who are tormented by hunger (1 Sam. 2:5). The barren and the hungry cannot change their lot; they can only call to God for help. But this cry to God accomplishes something; it changes the real situation of oppression. In the legend of Hannah as told in 1 Samuel, her husband Elkanah supports his suffering partner and tries to ease her suffering by being doubly attentive to her. But her suffering ends only through her prayer and God's intervention: Hannah is given a son. The exaltation of the debased one, the barren woman's motherhood is, in other words, the restitution of the patriarchal order. And yet the tradition of Hannah and its Jewish history of interpretation again and again alert consciousness to the underside of patriarchal order and its effect on women: it inflicts serious injury on women.[41]

There is a vision of Zion in the second book of Esdras in which the suffering of barren women is described most vividly.

The Childless Mother of Zion

In 2 Esd. 9:26–10:59, there is a moving vision of Zion. The mediator of revelation sends Ezra into a field of flowers, where no houses had yet been built, and tells him that he will come and talk to him again. Ezra repeats his lament, which is the basic theme of the whole book: Israel has received the law from God but people did not keep it, did not observe the commandments (9:33). Therefore "destruction will come upon" the people of Israel (9:36). They will perish before God and in actual reality, because death before God and the destruction of the people are closely connected, as will be shown later. But the law remains in its glory, since it comes from God (9:37).

Ezra's lament about the demise of the people of Israel is superceded by his vision of a lamenting woman. Her lament is violent, loud, and desperate. "Great is my distress," she cries (9:41). She tells of her misfortune: through thirty years of marriage she was barren and childless. Day and night she prayed to the Most High. Finally, after thirty years, God answered; God took note of her sorrow, had mercy on her distress, and gave her a son (9:45). Her fate is that of Hannah in 1 Sam. 1:2. The phrasing in 2 Esd. 9:45 is reminiscent of 1 Sam. 1:11 (cf. Luke 1:48). The lamenting woman then tells of the happiness of "her husband and . . . all our neighbors" (9:45) after the birth of the son. When the son comes of age, she chooses a wife for him[42] and arranges for the wedding. But the son dies as he enters his wedding chamber.[43] Nothing can comfort the mother. She flees from the town into the fields to starve herself to death. The old theme is retold in a new form: a barren woman in a patriarchal society suffers deep pain; a woman, who has lost her only son and is childless, has failed her social (and according to the understanding of the time, her God-given) destiny. To be without an heir means to be dead while one still lives.[44] What stands out in this text is that—even more than Hannah's husband in 1 Samuel 1—her husband is almost totally in the background. Given the logic of patriarchal societies, it is the children and heirs *of the man* to whom the woman needs to give birth. However, the perspective of this narrative, as in the story of Hannah in 1 Samuel 1, is that of a woman who is caught in the underside of patriarchal order, namely, in social death. Life has no place for her because she is without progeny.

Ezra angrily scolds the lamenting mother: "You are the most foolish woman in the world! Are you blind to the grief and suffering of our nation? Zion, the mother of us all, is in deep mourning" (10:6f.). His lament about the destruction of the people of Israel blinds him from recognizing the woman as the mother of Zion. He accuses the woman of mourning only for her son, whereas she should mourn for the entire nation (10:8). The greater pain of the mother of Zion should comfort her in her smaller pain (10:20). Her comfort (cf. 10:24, 41) is to come from the suffering of the mother of Zion. Both Ezra's anger and his comfort are quite odd, at least for modern sensibilities: on the one hand, there is arrogance (you mourn *only* for your son, not like Zion for the many); on the other, how is the *suffering* of one mother, of Zion, to be *comfort* for another mourning mother?

Ezra's speech of "comfort" is itself much more a moving lament about the fate of Israel/Jerusalem after the Romans had destroyed the Temple in 70 C.E. (cf. also 10:48):

> Our sanctuary has been laid waste,
> our altar demolished,
> our temple destroyed, . . .
>
> our virgins have been raped,
> our wives ravished,
> our God-fearing men carried off,
> our children abandoned,
> our youths enslaved. . . . (10:21–23)

Three laments have been artfully woven into one another in these two chapters of 2 Esdras: first, Ezra's lament about God's absence and the demise of the nation; second, a mother's lament about the death of her only and childless son; and finally, Ezra's lament about the suffering of the people after the destruction of the Temple in 70 C.E. The third lament is spoken by Ezra, but in its substance it is the lament of the mother of Zion. The three laments are, in the meaning of the whole text, three dimensions of the same misfortune: that of the mother of Zion, that is, of the people of Israel. The mother's lament over her only son's death at the threshold of the marriage chamber is the lament of the mother of Zion; only Ezra did not understand that he had met the mother of Zion.[45] The lament of the mother of Zion over the son's death is the lament about the misfortune of the people whose Temple has been destroyed and who are victims of war. And the lament over the sin of the people against God names God's absence as the cause (9:36) of the war being lost and of the destruction—very much in the sense of the prophetic tradition.[46] The people's future is death. Those who still live are dead in the midst of life, just like the mother who has lost her only son.

The meager comfort Ezra offers the lamenting mother does contain some hope for the future: "If you will accept God's decree as just, then in due time you will receive your son back again, and win an honored name among women" (10:16). Ezra offers this comfort without recognizing its real meaning.

For a childless woman, which is what he regards this lamenting woman to be, there is no more future; she is old and will have no more sons.[47] But the mother of Zion will again have many children. The suffering mother of Zion will give birth; her lament will become a liberating cry of birth, and she will be changed by God. In the vision, Ezra already sees the new, magnificent Jerusalem in the field of flowers. The interweaving of the three laments is also expressed in the continuity of the field, on which no houses have yet been built. The field is the place where Ezra has been sent to receive a revelation (9:23–28), where the childless mother awaits death (10:3–4), and where the new Jerusalem appears in the vision and where God will build it in the future (10:54). God gives the people a new future. People will once again live according to God's will. For them, "paradise lies open, the tree of life is planted, the age to come is made ready, and the rich abundance is in store; the city is already built" (8:52), home has been chosen. The age to come will also be *on this earth,* according to the eschatology of this text. It begins in the righ-teous action of the few who, in whatever misfortune, still cling to God's law.[48]

The description of misfortune and the twofold degradation of the mother of Zion, of her birth labor and of her transformation into the new Jerusalem as the exaltation of the debased, connects with a metaphorical interpretation of history widely held in Israel.[49] The fate of a woman becomes the embodiment of the fate of Israel. In antiquity, a people or a city was frequently embodied symbolically as a woman.[50] The idea of the exaltation of the debased, which Jewish tradition connects with that of embodiment as a woman, derives from the Jewish interpretation of the people's fate. And the fate of the symbolic figure of a woman is the fate of women in a patriarchal society. A woman without children is dead, though she lives. Her liberation is conceivable only through the birth of a son. The mother of Zion cries out in her labor pain when she is transformed into the new Jerusalem (10:26). Now she is the mother of many children. Within the framework of patriarchal ideas about the situation of a barren or childless woman, there is remarkably much being said from the perspective of a woman thus affected. The anguished lament expresses the deep pain of a woman who suffers social death, which the laws of a patriarchal society inflict on her. The text identifies itself with the woman's situation of suffering, just as 1 Samuel 1 seeks to be in solidarity with Hannah.

The suffering of the barren woman and her rescue through the birth of a son are a recurring motif in the description of Israel's fate[51] or of individual mothers who are important for Israel. Even if this tradition does not submit its patriarchal laws to critique—the laws that cause the suffering of barren or childless women—it does keep awake, as was shown here, a sensibility for that underside of patriarchal society which inflicts infinite suffering on women. In my judgment, the tradition of personifying the people in the fate of a barren or childless woman derives most profoundly from the people's experiences of suffering in Israel's history, beginning with the catastrophe of 587 B.C.E. Those experiences are recognized in

the suffering of women at the underside of patriarchy. Women's concrete experiences are taken seriously in that tradition as the people's history of suffering. In
many respects, this tradition is comparable to that of the Suffering Servant.[52]

Even though the story of Hannah in 1 Samuel 1 and 2 recognizably influenced the vision of Zion in 2 Esdras, from the perspective of social history, the
experience of degradation of the two women is quite different. Hannah's suffering and her prayer as a childless woman are the glorious prehistory of the birth
of a people's hero, Samuel. The mother of Zion bears the sufferings of a people
who live at the edge of their existence because of war and its consequences. That
towns are personified in the figures of women is significant but does not indicate a perception of experiences of suffering.

The fate of this personification of Zion connects women's experiences at the
underside of patriarchy with the suffering of the whole people. The men of this
people also identify themselves with this childless mother of Zion and not only
with the Suffering Servant or with Job. The male victims of Rome's violent domination become capable of perceiving the suffering of women at the underside
of patriarchy. Even in their word pictures they express the substantive connection between the suffering caused by war and the pain of a childless woman.
What they do not recognize is that the structures of patriarchy are made by human beings and therefore are changeable. Those structures can be clearly identified by listing the visible afflictions of women under patriarchy, which the narrative tradition recounts in stories of the exaltation of debased women. One need
only read down the first column in the list at the beginning of this chapter.

Judaea capta

From the year 71 C.E. there are in existence Roman coins that celebrate the
victory of Roman emperors over Jerusalem and the Jewish people in the war of
66–70 C.E. On one side, the coins depict *Judaea* as a figure of a woman in
mourning under a palm tree; sometimes there is the figure of a Roman standing in the pose of a conqueror. (In the example below, it is Titus in military
dress.) The depiction of a subjugated people in the form of a grieving and sometimes shackled woman—"Judaea capta," the inscription often reads—derives
from the grammatical gender of the inscribed *Judaea* and the frequent personification of regions and towns in female figures.[53] The Roman conquerors probably did not make a direct connection with the Jewish tradition of "the mother
of Zion." But for Jewish persons, *Judaea capta* must have signified the debased
mother of Zion, who in her deepest despair hopes in her God and in whose exaltation and liberation the people believe as long as they believe in their God.
The type of coin that depicts the Roman conqueror on the left side of the palm
tree also seeks to signal Rome's vigilance that will prevent any further Jewish rebellion. For many Jewish persons it was beyond doubt that God would lift up
the people and the head of *Judaea capta* once again; they supplemented the

coin's inscription with the content of their own tradition. When the Gospels, whose final form came into existence after the war of 66–70 C.E., speak of the suffering and the messianic hopes of the people (e.g., Luke 1:2), one should keep in mind that the women and men who speak in the Gospels would have known the tradition of the degradation and exaltation of the mother of Zion and these coins.

Mary's Degradation and Exaltation (Luke 1:48) in the Context of Matthew's and Luke's Accounts of Her Pregnancy

Mary and Elizabeth

A clear connection is made in the story of Mary, as Luke tells it, to the tradition of the exaltation of debased women: Mary's story is tightly interwoven with that of Elizabeth. Elizabeth's story tells of an old and childless woman who gives birth to a son who is important for the life of his people; the story is in the tradition of the story of Hannah or in that of the often-cited view within Judaism that important men are born to women who are no longer expected to have children. The Magnificat of Mary (Luke 1:46–55) also refers extensively to the Song of Hannah (1 Sam. 2:1–10), as well as to one line of the Hannah narrative: Luke 1:48—"You have regarded the low estate of your maiden slave"—is almost identical in its wording to 1 Sam. 1:11 in the Septuagint. Since the first two chapters of Luke do not describe Mary's low estate, her degradation (*tapeinōsis*), one can understand why some manuscripts of the text speak of Elizabeth in Luke 1:46 rather than of Mary, as it would appear that the Magnificat suits her situation better than Mary's. But such a change does not solve the problem. The degradation of Mary is in substantive connection with that of Elizabeth and with the tradition discussed above; what that degradation means in terms of the text needs still to be established.

The paths of Mary and Elizabeth are intertwined to a remarkable extent in the text. Elizabeth goes into hiding for the first five months of her pregnancy (Luke 1:25), offering her praise to God, *her* magnificat: "Thus the Lord has done to me in the days he looked on me, to take away my shame [my reproach] among people." This sentence takes up Rachel's words at the birth of Joseph (Gen. 30:23, LXX). It was in the sixth month of Elizabeth's pregnancy that the angel announced to Mary that she would have a child (Luke 1:26). After the angel had departed, Mary hurried to Zechariah's house in Judah to see Elizabeth, her relative (1:36, 39). In the scene describing their meeting (1:40–45), the unborn John and his Spirit-filled mother, Elizabeth, are portrayed giving praise for Mary's pregnancy and hail her as "the mother of my Lord" (1:43). The divine miracle of Mary's pregnancy continues and heightens the miracle of Elizabeth's pregnancy. The two women spend the first three months of Mary's and the last three of Elizabeth's pregnancy together (1:56). Mary offers her praise to God after hearing Elizabeth's greeting. It was Gabriel's—that is, God's—will that the women spend this time together. Gabriel tells Mary of Elizabeth's pregnancy, declaring it to be a divine miracle (1:36): Just as Elizabeth, an elderly, childless woman, had a child, you also can become pregnant, even when you have had no sexual relation with a man (1:34). The text presumes that, under normal circumstances, old women do not have children and that, similarly, it is normal for a woman and a man to have sexual union in order for her to conceive. But God's intervention breaks through the normal. The divine miracle of a fatherless pregnancy parallels and heightens the divine miracle of an aged woman's pregnancy, just as John the Baptist—like Jesus, a liberator of the people (1:68 and 2:32)—prepares the way (1:17, 76) for the Davidic Messiah (1:32f.). We shall return to the notion of a fatherless pregnancy.

The story of Elizabeth and Mary is told in an entirely gynocentric manner (1:24–56). The references to the months of pregnancy not only provide a chronological frame; they bind both women in a sisterhood that God wants and blesses, a relationship that repeats itself in the revelation between the two sons. Subdividing the pregnancies (the third, sixth, and ninth months are mentioned, the sixth as the month of the child's first movements) probably reflects traditions of how women saw the phases of pregnancy. To date, I am not able to explain satisfactorily why Elizabeth went into hiding for five months.[54]

Degradation of Mary—
Degradation of the People

The whole scene of Luke 1:24–56 presupposes a situation inside a house; at the same time, it contains numerous references to the political and social fate of the whole people of Israel and its future (Gabriel's speech, Elizabeth's words to Mary, Mary's Magnificat). The two women's sisterhood and their fate are interwoven with each other and with the *fate of the people* as the exaltation of the debased. This is particularly apparent in the parallelism of the praises the two women offer to God; Elizabeth's praise begins: "He has regarded the low estate of his maiden slave" (1:48; cf. 1:25); "he has turned to his people and set them free" (1:68). God's "regarding" (*epiblepein*) is for these women and for the people.

The *degradation of women* and the *degradation of the people* belong together. The following is being said about the latter: the people are disunited (fathers against children), and there are many who do not obey God (1:17, 77); people suffer from unjust rulers (1:52), from hunger, and from the rich among them (1:53), oppressed (1:68) by enemies and others who hate them (1:71, 74). The people live in darkness and under the shadow of death (1:79). Such expressions make use of biblical language, but it would be inappropriate to dismiss them as mere formulas; for the situation of the Jewish people as it existed when the text was written or handed on is recounted here in biblical terminology. The text is about people's degradation at the time when the Gospel was composed and when its oral and written sources came into being; it is about the Jewish people during the Pax Romana. The Magnificat and the other hymns need to be read and classified from a social-historical perspective. The people's return to God, their political liberation, and their social justice go together, one with the other. Mary's degradation is not described in the Magnificat, but it is seen as part of the people's degradation.

Just as the people's liberation calls for the people's active turning back to God, the liberation of debased women is connected with women's *liberating actions*. Such actions are at the core of the gynocentric narrative of Elizabeth and Mary. Elizabeth praises God (1:25) and becomes a Spirit-filled prophet (1:41–45). Mary trusts that God's word will come true (1:37, 45), even if it appears impossible in light of the laws of nature and in the face of political realities. Mary trusted that she would bring a child into this world without the involvement of a man and that this child was to bring God's indestructible reign to the people of Israel (1:33). She is strong where Zechariah was weak (1:20). Her praise of God, the Magnificat, is also a prophetic announcement of the people's liberation; she too speaks as a Spirit-filled prophet (1:46–55). The two pregnant women beat the drum of God's world revolution. I use the metaphor of beating the drum in order to emphasize how very much the situation described contradicts what Western culture has itself drummed into our heads about Mary's humility before God and the intimacy and private nature of Mary's visit to Elizabeth. The two women prophetically herald God's world revolution, God's option for the poor, which begins as an option for Mary and for women; she is "blessed *among women*" (1:42),[55] all generations to come shall call her blessed (1:48). The exaltation of debased Mary begins the liberation of the people, begins the actualization of the option for women and the poor. Mary's experience of oppression is not specifically mentioned; it is part of women's experience of degradation, for example, that of childless women, and that which a politically oppressed or a predominantly hungry people endure. Mary is one of such women, one of such a people. She heralds the world revolution and gives liberation a name: Jesus (1:31).

Here is a gynocentric event in an androcentric literary context. That Mary will be the one to give the name (1:31) and thereby plant the first sign of God's liberation is no longer quite so clear in 2:21. In the thoroughly androcentric parallel in Matthew, it is Joseph who gives Jesus his name (Matt. 1:21). In my view, it is not appropriate to the text to lift gynocentric content out of its androcentric context by means of literary criticism. There are still numerous patriarchal set pieces in the gynocentric passage, for example, in the conception of the Messiah (1:32f.). What I perceive in this gynocentric piece of narrative is rather that the patriarchal world is not really as invincible and seamless as it makes itself out to be in its language and conceptuality.

Pregnancy without a Man

I return to the fatherlessness of the unborn Jesus in light of these reflections. Mary becomes pregnant without a man. There were in the ancient world enlightened people who took it to be a law of nature that to produce a child, a woman and a man were required.[56] The text itself presupposes this common opinion. Mary boldly disregards a certainty that she had previously shared (1:34). But discussions in antiquity concerning procreation and conception rested on a spectrum broader than the specific idea of a man and a woman together, equally contributing to procreation. There was the explicit rejection of woman's participation in the origin of the embryo; it served the misogynist preservation of patriarchal interests. Aristotle rejects the theory[57] that women have seed and regards male seed as the real and decisive component in the origin of an embryo, while the woman merely provides the embryo's matter and nourishment. Predating Aristotle, the theory that the mother is really not a parent and that it was the father who procreated the child was very influential, right up to the days of the church fathers.[58]

Contrary and opposed to this explicitly misogynist tradition is the idea that women can procreate children alone, without a male partner. The patriarchal texts from which we learn of such theories describe the women who conceive children without a man as hussies and their children as monsters.[59] Gnostic mythology even pronounces decidedly that the father's will must be resolutely enforced against this female insubordination.[60] From a social-historical perspective, such theories signal, on the one hand, incipient liberation of women and, on the other, the defamation and oppression of women. These theories assume that there are women (and perhaps also men) who claim that women can have children without a man and, in so doing, liberate themselves from dependency and patriarchal oppression.

One has to keep the understanding of Luke 1—that a woman conceives a child without a man's involvement and that the child is by God's will the liberator of the people—within the context of that time's *understanding of procreation*. Scholars in the history of religion assign this story to the tradition of the holy marriage or divine procreation (a god procreates a child with a female human)[61] or to the tradition of the refusal of sexual relations (virginity means the absence of sexual intercourse); such classification, in my view, is not appropriate to the text. Mary is pregnant like any other woman and later has other children with Joseph (Luke 8:19–21 and par.) without having her life as a woman spoken of as disparate from her "virginal" phase of life. The text does not speak of divine procreation, even though that notion is read into it again and again (cf. below at IV.1.C).

From the perspective of social history, the gynocentric stories of Elizabeth's and Mary's pregnancies are a document of the liberating work of Jewish women (and men) at the time of Pax Romana. Their understanding of God, which rules out the notion of God as a procreating man, and their hope in God's world revolution are expressed not only in the hymns at the beginning of Luke's narrative but also in the notion that the liberator-child begins miraculously without a man. That in the history of Christian doctrine this, of all stories, came to serve the oppression of women is especially painful.

Mary's Pregnancy in Matthew 1

The text that parallels the Lukan narrative is highly androcentric and misogynist. Mary does not open her mouth; Joseph makes all the decisions. God addresses only him. But interestingly, both Matthew 1 and Luke 1 presuppose the same narrative. Joseph is not the father of this child. He first suspects adultery on the part of his betrothed and wants to divorce her secretly (Matt. 1:19) and spare her and himself the public deliberation about her adultery (or rape).[62] The text indicates that he is mistaken. Mary was not raped, and she did not commit adultery. She is pregnant by the Holy Spirit (Matt. 1:20; cf. Luke 1:35), who is not to be regarded as a kind of divine surrogate "procreator."[63] The child came into being without sexual intercourse, without a man; there is no repudiation of sexuality in the text either. That Joseph did not sleep with Mary until the birth of the child is said to guarantee that no man was in any way involved. Later on, Mary is a woman with a husband and children, and her virginity is not set over and against her being a woman.

Even the highly patriarchal "Matthew" can imagine a woman bringing children into the world who were not procreated by a man, if this is what God wishes. Soranus, a physician of antiquity, would have smiled at this story and said that Mary cleverly hushed up an indiscretion or a rape. Aristotle would have said that the truth had been violated, since only men procreate children. In its various versions, Christian dogmatics has eliminated the gynocentrism of this narrative, which is still present in Matthew, for example, by setting Mary apart from normal women. Neither Matthew nor Luke, however, does that.

The four ancestral mothers whom Matthew names are prototypes for

Mary's situation. When people do not know God's will, they may readily *mis-interpret* the actions of these women as prostitution (Tamar, Rahab, Ruth) and adultery (the "wife of Uriah"). According to the text, they are, in truth, the ancestral mothers of Israel, who are without blame. Their partners are examples for Joseph, who saves a situation open to misinterpretation by reintegrating Mary into the patriarchal order, just as the old patriarchs reintegrated the four ancestral mothers. Luke writes of Joseph that he was supposed to be Jesus' father (3:23); unlike Matthew, Luke keeps Joseph very much in the background, even though Jesus' lineage includes him (3:23–37) as it does in Matthew.

C. FEMINIST OBSERVATIONS ON THE
HISTORY OF INTERPRETATION

Traditional—that is, patriarchal—history of interpretation obscures the liberating substance of what this tradition has to tell about the exaltation of debased women and instead uses the content, contrary to the texts, as a means of oppressing women.

The Adulterous Woman:
Jesus Does Not Question "the Law"

As a rule, exegetical tradition does not name the *injustice* toward the woman who is to be stoned as an *adulteress*. By injustice I do not mean only the fact that she was deliberately trapped in order that she could be killed, as the appearance of the witnesses indicates (see above), but also the "routine" injustice that consists in threatening a woman's adultery with death and, in fact, prosecuting only the woman for adultery.

I have chosen as an example one interpretation that shows concern for *the adulterous woman as a person*, that is, which does not see her merely as an illustration of the sinner before God and Jesus' readiness to forgive.[64] It is the interpretation by Heinrich Baltensweiler (1967). He says explicitly that, for Jesus, "the person of the woman stands in the forefront, as do the persons of her accusers" (p. 131). In contrast to Jesus' response to her, the accusers treat her merely as an "object of demonstration" (p. 125; cf. p. 131) because they want to catch Jesus in a trap with their question. But in Baltensweiler's interpretation I search in vain for statements about or in support of the woman. On the contrary: in 8: 7, "in a strictly legal sense, Jesus acknowledges that in this case stoning is called for"! There is "no denigration of justice" (p. 132). Baltensweiler does not rule out, in principle, that the stoning was merely postponed to a later time (p. 132). Jesus' forgiveness (v. 11) "is an expression of his authority." "Forgiveness is unrestricted and comes upon her unexpectedly" (p. 132).

What words! Forgiveness comes like a bullet from an ambush—unexpectedly.

As Baltensweiler sees it, Jesus would calmly watch later on as the woman was stoned after all. Jesus contributes forgiveness. *Fiat iustitia!* The guiding principles of such an interpretation are anti-Judaism (the dispute with Jesus), a Christology of sovereignty (forgiveness), and the preservation of the social function of "the law." That stoning an adulterous woman constitutes a patriarchal-legal injustice like the crucifixion of Jesus and that early Christianity was very much aware of this does not, and could not, prevent Jesus from becoming the guarantor of public patriarchal justice, precisely on the basis of a narrative such as this.[65]

Since such an interpretation and its loyalty to the law are, in my view, relevant for and typical of the theological development in Germany, I would like to discuss an interpretation that goes a step farther in this direction. It is an interpretation of this text written by Hans von Campenhausen in 1977. He regards John 7:53–8:11 as a legend of the second century; it raises no questions at all about the fact that adultery is "a sin against God" (p. 172) or that it is a "grave offense" (p. 168) which, "according to the standards of that time—and not only of that time—must be punished" (p. 168). The intent of the legend was to foster a readiness *within the church* to forgive repentant sinners, including those who had committed adultery—but only once (p. 172). Von Campenhausen is obviously thinking of a man's one-time adultery, which, if he repents, may be forgiven in the church. "A Christian . . . may not throw a stone at a sinful brother" (p. 170). Since v. 7 is suspect, as if it questioned the law (p. 168f.), von Campenhausen uses the historical Jesus as his state-witness against that verse and the pericope of the adulterous woman. The historical Jesus normally stood aside from citizens' legal battles and from political disputes (p. 169). When persons outside his circle brought a political issue to him, "he responded in terms of the ruling authorities and the existing order" (p. 169f.).[66] For that reason, this legend has nothing to do with the historical Jesus. In Jesus' vicinity there are, "contrary to this legend and modern expectations (which are based not least on this pericope), almost no sinful women at all" (p. 171).[67]

Neither of these two interpretations questions the state's claim on punishing an adulterous woman. The relevant social function of punishing a woman's adultery is not discussed, even though the story's failure to mention the male adulterer would seem to have made that obvious. The important encyclopedic work *Die Religion in Geschichte und Gegenwart* (third edition, 1958) even praises the misogynist function of this justice: "The religions [of the world] determine *adultery* through the woman and prove it with reference only to her. This does not reflect an inferior view of woman but, rather, her dignity."[68]

David Daube's interpretation is an exception in this torrent of misogynist theological statements about adultery by women.[69] He understands John 8:7 as a critique, based in Judaism of tannaitic times,[70] of the legally structured injustice that men do to women. His interpretation of this pericope is both non-anti-Judaistic and critical of patriarchy; unfortunately, it has not been taken up in dominant exegesis.[71]

The Humble Virgin

The critical study by feminists of how the history of interpretation has dealt with the Lukan and Matthean descriptions of Mary is not focused here on the history of the church's doctrine[72] but only on what calls itself the historical interpretation of New Testament texts. (One must, of course, reckon with a close substantive connection between the church's history of dogma and the historical interpretation of New Testament texts, even when the argumentation consciously distances itself from the church's dogma and stays with the terms of history of religion.) Our task here must remain limited. In my view, and from the perspective of feminism, there are two central aspects in the interpretation of texts in dominant New Testament scholarship:

1. What do the interpreters mean by "virgin"? Or how do they interpret the idea that Jesus, in the sense of the texts, had no biological father?

2. How do they deal with the fact that the fate of Mary is identified with that of the people?

Virgin and Superman

According to Gerhard Delling,[73] Mary's being an untouched young woman is significant only for Christology. Writing in 1954, he said: "The concept of the virgin birth of Jesus is not meant to disparage the marriage bond. Its reference is to Jesus, not Mary. . . . Thus expression is given to the uniqueness of Jesus even from the physical standpoint" (p. 834f.).

Even though I agree with what Delling has to say, in terms of history of religion (no holy marriage, no *procreation* with God or the Spirit, but an understanding of God's Spirit as creative power)[74] it is the Protestant, institutional church-oriented interest in a Christology of sovereignty that guides his thought. This interpretation rightly rejects the idea that the texts speak of procreation by God but proceeds to create a superman on the level of Christology. What the notion of a fatherless pregnancy means to Mary and other women is a question that does not occur to these interpreters.

The book *Mary in the New Testament*,[75] by an ecumenical group of scholars in the United States, assesses the text from the perspective, like Delling's, of history of religion; yet it is so man-centered that while *procreation* by God or the Spirit is recognized as inappropriate in terms of the history of religion, it is finally posited once again.[76] Where Delling said that virginity does not disparage "the marriage bond," this study says that virginity "reflects no downgrading of human generation" (p. 122). Mary is "God's instrument" (p. 125). This actually cancels out their own insight from the history of religion, making God, in one way or another, the superman and Mary the vessel. One may read comparable ideas in Martin Dibelius's classic article about virgin birth.[77] In light of the foregoing discussion of the history of religion, François Bovon's work (1989) deals with the notion of procreation by God in a relatively cavalier manner. For him, the man's procreation is replaced in Luke 1:35 by God's power (p. 76), but in the sense of *procreation by God* (cf. esp. p. 69).

There are other interpretations besides that of a fatherless pregnancy as divine procreation (however much the text asserts that from the point of view of the history of religion, this notion is inappropriate). Divine conception does not rule out participation of an earthly procreator. The male, earthly procreators whom I have found in the literature are Joseph,[78] Zechariah,[79] and an unknown seducer or rapist.[80] The basis of these interpretive attempts, however, is enlightened ancient and modern biological theory, which holds that the production of a child necessitates both a woman and a man—exactly what the New Testament's legend of Mary disputes. An analysis of patriarchy has to critique both the notion of divine conception and enlightened biology: What understanding of man and his procreative capacity is presupposed in each instance? Why were ancient ideas about procreation not taken into consideration in this context? Their misogynist substance makes it necessary not only to critique the divinization of male procreation but also to acknowledge that, in early Christianity, the legend of Mary attacked the notion of such divinization. This critique raises the question whether enlightened biology is still subject to patriarchal androcentric conception. I do not doubt men's participation in the origin of children; I question the roles assigned to women and men even in an enlightened biology. Why is it that enlightened, rational biology reintroduces into a legend a procreating male who is conspicuous by his absence from it?

Humility or Oppression?

As I have clearly indicated, it is my thesis that in the Gospel of Luke, the woman Mary represents in her fate and prophecy God's option for the poor, an option that is decided in the option for women. In the sense of the early Christian gospel of the poor, the poor are the destitute majority of the Jewish people; they are—not only in Luke—the people itself. This view is also clearly discernible in the Magnificat. The young Jewish woman from the country beats the drum of God's world revolution—as did Hannah before her and Elizabeth with her. Mary's degradation is both a part and an expression of the people's oppression.

The tradition of interpretation in New Testament scholarship is guided by interests that were critically analyzed earlier (III.2.C); the text of the Magnificat is depoliticized. In addition, Mary's degradation is not understood as a real experience of oppression but primarily as an expression of her humility before God. Even when the connection between the social reality of Mary's life and her *tapeinōsis* is perceived, her social reality may still be the by-product of her humility[81] or becomes a symbol for the "condition of the human being as such."[82] This tradition of interpretation manifests itself in the translation of *tapeinōsis* as "low estate": "He has regarded the low estate of his handmaiden" (Luke 1:48, RSV; the same applies to the German translation of Luther, the Zurich Bible, Stier [1989], the ecumenical translation, all scholarly translations in the commentaries on Luke that I have consulted, and Bovon,[83] who wants to interpret the Magnificat in a liberation theology perspective). In Luke 1:48, 1 Sam. 1:11 is quoted. But the translations referred to, which speak of the low estate of the handmaiden in Luke 1:48, speak of "the affliction of thy maidservant" (RSV). It seems to make sense here that Hannah's barrenness be understood as an "affliction." In the eyes of this tradition of translation, Mary suffers no affliction; she is humble. In future, Luke 1:48 has to be translated differently: "He has regarded the humiliation [or degradation or oppression] of his maiden slave." That she is God's maiden slave—and no one else's—means that she is God's messenger and prophet.

When Paul refers to himself as God's slave (most often translated as "servant"; e.g., Rom. 1:1), no Christian ear hears "humility"; one rather hears "officebearer."[84] When Mary calls herself "maiden slave," the trained Christian ear hears "maidservant" in the sense of "humility." The false translation of Luke 1:48 harbors an obviously deep-rooted Christian ideology: "the low estate of your handmaiden"; humble women, the humility of the pious before God, and so forth. No thought here of degradation *and* exaltation or of oppression *and* liberation.

When the connection is seen at all, in the interpretation of the legend of Mary, between her and the people, the people are interpreted ecclesiologically; that is to say, the Jewish people, whose oppression and liberation are at issue here, are co-opted by the Christian church in a most anti-Judaistic fashion.[85]

D. FEMINIST PERSPECTIVES:
A PREGNANT CRONE AND AN
UNMARRIED, PREGNANT BRIDE
SUSPECTED OF ADULTERY

In 1987, Jane Schaberg wrote a book that is foundational for feminist theology; it is about the legends of Mary in the Lukan and Matthean narratives. The thesis of the book is that the New Testament's birth narratives of Jesus (Matthew 1 and Luke 1—2) indicate that their understanding of Mary's conception is not that of a miraculous virginal conception. Rather, both texts think, according to Schaberg, that during her engagement, the virginal Mary was seduced or sexually assaulted. In Matthew 1, "God 'acts' in a radically new way, outside the patriarchal norm but within the natural event of human conception. The story of the illegitimacy of Jesus supports the claim that Luke makes, that Mary represents the oppressed who have been liberated."[86]

Schaberg interprets the degradation of Mary (Luke 1:48) in terms of what it says about women's experience of injustice. She rightly shows that the words *tapeinoō/tapeinōsis* may refer to sexual humiliation. But she wants to exclude the meaning of the words "humiliation through poverty."[87] This establishes an either/or dichotomy (either sexual humiliation of women *or* humiliation of the poor) that finally fails to do justice to the overall text of the Magnificat. The humiliation of poor women includes sexual humiliation.

I respect the liberating power for women of the interpretation that Jesus was an illegitimate child. It is possible, in my view, that the historical Jesus was an illegitimate child and that the historical Mary was seduced or sexually assaulted. I agree with many of her book's individual interpretations. But *measured against the texts*, I find that Schaberg's thesis fails to fit. As the text indicates, it was Joseph's mistaken belief (Matt. 1:19) that Mary had been seduced or sexually assaulted. Divine revelation corrects this false assumption (Matt. 1:20). That a woman cannot become pregnant without a man had been Mary's mistaken belief, according to the text; encouraged by the angel Gabriel ("with God nothing will be impossible," Luke 1:37), she boldly casts that belief aside (Luke 1:38) and becomes a prophet of God's liberation. The texts want to speak of a miracle (pregnancy without a procreating man). Against the background of ancient biology (theories of procreation) and mythology (*hieros gamos*, procreation by God), a legend is told that, even in its highly androcentric Matthean version, has a catch: patriarchy is criticized. Given the significance attributed to male procreation in patriarchy and to the role of the father as the pivotal bearer of power in heaven and on earth, one cannot call this legend less than daring.[89] It is a miracle itself that the legend did not become unrecognizable in Matthew. Elaine Mary Wainwright provides a convincing explanation:[90] the Gospels, even the Gospel according to Matthew, presuppose communities in which there was a living praxis of women's liberation, albeit facing huge opposition.

The motif of the exaltation of the debased women and its tradition of which this chapter speaks must, from a feminist perspective, be examined critically in each individual case. This tradition may assert that an "abnormal" woman (in the patriarchal sense of that term) is generously reintegrated into the order of patriarchy by a man. In the list at the beginning of the chapter, I have tried, in the final column, to evaluate the individual narratives in this sense; my evaluations are individually open to correction, I am sure. But one should accept on principle that in this narrative tradition, the reestablishing of patriarchal order may be the foremost concern; or else the focus is on its injustice and the critique of patriarchy itself.

Jane Schaberg reads the stories of Jesus' ancestral mothers (Matt. 1:1–17) as critical of patriarchy: "All four find themselves outside patriarchal family structure.

. . . All four are 'wronged' or thwarted by the male world. . . . In their sexual activity all four risk damage to the social order. . . . The situations of all four are righted by the actions of men who acknowledge guilt and/or accept responsibility for the women."[91] Mary is to be seen as the fifth woman in this line. But—unfortunately—I read Matthew 1 differently: the misery of the ancestral women is interpreted away in these stories. According to the text, they really are heroes and ancestral mothers of the people, thanks to Judah, Salmon, David, Boaz, and Joseph. To understand them to be prostitutes or adulterous women is a *misunderstanding*, which in the sense of the text corresponds to that of Joseph. He at first took Mary to be an adulterous woman but then saw correctly that she had become pregnant without a man.

Texts such as Matthew 1 require creative expansion in order to be heard again as liberating gospel. I regard Jane Schaberg's book as a stimulus for such further creative expansion, for a feminist reimagining, even if I criticize her historically, for reasons of history of religion, and theologically, in view of the Gospel of the poor.

As I see it, the pericope of the adulterous woman is excellently suited for discerning in Western societies' discussion on abortion how essential the oppression of women is for patriarchy. Just like the criminal prosecution of termination of pregnancy, the penal claims of the state against the adulterous woman (much more rarely against the adulterous man) are an expression of a patriarchal society's all-embracing claim to have a right over women's bodies. These regulations of criminal law reach deeply into a woman's everyday life, and not only when adultery or abortion takes place. Marriage contracts in antiquity stipulated, for example, that a woman could not leave the house without the man's permission.[92] Adultery was alleged the moment the woman set an unsanctioned foot on the street. Thus the house becomes a woman's prison. The pericope of the adulterous woman recognizes and criticizes the misogynist intervention of criminal law into women's sexuality: the accusing men, the stoning executioners, find themselves guilty[93] and give up their murderous claim on putting the adulterous woman to death. "Nor do I condemn you; go, and sin no more" (John 8:11). Why is it that modern society cannot let go of condemning abortion? The women's movement does not want to dispute that adultery and abortion can mean guilt. But this guilt should be dealt with in a liberating way, as this story can teach it. Jesus separates guilt from the criminal law, and by speaking of guilt at the beginning of new life, he empowers the woman to live with existing guilt and walk in new ways.

The pericope of the adulterous woman and the legend of Mary belong together not only because they are pearls on the same string of this tradition (the exaltation of debased women) but also because they speak to adultery from different perspectives. In the eyes of patriarchal men, who have no inkling of God's miracle, Mary is an adulteress (Matt. 1:19). They learn from the legend of Mary, even in its deeply androcentric Matthean version, that their logic fails to do justice to God and Mary (and the four ancestral women), that in face of this event their logic even contradicts God. That is why the miracle of this pregnancy is critical of patriarchal logic, despite the reintegration of the ancestral women and Mary into the patriarchal order by the several men (like Joseph). In the pericope of the adulterous woman, the injustice of this patriarchal logic is unmasked at the moment when, on account of it, the woman is to be stoned. The critical observations on the history of interpretation of the two texts in New Testament scholarship show how powerful—or more accurately, how dominating—this logic still is. Procreation by God is spoken of even though the conclusions of religio-historical studies are clear. Again and again we hear of the humility of the handmaiden, even though Mary lives and speaks in the tradition of female Jewish prophets. And in spite of John 8:7, it is said that Jesus does not question "the law." The contradiction between the text and its interpretation is so blatant that I trust the liberating power of these narratives even where people read them in terms of a patriarchal hermeneutics because they know nothing else. But even today, these texts can clear a space in the midst of patriarchy for a liberating praxis of women and men.

Despite Matthew's enormous androcentrism, the symbolic power of the birth narratives of the Baptist and Jesus is, from a feminist perspective, quite magnificent. Elizabeth is an old woman (Luke 1:7, 18). An old woman is taken to be a superfluous being, about whose wrinkled skin people customarily would laugh.[94] Some features about her remind them that she was once a woman. But in the perception of ancient society, she is no longer a "real" woman; being barren, she is much more a "nonwoman."

At the onset of Jesus' life, the pregnant crone and the young bride, pregnant out of wedlock, sing praises to God and God's world revolution (Luke 1). As a result of the financial imposition on the oppressed Jewish people by superpower Rome, the highly pregnant Mary has to walk from Nazareth to Bethlehem (Luke 2). In Matthew, the pregnant bride, suspected of adultery, is protected by her fiancé. Both have to leave home with their infant for political reasons. Herod fears for his power should a messianic child be born. Jesus' mother and his putative father are homeless on account of politically motivated infanticide and find asylum in Egypt and, later, in Nazareth (Matthew 1—2).

These are legends and miracle stories that seek to bring God down to earth; they still want to do that today. At that time, suspicion of adultery and execution for adultery were probably the most powerful weapons for enforcing women's oppression. What occurs today in the criminal prosecution of abortion corresponds to this. Furthermore, then and now, contempt for old women who are not even regarded as women anymore is, like contempt for old people in general, a phenomenon of massive proportion. That is why I am highly fascinated by the divine miracle that Elizabeth embodies: a pregnant crone!

2

"It Is Not So among You . . . "
(Mark 10:42–45 and par.):
Communion on the Way
to God's Reign

A. THE TEXT

With some divergences, especially in Luke, this saying is to be found in all three Synoptic Gospels. It is now mentioned specifically[95] because of its fundamental importance for the Christian community.[96] Orders of rank are structures of unjust violence (Mark 10:42 and par.) and are to be resisted; they are to have no place in the community because they express the deep divide in society between being "great" or "first" and being served, on the one hand, and being female or male slaves and serving, on the other. What Jesus demands is paradoxical: a community's order of rank is to be that every member be the slave[97] of all other members and serve them. There is no way of ranking, from below to above, that can correspond to or reverse a top-down order. So whoever is "great" in the community can no longer exercise dominion over others in the sense of "natural" orders of social rank; otherwise the text would be a farce. In the community, authority and power sharing have to develop differently and, in substance, look different from what exists in a society shaped by dominance. Minor details aside,[98] this is the text's meaning. The service to the community demanded of everyone is, first of all, readiness to take up the political conflict with Rome's interests of domination (Mark 10:38–39 and par.) and to be executed, like Jesus, as a martyr of the Jewish people (Mark 10:45 and par.).

As Matthew declares, women have an active part in the service as well. The "mother of the sons of Zebedee" (Matt. 20:20) is depicted as a woman disciple who agrees at first to go to Jesus on their behalf but then affirms with them her readiness to offer service like Jesus (Matt. 20:22). She then enters upon this path before her sons. Like the other male disciples, they flee, whereas she stands with other women under the cross and, in solidarity with Jesus, risks her life (Matt. 27:56).[99]

The text of Mark 10:42–45 and par. is usually attenuated by means of assigning a different meaning to serving and being a slave in the community.

204

(More on this in IV.2.C, below). Serving is understood only symbolically; it becomes "being of service." The perspective here is that of the powerful. In some symbolic sense, they understand themselves as "servants." But this only obfuscates the structures of domination.

If the text is to be taken seriously and if it has not been falsehood from its inception, its truth and overall claim must prove itself in relation to two questions: (1) Was the domination of men over women and that of men and women slave owners over slaves in fact perceived as unjust violence? (Or in different words: Did women and slaves, both female and male, serve while the men were merely "of service"?) (2) Can one match the overall claim of this text with the *structures* of early Christian communities, or was it a text with a lofty meaning but without practical results? I shall return to Christology, which is of fundamental importance for the text and its understanding of the community.

B. SOCIAL-HISTORICAL QUESTIONS

Lines of Social Distinction Drawn by "Service"

The verb *to serve (diakonein)*—and those that belong to this group—serves a key function in Mark 10:42–45, as in the entire New Testament. It is found often on almost every literary level (all told, the words in this group occur one hundred times).[100] It recedes into the background again in the Christian literature of the immediate post–New Testament period. The frequency alone of its usage indicates that the Christian community expressed its self-understanding in this term. To understand the meaning of the word within early Christianity, one needs to study the social reality that society then attached to this word and to study it in social-historical terms.

In my social-historical analysis I begin with the Septuagint, where the term is used sparingly but with a meaning that is nonetheless clear. This term refers to human beings who are in relationships of subjugation and whose work is that of performing *personal services.*[101] There are at least two instances where the word has a pejorative meaning.[102] It is not used in connection with the relationship to God, unlike the term *douleuein* (to serve as a female or male slave), which in its substance is closely related. I find this usage in the Septuagint helpful in bringing back down to earth what the Christian history of interpretation has to say about the meaning of "to be of service" (*diakonein*). It says that "being of service" relates to a group of words signifying "serving at table."[103] The words do indeed mean serving at table (among other things), but as the labor of people who are subjugated and often despised.

In extrabiblical usage, as in the Septuagint, "to serve" (*diakonein*) refers almost exclusively to the menial labor of women and slaves, performed for people of higher rank on whom they are economically dependent.

The New Testament uses *diakonein* to express what slaves do in preparing and serving food (Luke 17:8; 22:37). The *diakonoi*, the servants in John 2:5, 9 who bring in the jars of wine, are, like the steward who organizes the festivities (*architriklinos;* John 2:8f.), to be understood as slaves. In Matt. 22:13 the *diakonoi* have to shackle and then eject unwelcome guests during a feast. John 13:4ff. presumes that it is female and male slaves who wash the guests' feet at meals. They open the door (Mark 13:34; Acts 12:13) and announce the guests. There are sufficient extrabiblical parallels to these individual features that we shall look only at the labor of two slaves mentioned in ancient literature.

The slave woman Photis in Apuleius's *Metamorphoses* (1.21.4ff.) opens the door to the guest (1.22.1), announces him (1.22.3), carries the baggage (1.23.4), must bring in oil and linens and conduct the guest to the bath (1.23.4), buy feed for his horse (1.24.1), and finally, ask him to come to dinner (1.26.1). She covers him up upon his retirement to bed (2.6.4), she cooks for him (2.7.2), she sleeps with him (2.7.5), she attends her lady at bedside (2.16.1), and she clears the dishes from the table (2.17.1).[104]

Aesop describes a slave, also named Aesop, who does heavy field work (2.4.9; cf. Luke 17:8) and, on orders from his master, must beat other slaves (3). He complains: "How wearisome the slavery that has overcome us! Surely it is odious to the gods. 'Aesop, set the table; Aesop, heat the bath; Aesop, top off the water; Aesop, feed the animals!' Whatever is toilsome, strenuous, painful or demeaning, Aesop must do it all" (13). He must carry baggage on a long journey (17); in his satchel he carries the vegetables his master bought (34); he accompanies his master to the bath, carrying the oil jar and the linen (38); he must cook (39, 42), serve the drinks (40), wash his master's feet before meals (40), serve the food (41, 43); he goes shopping and prepares meals (51).[105]

I turn again to the New Testament to describe the menial work women had to do in connection with tending to people's needs. Mark 1:31 and par. and Mark 15:40f. should not be classified immediately with women's work in the house, since these statements are to be related to discipleship of Jesus (see below). In exegetical tradition, these texts have been understood frequently and without much reflection as women's housework.[106] In Luke 10:40 it is Martha who does the housework[107] that is needed when a guest is hosted, and which is no different from the corresponding work of slaves already described. Doing housework and learning are clearly distinguished. Mary sits at the feet of Jesus and listens to his word (Luke 10:39), that is to say, she is Jesus' student and for that reason lets Martha do the housework alone. In spite of the complicated history of the text of Luke 10:42 and its interpretation, it is clear that housework is not to be played off against Mary's learning on the basis of this saying: Mary has chosen "the good portion," the portion of God's salvation,[108] so that Martha too should become a learner. The text has an androcentric perspective. Like all men in patriarchy, Jesus (that is to say, Luke's Jesus) expects housework to be done quietly and out of sight, even though, according to Luke 10:38–42 and 11:27f., women are not to be confined to the patriarchal roles. But the story does reflect that women in the communities who had to do housework (in spite of the basic principle that everyone takes part in *diakonein*) did not always comply quietly, even though Martha's protest was directed unfortunately only against Mary and not also against Jesus.

The division of roles between Mary and Martha is less conflicted in John 12:1–8: Martha does the necessary preparations for the meal, Mary anoints the guest's feet, a task that a host/hostess would assign to the housewife, a female or male slave, or even do him- or herself.[109] Jesus interprets this act as an anointing for his burial and, as such, as a prophetic deed in recognition of the Son of God and his way. The text does have in mind the traditional work of anointing and foot washing, but in many ways it falsifies that work and raises it to another level. Martha's work, by contrast, remains the work of housewives and does not transcend its customary place in society.

In their instruction to women, the household codes presuppose housework; in two instances it is not named (Eph. 6:7; Col. 3:18) as is the work of slaves (Eph. 6:7; Col. 3:22). The *diakonein* of women is so much taken for granted in this seamless patriarchal context that is has become an unspoken dimension of the admonition to be submissive. First Timothy 5:8, 10, and 13 indicate that there were conflicts about women's housework in Christian communities. Obviously there were women who were opposed to being confined to housework, a restriction that the author of this epistle seeks to enforce in relation to widows. In Titus 2:5 female presbyters are called on to train young women for housework in the patriarchal household. The Greek text refers to housework (*oikourgos*), which has been made invisible again in many translations ("domestic" [RSV] or similar expressions) and in part of the manuscript tradition (*oikouros*, "domestic," "housekeeping"). What the New Testament has to say about women's housework (*diakonein*) in the sense of the patriarchal household shows that the work is even less visible than the work of female and male slaves. It shows also that women in Christian communities were opposed to this patriarchal arrangement (Luke 10:40; 1 Tim. 5:8, 10, 13), that women in early Christianity had begun to break out of patriarchal oppression.

Because of the text's misogyny, in which it is not untypical for imperial Rome, it is difficult to discern what role women's housework has in Apuleius's *Metamorphoses*. The miller's wife, who had become Jewish or Christian (9.14f.: "who substituted for appearance's sake a safe religion with the impious embrace, as she called it, of the one and only God"), watches over the donkeys as they drive the mill. Another woman is supervised by a slave, on orders of his master who is absent, effectively "shackling her to her work with wool inside the house" (9.17.3–6). A woman prepares meals (9.22.3); another serves them (9.26.4).

The difference in status between free women and slaves is significant. Nevertheless, when there are no female slaves available, free women must do their work. But when female slaves are available, the difference in status is honored. Aesop relates a prank that is of interest here. The slave Aesop is to find for his master someone who is utterly indifferent or else receive a lashing. Aesop chooses a farmer whom he judges to be indifferent. His master schemes with his wife on how they might trick Aesop:

> Get up and take a bowl to this stranger to wash his feet. Because you are the mistress of the house, he will consider your dignity and not permit it; he will say: "my lady, is there not a slave (other texts write: a female servant) who can wash my feet?" He is not indifferent and, therefore, Aesop will receive his lashing. (61)[110]

In its different versions, this story speculates about what it might mean for the mistress of the house to wash the guest's feet. Either there is no female or male slave or the master of the house wants to honor the guest in a special way and forces (*enagkasen*) his wife to do this task, or she wants to honor the guest by washing his feet herself.[111]

Housework that has to be done in connection with cultic meals (*diakonein* in the sense of "to serve") is at times, but falsely, said to be done by those who bear "office." What female or male deacons (*ministrae, ministri*) do for the cultic meal is work of slaves or women, work that is not dignified with honor or power.[112] Such work is also associated in this context with the lowest places in society.

What this shows concerning the work (*diakonein*) done by slaves and women in looking after others is that *diakonein* delineates a sharp social boundary. Like manual labor, such *diakonein* is beneath the dignity of a free, affluent man. But even a poor man, a daily-wage earner or manual laborer, finds his world in order only when he is being served and does not have to do the work needed to look after himself. Such work is often unpaid, and as a rule, no one takes notice of it.

As already noted, foot washing is part of the menial labor performed by female and male slaves and women.[113] But it also embodies a particular symbolic value for expressing submission and domination and, consequently, for honoring someone.[114] In this context as well, the New Testament employs the ambiguous terminology that we have already noticed in connection with "being of service." On the one hand, Jesus' foot washing becomes an example for all members of the community (John 13:14). To wash one another's feet means that *all* move down to the lowest place. The narrative of the foot washing in John 13 is based on the same fundamental idea as Mark 10:42–45 and par. On the other hand, language is used that expresses the opposite of *diakonein* in the sense of "to serve." First Timothy 5:10 instructs a group of Christian women to wash "the saints' " feet, without indicating that all are to wash each other's feet. But 1 Timothy limits foot washing in the community to women, thereby reinforcing the usual social structure of submission. Like the veil in 1 Cor. 11:2–16, foot washing is here an expression of women's subjugation by men in the Christian community.

The social-historical evidence presented shows that work which attends to someone's personal needs—from serving meals to washing clothes—is done by slaves and women and is understood as submission to domination. The New Testament uses ambiguous language: the group of words involved refers on the one hand to the service of all to everyone else and on the other to the submissive service of slaves and women.

Did Free Men in the Communities Serve Slaves and Free Women?

The basic questions raised above (in IV.2.A) can hardly be answered because of androcentricity of language. Mark 10:42–45 and par., Jesus' foot washing in John 13, and other services yet to be discussed may be differently understood. Either the androcentrism excludes from view women and slaves and the text signals the abandonment of rank among men only,[115] or free men actually assume a serving role toward female and male slaves and women. That would mean that men serve at table, and wash feet and clothes, even when slaves and free women are present. "To serve" (*diakonein*) in early Christianity would then have been filled with new meaning and lived out in a novel manner. It would have meant participation in authority and in the work of looking after the needs of a circle of people without distinctions among slaves, women, and free men. The latter interpretation is supported by three considerations.

1. Free women and both female and male slaves participated in their communities' exercise of power; Elisabeth Schüssler Fiorenza has demonstrated this again and again. The primary example is found in Rom. 16:2; Phoebe is a *diakonos* in the community in the same manner as is, for example, Paul.[116]

2. There were conflicts in the communities that arose when women refused housework (Luke 10:38–42; 1 Tim. 5:8, 10, 13). A similar conflict is described in Acts 6:1ff.; the "Twelve" tried to distribute to different groups of people the *diakonia* of the word and the *diakonia* of looking after people's needs. Men were involved in the latter as well (the seven from among the "Hellenists"). But the Hellenists seem not to have settled for this separation of the service of preaching and the service of providing (cf. Acts 6:8; 8:4f.; 11:19). Men's domination of women did play a part in this conflict (Acts 6:1). I understand the phrase that "their widows" (i.e., those of the Hellenists) were "overlooked" by the Hebrews in the daily *diakonia* to mean that men of the Hebrew groups refused to serve women (i.e., these widows) by not preparing food and serving it to them. Those widows were not recipients of alms but participants in the exercise of the community's powers.[117]

3. Due to societies' hierarchical gender divisions of labor, the *diakonia* (Matt. 25:44) to the hungry, thirsty, naked, sick, and imprisoned was performed primarily by women; Matt. 25:31–46, however, regards it to be the praxis of all Christians. One could hardly assume that men were excluded from that praxis.

The language of the text is androcentric, as usual. But it is also not likely that it thinks of women engaging in a different *diakonia* than men. Rather, I regard the assertiveness of Jewish housewives toward their husbands, manifested in their diaconal praxis, as evidence that the work which had to be done in the home and in looking after people's needs was in fact a part of *everyone's* praxis of faith.

The connection between Jewish (and subsequently, also Christian) charitable work and the housework of Jewish women becomes apparent when one reads of the conflicts between women and men that arose because Jewish housewives independently and assertively carried out charitable work:

> A certain teacher was excessively timid in doing good. Every day he surreptitiously slipped four coins under the door of a poor man's house in the neighborhood. One day the poor man wanted to find out who his benefactor was. That day the teacher returned late from school with his wife; the poor man noticed that he bent over at the door, whereupon he followed them. Unfortunately, the teacher fell into a burning oven and burned his feet. He had his wife carry him away, still wanting to remain anonymous. Because he was concerned about the accident, his wife said that she was really doing more good because when a poor person came to her at home, she would provide something which that person could consume right away: "Bread, meat, salt, etc., whereas this poor man first has to go out and buy something with your money."[118]

The woman's sense of herself comes from knowing that her whole person is involved and not just the gift of money:

> Doing good (almsgiving) and works of love make up for all the commandments in the Torah, except that doing good is done to the living, while works of love are done to the living and the dead; doing good is done for the poor, while works of love are for the poor and the rich; doing good is done with money, works of love with one's whole person and with money.[119]

The connection between women's works of love and their housework means that they are engaged in the giving not only of money but also of their whole person as well as money. "Why did the clouds rise up first on the side where the master's wife stood and only after on the side of the master? Because the wife is always at home and gives the poor bread that they can eat right away, whereas I give them money that they cannot consume right away" (*b. Ta'an.* 23b). It is women's work to care for poor people and guests (*b. Ketubot* 61a). Many other sources speak of the greater intimacy that exists in the work of providing for others' needs; they speak similarly of the independence of women in their work of love.[120] In light of this, should not Luke 8:3 ("who provided for them *ek tōn hyparchontōn autais*") be translated as "according to what was possible for them in their circumstances,"[121] instead of "out of their own resources," as is done generally today?[122] What those women are doing is in the Jewish tradition of "good works"; Acts 9:36 alone would indicate that Luke also sees it that way.

The three considerations just outlined support the view that in the early Christian communities, the lines of social distinctions drawn by service had become problematic and were partially erased (e.g., by Hellenists, that is, Greek-speaking Jewish women and men; Acts 6:1ff.). The strongest arguments *in support* of this view are the signs of resulting conflicts about the issue. They indicate that struggling for changes in the hierarchy of service, for free men's participation in the work of looking after people's needs, is a most touchy issue. There were communities who learned that women no longer tolerated the mendacity of a praxis of justice that bracketed out their housework (Luke 10:38–42; 1 Timothy 5). These conflicts manifest how aggressively men fight for their privileges (Acts 6:1 ff.; but also 1 Cor. 11:2–16). Fortunately, they also show that Jesus' sayings, such as Mark 10:42–45 and par., are not intended merely to modify a loose order of rank among free men, thereby acquiring a token or farcical meaning. And they also hold up embarrassing pictures such as that of Jesus in Luke 10:38–42, in which, of course, he is out of touch with kitchen work and makes the conflict between looking after people and being about the word Martha's problem, no matter how gently he does so.

Against this background we may read the overall New Testament material with equanimity, detecting both the recognition of unjust structures of domination and Christian actions against them. On the one hand, we may read it with the suspicion that, by some trick or other, free men regain their privileges; on the other hand, we may read in the hope that there are practical foundations not for an early Christian world where all was well but for a praxis of justice that, albeit imperfect, is honest and, from a contemporary perspective, inspiring and practicable for the future of Christian communities.

The Perception of Unjust Structures of Domination and Christian Actions against Them

In many places in the New Testament, there is pervasive evidence that unjust social structures are perceived, while in others, textual material appears to strengthen unjust dominance. In Paul this phenomenon is almost nonexistent in relation to male slaves but very obvious in relation to free women and female slaves (blatantly so in relation to Hagar; Gal. 4:21–31).[123] In the other epistolary literature, structures of injustice are bolstered in the name of God or Christ (cf. at II.1 above), most plainly in the household codes and the pastorals. The gospel of the poor and the option for women pervade the Gospels. More than anyone else, it is free women, slaves, and children, but also those men who live near starvation as beggars or underemployed wage earners, who are victims of social structures of injustice. It is in the context of the numerous and diverse actions by Christians against injustice that we may see just how clearly these structures were recognized. When just relationships with one another are not practiced and there is no opposition to injustice, the presence of oppression goes unnoticed.[124] I want to elucidate what such opposition looks like with reference to two important examples; both are of central significance to the praxis of faith: mutuality and sister/brotherliness.

Mutuality

On every literary level, the New Testament affirms that mutuality is basic to every relationship in the Christian community. Just how much importance was attached to a praxis of mutuality may be determined from the frequent use of the Greek word *allēlous,* translated most often as "one another." In addition to the use of the reciprocal pronoun *one another* (*allēlous*), there is frequent use of composite words with the preposition *syn* (with) that refer to the qualitative communal sense of the community of faith. Both reflect linguistically the labor involved in achieving true communion. Some of the words composed with the preposition *syn* (with) were invented by Christian communities (e.g., *sym-mimē tes*—women and men imitators, Phil. 3:17;[125] *syzōopoieō*—to be made alive together, Eph. 2:5; Col. 2:13; *sygkakoucheomai*—to be ill-treated along with others, Heb. 11:25; etc.). Whenever new words are invented or existing words receive new meaning, the intensity of collective effort and common goals can be easily discerned.

The understanding of relationships of mutuality is based on the tradition of communion of Israel as a people of God. That is why the mutuality of serving in love of one another (*douleuein*) is paralleled with the commandment of love for the neighbor in Lev. 19:18 (Gal. 5:13f.). Acts 7:26 may serve as an elucidation of this Jewish tradition. Moses speaks against the conflict among the people. Because those engaged in conflict are brothers, they are not to do each other injustice. It is necessary at this point to know more than I do (or have been able to find in the scholarly literature) about the communal sense of Jewish diaspora communities;[126] for it is quite likely that the early Christian communities, in the lively formation of their internal structures, drew on the tradition of the Jewish diaspora communities. The work of creating communities that do not reconstruct social injustice but build up just structures is without doubt rooted in the tradition of Judaism.

The metaphors for the community as the body of Christ[127] and as a brotherhood[128] are used a number of times to explain that its internal structures are defined in terms of a praxis of mutuality. Individuals in the community understand themselves as members and as brothers and sisters among brothers and sisters. For good reasons, I interpret "brotherhood" as sister/brotherhood. The understanding of mutuality and sister/brotherliness is indeed androcentric (brother in mutual relation with brother; cf. Rom. 14:13), but the interest in mutuality is emphatically holistic. *All* participants are "members," sisters or brothers. Mutuality applies explicitly to all.[129] The word *panton* (all) in Mark 10:44 is an attempt to express the comprehensive character of the cancellation of social distinctions among Christians. Mark 10:42–45 and par. and the word *mutual* (or *one another*) refer to the same thing: everyone without exception participates in the labor against structures of domination. And that is why it is necessary to translate *brotherhood* as *sister/brotherhood,* despite the androcentric language about it.[130]

It is remarkable that the word *allēlous* is applied to such utterly different aspects of structures of relationship. This reciprocal pronoun is associated with a great number of words. The phrase "to love one another," which occurs fifteen times, is the only firm linguistic complex. It is absent from the Synoptic Gospels but is used frequently in the Johannine writings and has a firm place in Paul's epistles.[131] The admonition to do away with orders of rank is phrased differently but conveys identical meaning; it is found in connection with the upbuilding of structures of mutuality. "Outdo one another in showing honor" (Rom. 12:10); "Serve one another [like slaves] through love" (Gal. 5:13); "In humility count others as better than yourselves" (Phil. 2:3); "Clothe yourselves with humility toward one another" (1 Peter 5:5). This diversity shows what Mark 10:42–45 and par. and John 13 had already made plain: everyone moves downward in the given social structures; no one claims superior rank. This makes an authoritarian structure impossible.

The admonition to greet one another with a holy kiss is given in a linguistically identical manner (Rom. 16:16; 1 Cor. 16:20; 2 Cor. 13:12; 1 Peter 5:14; cf. 1 Thess. 5:26—an androcentric version of the admonition that means to include *all* even though it refers to them as "brothers"). Especially in connection with the eucharistic celebrations, the holy kiss "stresses the witness of the mutual relationship in the realm of the eschatological fellowship of the saints. . . . It is not individuals, but the community as a whole which is to act."[132] As a sign of heartfelt affection, but even more of respect, the kiss unites all in mutuality and expresses, both symbolically and physically, their sense of community without structures of submission. Here it is not that only those of low rank kiss those of superior rank. The admonition is formulated in a comprehensive sense: no one is left out.

I shall list only some of the many expressions that inform the meaning of mutuality. "Be at peace with one another" (Mark 9:50); the community of comfort unites the believers as those who give and receive: "to be among you to be myself comforted by your faith as you are by mine" (Rom. 1:12). Not only love but also faith (*pistis*) has a dimension of relationship with the sisters and brothers. Sisterly/brotherly love is mutual (Rom. 12:10); believers accept one another as Christ has accepted them (Rom. 15:7). They care for one another in concord (1 Cor. 12:25) and in mutuality bear one another's burdens (Gal. 6:2). One may round out this picture with the use of a Greek concordance, under *allēlous.*

As can be seen, mutuality is a dimension of the relationship with Christ or God. "It is not to be so among you" (Mark 10:43 and par.), "for the Human One[133] [literally, "the Son of man"] did not come either to be served . . . "

Christ and mutuality are often linked in the New Testament in the understanding that mutuality is Christlike. For example: "Welcome one another, therefore, as [*kathōs*] Christ has welcomed you" (Rom. 15:7). It is not enough to see Christ as the "ground and measure"[134] of mutuality. Rather, *kathōs* and similar terms put Christ's welcoming and that of the community on the same level. The Christology of this idea does not isolate Christ from believers but draws him into a circle with the community of the faithful.[135]

Mutuality of relationships in the community and its strict rejection of structures of domination are in contrast to hate and strife, which are also mutual relationships (e.g., Gal. 5:15, 17). Being of one mind with another does not come about through denying conflicts, for conflicts do arise frequently within communities. Even mutuality and the removal of differences in rank are opposed, as can be seen in the narrative in which Jesus' saying is reported (Mark 10:42–45). The sons of Zebedee surely are not the only ones who try to gain privileges—even privileges in God's reign (Mark 10:35–40 and par.). As the conflicts about serving, about *diakonia,* referred to above indicate, it is difficult even in small, manageable communities to establish new structures of life. Like the sons of Zebedee or the apostles of Jerusalem (Acts 6:1ff.), men fight for predominance; they do not recognize the injustice of the hierarchical gender division of labor (which is ultimately true also of Jesus, according to Luke 10:42). They fight for their privileges over women (like the unknown author of 1 Timothy). Like the mother of the sons of Zebedee (Matt. 20:20), women allow themselves to be used for men's power interests. And women, like Mary in Luke 10:38–42, feel honored when they are allowed to be pupils and do not notice how they betray their sister who is busy with housework. But Martha learns how to defend herself. She, too, represents in her contentiousness the experiences of many women in the communities. I see much strife in the early Christian communities, but it is fruitful strife, for it is a stage on the way to God's reign and it serves to shape mutuality.

On the basis of the fundamental importance of Mark 10:42–45 and par. (or John 13) and of mutuality in the New Testament, I not only confirm once again that free men did serve slaves and free women in terms of domestic work; I also note that a comprehensive understanding of "to serve" marks early Christianity: men do take care of each other's needs; free women and slaves do have authority and take part actively in proclamation of the gospel and administration of the community. That is why usages of "to serve" in the context of women's discipleship (Mark 1:31 and par.; Mark 15:41 and par.) are to be understood as denoting discipleship, and not a hierarchical gender division of labor in which women do all the work of looking after other people's needs.

Sister/Brotherliness

When early Christianity speaks of the relationship among members of the community in terms of sister/brotherliness (of the love of sisters/brothers—

philadelphia), it envisions the equality of rank of all brothers and sisters. That is why no one among them should be called father, since God alone is Father.[136] The conception of all being sisters and brothers, ruling out dominance on anyone's part, is found throughout early Christian literature. The house church replaces the biological and economic "family" as the primary social relation.

The word *family* is used here as a translation of the concept "house" (in Greek, *oikos;* Latin, *domus*), referring to the people who live together in the house. (It also refers to the building by that name.) In a figurative sense, "house," as family, comprises the nuclear family and often persons from the larger family circle and, in certain instances, female and male slaves. Living together as a house is the economic foundation of the lives of those who belong to the house. The early Christian house churches (e.g., *kat' oikon ekklēsia*)[137] were the places of assembly and the gathered people were, as a house, the family of God. Like the patriarchal house, the house church is the economic foundation of those who live together as God's family. But the house church is not organized along patriarchal lines. In the Christian house, being in Christ determines to what family one belongs, not the biological or economical family structures known in society (Mark 3:31–35 and par.).

Theological language about *familia dei* has proven to be more of a hindrance to understanding the meaning of relationships in the community, that is, sister/brotherliness. With the designation of the community as *familia dei*, patriarchal structures were brought back into Christian ecclesiology without examination. However, it is an established fact that early Christianity criticized patriarchal marriage. Its social reality and high ideological valuation[138] notwithstanding, Christians dissolved it whenever there was conflict between following Christ and patriarchal family. There is no need here to discuss the material in detail;[139] the evidence in the sources speaks for itself. One dimension of the material is the whole discussion relating to divorce.[140] Christian women and men[141] frequently divorced. In Christian communities there were to be no remarriages after divorce. A second marriage after divorce is regarded as a breach of the first marriage. In early Christianity, celibacy is experienced and practiced, especially by women, as liberation through the gospel.[142]

Understanding the Christian community as a house community and characterizing the relationship of members one with another as sister/brotherliness does not mean a new and improved form of the patriarchal household. The *ekklēsia*/community's self-understanding is not based on the model of the patriarchal family but, like the synagogue community, on that of the communal assembly of free (male) citizens. When the members of the community call themselves brothers and sisters—as is customary among Jews—they do so on the basis of a clear and critical process of reflection in which a qualitative distinction is made between patriarchal family and community. What the New Testament has become in Christian hands represents a tragedy with incredible repercussions: that which was critical of the patriarchal family and sought to reestablish just structures of relationships in the community has been forcibly suppressed and given a different meaning.[143] It has become possible thereby to use the New Testament in beatifying the patriarchal family. In the way Christian women and men have interpreted the New Testament, Cicero has triumphed over Jesus for centuries and rendered Jesus invisible (as was already shown in Part I).

It is from this perspective that we have to understand what it meant for Christians at that time to marry and have children. We know about Christian couples, working together for Jesus' message, in which the woman did not become an appendage of the man.[144] Their relationship was not defined in the interests of legitimate progeny and the continuity of property rights but in terms of their inclusion in the mutuality and sister/brotherliness of the community.[145] Mark 10:2–12 and par. records a tradition of Jesus that lauds a man and a woman's marital relationship as a relationship of deepest intimacy but without inclinations of domination and concern for the social obligation of producing children. God's will in creation for an inseparable relationship is set over against a misogynist and hardhearted patriarchal praxis of divorce: "the two shall be one flesh" (Mark 10:8 and par., from Gen. 2:24). This did not mean what was made of it later: a married couple cannot be divorced. (One has only to read how the text continues, Mark 10:11f., which accepts divorce and speaks only against second marriages.) Nor did it mean that real humanness is actualized only in the relationship of couples, although that is what later ages made of it. In Christian communities there are a significant number of women and men who do not live in a marriage relationship. Celibacy is supported and promoted. The praise of the inseparable marriage relationship between a woman and a man in Mark 10:2–10 and par. is not a law for everyone but a vision, a utopia of intimacy, which does not seek to oppress people but to give them courage. When two people marry and live together, they do not have to orient themselves by patriarchal marriage but may live according to this alternate vision of marriage in mutuality.

Sister/brotherliness within the community is not oriented by the structures of oppression that pertain to the patriarchal family; it is oriented instead by mutuality and the critique of domination, for only Christ is Lord (*Kyrios*) and only God is Father. But it also shows that life together in that community excludes life together in *patriarchal* family relationships. However, it also means that the congregation takes over from the patriarchal family its economic and emotional function of assuring the survival of its members, unless poverty is overwhelming.

Eucharist and Community of Goods

Early Christian communities were small, decentralized communes, usually in the house of one of the members. At night, sisters and brothers gathered for a common meal, to study Torah, and to take counsel together. The common meal was also the time for communal prayer and remembrance of Christ's death. The history of the Eucharist in earliest times has been written often enough. It is my concern now to show that this common meal was (and is), with its cultic, practical, emotional, and political aspects, the foundation of the communities and their path to the reign of God. The separation of cultic meal and supper, an idea that Paul already entertains,[146] spells the loss of the true sense of communion. It also opens the door to the separation of faith and politics and of faith and economics.

The book of Acts is often accused in modern interpretation of idealizing the first Jerusalemite community. The phrase "they had everything in common" (Acts 2:44; 4:32) is without doubt very general and imprecise. It is more likely, as the text itself indicates, that members *voluntarily and as the need arose* gave up private property in favor of the cooperative efforts of the community.[147] The community had a common money chest and considered itself responsible for the economic needs of its members, those of other communities, and itinerant prophets. The common meal is the expression of their economic sharing, their communion in the faith, and their emotional bondedness. The book of Acts portrays this with sensitivity and an accuracy that may be substantiated from other sources. In spite of the basic importance of the daily shared Eucharist, early Christian communities did not succeed in recognizing that their ritual of breaking bread symbolizes how patriarchy expropriates the labor of women (as I have shown above at II.2.B).

The early Christian Eucharist has a number of aspects: eating together, remembering Christ's death together, caring together for the members of the body of Christ, celebrating together the hope in God's reign. As if in a prism, the various facets of communal life are caught in the common meal. The word *communion* (*koinōnia*) may serve to guide us through the diverse aspects of community life and the Eucharist.

Outside the Bible, *koinōnia* refers usually to two or more people's joint sharing of a common property, whether it be in legal[148] or other terms.[149] It rarely refers to someone receiving a share in something that did not belong to her before.[150] Paul speaks of *koinōnia* within the terms of reference of early Christianity and not those historically associated with that concept. He uses it to speak of the relationship among Christian communities or individual Christians in which both sides give and take so that want is turned into abundance. That is how he understands the collection for Jerusalem; the poor communities there do not by any means merely receive but also give of their (spiritual) abundance (Rom. 15:27; 2 Cor. 8:13–15). The relationships among the communities are based in a mutuality that turns deprivation on either side into abundance. Each side enriches the other. In 2 Cor. 8:9, this idea is applied to the relationship of Christ to human beings: he became poor voluntarily so that others would become rich through his poverty. The mutuality of that relationship is not explained in this text but may be discerned in Paul's intent: And you give yourselves to God (cf. 2 Cor. 8:5), who through the gift of your bodies can spread the riches of God's love, transforming God's anger into goodness. Paul shows no hesitation in this context to make use of the idea of retribution; for the arrangement of mutual giving and receiving (as he formulates it in Phil. 4:15), *koinōnia* in the sense of mutuality, is not one-sided at all, that is, top-down.

The concept is also the key to the interpretation of the Eucharist in Paul and Acts. Eucharist creates community with Christ and with one another; it makes of the faithful the body of Christ (1 Cor. 10:16f.). This communion comes about through eating and drinking; it is physical, sensuous, and observable in its reality. In Acts 2:42, the word *koinōnia* means both common meal and "breaking bread." And these are the aspects of communion that the text lists: life together, community of goods, daily common prayer in the Temple, breaking bread together in the "house," rejoicing together in the nearness of God's reign, common praise of God (Acts 2:42–47; cf. Acts 4:32–37).

C. FEMINIST OBSERVATIONS ON THE
HISTORY OF INTERPRETATION

One notices a deep gulf between early Christianity's conceptions of life together in communities and how they are perceived in Christian theology. Generally speaking, the ideology of patriarchy, as portrayed earlier in this book in relation to Cicero, shapes how Christian theology perceives the traditions of the New Testament. This patriarchal hermeneutics resolutely pushes aside any clear notion that conflicts with its interests; because of the single-mindedness of its interests, it has no sensitivity for breaks or tensions in a text. Such textual anomalies indicate how much communities were subject to contradictions. They cannot be interpreted away as problems of "heretics" or "opponents" who were on the wrong side anyway and whose position and praxis of life need not be taken seriously in theology. In what follows here, I give some examples that manifest these patriarchal interests and prejudices and show how they function in the interpretation of the New Testament to obscure the truth of the texts.

First, one can discern a prevailing rule of thumb that *as a matter of course, one needs to distinguish between the service rendered by women and the office performed by men, even when the same word is used to describe them* (diakonein, diakonia, diakonos).

The hierarchical gender and "racist"[151] division of labor that assigns housework to women and slaves and permits free men to claim for themselves the right to be served by that work is accepted without discussion as a normal, given reality in early Christianity. Mark 10:42–45 and par., John 13, and Acts 6:2 should disturb the confidence of such an assumption. There is Jesus' action of comparing himself to a slave and then performing a slave's work of washing feet, but also his admonition to all his followers that only those who are slaves or the *diakonos* of all (of all other members) have rank in the community. Both of these initiatives fundamentally question the hierarchical gender and "racist" division of labor. The tradition of scholarly research functions with a double meaning of *diakonein* (to serve): men's *diakonia* is obviously something quite different from the *diakonia* of women and slaves.

I name some examples for purposes of clarification. Concerning Acts 6:2 (serving at tables), H. W. Beyer writes:

> The reference is not merely to the provision of food but to the daily preparation and organization. H. J. Holtzmann describes the men to whom this task was committed as organizers, dispensers, and overseers of meals, *trapezopoioi* [the table arrangers]. The *diakonein trapezais* [to serve at table] is brought into emphatic contrast with the *diakonia tou logou* [service of the Word] and embraces practical love rather than the proclamation of the Word.[152]

In other words, serving at tables, when it comes to men, is an office of leadership performed in the community's charitable activities. The question of who sets the tables, cooks, cleans up, and washes the dishes does not even come up; obviously, it has no connection with men's serving at table.

Here is what J. Gnilka writes about Mark 10:43: "*Diakonos* does not yet refer to an office conferred but to service given in administration, preaching, caring for the poor and waiting on tables during community assemblies." In this list serving at tables has a symbolic meaning, however; it is supposed to give evidence of a Christian man's readiness to offer service. As far as I am able to survey exegetical literature, it consistently refers to *diakonein* as meaning literally "serving at table," stressing its theological significance for the office of service men perform in the community, while it is taken for granted that it could not have been men's work to prepare the actual meal. Jesus' foot washing in John 13 is said to be a christological "sign" of his death on the cross; it is not seen that here the work of slaves receives a sacramental quality and that this draws the community into a new and just exercise of power.[153] The unspecified statements about women's *diakonia* (Mark 1:31 and par., etc.) are similarly interpreted—at least until the emergence of feminist theology discussions—as references to housework or, on account of Luke 8:3, as caring for others with material goods.

As an "office," the *diakonia* of women is a *marginal phenomenon* among the "real offices" in the community. And the content of women's *diakonia* is said to have a qualitative difference from the *diakonia* of Paul (he proclaims the word) or from the *diakonia* of men in the sense of a specific office conferred. J. Roloff interprets 1 Tim. 3:11 as an instruction to female deacons, saying that "the instructions for female deacons mentioned do not manifest a directly gender-specific orientation. But one must not conclude from their general, ethical content that this service is in fact equal to that of men."[154]

Speaking of Phoebe in Rom. 16:1, U. Wilckens recalls that her *diakonia* is an "office" and that it includes charitable work in the slums of Cenchreae and various tasks related to providing for itinerant Christians. He emphasizes that this *diakonia* is different from the functions of missionaries (like Paul) and their assistants, described in the same term.[155] One could easily multiply the number of such examples; they suffice to indicate that exegetical research separates women's *diakonia* and that of men in the community. The texts show no such separation; it has to be imported into them from the outset.

The scholarly tradition on the subject of women's *diakonia* (in fact, on *diakonia* in general) in the New Testament is recognizably burdened with a patriarchal outlook; the differentiated quality of woman's "office" and man's "office" is *presupposed,* as is a hierarchical gender and "racist" division of labor. In addition, the New Testament's androcentric perspective has been adopted without question. One recognizes that New Testament texts themselves partially resist this patriarchal outlook in that the interpretation introduces separations (*diakonia* of women vs. *diakonia* of men) that the texts do not mention. A reading of Mark 10:42–45 and par. that is critical of patriarchy shows that early Christianity understands *diakonein* as something every Christian owes every other Christian, without introducing any separation between housework and preaching the word as *diakonia,* the diaconate of women and that of men.

A second example of patriarchal prejudice in the interpretation of the New Testament is the notion that *mutuality is no biblical subject.*

One may observe here three patriarchal tendencies in the interpretation of New Testament texts that speak of mutuality and sisterly/brotherly love. The *first* tendency is the androcentrism that gives a male-centered rendition of a text even when it is not formulated in androcentric terms. For example, *koinōnia* (communion) appears as "brotherliness."[156]

The *second* tendency is not to acknowledge the mutuality of relationships even when the text explicitly demonstrates it, which allows for unequal power relationships to be introduced in the name of "brotherliness." Often enough, I have experienced that the church's practice of "brotherliness" among the ordained has been (and is?) a source of suffering for those in lesser positions. Behind the veil of brotherliness, which functions as the brotherhood of men in leadership positions, the lesser ones are supposed to tolerate rather than protest against this injustice. Scholarly and ecclesiastical interpretation of the New Testament, as far as I can gauge it, does not differentiate between a relationship among equals and one among unequals when it speaks of brotherliness—even when nowadays, as a concession to the women's movement, it is referred to occasionally as sister/brotherliness. The relationship among equals is a relationship of mutuality that is not one-way.

The *third* tendency of patriarchal interpretation being examined here is to regard mutuality as a sub-Christian notion of retribution. Accordingly, François

Bovon differentiates Christian mutuality from human, and therefore calculated, mutuality. Christian mutuality consists of the selflessness of God, who remains gracious to the wicked, and the analogous behavior of Christians toward their enemies. "This is where Christian ethics vehemently criticizes Hellenistic and utilitarian Jewish ethics."[157] Christian anti-Judaism has always disqualified retribution, in connection with both God's activity and human interaction, calling it scheming, sub-Christian, Jewish. *Do ut des* (I give so that you will also) is recited constantly as the opposite to Christian thinking. The Golden Rule reaps little affirmation, even though it is given in the Sermon on the Mount (Matt. 7:12; cf. Luke 6:31). It is currently fashionable to interpret the commandment to love the neighbor "as oneself" as an invitation to self-love, from which love of the neighbor will *subsequently* arise.[158] This interpretation is hopelessly lacking in insight concerning mutuality, which should mean, rather, that self-love is a by-product of giving love: that is, because I learn to bestow the goodness of loving, I also learn, *in so doing,* to receive love and to love myself as the recipient of love from another.

In terms of method, this third tendency in patriarchal interpretation shows most blatantly a lack of social-historical reflection on the meaning of mutuality and retribution. It needs to distinguish a mutuality in which people discover their power to love from banal social customs, for example, reciprocating hospitality. It must differentiate between God's retribution (*ekdikēsis*) in the eschatological judgment on which Jewish and Christian martyrs relied and the impulse to retaliate on the highway or in other human power struggles. In the tradition of Jesus, love for those who already love (Luke 6:32–34; Matt. 5:46) is set apart from the love of enemies. This does not make a distinction between non-Christian mutuality and Christian selflessness;[159] it does explicate the love of enemies, which takes the initiative and does not move in existing social grooves. Mutuality does not envision taking a defensive stance which first seeks to ensure that no risks are involved.

The third of my examples of patriarchal interests and prejudice in interpretation of the New Testament is the *treatment of the Eucharist.*

What the tradition of interpretation has to say about the Eucharist needs especially to be submitted to a critique from the feminist perspective. This is necessary because the important questions relating to the meaning of eating together and how the Eucharist is connected with the qualitative, comprehensive meaning of being a community have received scant interpretive attention. Worthy men have poured much sweat into the question of what the oldest form of the words of institution might have been in terms of the history of the Eucharist as a tradition. In their research, the early Christians' eating together is most often referred to as the *Sättigungsmahl* (eating to relieve hunger)[160] and is treated as if it were an incidental necessity or bother. What is really more important to the scholars is the Christology of the actual eucharistic words. The exegetical jargon, *Sättigungsmahl,* always reminds me of the language of restaurants in the former German Democratic Republic, where one's serving could be supplemented by a *Sättigungsbeilage* (an additional portion without extra charge) so that one would have enough to eat. That eating together is an elementary step toward communion in a comprehensive sense was taken very seriously in early Christianity.

Western tradition of interpretation has treated the community of goods in a most perfunctory fashion, as it has the gospel of the poor. Having discussed this extensively above (I.2.A and III.2.C), I need not provide further details here.

D. FEMINIST PERSPECTIVES

For the women who belong to the recent women's movement, mutuality is one of the basic essentials. A praxis of mutuality was and still is being lived there. For me, this praxis has become the distinctive mark of women who are moved by other women. They criticize concealed or visible structures of domination. In relating to one another, women try to take seriously, as a subject, the one who is before them. We ask questions of those who are before us, and we listen to their responses. Any decisions taken presuppose that all participants are able to state their views and name their interests. It is not my intention here to glorify what goes on within the women's movement. How to deal with conflicts and competition among us is a topic often proposed but not really addressed in discussion. But I see a profound and important connection between the interest in mutuality as a pivotal concept in feminist theology and the praxis of the women's movement. While the word *mutuality* lives a shadowy existence in traditional theology, it has been put to creative use in feminist theology to depict both God's or Christ's relationship to human beings and human interrelationship. It is the work of Martin Buber in particular and its reception on the part of feminist theologians that has enriched the "theology of mutual relation."[161] Carter Heyward, Beverly Harrison, and Dorothee Soelle[162] have expressed in theological language what many women in the movement think and practice.

"We are blessed if we have friends who are lovers of humanity. . . . Mutually, we may push one another beyond present hesitation; mutually, we may comfort one another; mutually, we may be blessed by one another. If so, it is very good."[163] Carter Heyward describes the fear and the injustice that human beings actually experience every day: "a lack of belief in mutuality that continues to thwart most of the rare possibilities for cultivating the mutuality that we have."[164] Christ does not come down from above as our savior but is there where people are the saviors of God.[165] Feminist theological reflection on mutuality makes biblical connections, particularly to the narratives of encounters between women and Jesus. In the biblically oriented women's movement, those Gospel stories have been the midwives to the birth of a growing (self-) awareness among women. But unfortunately—under the weight of traditional theology—the substantial evidence provided in the New Testament in support of mutuality, as I have described it, has not been seen and has not borne fruit.

The word *love* is usable only with much clarification, while the word *mutuality* is fresh and unambiguous because it cannot be used to obfuscate oppression. Love has first to be freed of its misuse: we want no separation of *erōs* and *agapē*, we want no sacrificial selflessness that in actuality means oppression. Even the word *communion* is tainted from abuse. Today, "the communion of women and men in the church" signifies a structure of injustice that is not worthy of the name *communion*. The word conceals the domination of the men's fraternity in theology and church.

"It belongs to the foundation of feminist theology . . . to regard the relationship between human beings not as an addition to the essence, as something to be actualized now and then, but to understand it as the *archē*, the origin, what the creation narrative calls 'in the beginning.' "[166] Mutuality is close at hand. We can mutually support one another, help, criticize, comfort, and create clarity for one another. It is enough when two people make a beginning. The reign of God can be felt when a community of mutuality comes into being. The New Testament tells of the sisters and brothers of Christ eating together every day. Eating together is the place of the communion of Christ's disciples, who take responsibility for the bread and who do not permit the earth in which the grain grows to be poisoned. It does not permit the women and men whose labor brought forth the bread to be turned into second-class citizens. The living source of justice for all of creation and for mutuality among human beings was and is the mutuality between women and men and the God who is before them.

Abbreviations

ANRW	*Aufstieg und Niedergang der römischen Welt*
b.	Babylonian Talmud
Ber.	*Berakot*
BHH	*Biblisch-Historisches Handwörterbuch*
B.M.	*Baba Meṣia*
B.Q.	*Baba Qamma*
BZNW	Beihefte zur Zeitschrift für die neutestamentliche Wissenschaft
CIG	*Corpus inscriptionum graecarum*
CIL	*Corpus inscriptionum latinarum*
Dtn	Deuteronomy, Deuteronomic
EKL	*Evangelisches Kirchenlexikon*
'Erub.	*'Erubin*
ET	English translation
Ev. Theol.	*Evangelische Theologie*
FRLANT	Forschungen zur Religion und Literatur des Alten und Neuen Testaments
ICC	International Critical Commentary
JAC	Jahrbuch für Antike und Christentum
JBL	*Journal of Biblical Literature*
Ketub.	*Ketubot*
LXX	Septuagint
m.	Mishnah
NEB	New English Bible
NF	neue Folge (new series)
NRSV	New Revised Standard Version
NTS	*New Testament Studies*
par.	parallel(s)
parag.	paragraph(s)

224

Pesaḥ	*Pesaḥim*
praef.	praefatio (preface)
RAC	*Reallexikon für Antike und Christentum*
RGG	*Die Religion in Geschichte und Gegenwart*
RSV	Revised Standard Version
Šabb.	*Šabbat*
Sanh.	*Sanhedrin*
t.	Tosephta
Ta'an.	*Ta'anit*
ThWNT	*Theologisches Wörterbuch zum Neuen Testament* (ET: *Theological Dictionary of the New Testament*)
ThZ	*Theologische Zeitschrift*
TRE	*Theologische Realenzyklopädie*
TU	Texte und Untersuchungen
WBFTh	*Wörterbuch der feministischen Theologie*
y.	Jerusalem Talmud
Yeb.	*Yebamot*
ZAW	*Zeitschrift für die alttestamentliche Wissenschaft*
ZNW	*Zeitschrift für die neutestamentliche Wissenschaft*
ZThK	*Zeitschrift für Theologie und Kirche*

Notes

PART I
Feminist Social History

1. *ZThK* 70 (1973): 245–71; ET: Theissen 1992, pp. 33–59.
2. Cf. Theissen 1992, p. 56n67, concerning "love patriarchalism," in reference to Troeltsch 1931.
3. Meeks 1983, pp. 52f. Horsley (1989) is an exception, in that he does not share in this consensus. I agree with his critique of both the notion of a radical itinerant elite and Theissen's conservative view of the Jesus movement.
4. Meeks 1983, pp. 52f.
5. Theissen 1992, p. 58. The upper-class orientation of this social history is discussed below at III.2.C.
6. This discussion was initiated by Rudolph Sohm (1841–1917); see S. Grundmann, *RGG*, 3d ed., vol. 6, cols. 116f. The presence of hierarchy in the early church was questioned especially by Ernst Käsemann on the basis of his experience of the church struggle in the Third Reich. He rejected the alternative between "charisma" and "office" in discussions of the early church. However, he was concerned only with the hierarchy of ecclesial officebearers and laypersons (itself an androcentric notion) and not with the hierarchies resulting from affluence and poverty. Hans Conzelmann provides an overview of this discussion in G. Kittel and G. Friedrich, eds., *Theological Dictionary of the New Testament* (cited as *ThWNT*), 9: 402–6; cf. nn. 32–34.
7. Theissen 1992, p. 52.
8. Theissen 1992, p. 51.
9. Theissen 1992, p .40.
10. On the history of the interpretation of the Sermon on the Mount, see Luz 1992, 1:218ff. Theissen's position on the Sermon on the Mount is discussed below.
11. Theissen 1992, p. 59; cf. the similar view of Luz 1985, 1:196f.
12. Theissen 1987, pp. 87, 95. I have discussed this book at length in L. Schottroff 1992b. Cf. below at II.4.C.
13. Theissen 1978, p. 125.
14. Braun 1958, 1:91. The term *attenuation* is anti-Judaistic, as is *late Judaism*, which was used regularly in German theology when Braun wrote this work.
15. Cf. L. Schottroff 1992b.
16. Theissen 1987, p. 95.

17. Theissen 1987, p. 164.
18. Theissen 1987, p. 164.
19. See the relevant contributions in the documentation of Aktion Sühnezeichen/ Friedensdienste (ed.) 1982.
20. Gerd Theissen, *Novum Testamentum* 19 (1977): 161–96.
21. Theissen 1992, p. 93.
22. Theissen 1992, p. 79.
23. Theissen 1992, p. 89.
24. Theissen 1992, p. 93.
25. Theissen 1987, pp. 92–93.
26. Theissen 1987, p. 177.
27. Theissen 1987, p. 180.
28. Theissen 1987, p. 186.
29. Cf. Theissen 1987, chap. 1 and pp. 25f., 21, 65.
30. See, e.g., the phrasing of note 9.3 on p. 204, "portion of happiness," and p. 114, "good fortune," relating to L. Schottroff in L. Schottroff/Stegemann 1986, p. 32.
31. Theissen 1987, p. 189.
32. Cf. L. Schottroff, "Die Schreckensherrschaft der Sünde und die Befreiung durch Christus nach dem Römerbrief des Paulus," in *Evangelische Theologie*, 1979, pp. 497–510, reprinted in L. Schottroff 1990a, pp. 57–72; also Wengst 1987.
33. Theissen 1987, p. 83.
34. See Meeks 1983, p. 70, where he criticizes the one-dimensional nature of Theissen's determination of social status (high status reflects a high degree of social integration). Meeks himself works with the notion of "status inconsistency"; e.g., a rich woman does belong to the upper class but, as a woman, is in many respects on a lower level than a rich man. According to Meeks, Christianity at the time of Paul was constituted by groups of persons characterized by this status inconsistency; cf. Meeks 1983, p. 73. I refer to Meeks because he represents the broad social-historical discussion in North America about the Jesus movement and the early Christian communities. This discussion is carried forth within the framework of the new consensus, that is to say, the model I have described in reference to Theissen. Individual aspects are criticized on the basis of this model, but the model itself is not questioned.
35. In L. Schottroff/Stegemann 1986, p. 47. Horsley (1989) argues similarly.
36. Cardenal 1976, 1978.
37. Stegemann 1984.
38. Schüssler Fiorenza understands the Jesus movement as a movement of the poor, which in her view also included "the marginal" (1983, p. 141). She accepts the view that the itinerant radicals and "local . . . sympathizers" belong together; she, too, questions the notion of itinerant radical outsiders (1983, p. 145).
39. Schüssler Fiorenza 1983, p. 145.
40. Schüssler Fiorenza 1983, pp. 76–80.
41. L. Schottroff 1990a, p. 252.
42. L. Schottroff 1990a, p. 252; Seneca, *De clementia principiis,* is a historical example of this. Cf. also below at I.2.D.
43. Schüssler Fiorenza 1983, pp. 105ff.
44. Schüssler Fiorenza 1983, pp. 72–76.
45. Schüssler Fiorenza 1983, p. 285, where the title of the chapter names this distinction. This means that she basically accepts an approach that distinguishes between a

church guided by the Spirit and early Catholicism, or a church structured in terms of offices. Her view of Paul is more differentiated, however (cf. Schüssler Fiorenza 1984, p. 236), than is customary in the traditional distinction between the (Pauline) church of the Spirit and the patriarchal church and its offices. Cf. below at III.1 in relation to Paul.

46. L. Schottroff 1990a, p. 253.

47. As far as traditional theology is concerned, Ernst Käsemann is the most important proponent of a nonhierarchical understanding of "office," even though his conception is androcentric and he considers only the aspect of officebearer, as already indicated above in n. 6. Cf. Käsemann 1960, 1964. This understanding is found throughout his corpus.

48. For details, see W. Schottroff 1994.

49. The basic study here continues to be R. Meyer 1940 (reprint, 1970).

50. In my view, the Greek concept *oikos* (house) depicts, in a manner appropriate to the texts, the residential sympathizers and their transformation of the patriarchal household into a community of Christ.

51. In connection with flight for social reasons, see L. Schottroff, in L. Schottroff/ Stegemann 1986, p. 46.

52. For relevant social-historical material, see L. Schottroff in L. Schottroff/Stegemann 1986 and L. Schottroff 1983.

53. Cf. below at IV.1.B.

54. Cf. below at III.3 on this understanding of eschatology.

55. Cf. Bock 1987, pp. 40f., for a feminist critique of thinking in terms of epochs of time.

56. This metaphor, I believe, was first used in German by Christel Neusüss.

57. Cf. below, esp. at III.2.

58. See Richter Reimer 1992, pp. 114–23.

59. See, e.g., Roloff 1985, p. 47: the apostolic council in Acts 15:1–29 renounces circumcision and other legal instructions and, therefore, basically the whole law. But the Torah is not at all renounced, only certain aspects of the Jewish practice of faith, as 15:20 indicates.

60. Walking in newness of life (Rom. 6:4) and proving the will of God (Rom. 12:3) mean to orient oneself according to the Torah, which no longer leads to death because in Christ it no longer must be transgressed. As long as sin rules, God's will, the Torah, is transgressed. Christ has taken away the power of sin. For this interpretation of Paul, see L. Schottroff in Schaumberger/Schottroff 1988.

61. E.g., Josephus, *Ant.* 20.38ff.

62. See L. Schottroff in Schaumberger/Schottroff 1988 on this matter.

63. Cf. L. Schottroff 1990, pp. 291–304 (ET: 1993, pp. 60–79); Langford 1992; Richter Reimer 1992, pp. 114–23.

64. E.g., Roloff 1985, pp. 67–71.

65. This is true also when the term *(love) patriarchalism* is not mentioned. As was already shown, this critique applies to every understanding of Gentile Christianity as love patriarchalism.

66. From the perspective of the history of interpretation, this understanding is situated within the tradition of Käsemann; cf. n. 6 above.

67. Felder 1991, p. 144.

68. If one thinks of him as one "who feared God," he would be the first representative of the church of the nations, with as much right as Cornelius (Acts 10:11ff.).

69. E.g., Schille 1984 on Acts 16:9.

70. E.g., Roloff on Acts 16.

71. Richter Reimer discusses extensively and critically the interpretation of Lydia as a middle-class person.

72. I am addressing her overall understanding of the issue. I return in I.3 to how texts, particularly of the New Testament, are addressed. I do not want to create a gulf between people's liberation work and their own texts.

73. Gotthold Ephraim Lessing, "On the Proof of the Spirit and Power," in *Lessing's Theological Writings,* trans. Henry Chadwick (Stanford, Calif.: Stanford University Press, 1957), p. 55.

74. L. Schottroff 1990a, pp. 226–28. In discussing my position, Schüssler Fiorenza (1989, p. 320) fails to take notice that I very clearly see the problem of anti-Judaism in relation to the Gospel of John—not on the level of the text, for social-historical reasons, but on that of the contemporary use of those texts in the Christian context.

75. L. Schottroff 1990a, pp. 170ff. and 334.

76. See Adler 1975 and Beckmann 1971 for information on the history of the Program to Combat Racism.

77. Gustavo Gutiérrez's book *A Theology of Liberation* appeared in English in 1973 and gave a picture of the comprehensive character of liberation theology. The texts of the peasants of Solentiname and their interpretation of scripture, collected by Ernesto Cardenal, appeared in English between 1972 and 1982.

78. Cf. above at I.1.A on the interpretation of the gospel of the poor and the renunciation of their possessions on the part of individual people. It was, and is, a rule of Western theology to interpret the synoptic gospel of the poor in the sense of individual people's renunciation of their possessions or in the sense of humility before God.

79. L. Schottroff 1978.

80. Erich Grasser and Werner Georg Kümmel, *Theologische Rundschau* 40 (1975): 307.

81. The words *elite* and *establishment* occur in this context, including as a self-definition.

82. Christina Thürmer-Rohr's analysis of women's complicity is ground-breaking in its scope. One would need to reflect on men's complicity.

83. C. Klein 1975 (ET: 1978).

84. Cf. L. Schottroff 1990a, pp. 354f.; and Hedwig-Drausfeld Haus e.V., Bendorf am Rhein, eds., *Charlotte Klein—"Pionierin der Verständigung." Ein Beitrag zum jüdisch-christlichen Gespräch* (1992).

85. Cf. Schaumberger/Schottroff 1988.

86. Cf. esp. Schaumberger's article "Patriarchat als feministischer Begriff," in *WBFTh,* pp. 321–23.

87. Hausen 1986.

88. Schüssler Fiorenza 1985, p. 388.

89. See, e.g., Ruether 1992.

90. Thürmer-Rohr 1987 (ET: 1991).

91. Jesus' eschatological prophecy that the last shall be the first in God's reign (Matt. 20:16 and elsewhere) provides the analysis of patriarchy and the praxis of liberation with an unambiguous perspective.

92. See, e.g., Acts 7:8f. in connection with the New Testament; in connection with Christian bishops, see Liddell/Scott 1961 on *patriarchēs;* and G.W.H. Lampe, *A*

Patristic Greek Lexicon (Oxford: Oxford University Press, 1961), on *patriarchēs, patriarcha*. The Christian church initially did not use the title *father* for its men in leadership positions; cf. Matt. 23:9 and the overall absence of this title in the Christian testament. It was only in the third century C.E. that this title came into use for ecclesial officebearers and was given special definition; see A. Schindler, in Tellenbach 1978, p. 72.

93. E.g., Xenophon; cf. K. Meyer 1975. See Victor 1983 on Aristotle's economics. The great amount of literature that deals with this subject corresponds to the fundamental importance it has in patriarchal domination. There exist writings on women and economy, written sometimes by women with fictive names: for example, the work by Perictione (Plato's mother) on "The Harmony of Women," which is a neo-Pythagorean text (the Greek text is in Holger Thesleff, *The Pythagorean Texts of the Hellenistic Period* [Abo, 1965], pp. 142–46 = *Stobaios* 4.28.19). See Wilhelm 1915 and its rich collection of materials related to this subject.

94. Aristotle, *Pol.*; cf. Schüssler Fiorenza 1983, pp. 254–57.

95. Cicero's writings on this subject will be analyzed below from the perspective of his concept of patriarchy.

96. Hausen 1986, e.g., has called for such a differentiation.

97. A social-historical interpretation of Rom. 13:17 is found in L. Schottroff 1990a, pp. 184–216.

98. Cicero, *De re publica*, trans. C. W. Keyes (Cambridge, Mass.: Harvard University Press, 1951).

99. The citations from Cicero's *De officiis* are taken from the translation by Harry G. Edinger (Indianapolis and New York: Bobbs-Merrill Co., 1974).

100. The context suggests a positive assessment by Cicero. See Pomeroy 1975, p. 162, on the Voconian legislation.

101. Or only limited amounts; the text suggests both readings.

102. In this text, Plato is criticized. (*Translators' note:* The author used a German text edition of Cicero's *De re publica* that included this fragment. The translators failed to locate an English text that included this section. The entire citation is, therefore, translated from the German as cited by the author.)

103. Varro, *De re rust.* 1.17.2–3; cf. Columella, *De re rustica* 1.7.4; and L. Schottroff 1990a, pp. 36–56.

104. Mark 3:6.

105. See, e.g., L. Schottroff 1990a, pp. 184–216.

106. Cf. note 92, above, on the reticence of early Christianity regarding the power of fathers. Christian theology's "wholehearted" embrace of Roman ideas of the father is described by Antonic Wlosok in relation to Lactantius; see Tellenbach 1978, pp. 48ff.

107. Trans. Heinrich Dittrich (Berlin and Weimar, 1978).

108. Additional material may be found in commentaries on 1 Cor. 12:14ff.

109. John Chrysostom, *Orationes* 48.7.

110. In dominant exegesis this perception is the rule, e.g., in the interpretation of Gal. 3:28.

111. The nineteenth century laid much stress on the harmonious unity that is achieved when woman completes man; see Hausen, p. 170. But cf. also harmony as the guiding concept of Perictione (note 93, above), where it is applied not only to the man but also to the house.

112. Cited in Adler 1975, p. 65.

113. Troeltsch (1912) and Theissen (1979; ET: 1992; cf. above at I.1.A) interpret

"love" in Christian love patriarchalism (in its substance, this term goes back to Troeltsch, although Theissen invented it) to be a unique Christian feature. Love patriarchalism "acquired a special coloring through the warmth of the Christian idea of love" (Theissen 1992, p. 56n67); this is how Theissen summarizes Troeltsch and gives his term its meaning. What Troeltsch, Theissen, and the "new consensus" (cf. above at I.1.A) have in fact done is depict the social history of the early church in terms of ancient economics.

114. Aelius Aristides, *Oration on Rome* 26.66.

115. The word *kyriocentrism* may mislead Christian readers, who may assume that it means Christocentrism, Christ being *kyrios*. What it actually means is society's orientation in terms of the class of ruling men. Christocentrism may well be an expression of kyriocentrism, as is discussed below.

116. As a generic concept, *brothers* encompasses both brothers and sisters, just as the term *applicant* refers to both female and male persons. An analysis of German as a masculine language is provided by Pusch 1984. Cf. also Otto Jespersen, *Growth and Structure of the English Language* (Oxford: Basil Blackwell, 1955).

117. As far as I know, there is still no feminist analysis of the linguistic usage of "men, brothers" in Acts and of the word *man* (the male person) in Acts and in the whole New Testament. There are initial attempts in Quesnell 1983; Richter Reimer 1992, pp. 34, 235ff.; O'Day in Newsom/Ringe 1992; D'Angelo 1990. R. Pesch's comment on Acts 1:16 is incorrect: Luke's stylized address *andres adelphoi* "hardly insinuates that . . . only the men in the assembly were being spoken to."

118. The word *inclusive* is used both for androcentric language that speaks also of women but without naming them and for nonsexist language, which does name women. The NRSV, e.g., understands "inclusiveness" as a way of overcoming androcentric language (1989 Preface).

119. It follows from Acts 1 that women met the conditions for both the apostolate and the diaconate, as stipulated in Acts 1:21–25, and yet Luke pays *no* heed to them; cf. Richter Reimer 1992, p. 237. One might object to my assumption that in the address "brothers," women are not thought of by saying that the harsh phrase "men, brothers" is a Lukan idiosyncrasy. His use of language, however, makes plain the real intentions of androcentric language.

120. Schüssler Fiorenza 1983, p. 45.

121. The NRSV resorts to "friends" in an effort to solve the problem. This is not possible for the German language.

122. Androcentric language should always be translated in terms of reference to both women and men as long as it has not been proven that no women were present in the actual situation; cf. below at II.2.B. The burden of proof that no women were present must rest on those who insist on a literal translation of androcentric language.

123. E.g., by translating the misogynist word *skeuos* (vessel) in 1 Thess. 4:4 as "woman" (cf. the German ecumenical translation of the Bible). On this text, cf. below; and L. Schottroff, in *Junge Kirche* no. 8/9 (1992): 500f.

124. Karl Marx's analysis continues to have historical merit, even though feminist discussion has shown that his analysis of capitalism does not take women's housework and unpaid labor into consideration. He failed to recognize that unpaid labor is also productive labor and is being exploited. A summary of the feminist discussion on women's work is provided in Mies 1988, pp. 46–58.

125. This phenomenon of the language of domination is still to be found today. Books dealing with the grammar of ancient languages have even discovered a euphemism

that conceals what really is going on, namely, that the overlords want to make it look as if they were doing the actual work. These books speak of the "causative active." Even when using texts of grammar or lexica, one must critically analyze androcentrism and kyriocentrism.

126. The ancient world paid close attention to the boundary that separated the labor of free men from that of all those below them. Female and male slaves and free women, unless they lived in upper-class circumstances, performed the invisible labor of *diakonein* (serving), of housework; cf. below at II.2 and IV.2, and L. Schottroff 1990c, pp. 226–33. Cf. note 124 above, on the feminist discussion of housework.

127. See Martin 1990, pp. 43ff.

128. Cf. Heyward 1982, for a critique of such a Christology.

129. Cf. esp. Cordelia Kopsch, "Schlag auf Schlag und Schritt für Schritt. Militärisches in unserer Alltagssprache," in Wegener et al. 1990, pp. 55–72.

130. Cf. above at pp. 10f. and III.2.

131. Cf. below at I.2.E.

132. B. Brecht, "Fragen eines lesenden Arbeiters," in *Gesammelte Werke in 20 Bänden* (1967), 9:656f.

133. Adaptation of a folk song, prepared by a Brazilian women's group; see Schaumberger/Maassen 1986, pp. 75f.

134. Cf. Angela Bauer's article "Sexismus," in *WBFTh,* pp. 367–70.

135. Cf. above at I.2.C.

136. Cf. esp. Bieler 1993 on the feminist discussion; she provides an overview of that discussion and extends it. A critique of the concept of "the role of woman" is found in Bock 1987, pp. 41f. The distinction between "sex" and "gender" is useful inasmuch as it clarifies that "gender" is no biological category. The problem with the distinction is that it may objectify sexuality; cf. Mies 1988, p. 36.

137. Cf. L. Schottroff, in Schaumberger/Schottroff 1988, pp. 37–55.

138. The following reflections on Rom. 1:26ff. are in a preliminary stage, awaiting the forthcoming extensive monograph by Bernadette Brooten; but see the foundational proposals in Brooten 1985.

139. Aristophanes, *Thesmophor.* 835–41; Tacitus, *Germ.* 19. First Corinthians 11:5f. talks of the kind of dishonoring of women and not, as is alleged in some commentaries, that women had their hair cut like men in order to look like them and therefore to protect themselves, e.g., on a voyage. It is perverse that texts such as Apuleius, 7.32; Lucian, *Fugit.* 27; or his *Hetairikoi dialogoi* 5.3 are drawn upon to support the claim that in 1 Cor 11:5f. Paul refers to "the perverse women who practice the vice of lesbianism" and who act as if they were men; cf. Weiss (1910) 1970, commenting on this text. In the interpretation of Paul it is commonplace to intensify Paul's own misogyny.

140. Cf. Wegner 1988.

141. Cf. above at I.2.C.

142. Cf. L. Schottroff, in Schaumberger/Schottroff 1988, pp. 49f.

143. Xenophon, *Oec.* 3.11.

144. Cf below at II.1.B.

145. Cf. Columella 12 praef.

146. Cf. below at II.2.B.

147. See, e.g., Ruth 2:9.

148. Cf. below at II.2.D.

149. Cf. below at III.1.B.

150. Cf. III. 3 on early Christian eschatology.

151. A survey of the diverse concepts of Women-Church and a bibliography is found in *Schlangenbrut* 9 (1991): 5–20, and in the article by Hedwig Meyer-Wilms in *WBFTh,* pp. 213–15.

152. From the point of view of history, the distinction between humanistic and gynocentric (or gynaikocentric) feminism refers much less to a contrast than it does to a certain phase in the discussion: I mean the phase from the discovery of women's oppression through heteronomous stereotypes of femininity to the discovery of "the rejection and devaluation of specific virtues and activities of women on the part of a highly instrumentalistic and authoritarian male culture" (Iris Marion Young, "Humanismus, Gynozentrismus und feministische Politik" in List/Studer 1989, pp. 37–65, esp. 46.) Cf. also Ina Praetorius's article "Androzentrismus" in *WBFTh,* pp. 14f.

153. Ruether 1992, p. 251.

154. On this and other visionary pictures in the Christian testament, cf. L. Schottroff, in Schaumberger/Schottroff 1988.

155. This expression in 1 Cor. 15:28 refers to the eschatological end of domination and struggle; 1 Cor. 8:6 thinks of creation and its relation to the faithful, and 1 Cor. 11:11 speaks of the end of men's domination of women in the sense of Gal. 3:28.

156. Cf. L. Schottroff, in Schaumberger/Schottroff 1988, pp. 99ff.

157. I refer the reader to the important article "Kreuz" in *WBFTh.*

158. Cf. below at III.3.

159. Briggs 1989.

160. Emphasis added (L.S.).

161. Emphasis added (L.S.).

162. Commentaries in the Western tradition of scholarship usually relate Christ's becoming poor to his becoming human, thereby leaving his humanity abstract and with no connection to the economic poverty of his people. When economic poverty is taken into consideration, it is interpreted as renunciation of property; cf. Klauck 1986 on the Philippian text.

163. Western tradition of interpretation usually understands Christ's becoming a slave also as his becoming *human* (the slavery of human existence) by referring to v. 7b. Being a slave is understood, in other words, as a metaphor that does not relate Christ to the experiences of female and male slaves. Such a dualistic interpretation of metaphorical language, which separates "image" and "thing," is not appropriate. (Cf. below in relation to the theory of parables that I employ in connection with metaphorical language.) See L. Schottroff 1990a, pp. 57–72; and L. Schrottroff 1988b, as well as below at III.1.B on the connection between Pauline metaphors of slavery and social reality.

164. Cf. in particular Mesters 1983.

165. Cf. below at III.1.B.

166. Cf. only the epistle to Philemon. It is essential to question the automatic assumption that owners of slaves were affluent people.

167. Cf. Theissen 1989 on this aspect.

168. Cf. above at I.1.

169. The "we" refers to the Heidelberg Working Circle, which has been working together since 1977 and has published its studies primarily through the Christian Kaiser Verlag in Munich. I cite the titles of our books, since they express the direction of our work: W. Schottroff and W. Stegemann, eds., *Der Gott der kleinen Leute. Sozialgeschichtliche Auslegungen,* 2 vols. (Munich and Gelnhausen, 1979), ET selections from *God of the Lowly,*

trans. Matthew J. O'Connell (Maryknoll, N.Y.: Maryknoll Publishers, 1984); W. Schott-roff and W. Stegemann, eds., *Traditionen der Befreiung* (Traditions of liberation), 2 vols. (Munich and Gelnhausen, 1980); L. Schottroff and W. Schottroff, eds., *Mitarbeiter der Schöpfung. Bibel und Arbeitswelt* (Coworkers of creation: The Bible and the world of work) (Munich, 1983); L. Schottroff and W. Schottroff, eds., *Wer ist unser Gott? Beiträge zu einer Befreiungstheologie im Kontext der "ersten" Welt* (Who is our God? Contributions to a theology of liberation in the context of the "first" world) (Munich, 1986); M. Crüsemann and W. Schottroff, eds., *Schuld und Schulden. Biblische Traditionen in gegenwärtigen Konflikten* (Guilt and debts: Biblical traditions in contemporary conflicts) (Munich, 1992).

170. On the relation to materialistic interpretation of scripture, see in particular W. Schottroff, Preface to W. Schottroff/W. Stegemann 1984.

171. The pressure to distance oneself from communism is one of the instruments of domination employed by capitalism, even now when there is no more Communist Eastern bloc.

172. Cf. in particular L. Schottroff/W. Schottroff 1984, Preface.

173. Cf. W. Schottroff 1980 on the questions of biblical methodology.

174. It is mistaken to view feminist historiography as an alternative to social history. A distinction must be made, rather, between an androcentric and a feminist social history, after which one must determine whether or not such history is oriented by liberation theology.

175. This has happened in the discussion of these so-called new approaches to scripture; cf. the studies referred to in note 177, as well as Wolfgang Langen, ed., *Handbuch der Bibelarbeit* (Munich, 1987).

176. This concept was coined by Joachim Scharfenberg in 1972; he gave it a positive meaning, whereas others have used it as a term of disqualification. Cf. Joachim Scharfenberg, *Religion zwischen Wahn und Wirklichkeit* (Hamburg, 1972), pp. 281ff.

177. The attempts of the journal *Evangelische Theologie* 45, 6 (1985) and of the theological commission of the Arnoldshainer Konferenz 1992 to describe social-historical interpretation of scripture within the domain of "new approaches" are, unfortunately, utterly superficial. The assessment of the theological commission was published in 1992 by Neukirchener Verlag under the title *Das Buch Gottes*. Another example of how superficial the so-called experts' discussion of "social-historical interpretation" can be is Peter Muller, *In der Mitte der Gemeinde. Kinder im Neuen Testament* (Neukirchen, 1992), pp. 86f. In this study, imputation becomes critique, while no attempt is made to substantiate this on the basis of texts from social-historical studies of scripture.

178. Hermann Gunkel made the following basic assertion in 1913: "Every ancient literary genre was initially located in a very particular place in the ordinary life of the people of Israel. Just as today the sermon still belongs to the pulpit, while fairy tales are told to the children, so in ancient Israel young women sang the hymn of victory as the army was marching homeward; the hired woman mourner sang dirges at the bier of the dead; the priest proclaimed the Torah to the layfolk who had come to the sanctuary; the judge rendered the judgment (*mispat*) in court to explain his decision; the prophet speaks his message in the outer court of the temple; the aged enjoy expressions of wisdom as they sit in the gate; etc. Those who want to understand the genre must make the entire situation plain to themselves and ask: Who it is who speaks? Who are the listeners? What mood governs the situation? What effect is to be achieved? Often, the genre is represented by a particular vocation that characterizes the genre: today the sermon is represented by the clergy, while long ago the Torah was represented by the priest, wisdom

sayings by the "wise," songs by the singer, etc. There may have been a vocation of itin-erant peoples' storytellers. Whoever studies this origin of genres will discover that almost all originally did not exist *in written but in spoken* form. For this, too, is a major differ-ence between ancient Israelite and modern nature, that writing determined culture as well as 'literature' far less in those days than it does now among us. That explains the *very paltry extent* of ancient output in writing" (*Reden und Aufsätze*, 1913, p. 33). When it comes to the *Sitz im Leben,* Gunkel understands "life" in a romanticizing sense, as the ordinary life of people (*Volksleben*).

179. As Bultmann (1963) puts it, "The miraculous deeds are not proof of [Jesus'] character but of his messianic authority, or his divine power" (p. 219).

180. Cf. Heyward 1982; Strahm/Strobel 1991.

181. Here Comblin (1988, p. 40) describes Latin American base communities' ex-periences of the Spirit. The New Testament's miracle stories also express these experi-ences.

182. See L. Schottroff/W. Schottroff 1991b, pp. 13ff., for a more extensive treat-ment.

183. Bultmann 1963, pp. 221ff. My discussion with Bultmann exemplifies my re-sponse to current patterns of miracle interpretation, which, albeit more differentiated than his, essentially replicate his basic position.

184. Schmithals (1979) 1985 on the text.

185. Bultmann 1963, p. 198.

186. Bultmann 1963, p. 174.

187. Ricoeur 1974, pp. 45–70.

188. Harnisch 1985, p. 188; cf. Weder 1978, p. 226, and II.2 below on Funk's (1971) interpretation of the parable of the leaven.

189. Weder 1978, p. 226.

190. Weder 1978, p. 225.

191. Weder 1978, p. 226; Harnisch 1985, p. 196.

192. In these narratives plants are viewed from the point of view of those who de-pend on them for food; cf., e.g., the metaphors of fruitfulness and unfruitfulness (seeds: Mark 4:3–8 and par.; fig trees: Luke 13:6–9; etc.).

193. Cf. below at II.3.

194. As will be shown, e.g., in the analysis of the parable of the leaven, below at II.2.

195. Cf. below at II.3.

196. In addition to the parables of nature, see also Matt. 6:25–34 and par.; 5:45 and par.; and 1 Cor. 3:6.

197. Cf. II.2.C on the approach to the theory of the parables, which is close to my own approach.

198. Some specialists use the tools of linguistics to answer these questions.

199. Jülicher (1910) 1963.

200. Cf. esp. Tamez 1993.

201. B. Brecht, "Notizen zur Philosophie 1929 bis 1941," in *Gesammelte Werke* (Frankfurt, 1967), 20:174.

203. Between 1987 and 1991, the University of Kassel conducted special summer sessions of its institute on research in feminist liberation theology. The work of the many women who participated in this project is of fundamental importance for the composi-tion of this book.

204. In the German-speaking context, the numbers on scripture of the feminist jour-

nals *FAMA* and *Schlangenbrut* offer good surveys on this point; cf. "Wenn Frauen kri-
tisch die Bibel lesen," *FAMA* 5 (September 1989); and "Schwerpunkt: im Anfang war
. . . feministische Bibelauslegung," *Schlangenbrut* 2 (February 1993).

205. Godel (1992) analyzes feminist Bible studies presented at the biennial German
Evangelischen Kirchentagen; her study gives publicity to one aspect of feminist biblical
interpretation. The development of a hermeneutical concept that could assist in advanc-
ing this aspect of Bible study was not her concern. A survey of current discussions is provided in Schroer 1992, 1993, as well as in Wacker 1988.

206. For a German-language overview of liberation-theological Bible readings in different contexts, see *Katechetische Blätter* 6 (1992).

207. Mesters 1983, 1991.

208. Schwantes 1991.

209. Lamb 1986.

210. Richter Reimer 1992.

211. Gebara/Lucchetti Bingemer 1988.

212. Schwantes 1991, p. 10.

213. Mesters 1983, pp. 19–21.

214. Schwantes 1991, p. 18. The concept of "consciousness-raising" is now customarily used in liberation theology and in feminist theory and theology to refer to this
hermeneutical step.

215. Mesters 1991, p. 4.

216. Gebara/Lucchetti Bingemer 1988, p. 40.

217. Lamb 1986, p. 77.

218. Schwantes 1991, p. 10; L. Schottroff/W. Schottroff 1984, pp. 7–12.

219. Mesters 1991, p. 3.

220. Dorothee Soelle, *On Earth as in Heaven: A Liberation Spirituality of Sharing,*
trans. Marc Batko (Louisville, Ky.: Westminster John Knox Press, 1993), pp. x–xi; cf.
also her *Thinking about God: An Introduction to Theology,* trans. John Bowden (Philadelphia: Trinity Press International, 1990), and *Stations of the Cross: A Latin American Pilgrimage,* trans. Joyce Irwin (Minneapolis: Fortress Press, 1993).

221. Mies 1984, p. 45.

222. Mies 1984, p. 45.

223. Christine Schaumberger, "Erfahrung," in *WBFTh,* pp. 73–78, esp. 74.

224. Schaumberger, "Erfahrung," p. 74.

225. Schaumberger, "Erfahrung," p. 74.

226. Cf., e.g., the two works by Karin Walter (1986 and 1988), and Eva Renate
Schmidt, Mieke Korenhof, and Renate Jost, eds., *Feministisch gelesen* (Stuttgart: Kreuz
Verlag, 1988 and 1989).

227. Cf. Heidemarie Langer, "Bibliodrama als Prozess," in Antje Kiehn et al., *Bibliodrama* (Stuttgart, 1987), pp. 65–90.

228. Schüssler Fiorenza 1983, pp. 15ff.

229. In an article published in 1988, she frequently uses the term *critique of ideology*
in this context.

230. Cf. above at I.2.B.

231. Schüssler Fiorenza 1983, p. 19.

232. Schüssler Fiorenza 1983, pp. 18–19.

233. Ricoeur 1970, pp. 32ff.

234. What Bultmann calls "substance critique" (*Sachkritik*) has the task of distin-

guishing what is theologically inappropriate in the biblical text from what is appropriate, drawing the criteria for appropriateness from the text itself. Cf. Bultmann 1954, p. 44.

235. Schüssler Fiorenza 1983, p. 6.

PART II
The Everyday Life of Women

1. What is meant is dignified demeanor and attire. Against the background of the history of interpretation, for which the inward disposition of Christian women is the chief issue of this text, to refer only to "demeanor" would obscure that the text also deals with instructions concerning attire.

2. The word *silence* here and in v. 12, in conjunction with 2:2, refers not only to being silent (during the worship of God) but also to the demeanor appropriate to submissiveness, one aspect of which is that women keep silent *also* in public.

3. For parallels of this bossy style of language, cf. Schrenk, in *ThWNT*, 1:629f. The counterproposal to the claim that this is the very language of dominance ("one should be more spiritual in thinking about this"—Holtz 1986, p. 64n57) assumes that when someone in the Spirit talks in the form of royal decrees, it is not language of dominance.

4. Cf. Roloff 1988, pp. 23ff., on the time of this letter's composition and its use of a pseudonym.

5. The change from the plural in v. 9 to the singular in v. 11—"woman"— and the quite naturally asserted connection between the first woman's guilt (Eve; v. 13f.) and the proscribed demeanor of women (i.e., all women who do not want to be disqualified as evil and beyond salvation) show that the text presupposes all women to have a common nature, bestowed on them at creation, and that a normative demeanor corresponds to that nature. Other cultures and religions speak in this context of the essence of woman given by nature (*conditio naturae*, e.g.; Valerius Maximus, 8.3). Küchler (1986, p. 12)— in my judgment, incorrectly—interprets the change from the plural to the singular (v. 11, and conversely in v. 15) as a change from the praxis of women or some actual ones (plural) to theory (singular). The manner of speaking in this text is, from head to toe, that of patriarchy defining what "the woman's" nature and conduct are.

6. The translation "I want . . . that women (offer prayer) in fine attire" (Küchler 1986, p. 11 and elsewhere) supplements the infinitive "to pray" from v. 8 in v. 9, which is linguistically inappropriate. Roloff (1988, p. 126n83) correctly assesses the linguistic aspect but insists nevertheless that, on account of v. 8, vv. 9–15 are about the service of worship (p. 132). However, the instructions about attire in v. 9f. are not to be interpreted as governing only worship.

7. Roloff 1986, pp. 132, 138.

8. Thraede (1980, p. 365) uses "conservative" in a positive sense for his middle-of-the-road position toward the oppression of women; cf. below at II.1.C. Speaking of the "traditional" image of women similarly serves to excuse misogynist propaganda since Augustus; cf., e.g., Blank-Sangmeister 1991, p. 341.

9. The Oppian Laws were promulgated in 215 B.C.E. Among other things, they restricted a woman's possession of gold to one half-ounce, meaning that women were deprived of the possessions they accrued because of the death of so many men during the wars against Hannibal. See Livy, 34.1–8; Tacitus, *Ann.* 3.33 (cited here); Valerius Maximus, 9.1.3; Orosius, 4.20.14; Zonaras, 9.17.1; Pomeroy 1975, pp. 177ff. Twenty

years later, when the laws were to be abrogated, there was a large demonstration by women.

10. Tacitus, *Ann.* 3.33.

11. Tacitus, *Ann.* 3.34.

12. Valerius Maximus's collection of vignettes appeared in 31 B.C.E.

13. Valerius Maximus, 9.1.3.

14. Valerius Maximus, 8.3; 3.2.15; 6.1.1; 9.12.2; and elsewhere.

15. Valerius Maximus, 6.3.9.

16. Valerius Maximus, 6.3.12: "P. Sempronius Soplius . . . inflicted the opprobrium of divorce on his wife for no other reason than that she had dared to watch the games without his knowledge. As long as women were treated like that, they would clearly not be disposed to do something wrong"; cf. 2.5.5; 6.3.9; 6.3.6; 8.1.1. Valerius Maximus is not the only source to show that injustice against women was governed by the principle of not letting an individual woman succeed in offering resistance against patriarchal domination; such a woman would be cruelly punished in order to warn all women and force their submission. Cf. the *Acts of Thecla* 2.219; Esth. 1:20; and at II.4.B below.

17. Tacitus, *Ann.* 3.24.

18. Tacitus, *Ann.* 3.25, 28.

19. Tacitus, *Ann.* (2.85) 3.22; 4.22, 52; and elsewhere.

20. I have chosen Tacitus and Valerius Maximus as typical representatives of misogynist propaganda since the time of Augustus. Cf. Friedländer (1922) 1964, 1:283ff.; Kiefer 1933, pp. 48–57; Bornemann 1975, pp. 385–412; Thraede 1977, pp. 79–87; Hatebur 1987; Elias 1986; Küchler (1986) discusses Jewish parallels—cf. at II.1.C below on this aspect. See also L. Schottroff 1990a, pp. 100–104 (ET: 1993, pp. 84–88); L. Schottroff 1988b, pp. 37–55, citing Christian and Gnostic parallels.

21. Cf. Balch 1988, pp. 25–36, for a survey of this discussion in research.

22. Cf. above at I.2.C.

23. Cf. 1 Peter 3:3; 1 Tim. 2:9; Rev. 17:4; and the extra–New Testament materials in the scholarly commentaries on those texts, such as Windisch 1951 (on 1 Peter 3:3) and Kiefer 1933, pp. 149–50, whose materials relating to Rome are gathered without any critical perspective. Küchler (1986, passim) has assembled pareneses from postbiblical Jewish and Christian literature on the instructions governing adornments; Friedländer ([1922] 1964, 2:324–29) has a rich collection of materials relating to Rome. From an archaeological-aesthetic perspective, Böhme 1974; Krauss (1910) 1966, 1:190ff.; on p. 198, he cites Jewish materials that *praise* women for adorning themselves.

24. Misogynist polemics accuse all women of being addicted to extravagance. Cf. Tacitus, *Ann.* 3.34; Valerius Maximus, 9.1.3. The attack on women's finery in 1 Tim. 2:9 is often interpreted as being about the (exaggerated) wearing of jewelry on the part of rich women; cf. Holtz 1986, p. 66; Roloff 1988, p. 134 (despite his insight into the "conventional" nature of the admonition); Schüssler Fiorenza 1983, p. 290. The attacks on women who adorn themselves paint the picture of a bedecked, well-off woman in order to intimidate *all* women. Poor women, too, tried to adorn themselves; cf. Friedländer (1922) 1964, pp. 328ff.; Blanck 1976, p. 72.

25. *katastrēnian;* cf. Bauer 1979, s.v. *katastrēnian* and *strēnian*. The word contains a misogynist imputation, namely, that women crave luxuries and sex, for which reason young widows are drawn away from Christ.

26. Valerius Maximus, 2.1.3–6.

27. Valerius Maximus, 4.3.3; Tacitus, *Ann.* 2.73.

28. Valerius Maximus, 6.7.1.

29. Roman morality often idealized individual men who remained lifelong the husbands of one woman only, men who, e.g., did not remarry when they were widowed (cf. note 27 above). This moral attitude is quite likely behind the epistle's admonition to leading Christian men. The discussion of these texts raises the question whether they imply simultaneous or serial polygyny; cf. Roloff 1988, pp. 155ff.

30. See also Titus 1:6.

31. Cf. Bauer 1979, s.v. *periergos;* and the cases against women to which Tacitus refers (see note 19, above).

32. To criticize women who speak in public is part of Rome's propagation of misogyny; cf. Livy, 34.2.10; 1 Cor. 14:34–35 (Cato, in the citation from Livy just given, as well as Paul, refers to the "proper" conduct of women: "ask your husband at home"— Livy); Valerius Maximus, 3.8.6; 8.8; 8.3. Cf. above at notes 1 and 2. See Schottroff 1990a, p. 100 (ET: 1993, p. 84); additional material in commentaries on 1 Cor. 14:35 and in Dautzenberg, in Dautzenberg et al. 1983, pp. 196–205.

33. Cf. L. Schottroff 1988b, pp. 36–55; Schüngel-Straumann 1989.

34. What rarely disturbs exegetes in this unambiguous assertion of 1 Tim. 2:15 is that it calls for women in patriarchy to be obliged to have children. What is problematic for them is the notion that giving birth should secure salvation (which really is God's gift). An attempt to get away from such theological embarrassment is found in Roloff (1988, pp. 140–41), whose solution, however, does not go beyond the indicated parameters. The enormity of the misogynist assertion of 1 Tim. 2:15 is heightened when the pains of giving birth are understood as erasing the guilt of Eve; cf. L. Schottroff 1988b, pp. 38–39 n35.

35. Roloff 1988, p. 243, on 1 Tim. 4:7: "It is chatter of the kind old women make, silly and abstruse." There is no critical distancing from the text here. Holtz 1986, p. 105: "Since woman receives high valuation in the pastoral epistles, one must not presume any misogynist features in the text." He believes the text to be about old women's "heretical chatter." What is being asserted here about the pastoral epistles is simply grotesque as is how unsuspecting the author is of his misogyny. (Jeremias/Strobel 1975 do not comment on the word but translate it as "childish," which is impossible linguistically; *graōdēs* means "old woman–like" and is a discriminatory term—as if it would help to have children, instead of old women, discriminated against.)

36. I refer to two areas and their relevant materials: pictorial presentations (cf. Zanker 1989) and literary texts (cf. the collection *Anthologia graeca*).

37. Cf. above at note 2.

38. Cf. 1 Tim. 2:12: *authentein.*

39. Tacitus, *Ann.* 1.68; 2.55, 72; 12.1, 7, 37.

40. In 1 Cor. 14:35; 1 Tim. 2:11; 5:13; and 2 Tim. 3:7, the verb *to learn* is used polemically by patriarchally oriented Christian men against the Christian women who defend their independence by means of the right "to learn" independently from the patriarchal household.

41. This is suggested indirectly by 1 Tim. 2:12 and 5:13; cf. 1 Cor. 14:35, in connection with the use of *lalein* in 1 Corinthians 14.

42. This is suggested indirectly by the attack on women's teaching in 1 Tim. 2:12 but also by Titus 2:3–5, where old women are permitted to teach young women their role in the patriarchal household. Cf. Schüssler Fiorenza 1983, p. 290.

43. Valerius Maximus frequently sketches the "horror show" of collective women's

resistance against the subjugation of women on the part of the state: women are prohibited from public mourning over the loss of their husbands in war (1.1.15); a law is passed against preparation of poisons because 170 women allegedly poisoned their husbands (2.5.3). (Legislation was an often used tool against women, cf. note 9, above.) The author's polemic throughout his work reveals a history of women's resistance that, on account of its collective nature, had a political character.

44. Col. 3:18–4:1; Eph. 5:22–6:9; 1 Peter 2:18–3:7; 1 Tim 2:11–15; 5:3–8; 6:1–2; Titus 2:2–10; 3:1–2; *1 Clem.* 21:6–8; Ignatius, *Poly.* 4:1–6:2; *Did.* 4:9–11; *Barn.* 19:5–7.

45. Schüssler Fiorenza 1983, pp. 79f.

46. Schüssler Fiorenza 1983, p. 88.

47. Schüssler Fiorenza 1983, p. 78.

48. Schüssler Fiorenza 1983, p. 78. Thraede regards the household codes as a middle position that, measured against the position of "conservative counterproposals" of the time to egalitarian tendencies, is to be judged Christian and humane (p. 365 and elsewhere). However, they are less useful for a democratic position today than is the historic Paul (pp. 367f.). The justification for such demands for obedience must be subjected to feminist critique. Cf. Balch 1988, pp. 26f. and 31f., on the history of the critique of this apologetic construction.

49. Schüssler Fiorenza 1983, p. 266.

50. Schüssler Fiorenza 1983, p. 289.

51. Schüssler Fiorenza 1983, p. 291.

52. Schüssler Fiorenza 1983, p. 87.

53. Cf. below at III.2.C.

54. Page numbers in the following text refer to Roloff 1988.

55. Page numbers in the following text refer to Küchler 1986.

56. Cf. above at note 20.

57. Thraede 1987, p. 115n3.

58. Thraede 1977, pp. 124f.

59. Thraede 1987, pp. 109 and 113f.

60. Cf. above at note 48.

61. *Stellungnahme* 1990, p. 9.

62. Cf. *Stellungnahme* 1990, p. 9, against Gnosticism and its success among women, and the subsequent critique in the rest of the text against feminist theology (pp. 13f.). It is an old trick of dominant exegesis to disqualify whatever the exegetes of contemporary women's movements encounter by recalling the women who opposed Paul in Corinth (cf. L. Schottroff 1988b, pp. 57ff.) or the Gnostic heresy against which 1 Timothy defends itself.

63. One might evaluate positively, e.g., that the household codes *address* slaves (Col. 3:22 and elsewhere), in other words, that their obedience is demanded not merely in *speech about them;* it is positive as well that husbands are called on to love their wives (Eph. 5:25; Col. 3:19) and not only wives to be obedient to their husbands (Eph. 5:22–24; Col. 3:18). Balch (1988, p. 33) discusses such positive evaluations. He speaks in favor of them and refers to the earliest Christian communities' "integrating power" in their "selective acculturation" of prevailing Roman culture. (This is type of interpretation 1b, in reference to 1 Peter.)

64. This is correctly identified in Balch 1988, p. 32, and his supporting evidence.

65. *Oikodespotein* (1 Tim. 5:14), refers to the married woman's governance of the patriarchal household and her rule over the slaves, in other words, to the role she has in

the household subordinate to the man. Holtz (1986, p. 121) asserts—incorrectly—that here the text thinks of women being placed on an equal level with men (cf. also Roloff 1988, p. 299n391, in opposition to that view).

66. See, e.g., Bauer 1979, s.v. *aphormē;* or Roloff 1988 on the text.

67. Bauer 1979 considers this possibility, s.v. *loidoria.*

68. Roloff 1988, p. 300.

69. See L. Schottroff 1990a, pp. 100–104 (ET: 1993, pp. 84–88), for documentary material, as well as Luke 23:2, 5 in some of the manuscript traditions.

70. See L. Schottroff 1994.

71. The word *anthrōpos* (human being) in the parable of the mustard seed, Matt. 13:31 and Luke 13:19, clearly means the male human being when seen next to *gynē* (woman) in the parable of the leaven.

72. In connection with the first usage of the names of the evangelists, I would like to recall what I already sketched out in I.3.D: the tradition of the ancient church, as well as Christian scholarship, assumes that the author, redactor, or writer of a Gospel is a man. Even if the authorship of the legendary men Matthew, Mark, Luke, and John is ques tioned by scholarship, people continue to assume that a man was the redactor or the like. What needs to be criticized is how it is taken for granted that an individual male person is responsible. On every level of the synoptic tradition, we must assume a collective process of transmission of the words and stories of Jesus. Women and men participated in this process. We must assume the participation of women even in the writing and the formation of the overall product called "the Gospel." The texts in their final form also are products of Christian *communities.*

73. It makes no difference to the content of the narratives whether Luke uses *enekrypsen* or *ekrypsen.*

74. Bauer (1979) suggests that "to mix into" is meant (s.v. *kryptō*); "to hide" is of- ten assumed to be the meaning, as metaphor for the hiddenness of God's reign (cf., e.g., notes 120 and 121 below).

75. Caspari/Kleemann 1918, p. 229. One may ask whether sourdough bread was prepared in Germany at the beginning of this century as it was in first-century Palestine. Evidence from geography and the history of technology supports an affirmative answer; cf. below at notes 76 and 77. The only uncertain matter is the moment when the dough was covered up.

76. Dalman 1935, 4:46; Krauss 1910, 1:99ff.

77. Blümner 1912, 1:60f.; this source includes pictorial presentations of women at their work in preparing bread (figs. 25–30).

78. Jülicher 1910, p. 578; Jeremias 1963, pp. 146f.

79. Jeremias 1963, p. 147; Funk 1971, pp. 159f. On the calculation of the amounts, see Billerbeck 1926, 1:669f.; Krauss 1911, 2:394f. Genesis 18:6 is not about sourdough bread (cf. in particular Dalman 1935, 4.34f.); the verse is therefore not suited to calcu- lating how much flour is spoken of in the parable of the leaven.

80. E.g., Jeremias 1963, pp. 147f.

81. Apuleius, *Metamorph.* 10.16.2.

82. Cf. L. Schottroff 1983, p. 182; and at I.2.D above.

83. Matt. 6:28 and Luke 12:27 parallel the work of men in the fields as depicted in Matt. 6:26 and Luke 12:24. The work of women spinning is paralleled in Matt. 6:28 and Luke 12:27 to *kopian* (doing heavy physical work). *Kopian* either refers once again to men's work, which would parallel the men's work with that of women spinning, or,

more likely, women's work is called *kopian*. Both times women's work is judged to be similarly demanding as that of men. The text's own history reveals some variety. There is the attempt to present women's work in a wording that would make it more clearly parallel the work of men ("they do not comb wool, do not spin, do not labor hard"— a three-part description like that of the work of men; this is most likely the first hand-written form of Sinaiticus). In the transmission of the text of Luke 12:27, there is a version that speaks of "spinning and weaving" but leaves out the *kopian,* probably because it did not want to use the word for the labor of women. This has to be seen as an attenuation of the text.

84. In Matt. 24:41 and Luke 17:35, women's work at the mill is paralleled either to men's work in the fields (Matthew) or to men's sleeping (Luke); Luke 17:31 (from Mark 13:16) may be the reason for the Lukan change of the Q text.

85. Friedrich Schiller, "Das Lied von der Glocke": "The man goes out into hostile life, must labor and strive, plant and produce, . . . inside rules the respected housewife." That is how I learned patriarchal hierarchy of work in my school years. When Christianity came into existence, this ideology did not look much different: "Thus was woman created, rightly and justly, to rule the household with order, while the man must bestir himself in the marketplace and faraway lands" (Columella 12, praef.)

86. *Purpuraria* next to *purpurarius* (a female and a male dealer in purple goods or someone, female or male, who dyes these goods); see *CIG,* 2159.

87. A relief in Budapest, dated between 110 and 130 C.E., shows a blacksmith and a woman (his wife?) in the workshop; he is the major figure, shown at his work, while she is a secondary figure doing work of lesser importance (she seems to be arranging things in their proper place); see Zimmer 1982, no. 123, pp. 193f.

88. Zimmer 1982, no. 133, pp. 193f.

89. Cf. the material and critical reflection in Eichenauer 1988, pp. 34ff., and p. 92 on the *quasillariae,* women who by profession worked in spinning, mostly slaves, whose work was distinguished on ideological grounds from that of the matron, which was given the "honorable title" of *lanificium.*

90. The literature of antiquity dealing with economics speaks of women's work in the house on parallel terms with the work of men outside the house. It is plain that such associating does not mean equality. Nature prescribes the division of labor, woman's anxiousness qualifies her for the tasks she is given, and man's resoluteness qualifies him for his. In addition, by her efforts, woman helps her husband's activities achieve greater success; she is the helpmate of his work. This is how Columella expresses it (12, praef.).

91. See Zimmer 1982, p. 26.

92. See, in particular, Scheidel 1990; Herfst 1992, pp. 13ff.

93. See L. Schottroff 1990a, pp. 310–23, esp. pp. 319–23 (ET: 1993, pp. 138–57, esp. pp. 150–55), on the work of women in the sex trade and on the interpretation of Luke 7:36–50 in relation to that work.

94. See L. Schottroff 1992a on John 4 and the work of the Samaritan woman.

95. See Richter Reimer 1992, p. 69.

96. See L. Schottroff 1990a, pp. 305–9 (ET: 1993, pp. 131–37); Richter Reimer 1992, pp. 123ff.

97. Richter Reimer (1992, pp. 146ff.) rightly calls attention to the fact that the text does not present Rhoda (Acts 12:12ff.) as a slave whose job it was to open the gate; see also below at III.1.B.

98. Richter Reimer 1992, pp. 162ff.

99. See L. Schottroff 1988a, p. 252; and below at II.1.C.
100. Cf. below at IV.2.
101. Cf. below at IV.2.
102. Cf. Richter Reimer 1992, pp. 206ff., an extensive discussion of *skēnopoios* and the history of how this word was interpreted.
103. Cf. Bücher 1922, pp. 204ff., on paid skilled-trade work; see also Autorengruppe 1983, pp. 125ff. One often finds in the Christian history of interpretation that the idea of a middle-class, well-off skilled-trade establishment is read into statements in the New Testament about manual labor. Behind this is an idealization in the sense of patristic ideology; what is utterly lacking is social-historical analysis. Such an idealization matches that of the woman in the house who does not work.
104. Luke 12:46; on the absence of large estate owners from the lands, see Columella, 1.1, 18–20. On the work of female slaves, cf. below at III.1.B and IV.2.B; and Pomeroy 1975, pp. 191–92 and n3 (references to literature); Treggiari 1975b; Günther 1987, pp. 40ff.
105. Cf. above in this section.
106. See Eichenauer 1988, pp. 86f., on this inscription; Kampen 1981, p. 113; Günther 1987, p. 129; Treggiari 1979, p. 72.
107. Maxey 1938, p. 113; Eichenauer 1988, p. 86; Pliny the Elder (*Nat. hist.* 9.143) unmistakably supports the reading of "fisherwoman" for *piscatrix*. See Kampen 1985 on the women street vendors.
108. Autorengruppe 1983, fig. 38, shows the figure of an emaciated fisherman; cf. Maxey 1938, pp. 12ff., on the working conditions of those men; also L. Schottroff 1983, pp. 192ff.; Luke 5:1–11.
109. Heine 1990, p. 357. She focuses her critique particularly on women and men Pharisees, women and men Sadducees, women and men evangelists.
110. On women tax collectors, see P. J. Sijpestein, "A Female Tax Collector," *Zeitschrift für Papyrologie und Epigraphik* 61 (1985): 71–73; and his "Another Female Tax Collector," *Zeitschrift für Papyrologie und Epigraphik* 61 (1985): 121–22. (I am indebted to Martin Leutzsch for these references.) On women Pharisees, see *m. Soṭa* 3:4, where the word is used and has to be translated as "woman Pharisee," although some exegetes dispute this. Given the character of the Pharisaic movement, the participation of women in it can be taken for granted.
111. I restrict myself to the picture painted by the oldest Gospel, that of Mark; cf. L. Schottroff 1990a, pp. 134–59; (ET: 1993, pp. 168–203).
112. On Magdala, see the collection of sources in Avi-Yonah 1976, p. 99. Magdala was renowned for its production of salted fish.
113. L. Schottroff 1990a, p. 141 (ET: 1993, p. 175).
114. Marquardt (1886) 1975, 1:327.
115. Billerbeck 1961, 4:621, 62.
116. See Krauss (1910) 1966, 1:101f.; and below at II.3.B.
117. Cf. Blümner (1912) 1969, 1:65, for a sketch.
118. Ringe 1988, p. 159.
119. Emphasis added (L.S.).
120. Funk 1971, p. 158.
121. Luz 1990, 2:333.
122. Cf. also above in this section.
123. Jülicher (1910) 1963, 2:579.

124. Mesters 1983, 1:82.

125. Cf. above at II.2.B.

126. Weder 1978, p. 137.

127. Weder 1978, p. 136.

128. Based on the translation by E. Haenchen.

129. Jeremias 1963, p. 148; cf. above in this section.

130. See L. Schottroff/W. Schottroff 1983.

131. The so-called household codes (cf. above at II.1.C.) demand that slaves be submissive and do their work conscientiously (Eph. 6:5ff.; Col. 3:23) but that women only be submissive. Of course, in the tradition of these codes, it is expected that women labor their entire life. Cf. below at IV.2.B.

132. The only exception I know is the womanist New Testament scholar Clarice Martin (1990, pp. 43ff.). She correctly criticizes the translation of *doulē* as "servant" instead of "slave."

133. Harnack 1900a, p. 35. Harnack 1900b and Harnack 1904, 2:222, do not mention their work at all.

134. E.g., Lampe 1989, pp. 156ff.

135. Richter Reimer 1992.

136. The exception on this text is Schille 1984: "That Lydia was well off is not said in the text."

137. Cf. also the interpretation of Acts 9:39: Tabitha, who "sewed garments," becomes a well-off widow (G. Stählin, in *ThWNT*, 9:451n107) or "a gentlewoman (or virgin) who uses her wealth to support poor women" (Wikenhäuser 1961, p. 116). The interpretation of Preuschen (1912, p. 62) goes even more solidly against the text: "*chitonas kai himatia* are not, as it would appear from the common text, the items of clothing she had sewn and which she, in the manner of affluent women, would give to the poor but are her own clothes, which show off her wealth." One can observe here how the interpreters' wish to find rich and high-ranking people among Christians of New Testament times trespasses against the allegedly highly exalted scientific nature of their discipline. The text speaks of Tabitha's work, not of her wealth.

138. I find an eschatological interpretation of this parable more appropriate than an ecclesiological one. Cf. L. Schottroff 1988b, pp. 142f., where I offer a critique of the ecclesiological interpretation of the mustard seed, in which the group around Jesus is made invisible.

139. In contrast to traditional interpretation, the woman's action is at the center of feminist interpretation. Cf. Waller 1979–1980, pp. 99–109, esp. 107: "A woman is the locus of sacred activity." However, Waller's interest in the dimension of women's work is secondary; cf. Ringe 1988, p. 159. On the Lenten veil, see Misereor. Bischöfliches Hilfswerk, e.V., *Das Misereor-Hungertuch. Biblische Frauengestalten—Wegweiser zum Reich Gottes* (Aachen, 1989).

140. See Thürmer-Rohr 1991, a critique of the hope that is a dimension of women's complicity in the systemic injustice of patriarchy.

141. Mark 4:28 and the parable of the leaven are frequently used as the case against human cooperation in establishing God's reign; cf., e.g., Luz 1990, 2:335: " 'Eschatological' interpretations maintain that God's reign is promised to human beings but is not brought into being by them." Here "laboring in God's harvest" (Matt. 9:38; Luke 10:2) is set aside and a sharp alternative is set up: God's doing versus human action. Such an alternative has a significant place in Christian dogmatics but not in the New Testament.

142. That feminists have taken up the word *struggle* and are using it in a positive sense has become a matter of controversy; and yet the word is most useful, "in the first place, to identify women's efforts in finding ways to live and, in the second, to emphasize that feminist theology must, of necessity, confront the violence of patriarchy," as Christine Schaumberger (1991, pp. 31f.) rightly puts it.

143. See L. Schottroff 1983, p. 194f., on shepherds' working conditions.

144. On the value of one drachma, cf. below at II.3.B.

145. Jülicher ([1910] 1963, 2:318) speaks of the shepherds' "happy love" and "faithfulness"; Schulz (1972, p. 390) of "shepherd faithfulness." Many a hymn and spiritual song gives this rendition of Luke 15:5; on such interpretations of Psalm 23, see W. Schottroff 1980, pp. 78–113.

146. In the patriarchal sense of things, the women of the "house," i.e., of the family, are of no significance, as this parable indicates. It is focused on an event in the family but perceives the family utterly without women's involvement. Cf. above at I on the father–son relationship as the patriarchal center of power; cf. Gössmann 1989 on the interpretation of Luke 15:11–31 in terms of mother and daughter as given by Hildegard of Bingen.

147. Klostermann 1929, p. 157.

148. Cf. above at I.3.D. and II.2.B on the assumption that androcentric language means to include women in every instance until proven otherwise. One must therefore assume in relation to Luke 15:2 that women Pharisees and women scribes "murmured" against Jesus' action of justice.

149. See Krauss (1912) 1966, 3:22.

150. Social-historical materials on Matt. 20:1–16 are brought together in L. Schottroff 1990a, pp. 36–43; ET, W. Schottroff and W. Stegemann (eds.), *God of the Lowly* (Maryknoll, N.Y.: Orbis Books, 1984, pp. 129–35). My material was taken up and supplemented by Heszer 1990, pp. 50ff.

151. Ben David 1974, pp. 301f.

152. Ben-David 1974, pp. 152, 293.

153. t. B.M. 8.2; cf. Farbstein 1896, 45.5.

154. Cf. above at II.2.B. On aged women in the fields, see *Anthologia graeca* 9.89: "In order to fight hunger and other hardships, Niko, the old woman, went out to the fields with her daughter to gather ears of grain. She succumbed to the heat and died. As there was no wood, other young women helped heap straw and ears of corn on top of her for a pyre."

155. Tobit 2:11–14.

156. The *ketubbah,* a marriage bond, was a sum of money promised during the marriage ceremony by the groom to the bride for the eventuality of the marriage's ending in divorce or on account of his death.

157. *M. Ketub.* 1:2; cf. also Ben-David 1974, p. 293.

158. *M. Ketub.* 1:2.

159. Materials in Krauss (1911) 1966, 2:18f.

160. *M. Ketub.* 4:4; cf. also Krauss (1911) 1966, 2:20f.

161. Materials on child labor in agriculture in Scheidel 1990, pp. 422–24.

162. *Anthologia graeca* 14.134.

163. Lucian, *Hetairikoi dialogoi* 6.

164. Terence, *An.* 70ff.

165. Lauffer 1971.

166. Bücher 1922, p. 217: "It must be noted that a female weaver's pay, even when

she works with wool, remains pay on the basis of time, whereas that of a male weaver of woolen materials is for piecework. Furthermore, there are fewer pay levels for women than for men and the pay differential between fine and rough work is smaller than for male weavers." Cf. L. Schottroff 1990a, p. 106 (ET: 1993, pp. 89–90).

167. Avigad 1980, pp. 128, 137.

168. Ben-David 1974, pp. 300f.

169. Jeremias 1963, p. 134.

170. Jeremias himself acknowledges that as a dowry or emergency fund, the sum is really too small.

171. Luke 12:16–21 indicates that the price of grain was kept artificially elevated even in times of bumper crops.

172. Cf. above at II.2.B.

173. Cf., e.g., Krauss (1910) 1966, 1:101f., on the coexistence of domestic and commercial baking; H. Schneider 1980, pp. 111f. and 117.

174. H. Schneider 1980, p. 98.

175. Dio Chrysostom, *Or.* 7.104.

176. Ben-David 1974, p. 306.

177. Cf. above in this section.

178. Cf. Krauss (1912) 1966, 3:22.

179. E.g., Grundmann n.d. and Kremer 1988 on this text.

180. The clearest observations I have found are in Weder 1978, p. 250f.; cf. also below.

181. Jülicher (1910) 1963, 2:321.

182. He refers to A. Plummer, *Gospel according to Luke,* 4th ed. (ICC; Edinburgh, 1908); J. T. Beck refers to Johann Tobias Beck (1804–1878). I have not researched to which of Beck's works he is referring.

183. The son is to seek wisdom: "If you seek it like silver, and search for it as for hidden treasures . . ."

184. *Midrash H. L.* 1.1 (79b), according to Billerbeck (1924) 1961, 2:212.

185. Weder 1978, pp. 250f.

186. Cf. Bultmann 1963, pp. 171f.

187. See Grundmann n.d. on this text.

188. Schlatter 1931, p. 347.

189. Material in Scheidel 1990, p. 427.

190. Greek philosopher, born ca. 135 B.C.E. The citation is from Strabo, *Geogr.* 3.4.17.

191. Material in Scheidel 1990, passim.

192. Scheidel (1990) cites additional parallels, p. 428.

193. Heszer (1990, pp. 85f.) refers to the version from Diodorus Siculus as a parallel to Matt. 20:1–16 in terms of substance.

194. The interpretation of angels' being God's "regal court" is highly inappropriate. Some examples of such a tradition of interpretation, which assumes a heavenly hierarchy contrary to the text, are Klostermann 1929 and also Wiefel 1988 on Luke 15:10. That verse provides no basis for the assumption that angels are to be seen as a regal court.

195. On this expression of misogyny, cf. Luke 24:11 and Schramm 1981, pp. 58f.

196. As the parable appears only in Luke, it is just as possible to consider that it came into existence only at the time of that Gospel as it is to consider it a part of an older tradition. This question in no way affects the significance of the parable's contents, because

I do not consider the Christian community at the end of the first century C.E. to be of smaller value in comparison to the Jesus movement of the historical Jesus. What is important is that the collective process of handing on the gospel be kept in sight, a process in which women and men always were involved.

197. On economic interference with widows' welfare according to the Hebrew scriptures, see the material gathered by Gustav Stählin, in *ThWNT*, 9:445; and the extensive analysis by W. Schottroff 1992. Undoubtedly there were rich widows in the ancient world. It could be that this widow wielded some power on account of her wealth; she does succeed in getting the unjust judge to render judgment in her favor. But the parable gives no indication that the widow is an exception to the rule of social reality: the majority of the population was poor, and the majority of widows were extremely exploited and oppressed on account of their class *and* gender. (The question of whether the parable of Luke 18:1–8 is of Lukan, pre-Lukan, or even Jesuanic origin should not give rise to arguments that do injustice to the text. If interpreters come to the conclusion that "Luke" is the preacher of the rich urban Romans and that the image of a successful, affluent widow fits the scene, it still does not answer why this parable gives such visibility to structural injustice through the widow's obtaining her rights, through the depiction of gender hierarchy and economic exploitation.)

198. Even if this parable were called a "simile," i.e., a singular narrated case (following Adolf Jülicher's categorization of the parables' genre, which I no longer regard as useful; cf. above at I.3.C), it would not alter the fact that this singular case derives its plausibility from the everyday reality of widows' hardships that was known to everyone.

199. Cf. W. Schottroff 1992.

200. E.g., Jeremias 1963, p. 156. Often the interpretation of this parable is based on arguments from literary criticism, e.g., that v. 1 is Lukan and therefore misses the point (Jeremias) or that v. 1 does not miss the point and vv. 6–8a are typically Jewish (Jülicher [1910] 1963, pp. 284, 286). I reply to such arguments that literary criticism and its hypotheses have proven to be unreliable tools and instruments for sustaining preconceived notions. The point is to understand the given text as a whole in its literary context. And even if I were to relativize the parable's context through literary criticism, it is the widow who is placed in the center, and our attention is called to drawing conclusions from her conduct for our lives. The judge responds only to the widow's actions.

201. *Egkakein* in v. 1 signifies the exact opposite of *hypomonē*, the patient power to resist; cf. L. Schottroff 1988b, pp. 103ff. Both words may find use in connection with the situation of women during childbirth; cf. Rom. 8:24, in the overall context of Rom. 8:18–25 (see L. Schottroff 1988b, pp. 110f.), and *2 Clem.* 2:2.

202. Cf. Holtzmann 1911, pp. 90–107.

203. Luke 18:1. On the connection of Luke 18:1 and the understanding of *hypomonē* and the patient power to resist, see note 201, above.

204. See L. Schottroff 1988b, pp. 103ff., on the eschatological basis and purpose of this power to resist.

205. See esp. Delling 1970, pp. 209ff., on *ekdikēsis*, vv. 3 and 7. The understanding has numerous levels here: God or the judge is to *avenge* the injustice done to the widow or the faithful and to reestablish justice; they are to *help* people obtain their *rights*. As the eschatological judge, God requites injustice. Once the anti-Judaistic notion of the God of Israel as a God of revenge had taken hold, this fundamental understanding in early Christianity was excluded from the Christian perception of the New Testament.

206. Brunner (1988, p. 359) dates this text in the Ninth or Tenth Dynasty (between 2155 and 2030 B.C.E.). It reports that the judge and the king wanted to fulfill the farmer's petition even after the first intervention but did not tell him so in order to hear further samples of his eloquence. This fictional situation may be left aside in the analysis of the farmer's conduct in the perspective of social history.

207. Erman (1923) 1971, p. 167.

208. Erman (1923) 1971, pp. 169f.

209. Erman (1923) 1971, p. 171.

210. Cf. Thierfelder 1963, p. 63.

211. H. Musurillo 1954, pp. 66f.; cf. also Carcopino 1979, p. 267; MacMullen 1966, pp. 84ff. Commodus was emperor in Rome from 180 to 192 C.E. The fourth book of Maccabees is part of this context.

212. There is an extended discussion among exegetes about the literary connection of the parable and the material that frames it and at which stages in the text's development the various parts of that material were added. The primary task does not change, however: to interpret the text in its given form; cf. above at note 200.

213. "Always to pray"—v. 1—and "cry to him [God] day and night"—v. 7— connect, among other things in the text, the woman's conduct in the parable with the believers' conduct and interpret her speaking, even though the words are addressed to the believers.

214. Cf. the cries of the group of women in the *Acts of Thecla* (cf. below). Jeremias (1963, p. 154n1) cites a parallel from Nisibis (Mesopotamia), probably from the end of the nineteenth century. A woman pressured the Cadi at court to pay attention to her; he was always too busy with something more important, but every day she came back and cried aloud. "She was sternly bidden to be quiet, and reproachfully told that she came every day. 'And so I will do,' she loudly exclaimed, 'until the Cadi hears my case.'"

215. Cf., e.g., Weder 1978, p. 270n139. It is doubtful that the narrator of the text portrays the judge ironically (e.g., Weder 1978) or that he is ridiculed by the narrator (e.g., Harnisch 1972, pp. 421ff. and 433). The so-called sarcasm of the judge is quite realistic: this is how judges react to stubborn women.

216. On this question see esp. Delling 1970, p. 213.

217. This is how Walter Bauer (1979, p. 848) weakens the meaning of the text. Cf. also J.D.M. Derrett 1972, pp. 178, 189–91: "otherwise she could blacken my face"— the woman might cause him to lose face before the people.

218. *Frauenwiderstand im Hunsrück. Frauengeschichte(n) 1983–1985* (Women's resistance in the Hunsrück region: Women's history (stories) 1983–1985) 1985, pp. 174f. The peace movement was dismissed in the courts and in public discussion under the comprehensive notion of "violence"; this was to refer to its symbolic activities and its sit-ins. But in the newspaper articles against women's resistance I see something that goes beyond this: it is sexism that uses the nonviolent "role" of women and the conduct of resisting women to create the impression that the latter are aggressive furies who are not satisfied with their private lives.

219. Harnack 1904, 2:234.

220. Harnack 1904, 2:234: "Neither in the pre-Decian period nor in subsequent years was there any difference made between men and women in a persecution." In a later German edition (1924), Harnack added to that sentence: "although the manner of punishment was frequently *different*" (p. 605 in vol. 2 of the German edition; emphasis added by L.S.).

221. Rome's persecution of Christians was a consequence of the resistance Christians offered to the everyday structures of violence in the empire. On this everyday resistance, see Schäfke 1979; L. Schottroff 1990a, pp. 184–216. See Augar 1905 on the persecution of Christian women.

222. Mark 15:40 and par.

223. L. Schottroff 1990a, pp. 134–59 (ET: 1993, pp. 168–203).

224. L. Schottroff 1988c.

225. The edition of the *Acts of Thecla* is that of R. A. Lipsius and M. Bonnet, *Acta apostolorum apocrypha,* vol. 1 (1891); ET in Schneemelcher 1991, pp. 239–46.

226. Davies (1980, p. 61) comes to a similar conclusion. On the discussion about the historical value of these apostolic acts, see the research survey of Albrecht 1986, pp. 246ff. Schneemelcher (note 225 above) criticizes such judgments of the text: "Above all we must be very cautious about any combination of these folk-lore hypotheses with the assumption of a liberated women's movement in the Church of the 2nd century as the *Sitz im Leben* for the APl. . . . On a sober treatment of the evidence, hypotheses of such a kind appear to be largely no more than the products of modern fancy, without any basis in the sources" (pp. 221f.). The *Acts of Thecla* is one example, next to others, of the basis in the sources that Schneemelcher finds missing. It all depends on one's method and perspective. Tertullian unwittingly provides more evidence of a women's liberation movement; cf. note 228, below.

227. *Acts of Thecla* 34.

228. Tertullian, *De bap.* 17. Cf. below at III.1.B.

229. *Acts of Thecla* 7, 9, 12, 15.

230. See Albrecht 1986, p. 256, on this hypothesis.

231. E.g., the accusation against Paul that his preaching had spoiled the virginity of women and therefore *the city* (15).

232. Cf. also the *Acts of Peter* 34. Peter is to be killed "so that we may recover our wives and in order to give satisfaction to those who cannot execute him, who have themselves been deprived of their wives by him." Cf. above at II.1.B.

233. This caused Christian men once again to adopt an ambiguous position: they would teach abstinence but repudiate it when women gave up their socially prescribed woman's role, which was said to have been divinely ordained. On the liberation of women through virginity, see Ruether 1979, pp. 72ff.; Jensen 1988, pp. 173ff.; Burrus 1987.

234. Lipsius/Bonnet, pp. 271f. (see note 225, above).

235. Cicero, *De re pub.* 1.38; *De off.* 1.54; and elsewhere. Cf. above at I.2.C.

236. Cf. above at II.1.B.

237. Albrecht 1986, p. 263, considers such a possibility.

238. Cf. Blandina's conduct during her martyrdom in Lyon; see Eusebius, *Hist. eccles.* 5.1.41.

239. Davies (1980, pp. 58ff.) accurately outlines the recognizable critique of Paul's conduct found in this text. Albrecht (1986, p. 259) judges more cautiously. Cf. MacDonald 1983, on the portrayal of Paul; also below at III.1.B.

240. See esp. Söder (1932) 1969, pp. 158ff.

241. On this anointing and its substantive parallel in Mark 14:3–9 and par., see L. Schottroff 1990c.

242. Josephus, *Bell. Jud.* 2.20.

243. Cf. L. Schottroff 1990a, pp. 291ff. (ET: 1993, pp. 60ff.).

244. It is closely related to other acts of apostles, with which it shares novel-like elements of narration; it is related as well to other extra-Christian novellas. (Cf. Söder [1932] 1969.) This in no way minimizes the particular quality of the *Acts of Thecla* as a document of the history of women and their resistance. The *Acts of Xanthippe and Polyxena* is, in like manner, an important source for the history of women's resistance; cf. Davies 1980, pp. 64–69, and below in this section.

245. Cf. above at II.1.B.

246. Davies (1980, p. 60), however, does speak of "a general opposition of males to females."

247. Cf. above at I.2.B on this particular approach.

248. See Schäfke 1979, pp. 502–6.

249. Cf. L. Schottroff 1990d.

250. Richter Reimer (1992, pp. 147ff.) has provided a thorough examination of this incident.

251. Richter Reimer 1992, p. 147.

252. Cf. *Acta Xanthippae et Polyxenae* 10: Xanthippe fears that her husband is about to refuse hospitality to Paul and that therefore the Christian community will be located in someone else's house. See the English translation in The Ante-Nicene Fathers, 10:204–17.

253. Richter Reimer 1992, p. 154n292.

254. Richter Reimer 1992, pp. 143ff.

255. On feminist-theological discussion of women's resistance, see the thematic issue *Frauenwiderstand* of the journal *FAMA* (December 1988); Harrison 1985; Thürmer-Rohr 1991.

256. See Deissmann 1923, pp. 94f.; Bauer 1979, s.v. *trachēlos*.

257. Deissmann (1923, p. 95) assumes that Paul is using a common expression in the sense of "sticking out one's neck for someone," which at one time referred to a legal procedure of being decapitated on behalf of someone else or to stand bail for someone by pledging one's own neck. The context of this remark by Paul (Rom. 16:4) suggests, however, that he faced prosecution by the state and imprisonment, given his previous experience (as suggested by Rom. 16:7).

258. Emphasis added.

259. Harnack 1904, 1:231f.

260. Cf. Lucian, *De morte Peregr.* 12–16; *Acts of Thecla* 31.

261. Rabbi Meir, her husband, is of the third generation of tannaitic Jews (130–160 C.E.) according to Strack/Stemberger 1982, p. 83. Goodblatt (1975/76) writes that only in the fourth or fifth century C.E. did the tradition arise that Beruriah was the wife of R. Meir and that she was a learned woman. In the following reflection, the attention is on Beruriah as a figure in legends and on her significance within women's history, not on the "historical" Beruriah.

262. *b.'Erub.* 53b.

263. Cf. *'Abot* 1.5; Goldfeld 1976, p. 263; Archer 1990, p. 97.

264. Goldfeld (1976, p. 266) cites a commentary from the eleventh century C.E. on *'Aboda Zara* of Rashi: "Once Beruriah scoffed at the rabbinical saying 'Women are light-minded' (Kiddushin 80b) and her husband warned her that her own end might yet testify to the truth of that saying. To put her virtue to the test, he charged one of his disci-

ples to seduce her. After repeated efforts she yielded and then shame drove her to commit suicide. R. Meir, tortured by remorse, fled from his home." This legend too portrays Beruriah as a critic of misogynist traditions within educated Judaism. Here she is severely punished for that. Her seduction presupposes an image of women that is set firmly against their emancipation (as discussed above in II.1).

265. Archer (1990, pp. 97ff.) contests the view that the historical Beruriah had received an education and that she may be used as evidence for women's education at the time. She doubts similarly that one may deduce from the legends that women at the time of the Babylonian Talmud received an education (p. 99). But she does not consider the critical substance of these traditions; cf. below, note 269. Goodblatt (1975/76) argues similarly.

266. *b. Pesaḥ* 62b.

267. Cf. particularly Goldfeld 1976.

268. It is not likely that only women transmitted the Babylonian Talmud.

269. *t. Pe'a* 4:12; cf. *b. Ta'an.* 23b (it is more meritorious in God's eyes for women to give alms than it is for men) and *b. Ta'an.* 23b; cf. also *b. Ber.* 10a (men pray for the demise of sinners; women pray for an end of sin—and that is the only way that sinners come to repent), all of which contain the same type of legend as does Mark 7:24–30 and par. The everyday experience of women is a source of wisdom that allows them to accomplish more in God's eyes than the men who are associated with them in each instance. This type of legend is critical of the belief of men that they are seen by God as the ones who really fulfill God's will. The very ones whom men deem inferior are superior to them; cf. the legends of *b. 'Erub.* 53b. These legends presuppose a social praxis in which women are refused an education; cf. Archer 1990, pp. 70–101; Goldfeld 1976. The controversy among scholars about women's education shows that subjugation and contempt of women did not go unopposed; cf. particularly *y. Pe'a* 1.1 (15c). Cf. Daube 1972 on Beruriah's resistance and other traditions of women's resistance.

270. Cf. L. Schottroff 1992b on the androcentrism of the Sayings Source and its traditions in the Sermon on the Mount.

271. Unlike the still-dominant tradition of interpretation, I do not regard the so-called antitheses of the Sermon on the Mount (Matt. 5:21–48) as Jesus' way of setting himself apart from the Torah of Moses or the rabbis' teaching. Rather, these antitheses are an actualizing interpretation, in the style of Jewish interpretation, of the Torah that God had given to Moses—a conviction Jesus shared. The Mishnah tractate *Baba Qamma* 8 stipulates the recompense for pains inflicted by injuries or insults, providing for an altered reading of the *lex talionis* of Ex. 21:24f.; Lev. 24:20; Deut. 19:21; cf. Gaius, 3.223, in Roman law. In its discussion of the law, the Mishnah manifests a clearly critical awareness of the fact that this law is very difficult to enforce in relation to poor people and women. A legend about R. Akiba in *Baba Qamma* 8:6 makes this plain. Matthew 5:38f. presupposes a situation that does not even envisage a judicial settlement of injustice, but rather that whoever has the opportunity will strike back. But like *Baba Qamma* 8 and Gaius, 3.223, Matt. 5:38f. understands itself to be a further development of the *lex talionis*.

272. This is a widely held interpretation; cf. L. Schottroff 1990a, pp. 12ff.

273. Wink 1987. My interpretation differs from his only in minor aspects; cf. L. Schottroff 1982, pp. 23ff. Cf. also Klassen 1984; Wengst 1987, pp. 68ff. Cf. note 277

below, on Hoffmann; he also belongs to this tradition of interpretation oriented toward the praxis of peace.

274. Wink 1987, p. 22.

275. Wink 1987, p. 26.

276. *Acts of Perpetua and Felicity* 10; cf. *Acts of Thecla* 22, 23, 34, 38. (Cf. also above in this section.) More evidence could be provided. Amnesty International reports that in many countries today (e.g., Turkey 1991), women face interrogation during which they are forced to strip naked and are raped by policemen.

277. Hoffmann (1981, p. 133) rightly observes: "The usual reaction would be that he hits back, fighting for his rights and denying himself to the other." One needs to add, however, that this is not, as Hoffmann puts it, "normal human behavior" but normal behavior of men on account of the social formation of the man's role.

278. Cf. Seneca, *De ira* 3.23.2; for more material and further discussion, cf. L. Schottroff 1990a, pp. 23ff.

279. Krauss (1912) 1966, 3:248n96.

280. Krauss (1912) 1966, 3:11.

281. Lazarus Goldschmidt's translation.

282. Cf. Krauss (1912) 1966, 3:228.

283. 2 Sam. 23:5.

284. Krauss (1912) 1966, 3:227.

285. Goldfeld (1976, p. 263) uses "rebuking" as her translation here. The Aramaic verb *batash* may mean both "to stamp" and—in a figurative sense—"to treat with contempt"; cf. Marcus Yastrow, *A Dictionary of the Targumim, the Talmud Babli and Yerushalmi, and the Midrashic Literature* (Israel: n.p., 1903), s.v. *batash.*

286. Cf. above at note 264 on Rashi's deprecation of Beruriah; cf. Krauss (1911) 1966, 2:47.

287. Krauss ([1912] 1966, 3:228) says that she had "reprimanded" the student.

288. *Acta Xanthippae et Polyxenae* 21; cf. above at note 253.

289. Zscharnack 1902, p. 88.

290. E.g., Luther's translation. To read this parable as an admonition to Christian conduct conforming to patriarchal structures requires that it be read *against its wording.* The widow in 1 Tim. 5:10, who is well conformed to patriarchy, surely prays day and night but does not defend herself against unjust judges, thereby giving visibility to unjust structures.

291. E.g., Luz 1989, pp. 329f.; Gnilka 1988, 1:181; Schweizer 1975, p. 129.

292. Cf. above at note 273.

293. So, e.g., the widely read book by Theissen (1987) on Jesus; cf. above at I.1.A.

294. Cf. Thürmer-Rohr 1991; on the feminist-theological discussion about complicity, see Schaumberger/Schottroff 1988. Cf. Barbara Welter's article on the feminization of religion in the nineteenth-century United States, "'Frauenwille ist Gottes Wille.' Die Feminisierung der Religion in Amerika 1800–1860," in Claudia Honegger and Bettina Heintz, eds., *Listen der Ohnmacht. Zur Sozialgeschichte weiblicher Widerstandsformen* (Frankfurt, 1981), pp. 326–54.

295. Cf. the third chap. of the KAIROS Document and its liberation-theological critique of Christian ideologies of nonviolence and reconciliation that do not resolve the power problem; L. Schottroff 1990b, pp. 281–83.

296. Cf. Wink 1987.

297. Harrison 1985, p. 238.

298. *b. Ber.* 10a; on this passage, cf. Goldfeld 1976, p. 265. Parallels to R. Hilkia's wife are found in *b. Ta'an.* 23a–23b; cf. Goldfeld 1976, pp. 267f. Cf. also above at note 269.

299. Schaumberger 1981, p. 87. Cf. also Wartenberg 1981, pp. 262–66.

PART III
The Critique of Patriarchy and the Power
to Become a New Being

1. This is the translation found in the Zurich Bible, 1931 revision. The ecumenical translation (Protestant-Catholic) renders the text: "Let each remain in the state in which the call of God reached you." The (German) Luther Bible of 1929 reads as follows: "Everyone remain in the vocation in which he is called." The 1964 version of this text says: "Everyone remain in the calling in which he was called."

To understand the term *vocation* in the Lutheran translation and the term *state*, which has the same meaning, it is useful to consult the Augsburg Confession of 1530, art. 16: "Our churches also condemn those who place the perfection of the gospel in forsaking home and property, wife and children. . . . The gospel does not teach an external and temporal but an internal and eternal righteousness of the heart and does not destroy worldly government, state, or family but requires that one preserve all as ordinances of God and that everyone exercise Christian love and right good works in them, each according to his calling." The German word *Beruf* (calling) goes back to Luther's interpretation and translation of 1 Cor. 7:20; cf. K. L. Schmidt, in *ThWNT*, 3.491f.n1.

The 1971 version of the RSV reads: "Every one should remain in the state in which he was called." The 1990 RSV version is as follows: "Let each of you remain in the condition in which you were called." The word *condition* in place of *state* at best attenuates the solidity of the status quo but changes nothing in the false translation. This resembles what is observable in German translations: uneasy about solidifying the "state" of things, one switches to "condition" but only goes on to solidify the social "condition"; e.g., Thyen 1978, pp. 158, 160.

The interpretations and translations of 1 Cor. 7:20 in the context of theological scholarship are to be discussed below. I want to refer here to the only exception known to me in which the state or condition at the time of conversion is not theologically solidified in the name of Paul—Schüssler Fiorenza 1983, pp. 220–21: "Exegetes misread Paul's advice to Jewish or gentile Christians, when they argue that Paul here means to say that they should remain in the social state and religious role they had when they heard the call to conversion." For an exception in the translation of this text, cf. below at III.1.D.

2. Even in the ancient church there were exegetes who supplemented the phrase in 1 Cor. 7:21, "avail yourself of the opportunity," with "to be free from slavery." Others added: "to make use of your freedom." Bartchy (1973, pp. 6f.) provides a helpful survey of such diverse additions in the history of interpretation. In current discussions in the Western world about Paul, the addition to v. 21, "to make use of your freedom," in no way alters the interpretation of v. 20; it remains an admonition "to remain in one's status."

3. Representatives of status quo theology are named in III.1.C.

4. Wire (1990, p. 86) understands the Pauline solidification of the status quo—which she does not critique exegetically—as an argument directed (chiefly) against women who want to be divorced; cf. note 7, below. She rightly seeks to criticize traditional doctrinal

hermeneutics, according to which Paul is an unassailable authority who had many Christian opponents in Corinth who *cannot but be* theologically mistaken. On hermeneutical questions, see Schüssler Fiorenza 1987 and below at III.1.D. On Wire's thesis concerning the Corinthian women, see III.2.C.

5. Bauer 1979, p. 435, s.v. *klēsis:* "1. call, calling, invitation. In our lit. almost exclusively in a religious sense . . . of divine call. . . . 2. station in life, position, vocation." The latter meaning is applied by him only to 1 Cor. 7:20. On Bauer's arguments and the overall meaning of the word, see Bartchy 1973, p. 136n480–82.

6. See Schaumberger 1991, pp. 25ff. and n17, on the discussion of the "paradigm shift."

7. Nowhere did Jesus fundamentally prohibit divorce; he clearly rejected a remarriage after divorce as adultery. Paul rephrases the formulation of Jesus' sayings in such a way that it appears as if Christians ought not to divorce. And yet his responses to individual cases indicate that Christians divorced frequently. One could conclude from 1 Cor. 7:10–11 that women pushed to have a divorce more often than men. We know from Justin (*Apologia* 2.2) and Tertullian (*Ad uxorem* 2.4) how difficult it was for Christian women to live together with non-Christian men. I regard Paul's excursus in 1 Cor. 7:17–24 on basic principles as an argument with which a Christian's divorce from a non-Christian partner could be defended by Christians themselves. Verse 15 speaks of the unfreedom that results from a Christian's insistence on maintaining the marriage against the wishes of the non-Christian partner. In *Apologia* 2.2 Justin reports about the pressure exerted by the Christian community on a Christian woman: "Pressured by the others of her community to remain in her marriage because there was still hope that her husband would amend his ways, she desisted and remained," at least for some time. In 1 Cor. 7:17–24, Paul wants to assert that the real issue is for people to live according to God's call. In particular cases this may mean divorce, so as to avoid becoming a slave to another human being.

Schüssler Fiorenza (1983, p. 223) suggests that the manner in which Paul reduces, in 1 Cor. 7:12–15, the range of options open to Christians in a mixed marriage creates more problems for Christian women than for Christian men. As I see it, Paul was arguing, in vv. 15, 16, 17–24, much more *against* the pressure that Christians exerted on other Christians, presumably more on women than on men, as the verb *to enslave* in vv. 15 and 16 would indicate. Wire (1990, pp. 86f.) understands 1 Cor. 7:17–24 to be an argument "to stop and then reverse a movement away from marriage by those, especially women, who seek independence from their sexual partners." An erroneous interpretation of 1 Cor. 7:13–16 such as this results from the false translation of 1 Cor. 7:20 and the misinterpretation of 1 Cor. 7:17–24 as "remain in your state."

8. As in 1 Thess. 4:7 and Eph. 4:4, the dative of *kalein* is used here. This calling is thought of as a process that God initiates and accompanies and that is actualized by believers and their conduct of life; cf. Eph. 4:1. It is similar for the datives in 1 Cor. 7:20, 24.

9. Blass-Debrunner, parag. 449.4 on *ei mē = plēn*. I have attempted to indicate in this rendition that now Paul speaks no longer about individual cases.

10. The use of the plural appears to me to be the best way to eliminate the androcentrism in the Greek text. Paul thinks from the position of men but wants women too to be covered by these principles. It is interesting to note that when it came to individual cases, androcentric language no longer sufficed for his purposes (7:1–16).

11. I relate God's apportioning in substance to the spiritual gifts (cf. 1 Cor. 7:7, 12) and to the Spirit; cf. also Rom. 12:3.

12. *kyrios* refers to God.

13. *diatassomai* = "to instruct, command." In terms of its substance, it means something authoritatively taught. The translation I propose seeks to avoid the confusion with military orders. Paul's authoritarian language could indicate that he wants to establish himself as the only authority in Corinth (Schüssler Fiorenza 1987), but then there would be no real power behind his authoritarian language. His language, rather, is in an overall context in which he argues quite erratically precisely because he has no more power in the community he is addressing.

14. On this translation, see note 8, above.

15. The context shows clearly that *kyrios* here refers to Christ.

16. On this translation, see note 7, above.

17. Cf. note 7, above, on this point.

18. Schüssler Fiorenza 1983, p. 210. That such a conclusion was actually under discussion in early Christianity is shown in Justin, *Dialogue with Trypho* 23.5. In Justin, the subject is already marked by anti-Judaism. On what the Jewish circumcision of men meant to women, see the Christian views collected in L. Schottroff 1990a, p. 299nn19 and 20 (ET: 1993, p. 77nn19 and 20).

19. On the application of personal rights in Roman law, see Gaius, 1.48f.: "Some persons are subject to their own law [*sui iuris*]; others are subject to the law of others [*alieno iuri subiecti*]." Cf. Kaser 1962, parag. 12ff. On the prescription of rights in Roman patriarchal households, see J. Gaudemet, in RAC (*Reallexikon für Antike und Christentum*, 1969), 7:319ff.

20. On the meaning of this concept in our context, cf. above at note 1.

21. See Bartchy 1973, pp. 87ff., on the process of being freed.

22. See Brooten 1982 on the right of Jewish women to initiate divorce.

23. 1 Macc. 1:15; Smallwood 1981, p. 376n74.

24. The patriarchal self-awareness of the free man who is fully conscious of his privileges is manifest in the "social types" of which the ancient world made use in its sociology— which was written from the perspective of the privileged (cf. below at III.2.A and B, on 1 Cor. 1:26ff.). People often cite parallels to Gal. 3:28 or 1 Cor. 7:17–24, from Jewish and non-Jewish sources, that in their substance relate to Paul's categories: e.g., Thyen 1978, p. 143; Schüssler Fiorenza 1983, pp. 213f. There is no warrant to make an anti-Judaistic use of Gal. 3:28 against the Jewish prayer found in *t. Ber.* 7:18 ("Blessed be the One who did not make me a Gentile, . . . who did not make me a woman, . . . who did not make me someone uncultured, . . . "). Paul does not warrant such use; nor does the history of Christianity, whose leading men have always been grateful to God that they were Christian, male, white, and well-off, as one may deduce from the Christian theology that dominates to this day and from the struggle waged against it by feminist liberation theology and its search for a new paradigm.

25. As far as I know, historically speaking, Schüssler Fiorenza (1984) is the first Christian theologian to concretely relate Gal. 3:28 to the life of a female slave.

26. Cf. Gal. 2:11–14.

27. Paul provides a legitimate basis for divorce in opposition to patriarchal pressure to live in marriage, a pressure exerted inside (and undoubtedly also outside) the Christian community; cf. above at note 7.

28. I use quotation marks to signal that I am describing the consciousness of androcentric language but that I do not share that consciousness.

29. Richter Reimer 1992, pp. 247f.

30. Richter Reimer (1992, p. 247) refers to the gate of Simon the tanner (Acts 10:17), which no one uses as evidence of Simon's affluence, whereas this is done often in relation to the gate of the house of Mary, mother of John Mark (Acts 12:13, 14).

31. It is the same verb used to give emphasis to how the non-Christian slave woman in Luke 22:59 persists in her opinion. In Acts 15:2 the verb describes Paul's insistence on non-Jewish men being fully Christian without circumcision and that they should "remain as they were when they came to faith"—a parallel in substance to 1 Cor. 7:17–24. According to the manuscript of Acts, Paul is addressing the concrete case of a Gentile Christian wanting to be circumcised; he is not propounding a general status quo theology.

32. Richter Reimer 1992, p. 248.

33. Schrage (1991, p. 141n261) interprets Rom. 16:10f. to refer to "members of house churches"; this would imply, however, that Paul is greeting only a part of the house community. The phrasing of Rom. 16:10f. most probably means that there are Christian and non-Christian slaves, both male and female, in Aristobulus's and Narcissus's households. The ecumenical translation (referred to in note 1, above) is mistaken in translating Rom. 16:10 as "greet the whole household of Aristobulus"; what it should literally say is "greet all of those who belong to Aristobulus." I am persuaded by the argument of Schüssler Fiorenza (1987, pp. 394f.), who goes counter to the usual view that Chloe (1 Cor. 1:11) was most likely a non-Christian owner of Christian slaves. On account of the similar construction of v. 12, she understands "Chloe's people" to be "people or followers of Chloe" (p. 395) who, as official messengers of the community, inform Paul by word of mouth and in writing about disputes, which he then interprets in 1 Cor. 1:12 as the quarreling among factions.

34. Pomeroy 1975, p. 192. On the work of female slaves, cf. above at II.2.B and below at IV.4.B. See Thierfelder 1963, pp. 121ff., on contracts relating to the sale of female slaves; Treggiari 1975a, pp. 400f., on the sale of female slaves.

35. See Taubenschlag 1930, p. 152. On a Christian slave woman as a nurse, see Tertullian, *Ad Scap.* 4. In certain situations slave owners were more interested in the usefulness of female slaves for sexual purposes than in their ability to work. Columella (1.9.18) relates that he had rewarded female slaves who had brought up several children (i.e., more slaves) with holidays or even freedom.

36. Names such as Ampliatus (Rom. 16:8), Urbanus (16:9), Stachys (16:9), Persis (16:12), and Phlegon (16:14) are associated with slaves, but it is difficult to conclude with certainty from those names that those people were slaves; cf. Bartchy 1973, p. 61; Lietzmann 1928, pp. 125f.; Gülzow (1969, p. 54n1) also counts Tryphaena and Tryphosa (Rom. 16:12) among slaves.

37. Richter Reimer 1992, pp. 197ff.

38. Richter Reimer 1992, pp. 182ff.

39. The exorcism is not told as a story of a female slave's liberation; cf. Richter Reimer 1992.

40. Acts 16:15; other Christian households where slaves lived as Christians are referred to in John 4:53; Acts 10:2; 11:14; 16:31, 32ff.; 1 Cor. 1:16; 16:15f. On *oikos* and *oikia*, see the discussion in Gülzow 1969, pp. 52f.

41. Gülzow 1969, p. 44n2.

42. The demand to be subject to *kopiontes*, 1 Cor. 16:16, must be seen as referring also to women who were engaged in leadership tasks, on account of the use of this verb for the work of women in Christian communities in Rom. 16:6, 12—if this point needs still to be made at all, since these women are also part of the *oikia* (16:15). The general-

ization of the demand in vv. 15 and 16 to subject oneself contradicts the notion that, as far as Paul is concerned, Stephanas is to be entrusted with an authority that is not to be entrusted to many women in Corinth; cf. Schüssler Fiorenza 1987, p. 397.

43. This is implied indirectly in 1 Tim. 6:1 and Ignatius, *Pol.* 4. Cf. Bartchy 1973, pp. 99ff.; Schäfke 1979, pp. 528ff.; and Harnack 1904, 1:232f.

44. See the references to texts in note 43, above.

45. The *Acta Pionii* tell of Sabina: "Pionius [a Christian] had said to Sabina that she should change her name so that she would not be subject once again to the brutality of her owner [Politta]; by naming herself Theodata she would escape the violence of brutality. The latter had tried in the days of Gordianus [ca. 240 C.E.] to bring Sabina to renounce her faith and banished her, in shackles, to the hill country; there she secretly received food from the brethren. Thereafter, they took care that she should be free of both Politta and the shackles. From then on she stayed with Pionius and was arrested with him in this persecution" (9). Cf. Gülzow 1969, p. 241n1; Schäfke 1979, p. 532. Schäfke is one who reads the text (p. 532) as saying that Sabina was taken to court because her change of name was illegal.

46. Lucian (*De morte Peregr.* 12f.) describes a comparable situation more accurately.

47. *Acta Pionii* 7.

48. Eusebius, *Hist. eccles.* 6.5.

49. Eusebius, *Hist. eccles.* 5.1.17.

50. Eusebius, *Hist. eccles.* 5.1.42.

51. The slave woman Biblis: cf. Eusebius, *Hist. eccles.* 5.1.25f.; Felicity: *Acts of Perpetua and Felicity* (2, 15, 18, 20). On whether she was a slave, see Gülzow 1969, pp. 130ff. (his arguments fail to persuade me, solely on account of the way *syndoulos* is used in the New Testament); and Schäfke 1979, pp. 535f.

52. Thus explicitly Eusebius, *Hist. eccles.* 5.1.14.

53. The *Acts of Pionius* suggests a period of ca. ten years between Sabina's liberation and her arrest; unfortunately, the text leaves in the dark her life as a liberated woman in the Christian community because of its interest in martyrdom.

54. The question was subject to controversy in antiquity; Bartchy (1973, pp. 64ff.) documents this. Cf. below, note 72, for the critique of slavery by the Essenes. In his homilies on Ephesians, John Chrysostom writes: "If anyone asks where slavery comes from and how it found entry into human life—I know well that many like to ask such questions—let me explain. It was greed that created it, weakness and insatiableness. Neither Noah, nor Abel, nor Seth had a slave, nor the people after them. Sin it was that created this condition" (22.2).

55. It is recognized that slavery (but not the oppression of women) is a matter of suffering. Galatians 3:28 holds up an eschatological vision and orientation for the praxis of the community. The hermeneutical prejudgment to separate eschatological statements from social praxis—as is still maintained in traditional theology—must be fundamentally challenged. One example of such a traditional hermeneutic in relation to Gal. 3:28 is Paulsen 1980, p. 88 (only enthusiasts draw direct conclusions from eschatology). On the praxis of the communities, see Philemon 16: "brother both in the flesh and in the Lord," i.e., no more slave–master relationship; Harnack (1904, 1:235f.) lists Christian parallels.

56. Gülzow (1969, pp. 94n1 and 96n4) lists materials documenting this point.

57. Cf., e.g., Luke 23:2, according to Marcion's text; and Origen, *Contra Celsum* 2:55.

58. Cf. above at II.1. "There are necklets and amulets of slaves, the wearers of which

identified themselves as Christians by the use of the Christ monogram or a decorative alpha and omega" (Schäfke 1979, pp. 534f.).

59. 1 Cor. 11:3, 7, 10 versus 1 Cor. 11:11–12; Gal. 3:28. Schüssler Fiorenza (1988a) rightly speaks of Paul's "ambiguity" (p. 241n98) and "double-edged[ness]" (p. 236) in relation to women.

60. See L. Schottroff 1990a, pp. 123ff. (ET: 1993, pp. 108ff.).

61. See L. Schottroff 1988b, p. 35; L. Schottroff 1990, pp. 61ff. The word *female slave* appears in Paul only with negative connotations, (Gal. 4:22–31).

62. Whether Colossians is an epistle written by Paul has no bearing on this text.

63. On Thecla and the *Acts of Thecla,* see above at II.4.B.

64. See above at II.4.B.

65. Both teaching and learning are prohibited to women: 1 Cor. 14:34f.; 1 Tim. 2:11f., 5:13.

66. Tertullian, *De bap.* 17. Schneemelcher (1991, 2:214f.) provides information about how this text has been discussed but fails to persuade me, because his judgments are directed by antifeminist interests; cf. above at II.4.

67. I use the word *conservative* because in everyday speech it is used to signify means for enforcing patriarchal structures, even though it is too good a word to be filled with an exclusively negative meaning.

68. Cf. Schulz 1972a, pp. 173f.

69. Schweitzer 1967, pp. 194.

70. See Schweitzer 1954, pp. 348–95.

71. See Schulz 1972a, p. 174.

72. According to Josephus (*Ant.* 18.21) and Philo (*Quod omnis probus liber sit* 79), the Essenes sharply rejected the possession of slaves as an injustice.

73. Käsemann 1964, 2:215. This manner of interpreting is widespread even today; it justifies Paul and other parts of the Christian testament as a middle road between extremes. Cf. above at II.1.C.

74. See Käsemann 1964, 2:215.

75. Stuhlmacher 1981, p. 48. This is a widely held interpretation.

76. Stuhlmacher 1981, p. 42.

77. Thyen (1978, p. 160) brusquely rejects this exegesis of 1 Cor. 7:17–24.

78. Wire (1990) offers no critique of traditional exegesis of Paul; she depicts him as an upper-class male who employs a status quo theology against women who want to change and improve their status (pp. 86, 66f., and 61 on 1:26) and who holds up his own loss of status brought about by his Christian faith. She understands the *liberation* of Christian women in Corinth as a *move upward* in society (cf. esp. p. 71). Cf. note 4, above, concerning her critical assessment of traditional hermeneutics of Paul. Her book contains important observations on the history of Christian women in Corinth; cf. below at III.2.B. My criticism is that the substance of dominant exegesis of Paul is not subject to critique, so that her hermeneutical critique touches only upon the preliminary ground of traditional exegesis of Paul (whether or not he is theologically justified). In addition, I find a view of women's liberation as a rise in social standing untenable.

Schüssler Fiorenza (1987) understands the theology and praxis of Corinthian women as an exaltation of the lowly but not, I would judge, in the sense of moving to a higher social status (pp. 399f.). But she too understands Paul to be an upper-class male who, on account of the Christian faith, experienced a loss of social status and criticized women of

Corinth on the basis of that loss. (In 1984, pp. 205ff., she outlines Paul's position in 1 Corinthians 1—4 fittingly.)

79. Stier 1989; cf. above at note 1 for an exception to current exegesis.

80. Cf. above at II.1.C.

81. The poor are addressed both in Matthew's indicative and in Luke's vocative form of speech.

82. Gnilka (1988, 1:121f.) interprets the beatitude of the poor in spirit according to Matthew as a spiritualization and assesses it positively as such. Ragaz (1948, pp. 47f.) offered a critique of the beatitude but also gave it a spiritualizing interpretation. Gnilka and Ragaz exemplify what is widely held in the discussions of both academy and church.

83. I have provided an extensive exegetical foundation for this interpretation of Matt. 5:3 in L. Schottroff 1983, pp.162–64.

84. Cf. esp. Mark 2:13–17 and par.; Luke 15:1–3; Mark 2:23–28 and par.

85. So Laureano in Cardenal 1978, 1:186, on Luke 6:24–26.

86. See L. Schottroff/W. Stegemann 1986, pp. 30f.

87. See L. Schottroff 1994 for a more extensive treatment of Matt. 11:25 and par. and the Sayings Source.

88. On the concept of "those of tender age," see L. Schottroff 1994.

89. There are two types of interpretation of Matt. 11:25 and par.: (1) Those of tender age become the truly wise as a result of revelation; they are very different from those whose wisdom is the fruit of their efforts. (2) Those of tender age become, as such, the subjects of God's relatedness; they have been empowered for liberating praxis in communities of solidarity. I identify myself with the latter type. For more on this type of interpretation, see L. Schottroff 1994.

90. On the history of the social concepts contained in 1 Cor. 1:26ff., see Bohatec 1948; and note 91, below. On the notion of the eschatological reversal of social conditions, see Dobschütz 1922; E. Peterson 1959; L. Schottroff 1978, pp. 43–45; L. Schottroff 1990a, pp. 251f. Kreissig (1967, p. 99) questions that the Corinthian community was composed primarily of lower-class people; he claims that Paul was exaggerating. There is, however, no persuasive basis for this assumption, even when one postulates a maximum of upper-class members, drawing on the names of people to whom Paul refers. On Kreissig's view, cf. L. Schottroff 1990a, pp. 248f.

91. In 1 Cor. 1:26ff., Paul makes use of concepts the ancient world employed to describe the vertical division of society; those concepts belong to the perspective of the upper class. Cf. Aelius Aristides, *Oratim on Rome* 26.39ff.; see L. Schottroff 1990a, pp. 249f.

92. In substance, this is a statement like Matt. 5:3 (cf. above at note 83): their social misery destroys also their relationship to God. On the exegetical and religio-historical discussion of this phrase, see L. Schottroff 1970, p. 177.

93. Cf. esp. Bohatec 1948, p. 269.

94. The eschatological saying in Matt. 19:30; 20:16; Mark 10:31; and Luke 13:30 presupposes that in the perspective of those "at the top," of the "first," the vast majority of the population is the "last."

95. The conflict mentioned in 1 Cor. 11:18f. had been initiated by the poor, who felt discriminated against by the behavior of the rich hinted at in 1 Cor. 11:21, 22, 34. Klauck (1987), commenting on the passage, describes the situation convincingly.

96. 1 Cor. 11:22, 34. The distinction between "the Lord's Supper" and the regu-

lar or ordinary meal is given here *in nuce*. From a feminist perspective, this was a fateful development; cf. Wire 1990, pp. 108–10. Theissen (1979, p. 312) justifies the Pauline solution, calling it "realistic and practicable"; it was a compromise in the terms of "love patriarchalism." This bans women, when they cook, back into the private sphere, and the human dignity of poor people is disregarded in the communal assemblies.

97. Acts 2:42–47; 4:32–37; 5:1–11.

98. Mark 10:17–22 and par.

99. There is a widely held perception that the book of Acts provides an unrealistic idealization of the community of goods. Such a perception fails to recognize that Mark 10:17–22 and par. or Paul's practice of gathering offerings (e.g., 2 Cor. 8:1–15) presuppose the same praxis of sharing, a praxis in which sharing among the poor worked with much less friction than the voluntary renunciation of possessions on the part of the rich. Cf. esp. Richter Reimer 1992, pp. 34ff.

100. Cf. James 2:1–4: a rich man, dressed accordingly, is met in the community with pronounced respect, while a poor person is pushed off into the corner. In its details, the situation differs here from that of 1 Cor. 11:17ff.; they are alike, however, in that the demeanor of the rich, used to the display of power, continued also in the communities of Christians, resulting in others' submissive demeanor.

101. This "shaming" and "bringing to nothing," the debunking of elitist claims, that is (1 Cor. 1:27–28), will take place in God's eschatological court, but it has implications already for the present.

102. Such an interpretation, in my view, fundamentally misunderstands the gospel of the poor; cf. above at III.1.C, note 78.

103. Under certain circumstances, one may see 1 Cor. 11:5 and 14:33–36 as being contradictory; it could mean, theoretically at least, that the latter passage is a secondary, post-Pauline text, inserted later. This creates the problem of using literary-critical "violence" to bring about a solution without any attempt to explain the existing difficulties (cf. Zscharnack 1902, p. 69). The text as it is composed now requires an explanation, whatever approach is taken. The most convincing solution, it seems to me, is that 1 Cor. 14:33–36 does not forbid women every manner of speaking but that the *lalein* (speaking and learning) refers specifically to women questioning prophets critically in public; cf. Zscharnack 1902, pp. 69f. Dautzenberg (1975, pp. 265f.) gives an overview of various possibilities for interpreting the juxtaposition of 1 Cor. 11:5 and 14:33–36.

104. Zscharnack 1902, pp. 58f.

105. Zscharnack (1902, pp. 58f.) draws parallels between the early Christian movement and the medieval and modern movement of mysticism.

106. Cited in Zscharnack 1902, p. 65. See Jensen 1992, pp. 62ff., on Philip's daughters as discussed by Eusebius.

107. Cf. Zscharnack 1902, esp. pp. 58ff.; Wire 1990; Jensen 1992, pp. 254ff.

108. I.e., the Messiah. I take the eighty-four years to refer to her age and not to how long she had been widowed.

109. The ET is from Harrington-Saldarini 1987. A Targum is a paraphrasing translation of the Hebrew text of scripture into Aramaic, which served as the language of everyday life since the time of the Persians. The paraphrase of the Song of Hannah dates from the period of Roman rule of the Jewish people.

110. Judith 9:10f.; cf. 8:33; 12:4; 13:14; 16:6. Deborah and Jael (Judges 5) too are

such antiheroines; cf. Kegler 1980, pp. 37–59. On Judith, see esp. Schüssler Fiorenza 1983, pp. 115–18. The tyrannicide of Judith and Jael is seen as the self-defense of a small nation against a far superior, unjust ruler, carried out by a woman, and not at all as a justification of militarism. In Judg. 5:30 women deride the men's military, which captures women as booty. Judith's deed too is regarded as a disarming of a large military contingent—by a woman's hand and by that of a God whose "superior power [lies not] in strong men" (9:11).

111. The *Kerygmata Petrou* are part of the Pseudo-Clementines; they come from Syria in the middle of the third century C.E. Cf. G. Strecker, in Schneemelcher 1991, 2:531ff.

112. Cf. L. Schottroff 1988b; and above at II.1.B.

113. Cf. Achelis/Flemming 1904, pp. 365ff.; also Bowman Thurston 1989, pp. 96ff.; and Jensen 1992, pp. 141ff.

114. Achelis/Flemming 1904, pp. 76 and 84.

115. See Achelis/Flemming 1904, p. 280.

116. Achelis/Flemming 1904, p. 77.

117. Achelis/Flemming 1904, pp. 78, 80, 82, 83.

118. Achelis/Flemming 1904, pp. 79, 80; cf. also p. 278.

119. Achelis/Flemming 1904, p. 78.

120. Achelis/Flemming 1904, p. 76.

121. Achelis/Flemming 1904, p. 80.

122. Achelis/Flemming 1904, pp. 80, 81.

123. Cf., e.g., the materials gathered by Wire (1990, pp. 250–53).

124. Cf. above at notes 98–100.

125. See L. Schottroff 1988a.

126. See Marcel Borret, *Origène contre Celse* (Paris, 1967), 1:15–21, on the dating of Origen's work.

127. Cf. Origen, *Contra Celsum*, 3.52.

128. The judgment of, e.g., Gülzow (1974, p. 222; cf. p. 220) is too simplistic: "the little people's gossip of pagan polemics"; on this, see also the discussion of Joseph Vogt later in this section.

129. There is a widely held notion, much taken for granted and rarely questioned, that itinerant prophets were men. Such a notion derives from the patriarchal assignment of women to the household; it fails to correspond, however, to the actual reality of patriarchy. Cf. L. Schottroff 1991.

130. See Josephus, *Ant.* 20.34, on Jewish missionary work in harems; on this subject, cf. L. Schottroff 1990a, pp. 291ff. (ET: 1993, pp. 60ff.). On the missionary work of the Cynics in workshops, see Hock 1979, pp. 438–50. The comparison with Cynic philosophy refers to their methods of missionizing and not to the idea, often derived from this comparison, of the poverty of the Jesus movement resulting from its renunciation of property. Cf. above at I.1.A.

131. Alföldy 1984; similarly MacMullen 1974, pp. 88ff.

132. On the concept "social types," see Welskopf 1981, passim.

133. See Wilken 1986, pp. 130f., on what Celsus sees as the political implications of Christianity.

134. Vogt 1975.

135. So says Caecilius, an enemy of Christians, in Minucius Felix, *Octavius* 8.4.

136. Three articles by Friedrich Engels, written in and after 1882, deal with early

Christianity: "Bruno Bauer and Early Christianity" (1882); "The Book of Revelation" (1883); and "On the History of Early Christianity" (1894)—ET: *Marx and Engels on Religion* (New York: Schocken Books, 1964), pp. 194ff., 205ff., and 316ff. respectively (ET hereafter cited as Engels 1964).

137. Kautsky 1953.

138. Rosa Luxemburg, "Socialism and the Churches," in Mary-Alice Waters, ed., *Rosa Luxemburg Speaks* (New York: Pathfinder Press, 1970), pp. 131ff.

139. Engels 1964, pp. 206 and 318.

140. See Engels 1964, p. 316.

141. Judge 1964, p. 50.

142. Troeltsch 1931. Concerning Troeltsch and the following discussion, cf. L. Schottroff 1990a, pp. 247–56; on the history of medieval interpretation of 1 Cor. 1:26ff. as a biblical legitimation of the aristocracy, see Schreiner 1974.

143. Theissen 1979 (ET: 1992).

144. E.g., Meeks 1983; Malherbe 1977.

145. Hock 1978 and 1979; many authors in the United States accepted this view.

146. Thus the current and dominant exegesis; cf. L. Schottroff 1988b, pp. 57ff.

147. Cf. above at III.1.C, note 78.

148. Pithan/Tamez 1992, p. 14.

149. Pithan/Tamez 1992, p. 12.

150. Cf. Gebara 1987; Lucchetti Bingemer 1988; Schaumberger 1987.

151. Cf. above at note 120.

152. In this discussion I consciously do *not* distinguish between eschatology and apocalyptic, or even between Christian eschatology and Jewish apocalyptic. From the point of view of history, early Christian eschatology is part of the Jewish apocalyptic of that time and is not fundamentally different from it, even if the resurrection of Jesus Christ is understood as an eschatological event. From the perspective of social history, Jewish and Christian apocalyptic have the same background. (Cf. below at III.3.B.)

153. Bultmann (1963, p. 117) refers to this genre as "warnings," thereby giving it an authoritarian appearance. The judgment of God declared in these texts is not an instrument of warning; rather, the judgment is awaited and announced. Even though individual details need to be questioned and his concept of demythologization needs to be subjected to feminist critique (cf. below at III.3.C and D), I still find Bultmann's arrangement and structuring of material helpful (1963, pp. 108–30).

154. The different verbs used in Matthew and Luke do not yield a substantial difference in the meaning.

155. Cf. Blass-Debrunner, *Grammatik des neutestamentlichen Griechisch,* sec. 101, as well as the exegetical discussion on 1 Cor. 7:38 concerning the verb *gamizein.* In relation to the texts from the Synoptic Gospels discussed here, there is no dispute that *gamizein* is a causative active and that *gamizesthai* means "to be married off." Wiefel's assumption (1988, p. 311) that the verb refers euphemistically to sexual intercourse is a misunderstanding to which an unsuitable tradition of interpretation gave rise (cf. below at III.3.C).

156. Matthew expresses the idea of the ongoing continuation of conduct in a periphrastic conjugation in the imperfect, while Luke uses the imperfect in his enumeration.

157. Examples of this tradition of interpretation are Gnilka 1979, 2:204; or Grässer 1960, pp. 77ff. and 81ff.

158. Gnilka (1979, 2:207) describes a broad consensus that—in an anti-Judaistic and historically unjustifiable manner—depicts Jewish apocalyptic as "calculating": "The repudiation of calculating times and dates, given here, may appropriately be called anti-apocalyptic."

159. On the understanding of *hypomonē* (patience) as power of resistance, cf. L. Schottroff 1988b, pp. 103ff.

160. Cf. Krauss (1911) 1966, 2:25: the important negotiations preceding the solemnization of marriage are "conducted in the case of a woman of the age of majority directly between her and her suitor."

161. It is quite problematic when translations of scripture render the androcentrism of the text invisible, as is done in the New English Bible, which is widely used in English-speaking churches. It translates Matt. 24:38 as "ate and drank and married, until the day . . . " Such "modernization" would be tenable only in a context in which the historical injustice of androcentrism toward women, found in numerous biblical texts and their interpretation in history, was clearly expressed.

162. L. Schottroff/Stegemann 1986, pp. 83f.; Schüssler Fiorenza 1983, p. 146.

163. Cf. Rom. 16:3, 7; 1 Cor. 7:10–16.

164. The excuses offered are not pretenses; rather, they describe necessary actions in the completion of transfers of property or marriages. Cf. L. Schottroff 1987, p. 206.

165. On the legal significance of the signet ring and of affixing a seal, see G. Fitzer, in *ThWNT*, 7:940f.

166. Consider only how Luke describes banquets (14:1ff. or 17:7–10).

167. In certain circles today, there is still abroad the notion that a man has fulfilled his destiny when he has fathered a son and planted a tree.

168. E.g., Cicero, *De re pub.* 5.7 and *De off.* 1.54.

169. Cf. 1 Cor. 7:1–7 or later stories of apostles, such as the *Acts of Thecla*.

170. On the separation of the patriarch's sexuality from marriage, the latter of which served the purpose of producing progeny but not his sexual interests, cf. Xenophon, *Oec.* 7.11; Cicero, *De off.* 1.12, 54 (for the patriarch, the procreative drive and the love of the father for his children go together); Reinsberg 1989, pp. 76ff. Plutarch thinks it ideal that a female marriage partner is attractive enough also to be a sexual partner, yet he counsels that "a man must think thus about an unfriendly, virtuous woman, 'I cannot have her as my wife and mistress at the same time' " (*Moralia* 142.30–33).

171. By this I mean types of sayings (cf. above at note 153) such as words of judgment, apocalyptic predictions, etc. I regard all New Testament texts, however, as apocalyptic/eschatological, since Christianity in New Testament times was marked throughout by the expectation of God's reign.

172. L. Schottroff 1990a, pp. 73–95; L. Schottroff 1988b, pp. 88–151. I build on the interpretation of apocalyptic provided by Jürgen Ebach (1985) and—critique notwithstanding—Ernst Käsemann (1960 and 1964).

173. Cf. above at I.3 and II.1.C on the theory of the parables.

174. E.g., Weder 1978, pp. 117–20; Gnilka 1978, 1:185, who provides further examples.

175. I have provided an extensive analysis in L. Schottroff 1988b, pp. 125–151.

176. The word *nature* in today's sense implies a dualistic theory (the separation of spirit and nature) and praxis (nature as an object at human beings' disposal). The New Testament knows no such word *nature;* instead, it speaks of *creation.* Cf. L. Schottroff 1989, pp. 130ff.

177. L. Schottroff 1988b, p. 125f.

178. See above at III.1.C.

179. There is a classic critique of parables that picture female and male slaves and workers as irresponsible people and that, as a result, have legitimated oppression. It is found in Bertolt Brecht's *Threepenny Novel,* trans. Desmond I. Vesey (New York: Grove Press, 1956): "And . . . all who relate such things [he refers to the parable of the talents], I condemn! And I'll go further: whoever listens to it and dares to refrain from taking immediate steps against it, him I also condemn!" (p. 396). I find this critique *qua* critique of what such parables have caused to happen quite justified; still, it fails to do justice to those parables' meaning within the context of early Christian eschatology and its idea of God's wrath.

180. See L. Schottroff 1990a, pp. 73ff., on the Roman persecution of Christians, which is presupposed in Mark 13.

181. E.g., Nickelsburg 1979, p. 649; or Kloppenborg 1987, pp. 166–70. This interpretative approach is critiqued by Mosala 1989, p. 64.

182. I share the research approach to apocalyptic taken by Wengst (ET: 1987); Ebach 1985. Cf. also the corresponding methodology of Bertholet 1907.

183. On the horrors of war in biblical times, see the summary study by W. Schottroff (1993). Josephus describes the crimes committed in war against women and children: e.g., *Bell. Jud.* 3.304 (enslavement); 4.82 (children are smashed to death); 4.560 (rape); 6.283 (people are burned alive).

184. Taken from the Michel-Bauernfeind (German) translation, which is also used in the citations that follow.

185. In relation to Acts 6:6, cf. esp. Stolle 1914 and Krauss 1909.

186. E.g., 25 B.C.E. (Josephus, *Ant.* 15.299ff.); 46–48 C.E. (*Ant.* 20: 52, 101).

187. Cf. *Bell. Jud.* 5.512f.

188. Thus Stolle 1914, pp. 62–65.

189. E.g., Lamentations 2.

190. Lam. 2:20; 4:3f., 10. Petronius, *Satyricon* 141.9–11; Deut. 28:53–57; rabbinical material is listed in Michel-Bauernfeind on that text and in vol. 2.1 (1963), p. 267. Further material in Hillers 1964, pp. 62ff.

191. 2 Kings 6:28f.

192. 2 Kings 3:27f.; Curtius Rufus, *Hist. Alex. Magni* 4.3.15, 23, and elsewhere.

193. Many commentaries state that the first horse referred to in Rev. 6:1–6 stands for the Parthians. But this fails to recognize the political perspective on Rome that the book of Revelation has taken (as has Jewish and Christian apocalyptic of the time).

194. Bultmann 1963, p. 117.

195. Schulz 1972, pp. 284f.

196. Zeller 1984, p. 91; Schenk 1981, p. 122; Lührmann 1969, pp. 73f.; Schneider 1984, 2:356; Theissen 1989, p. 288.

197. Wiefel 1988, p. 311.

198. Grundmann 1969, p. 343. More such citations could be easily provided.

199. Sato 1988, p. 285.

200. Tödt 1959, p. 46.

201. I refer to the article "Eschatologie IV. Im Urchristentum," by Hans Conzelmann, in *RGG,* 3d ed., vol. 2, cols. 665–72, as a representative example of the construction of New Testament eschatology in terms of an ideal type. Cf. above at III.3.A and B for corresponding interpretations of individual texts. A critique of such an interpretation may be found in L. Schottroff 1988a.

202. See above at III.2; and L. Schottroff 1988b.

203. Cf. above at note 158 in this section.

204. G. Klein 1982. Stuhlmacher (1981) also interprets the issue in this way; cf. above at III.1.C.

205. Cf. Libanio/Lucchetti Bingemer 1987 for an interpretation of eschatology in terms of liberation theology: hope arises from struggle. She cites (pp. 77f.) the song of a leper, dated to 1981: "We smile at life, and we shall live smiling when from the trimmed tree trunk new life springs forth."

206. I cannot deal here with the anti-Judaism of this article.

207. Also see below in section D.

208. Cf. above at III.3.A. Sutter Rehmann (1993) presents a feminist-theological study of basic apocalyptic texts from the New Testament.

209. Walter Benjamin, "Central Park." On the connection between Benjamin's critique and apocalyptic thinking, see Ebach 1985, pp. 5–61. On the critique of hope for immortality as the prolongation of the way things go now into infinity, see Theodor W. Adorno, *Negative Dialectics,* trans. E. B. Ashton (New York: Continuum, 1983), p. 371.

210. Current usage of "apocalypse" and "apocalyptic" tends to be misleading. The Greek word *apokalypsis* means "revelation."

211. Ruether 1983, p. 254.

212. Schüssler Fiorenza 1988a. Cf. above at note 59.

213. Bultmann 1984, p. 5. Cf. also Sutter Rehmann 1993 for a feminist critique of the program of demythologization.

214. Thürmer-Rohr 1991, pp. 26–28.

PART IV
Liberating Praxis of Women and Men

1. The text itself refers to the economic exploitation by physicians as a dire social consequence (Mark 5:26, but not the Lukan and Matthean parallels). Add to this that, on account of her impurity—as defined in Lev. 15:25ff.—she presumably experienced restrictions in several areas of her daily life and was excluded from the cult of the Temple. That women are "impure" longer and more frequently than men is reflected in their social inferiority, even though impurity, seen as such, is not to be regarded as social discrimination, nor does it correspond in any way to today's ideas about filth or moral disqualification. The social consequence of this illness, independent of the consequences of cultic impurity, is how the structures of patriarchy disqualified the sick woman: she is useless for bearing children. Her situation is comparable to that of a barren woman.

2. 1 Sam. 1:2.

3. Genesis 38.

4. John 4.

5. In this list I categorize God's action as "help of men," since in this tradition God often makes use of a man to help women.

6. Cf. the interpretation of L. Schottroff 1990a, pp. 310–23 (ET: 1993, pp. 138–57).

7. On John 4, see the interpretation of L. Schottroff 1992.

8. Wainwright (1991, p. 75) sees "the power and presence of women which critiques patriarchal exclusion" also in Matthew.

9. Becker 1963, p. 39.

10. Becker 1963, pp. 92ff.; he refers to arguments against the view that Papias was already familiar with this pericope; similarly, Campenhausen 1977, p. 165. In the context of my discussion of this text, the question of the conclusive dating of this pericope is secondary.

11. Becker 1963, p. 117, and cf. pp. 177f.

12. Augustine, *De adulterinis coniugiis* 2.6. More material from Augustine and an interpretation of his views are found in Becker 1963, pp. 24f.

13. The story cannot be explained at all in terms of the prevailing interests of the dominating circles in the ancient church. Cf. Becker 1963 and Campenhausen 1977 on this discussion.

14. A well-known example is the Susanna narrative appended to the book of Daniel. See Plöger 1973, pp. 65ff., on the question of sources. Cf. Diodorus Siculus, 10.2. Derrett (1963/64, pp. 5f.) extensively documents the assumption that the husband had set a trap for the adulterous woman. Sahebjam (1992) documents a parallel story from present-day Iran. By removing his wife by stoning, the husband can take up his business interests, for example. If all he wants is to be rid of his wife because of her ill repute, he may divorce her; cf. Derrett 1963/64, p. 6.

15. The question about the man who was involved in the adultery is often defused in this or a similar manner; cf., e.g., Baltensweiler 1967, p. 125. A different approach is taken by Derrett (1963/64, p. 7); he assumes that it was customary for the men who witnessed the adultery and the man who was actually involved to make prior arrangements. Cf. Sahebjam 1992.

16. E.g., Lev. 20:10; Deut. 22:22. Both texts prescribe the death penalty for the adulterous male. It is not my intention to legitimate patriarchal legislation; I wish to point out that in actual practice this legislation was still applied to women, but contrary to its meaning.

17. Campenhausen 1977, p. 168. Cf. below at IV.1.C.

18. See Sahebjam 1992. Given my methodical reticence about using ethnological material from a different historical context in explaining biblical subjects, I believe such use to be legitimate if, in every case, it can be justified from its contents. The more difficult problem connected with using a present-day murder of a woman in Iran is that such stories are read in a generalized, anti-Islamic fashion. Sahebjam's book does not generalize; it also makes reference to resistance within Islam against the praxis of stoning women.

19. An example is how the Gospel named after John speaks of "the Jews," which requires that the context be examined as to which concrete group of people is envisaged. John 7:53–8:11 has often been interpreted in an anti-Judaistic manner; yet it does not permit such a reading, since "the scribes and Pharisees" are dissuaded from stoning the woman, having made Jesus' position their own. Verse 6a, an addition to the text in some manuscripts, is not necessarily anti-Judaistic. Jesus himself makes use of the discussion procedure of setting a trap (Mark 11:27ff. and par.); this is not an attack on the opponent's life. Cf. Daube 1987, p. 31, on this point. The text does not say that they "stole away" (e.g., Schulz 1972, p. 124). Cf. note 32 below, on the anti-Judaistic interpretation of the text.

20. See esp. Wegner 1988, p. 47 (in relation to the Mishnah) and p. 13 (in relation to the Hebrew scriptures).

21. See Pomeroy 1975, pp. 153f. Justinian (*Digesta* 48.5.24) speaks of the father; he also states that only under certain circumstances may the husband kill the man involved

but not his own wife. Yet the husband or a third party is permitted to kill both if an example is to be set for others; cf. Delling 1959, p. 673; Diodorus Siculus, 10.20. Aelian even speaks of this matter in relation to animals, an elephant, to be precise (11.15).

22. Delling 1959, p. 666; W. Schottroff 1992, pp. 891f.

23. On group stoning, cf. Lev. 24:10–16, Deut. 22:20f., Ezek. 16:38ff. Such stonings correspond to the understanding of the deed as a threat to the community. Blinzler (1957/58, p. 43) states that adultery is not a private offense but rebellion against the God of the covenant. The same holds for an adultery verified by witnesses; cf. note 14 above, and Derrett 1963/64, p. 6.

24. Deut. 22:20f.; Sahebjam 1992.

25. Sahebjam 1992, pp. 85ff. and 124–27.

26. "Has no one condemned you?"— John 8:10—shows that the same group both judges and stones, for the woman is placed in the middle for her execution.

27. Cf. esp. Blinzler 1957/58, pp. 32–47.

28. Baltensweiler (1967, pp. 125–27) provides a survey of the various attempts to interpret the gesture.

29. I do not wish to be understood now as holding an anti-Judaistic picture of Jesus, one that sees him in opposition to all other Jewish men or all other Jews. As the end of the narrative itself indicates, other Jewish men came to share Jesus' critique of the stoning of the adulterous woman.

30. Nevertheless, I do not understand v. 5 as a theoretical exploration (to stone or not to stone the woman) or as an invitation to Jesus to add his views about an issue under dispute; rather, I see it as a summons to Jesus to become part of her condemnation (and stoning).

31. Sahebjam 1992, p. 124.

32. E.g., Mark 2:25–27 (28). Jesus does not differ fundamentally from other Jewish interpreters of scripture in relation to the independence of their interpretations. The ancient and often-repeated Christian assertion that Jesus' interlocutors in John 8:5 (or vv. 5 and 6a; cf. note 19, above) wanted to corner Jesus and get him to contradict the Bible is based on a purely formal and fundamentalist approach to the wording of scripture that is more Christian than Jewish (or at least Sadducean). An example of such an anti-Judaistic interpretation of John 8:1–11 is in Schnackenburg 1971, 2:228 ("If Jesus speaks against this, he questions the authority of Moses and, therefore, God").

33. Cf., e.g., Derrett 1963/64, pp. 10f.

34. Cf. note 21 above.

35. They were deemed capital crimes because they threatened the community as a whole.

36. Pseudo-Philo, *Antiquitates biblicae* 50; cf. C. A. Brown 1992, pp. 140ff.

37. On the question of its genre and other historical points, see W. Schottroff 1989, pp. 24–35, esp. pp. 28f.

38. Hannah even considers pretending to have committed adultery, in order to be subjected to a *sotah* according to Num. 5:12ff.; for she interprets Num. 5:28 that she can in this way force God to open her womb. This verse says "she is clean . . . and shall conceive children." In other words, God is obligated to her since she was unjustly subjected to the *sotah* (*b. Ber.* 31b).

39. Patai (1959) argues the opposite case. He presupposes that barrenness was regarded as the result of an individual's sexual "sins"; he then interprets certain texts in light of this presupposition. But one must distinguish between the barrenness of a peo-

ple, resulting from a disturbed relationship with God (e.g., Hosea 9), and the assignment of guilt to an individual childless woman, something that, according to my knowledge, the Hebrew scriptures do not do. The Mishnah too speaks quite differently about barren women (*m. Yeb.* 6): after ten years of childless marriage, a man must obtain a divorce in order to meet his duty, which is to procreate children, with another woman. The divorced woman may remarry and is given another period of ten years in her new marriage. Cf. Preuss 1905, pp. 449–52, on barrenness in biblical and postbiblical Jewish tradition. Women's barrenness is discussed throughout as that of married women; unmarried women are not spoken of in these sources.

40. *B. Yeb.* 6a: many of the tribes' ancestral mothers and fathers lived at first in childless marriages because God desires the prayers of the pious.

41. "Those women who somehow find themselves between categories are without protection and are, in a sense, misfits in the social structure" (Niditch 1979, p. 145) fittingly describes the social position of the childless married woman or of young childless widows such as Tamar and Ruth, who are refused levirate marriage. Cf. below at IV.1.C in connection with the important work of Schaberg 1987.

42. Even though the text presupposes that her husband is alive, she acts like a woman without a husband; cf. Gen. 21:21.

43. Cf. Tobit 3:7ff.

44. E.g., Gen. 30:1.

45. Harnisch (1983, p. 93) calls it an "ironic notion that Ezra should plead for the welfare of Zion before what he takes to be a woman but who in truth is Zion." I do not detect any irony but rather the belief in God's providence, which had given Ezra his task long before he realized it himself.

46. Cf., e.g., Isa. 63:17–19.

47. Gunkel surmises, inappropriately in my view, that the "woman" will come to understand that she shall have another son; he then, appropriately, concedes that the word is ambiguous; cited in Kautsch 1975, p. 387 note k. Cf. also Harnisch 1983, p. 87.

48. On the relation of apocalyptic notions of the future to present times, cf. Ebach 1985, pp. 5–61; L. Schottroff, in Schaumberger/Schottroff 1988; and L. Sutter Rehmann, in *WBFTh* 1991, pp. 86–89.

49. Cf., e.g., Isa. 54:1; Luke 1:46–54; the Song of Hannah in the *Targum Jonathan.* On this last, see W. Schottroff 1989, pp. 33f.

50. See esp. Stählin 1974, pp. 5–20, in relation to the biblical domain; note 24 there provides bibliographic materials on the personification of cities in the extrabiblical domain.

51. See esp. Isa. 54:1, and how postbiblical Jewish eschatology incorporated this promise, in Billerbeck 1961, 3:574f.

52. See L. Schottroff, in L. Schottroff/W. Schottroff 1988, pp. 27–38.

53. Cf. note 50, above. Concerning these coins, cf. Smallwood 1981, pp. 329f.; Radnoti-Alföldy 1978, p. 180. The coin reproduced here (from *BHH* [1964], 2:910) was struck after Vespasian's victory over the Jewish people in 70 C.E.

54. Bovon (1989) provides the following interpretation of Luke 1:24: on account of the "shame" of the childless woman, she remains in hiding for those five months until her pregnancy is visible; in addition, the period serves to make the connection with the Mary legend. But people do not have to see a pregnancy in order to praise someone hitherto childless. The argument about the connection with the Mary legend is purely formal. I know of no satisfactory explanation.

55. The explanation that *eulogēmenē en* is a Semiticizing form that gives what is in the

positive the meaning of the superlative does not persuade me; cf., e.g., Blass-Debrunner-Rehkopf, sec. 245.4. Grammatical arguments cannot determine whether Mary is blessed more than all other women or is blessed in the community of women; the text's own context alone can do so (cf., e.g., Rom. 1:12, where the preposition *en* refers to community). Mary's being blessed has significance for all women and for all generations (Luke 1:48) and does not at all isolate her from the community of women. Rather than setting the one woman against the rest of womankind, the text thinks of a women's community, a Women-Church. The formulation of Luke 1:42 is quite different from, e.g., that of Judith 13:18 (*para . . . tas gynaikas*), where the superlative is clearly implied.

56. Thus, e.g., Soranus, an enlightened physician (second century C.E.), in his *Gynecology* 1.7; but also Mary (Luke 1:34).

57. Writing on the genesis of the creatures, Aristotle's basic position is that "the female as such is the passive, the male as such the active one, the latter of whom gives origin to the movement" (*Gen. an.* 729b). His comparisons tell much: "just as a bed comes to be from the carpenter and the wood" (792b), "conception must accordingly occur in the female, for the carpenter has to be with the wood and the potter with the clay" (730b). The woman only makes available the requisite matter, while the male semen is the creator. On Aristotle's theory of conception, see Smith 1988, pp. 346f.; Castelli 1988, pp. 361f.; Lloyd (1983) 1986, pp. 86ff.

58. Clement of Alexandria, *Paedagogus* 1.6.48f. Paul, speaking of woman as the man's "vessel" (1 Thess. 4:4), presupposes the same understanding of conception as Aristotle.

59. Angry at Zeus for conceiving Athena in his own head without a woman, Hera conceives Hephaistos alone, but he turns out to be a weakling (Homer, *To Apollo* 300ff.; cf. Hesiod, *Theogony* 924ff.). Gnostic mythology tells of Sophia having brought forth without a partner an imperfect and ugly creature from whom derived the powers hostile to the light, those powers that are responsible for the dreadful condition of the world and for the captivity of light in the human body; cf. the *Apocryphon of John* (BG 8502) 36.15–37.20; 46.10ff. On this notion and its further development, see Pasquier 1988, pp. 47–66; Smith 1988, p. 354.

60. Cf. Smith 1988, p. 354; "A Valentinian Exposition" 36.25ff., in *The Nag Hammadi Library* 1977, p. 439.

61. Cf. the classic collection of relevant material in Dibelius (1932) 1953, pp. 1–78; cf. also Gerhard Delling's article "parthenos" in *ThWNT*, 5:826–37.

62. An extensive analysis of Joseph's thoughts is found in Schaberg 1987, pp. 42ff. On the history of the interpretation of this text, see Luz 1992, 1:119f.

63. L. Schottroff 1990a, pp. 259ff. (ET: 1993, pp. 160ff.). Cf. also below at IV.1.C on procreation by God (or the Spirit).

64. Thus, e.g., Schnackenburg.

65. Cf. Campenhausen 1977, pp. 168f., for a number of examples of the interpretation that Jesus did not question the law.

66. Matt. 22:15–22 and par.

67. Campenhausen 1977, p. 171. The woman who was a sinner (Luke 7:36–50) is said to be the only exception. She was, indeed, a "prostitute but no adulteress and was not part of the company at Jesus' table" (p. 171). Rankings such as this of sinful women (to be an adulterous woman is worse than being a prostitute) follow the interests of patriarchy, which von Campenhausen represents impeccably.

68. C. H. Ratschow, the article on "Ehebruch" (adultery), in *RGG* (3d ed., 1958), vol. 2, col. 335.

69. Daube 1987, pp. 29–31.

70. Daube bases himself on the reinterpretation of Num. 5:30f. in *Sipre on Num. 5:31* ("And if the man is free of sin, then shall the woman bear her sin") and on corresponding statements by Johanan ben Zakkai (Dtn rabbah on 10:1). I doubt, however, that John 8:7 thinks only of the sexual sins of the men involved, given the actual situation; cf. note 17, above.

71. Barrett (1978) opposes this conclusion; this pericope, he believes, makes no reference to Jesus' repudiation of injustice to women, even though such an idea is conceivable: "The story, it may be guessed, eventually reached the pages of the Fourth Gospel rather because it depicted Jesus as the merciful judge than because a Christian editor wished to attack discrimination against women" (pp. 590–91). As is so often the case, high Christology becomes a weapon against women.

72. Cf. Catharina Halke's article "Maria," in *WBFTh*, pp. 268–75.

73. "Parthenos," in *ThWNT*, 5:826–37.

74. Delling indicates that the grammatical gender of "spirit" in Hebrew (*ruach*) rules out an interpretation as procreative spirit (*ThWNT*, 5:835–36). Cf. L. Schottroff 1990a, p. 261 (ET: 1993, p. 164).

75. Brown 1978.

76. Brown 1978, p. 121n265.

77. Dibelius (1932) 1953, pp. 1–78, esp. pp. 35ff.

78. Ruether 1977, pp. 34ff. She correctly notes that the texts do not presuppose Joseph's natural paternity but does not rule out the possibility of an earlier Christian version of the legend of Mary that was rooted in such a presupposition.

79. Boston 1986.

80. Schaberg 1987.

81. E.g., Schürmann 1969 on Luke 1:48.

82. Schweizer 1984 on Luke 1:48.

83. Bovon 1989.

84. An example of this is Wilckens 1978 on Rom. 1:1: "Slave" is "a title applied to the missionary," as suggested by how the Hebrew scriptures speak of those individual men (*sic!*) "whom God uses in a special way as his salvation-history instruments."

85. This difficulty arises also for new feminist developments in Mariological ecclesiology (cf. Ruether 1977).

86. Schaberg 1989, p. 119.

87. Schaberg 1987, pp. 99–101.

88. Wainwright (1991, p. 74) also rejects Schaberg's thesis, but—unfortunately—without detailed reasons.

89. In her work on Luke 1:2, Kahl (1987) maintains that this text rejects any notion of paternity and does so for reasons of critique of patriarchy. She speaks of a "negation of the order based on fatherhood in the sense of that order's 'inversion' " (p. 98). Her analysis contains important observations .

90. Wainwright 1991, passim.

91. Schaberg 1989, pp. 113–14; similarly Wainwright 1991, pp. 67, 75, and passim.

92. E.g.: "Isidora [makes a commitment] to leave Dionysius's house neither during the day nor the night without his knowledge, so as not to bring dishonor on the household, nor to engage in extramarital relationships. . . ." (BGU [*Aegyptische Urkunden aus den Königlichen Museen zu Berlin, griechische Urkunden*] 4.1050, Alexandria at the time of Augustus).

93. Wahlberg (1975, p. 19) titles the story "Jesus and the Adulterous Men."

94. This is very apparent in paintings depicting an old drunk woman; cf. Zanker 1989. But there are also numerous literary examples, e.g., in the *Anthologia graeca*.

95. This saying of Jesus comes from a narrative (Mark 10:35–40 and par.) that tells of the power interests of two disciples, James and John. The rest of the "twelve" disciples are angry at them, whereupon Jesus utters a fundamental declaration on the question of hierarchy, a declaration which in its substance takes up the concrete answer to James and John's issue (Mark 10:38–40 and par.).

96. Within the context of the narrative itself, it is the "Twelve" (or in Luke, the "apostles") who are addressed. In terms of the Synoptic Gospels, they represent the community of Jesus' followers. The issue here is not their special power interests as office-bearers, since such a notion of "office" is an absurdity within the Gospels and the majority of other New Testament texts. The notion of office is a retrospective projection of institutional developments after the second and third centuries C.E.

97. Cf. below at IV.2.B for a translation of the androcentric language of this text.

98. Mark 10:42, "those who are supposed to rule" (cf. Gal. 2:9; and *ThWNT*, 2:233, pt. 3), is not an ironic expression, as Gnilka (1979), referring to this text, suggests. It designates, rather, those who rule and their authority. Unlike its parallels in Mark and Matthew, Luke 22:25 does not explicitly identify the violence of the rules as unjust, but this does not warrant the widely held conclusion that Luke is politically timid and conformist. He calls the Roman overlords who killed Jesus "lawless men" (Acts 2:23; cf. L. Schottroff 1990a, pp. 344ff.).

99. Cf. L. Schottroff 1990a, pp. 134ff. (ET: 1993, pp. 168ff.), in relation to the dangers that relatives and followers of crucified persons faced from Roman authorities. On "the mother of the sons of Zebedee" (Matt. 20:20), see the feminist interpretations of Moltmann-Wendel 1982, pp. 123ff.; and Wainwright 1991 on this text.

100. See the statistics provided in Kurt Aland, *Vollständige Konkordanz zum Griechischen Neuen Testament*, vol. 2 (Berlin: Walter de Gruyter, 1978), at the appropriate entry.

101. Esth. 6:1, 3, 5; 1:10; 2:2; 1 Macc. 11:58.

102. Prov. 10:4; 4 Macc. 9:17.

103. Cf. below at IV.2.C.

104. On the labor of female slaves, cf. above at II.2.B.

105. B. E. Perry, *Aesopica* (Urbana, Ill., 1952).

106. E.g., Gnilka 1978, 1:84, on Mark 1:31, "attending to the guests"; Gnilka 1979, 2:326, on Mark 15:41, "alluding to giving material assistance." Other examples and a discussion of this line of interpretation are found in L. Schottroff 1990a, pp. 142ff. (ET: 1993, pp. 176ff.). Cf. also E. Schweizer, "Scheidungsrecht der jüdischen Frau. Weibliche Jünger Jesu?" *Ev. Theol.* 42 (1982): 299: according to Mark, the "disciples" were only men. One argument to support this claim is that "wherever women are named in the company of Jesus, their 'serving' is also mentioned." Schweizer understands by serving "providing food and drink," in analogy with Mark 1:13. "That thereby they do what is most important and best" is obvious from the text.

107. Schüssler Fiorenza 1983, p. 165; Schüssler Fiorenza (1992, pp. 52ff.) rejects that Martha's "serving" was housework (in the sense of Luke 10:38–42) but considers that it has to be understood as community administration and that the juxtaposition with Mary was an attempt to play a submissive Mary off against a self-possessed Martha, with the intent of suppressing women's self-assertion. But Luke's high valuation of "listening," e.g., in 8:21, speaks against such a reading, as does the socially prevalent linguistic

usage of *diakonein,* which, set apart from the listening on the part of the women and men disciples (in the form of Mary), is all that is left for Martha to do: serve as a housewife does.

108. Cf. L. Schottroff 1990a, p. 131 (ET: 1993, p. 116).

109. Cf. below on the washing of feet as a menial task. Cf. Luke 7:44 on the host washing feet.

110. See note 105, above.

111. See the synopsis of the various versions of the *Aesopica* in H. Zeitz, "Die Fragmente des Äsopromans in Papyrushandschriften" (diss., University of Giessen, 1935), pp. 8ff.

112. F. Böhmer, *Untersuchungen über die Religion der Sklaven in Griechenland und Rom* (Wiesbaden, 1981), 1:9ff., 103, 154ff.; H. W. Beyer, in *ThWNT,* 2:93.

113. Cf. the article on foot washing by B. Kötting (D. Halama), in *RAC* (1972) 8:743–77.

114. It should not be rejected offhand, as Wagener (1993) does, that a free man or a free woman might honor a guest by washing the guest's feet him- or herself, as Luke 7:44 presupposes.

115. Such is the interpretation of Wagener 1993.

116. Cf., e.g., Schüssler Fiorenza 1983, p. 181; cf. below at IV.2. C for a critique of traditional interpretation.

117. Dominant tradition of interpretation takes for granted—with providing reasons —that widows are the only recipients of provisions. Schüssler Fiorenza (1983, pp. 162ff.) makes a very different case. She believes that the conflict described in Acts 6:1ff. is about the active participation of Hellenistic-Jewish Christian women in the celebration of the Eucharist. The connection between the daily common meal and the Eucharist is plausible, as is the assumption that the conflict was not about excluding some women from the distribution of food to the poor but about reducing the scope of their activities. Early Christianity provides us with no analogies to refusing bread to poor widows. The history of early Christianity, however, is rampant with attempts to remove women from all kinds of activities. See L. Schottroff 1990b, pp. 235f., on the participation of widows in the community.

118. *t. Pe'a* 4.12; Krauss (1912) 1966, 3:73.

119. *t. Pe'a* 4.19; Billerbeck 1961, 4:536f.

120. *b. Šabb.* 156b; *b. Berakot* 10b, 61a; *y. Terumot* 8.4–5; Krauss (1912) 1966, 3:71, 73, 25; Krauss (1911) 1966, 2:50.

121. Cf. Liddell/Scott 1961: "*ek tōn hyparchontōn* under the circumstances, according to one's means" in the general and not a specifically financial sense, which is also a possible rendition.

122. Unfortunately, I also shared that interpretation at first (L. Schottroff 1990a, p. 108 [ET: 1993, pp. 91f.]). I owe to D. Schirmer of Berlin the insight that *ek tōn hyparchontōn autais* is not limited linguistically to "from their resources" in a financial sense. Even though Luke frequently uses *ta hyparchonta* in the sense of material possessions (cf. esp. 12:15), one should not assume that sense without examination as applying also to 8:3.

123. See L. Schottroff 1993 on Gal. 4:21–31 as it relates to this matter; on female slaves in the community, cf. above at III.2.B.

124. Paul is a great theological teacher in relation to this aspect; cf. L. Schottroff, in Schaumberger/Schottroff 1988.

125. Cf. W. Michaelis, in *ThWNT,* 4:667n13.

126. Kraabel (in Gutmann 1981, p. 87) points in this direction in an interesting com-

ment: in late antiquity there were no regional hierarchies that exercised control over individual synagogue congregations; "to judge only from these buildings, the closest thing to a central authority was the scripture itself." This observation refers to a period later than that of the New Testament, when Christian communities already had rigid central hierarchies. Bernadette Brooten has examined the leadership functions in synagogue congregations, which were carried out also by women, and her findings point in a similar direction (Brooten 1982). Krauss ([1912] 1966, 3:103ff.) presents rich information on the life of those congregations, albeit from a different basis. Cf. also Richter Reimer 1992, esp. pp. 105ff., on the synagogue building in the Diaspora as the common center of a minority group.

127. Rom. 12:5; 1 Cor. 12:25; Eph. 4:25.

128. Rom. 12:10; 14:13.

129. Cf., e.g., Acts 2:44; 4:32. The comprehensive character of instructions for the praxis of life is quite clear throughout the New Testament. The special pareneses of the so-called household codes are formal and substantively foreign in relation to this broad tradition.

130. Cf. above at I.2.D on androcentric language.

131. John 13:34f.; 15:12, 17; 1 John 3:11, etc.; Rom. 13:8; 1 Thess. 3:12; 4:9, etc.

132. Käsemann 1980, p 415.

133. The concept "the Human One" ("the Son of man") in biblical tradition expresses primarily that "he" is part of humanity; cf. Dan. 7:13. The translation "the Human One" is appropriate, more embracing and less androcentric than "the Son of man."

134. Schnackenburg 1976, vol. 3, on John 13:55; similarly Käsemann 1980 on Rom. 15:7. The almost compulsive striving of traditional theology to depict Christ as the bringer of salvation blocks the view of Christ's nearness as brother and example.

135. On the feminist-theological discussion, see Heyward 1982; Strahm/Strobel 1991.

136. Matt. 23:9; cf. Mark 10:30 and the manuscripts with the patriarchal corrections of Mark 10:30; Tertullian, *Apologeticus* 39. On the subsequent introduction of the patriarchal title *father* into Christianity, cf. note 92 in Part I, above.

137. Cf. Klauck 1981 on terminology.

138. Cf. above at I.2.C on how the patriarchal household understood itself.

139. Cf. Matt. 10:34–36 and par. and the relevant material parallels. A short summary in found in L. Schottroff, pp. 338f.

140. Matt. 5:31–32 and par. and the relevant material parallels.

141. Cf. above at III.1.A.

142. Cf. above at II.4.B.

143. The most common way of giving a different meaning nowadays is by presupposing the ethos of an elite, namely, the itinerant radicals, which, although not being "antifamily," certainly was "a-family." This group and its ethos are said to have existed side by side with patriarchal Christian families and communities organized on patriarchal structures; cf. above at I.1. Another way of giving a different meaning is this: just as a *soldier* leaves his father's house in order to follow the call of the "fatherland," so a Christian (meaning Christian men, because Christian women do not enter this picture) follows the call of God and leaves his father's house (Matt. 10:34–36 and par.) for the sake of God's higher-ranking patriarchy.

144. Prisca and Aquila (Rom. 16:3–4 and elsewhere), Junia and Andronicus (Rom. 16:7).

145. Ananias and Sapphira's failings (Acts 5) in the patriarchal structures of marriage show implicitly what a successful inclusion of existing relationships looks like; cf. esp. Richter Reimer 1992 on this point.

146. 1 Cor. 11:22.

147. Cf. esp. Richter Reimer 1992 on this point.

148. According to Sampley (1980), there is a legal contract between Paul and the Philippian community in the sense of a *societas* as described in Roman law: a society that, for specific purposes, shares the requisite costs. It would, however, be a peculiar contract that could be broken with as few problems as Phil. 4:10 suggests. In addition, neither the voluntary nature of every gift made nor the understanding of *koinōnia* as the transformation of lack into abundance fits into the framework of a legal contract.

149. Cf. esp. F. Hauck, in *ThWNT*, 3:797ff.

150. F. Hauck, in *ThWNT*, 3:797, 808.

151. In the absence of a corresponding word that expresses the hierarchy of the division of labor between slaves and free persons, I use the word *racist* because the manner in which free persons at that time behaved toward slaves had the characteristics that are depicted today in the word *racist*.

152. H. W. Beyer, in *ThWNT*, 2:84 (*diakonein* in the New Testament). More material on this patriarchal tradition of interpretation in Schüssler Fiorenza 1983, e.g., on the interpretation of Rom. 16:1.

153. On the interpretation of John 13, cf. L. Schottroff 1986, p. 55.

154. Roloff 1988, p. 165.

155. Wilckens 1982, p. 131.

156. This is what one reads in standard commentaries on Acts 2:42.

157. Bovon 1989, p. 317.

158. This often-held view is historically incorrect (cf. Nissen 1974, p. 284): according to Lev. 19:18, securing one's own existence, not self-love, is the measure for one's actions toward the neighbor. On the interpretation of the commandment to love the neighbor in the context of the thesis of "self-love," cf. Dorothee Sölle, "Aussen- und Innenarbeit," in *Junge Kirche* (1993).

159. Bovon 1989 on this text.

160. I will not cite individual references here, as the word is found in almost all German commentaries on the Eucharist.

161. This is the subtitle of Heyward 1982.

162. Heyward 1982; Harrison 1985; and Dorothee Sölle, "Gerechtigkeit," in *WBFTh*.

163. Heyward 1982, p. 166.

164. Heyward 1982, p. 166.

165. Heyward 1982, p. 166.

166. Sölle, "Gerechtigkeit," in *WBFTh*.

Bibliography

Translators' Note: It is not customary in German publications to indicate the *name* of a publisher; only the *place* and *date* of publication are stated. In this literature list we have endeavored to provide as much information about works published in English translations or originally published in English as we were able to ascertain; in such cases, we have sought to provide the standard information customary in English-language scholarly works. We are aware that our search for works cited by Professor Schottroff that have appeared in translation may not be complete.

Achelis, Hans/Johs. Flemming. 1904. *Die syrische Didaskalia übersetzt und erklärt.* Leipzig.

Adler, Elisabeth. 1975. *Oekumene im Kampf gegen Rassismus. Ein erster Anfang* (= epd Dokumentation Bd. 14). Bielefeld and Frankfurt.

Aktion Sühnezeichen/Friedensdienste, eds. 1982. *Christen im Streit um den Frieden.* Freiburg.

Albrecht, Ruth. 1986. *Das Leben der heiligen Makrina auf dem Hintergrund der Thekla-Traditionen.* Göttingen.

Alföldy, Géza. 1984. *Römische Sozialgeschichte.* 3d ed. Wiesbaden.

Altaner, Berthold/Alfred Stuiber. 1978. *Patrologie.* Freiburg.

Apokryphon des Johannes (BG 8502) = Walter C. Till, ed., *Die gnostischen Schriften des koptischen Papyrus 8502* (Berlin, 1955), pp. 33ff.

Archer, Léonie J. 1990. *Her Price Is Beyond Rubies: The Jewish Woman in Graeco-Roman Palestine.* Sheffield: JSOT Press.

Augar, Friedrich. 1905. *Die Frau im römischen Christenprocess.* TU NF 13, 4. Leipzig.

Autorengruppe der Martin-Luther-Universität Halle-Wittenberg. 1983. *Die Arbeitswelt der Antike.* Leipzig.

Avigad, Nahman. 1980. *Discovering Jerusalem.* Jerusalem: Israel Exploration Society.

Avi-Yonah, Michael. 1976. *Gazetteer of Roman Palestine.* Jerusalem.

Balch, David L. 1988. "Household Codes." Pp. 25–50 in *Greco-Roman Literature and the New Testament, Selected Forms and Genres,* ed. David E. Aune. Atlanta: Scholars Press.

Baltensweiler, Heinrich. 1967. *Die Ehe im Neuen Testament.* Zurich and Stuttgart.

Barrett, Charles Kingsley. 1978. *The Gospel according to John.* 2d ed. Philadelphia: West-minster Press.

Bartchy, S. Scott. 1973. *Mallon Chresai: First-Century Slavery and the Interpretation of 1 Corinthians 7:21.* Missoula, Mont.: Scholars Press.

Bauer, Walter. 1979. *A Greek–English Lexicon of the New Testament and Other Early Christian Literature.* Edited and translated by W. F. Arndt and F. W. Gingrich. Chicago: University of Chicago Press.

Becker, Ulrich. 1963. *Jesus und die Ehebrecherin, Untersuchungen zur Text- und Über-lieferungsgeschichte von Joh. 7,53–8,11.* BZNW 28. Berlin.

Beckmann, Klaus-Martin, ed. 1971. *Rasse, Entwicklung und Revolution. Der Notting-Hill-Report und die zugehörigen Dokumente.* 4th ed. Stuttgart.

Ben-David, Arye. 1974. *Talmudische Oekonomie.* Vol. 1. Hildesheim and New York.

Bertholet, Alfred. 1907. *Daniel und die griechische Gefahr.* Tübingen.

Bieler, Andrea. 1993. "Konstruktionen des Weiblichen zwischen Zwang und Wider-spruch. Eine feministisch-befreiungstheologische Analyse des Werkes der Theolo-gin Anna Paulsen im Kontext der bürgerlichen Frauenbewegung der Weimarer Republik und verschiedener nationalsozialistischer Positionen." Diss., Kassel.

[Strack, Hermann L.]/Billerbeck, Paul. [1926] 1965 (vol. 1); [1924–1928] 1961 (vols. 2–4) *Kommentar zum Neuen Testament aus Talmud und Midrasch.* Munich.

Birckenbach, Hanne-Margret. 1990. *Friedensforschung und ihre feministischen Ansätze: Möglichkeiten der Integration* (= AFB-Texte). Arbeitsstelle Friedensforschung Bonn. November.

Blanck, Horst. 1976. *Einführung in das Privatleben der Griechen und Römer.* Darmstadt.

Blank-Sangmeister, Ursula, trans. and ed. 1991. *Valerius Maximus. Facta et dicta mem-orabilia.* Stuttgart.

Blass, Friedrich/Albert Debrunner. 1984. *Grammatik des neutestamentlichen Griechisch.* 16th ed. Bearbeitet von Friedrich Rehkopf, Göttingen: Vandenhoeck and Ruprecht.

Blinzler, Josef. 1957/58. "Die Strafe für Ehebruch in Bibel und Halacha." *NTS* 4:32–47.

Blümner, Hugo. 1969. *Technologie und Terminologie der Gewerbe und Künste bei Griechen und Römern.* 4 vols. Reprint Hildesheim. [Vol. 1, 2d ed., 1912; vol. 2, 1879; vol. 3, 1884; vol. 4, 1887.]

Bock, Gisela. 1987. "Historische Frauenforschung: Fragestellungen und Perspektiven." Pp. 24–62 in *Frauen suchen ihre Geschichte,* ed. Karin Hausen. 2d ed. Munich.

Böhme, Astrid. 1974. *Schmuck der römischen Frau.* Kleine Schriften zur Kenntnis der römischen Besetzungsgeschichte Südwestdeutschlands 11. Württembergisches Landesmuseum Stuttgart.

Bohatec, Josef. 1948. "Inhalt und Reihenfolge der 'Schlagworte der Erlösungsreligion' in 1. Kor. 1,26–31." *ThZ* 4:252–71.

Bornemann, Ernst. 1975. *Das Patriarchat: Ursprung und Zukunft unseres Gesellschaftssystems.* Frankfurt.

Boston, Gerald. 1986. "Virgin Birth or Human Conception." *Expository Times* 97:260–63.

Bovon, François. 1989. *Das Evangelium nach Lukas.* Vol. 1. Zurich and Neukirchen.

Bowman Thurston, Bonnie. 1989. *The Widows: A Women's Ministry in the Early Church.* Philadelphia: Fortress Press.

Braun, Herbert. 1958. *Spätjüdisch-häretischer und frühchristlicher Radikalismus.* 2 vols. Tübingen.

Briggs, Sheila. 1989. "Can an Enslaved God Liberate? Hermeneutical Reflections on Philippians 2:6–11." *Semeia* 47:137–53.

Brooten, Bernadette J. 1982. *Women Leaders in the Ancient Synagogue.* Chico, Calif.: Scholars Press.

———. 1982. "Konnten Frauen im alten Judentum die Scheidung betreiben? Überlegungen zu Mk 10,11–12 und 1 Kor 7,10–11." *Ev. Theol.* 42:65–80.

———. 1985. "Paul's Views on the Nature of Women and Female Homoeroticism." Pp. 61–87 in *Immaculate and Powerful: The Female in Sacred Image and Social Reality,* ed. Clarissa Atkinson et al. Boston: Beacon Press.

———. 1987. "Darum lieferte Gott sie entehrenden Leidenschaften aus. Die weibliche Homoerotik bei Paulus." Pp. 113–38 in: *Hättest du gedacht, dass wir so viele sind? Lesbische Frauen in der Kirche,* ed. Monika Barz, Herta Leistner, and Ute Wild. Stuttgart.

Brown, Cheryl Anne. 1992. *No Longer Be Silent: First Century Jewish Portraits of Biblical Women.* Louisville, Ky.: Westminster John Knox Press.

Brown, Raymond E., et al., eds. 1978. *Mary in the New Testament.* Philadelphia: Fortress Press.

Brunner, Hellmut. 1988. *Altägyptische Weisheit.* Darmstadt.

Bücher, K. 1922. *Beiträge zur Wirtschaftsgeschichte.* Tübingen.

Bultmann, Rudolf. 1941. "Neues Testament und Mythologie." Pp. 27–69 in idem, *Offenbarung und Heilsgeschehen.* Munich. (ET: *New Testament and Mythology and Other Basic Writings,* ed. and trans. Schubert Ogden. Philadelphia: Fortress Press, 1984.)

———. 1954. *Glauben und Verstehen.* Vol. 1. Tübingen.

———. 1963. *The History of the Synoptic Tradition.* Translated by John Marsh. Oxford: Basil Blackwell.

Burrus, Virginia. 1987. *Chastity as Autonomy: Women in the Stories of Apocryphal Acts.* Lewiston, N.Y. and Queenston, Ont.: Edwin Mellen Press.

Campenhausen, Hans Freiherr von. 1977. "Zur Perikope von der Ehebrecherin (Joh 7,53–8,11)." *ZNW* 68: 164–75.

Carcopino, Jérome. 1979. *Rom. Leben und Kultur in der Kaiserzeit.* 2d ed. Stuttgart.

Cardenal, Ernesto. 1976, 1978. *The Gospel in Solentiname.* Translated by Donald D. Walsh. Vols. 1 and 2. Maryknoll, N.Y.: Orbis Books.

Caspari, Helene/Elisabeth Kleemann. 1918. *Das Landkochbuch.* 2d ed. Berlin.

Castelli, Elizabeth A. 1988. "Response to 'Sex Education in Gnostic Schools' by Richard Smith." Pp. 361–66 in *Images of the Feminine in Gnosticism,* ed. Karen L. King. Philadelphia: Fortress Press.

Comblin, José. 1988. *Der Heilige Geist. Gott, der sein Volk befreit.* Düsseldorf.

Crüsemann, Marlene/Willy Schottroff, eds. 1992. *Schuld und Schulden. Biblische Traditionen in gegenwärtigen Konflikten.* Munich.

Dalman, Gustav. 1964. *Arbeit und Sitte in Palästina.* 7 vols. Reprint, Hildesheim. [Vols. 1–7, Gütersloh, 1928–1942.]

D'Angelo, Mary Rose. 1990. "Women in Luke-Acts: A Redactional View." *JBL* 109: 441–61.

Daube, David. 1956. *The New Testament and Rabbinic Judaism.* London.

———. 1972. *Civil Disobedience in Antiquity.* Edinburgh: Edinburgh University Press.

———. 1987. *Appeasement or Resistance and Other Essays on New Testament Judaism.* Berkeley: University of California Press.

Dautzenberg, Gerhard. 1975. *Urchristliche Prophetie*. Stuttgart.
Dautzenberg, Gerhard/Helmut Merklein/Karlheinz Müller, eds. 1983. *Die Frau im Urchristentum*. Freiburg.
Davies, Stevan L. 1980. *The Revolt of the Widows: The Social World of the Apocryphal Acts*. London and Carbondale: Southern Illinois University Press.
Deissmann, Adolf. 1923. *Licht vom Osten: Das Neue Testament und die neuentdeckten Texte der hellenistisch-römischen Welt*. Tübingen: J.C.B. Mohr.
Delling, Gerhard. 1959. "Ehebruch." *RAC* 4:666–77.
———. 1970. *Studien zum Neuen Testament und zum hellenistischen Judentum*. Göttingen.
Derrett, J. Duncan M. 1963/64. "Law in the New Testament: The Story of the Woman Taken in Adultery." *NTS* 10:1–26.
———. 1972. "Law in the New Testament: The Parable of the Unjust Judge." *NTS* 18:178–91.
Dibelius, Martin. [1932] 1953. "Jungfrauensohn und Krippenkind. Untersuchungen zur Geburtsgeschichte Jesu im Lukas-Evangelium." Pp. 1–78 in *Botschaft und Geschichte*. Vol. 1. Tübingen.
Dobschütz, Ernst von. 1922. "Religionsgeschichtliche Parallelen zum Neuen Testament." *ZNW* 21:69–72.
Ebach, Jürgen. 1985. "Apokalypse. Zum Ursprung einer Stimmung." *Einwürfe* 2:5–61. Munich.
Eichenauer, Monika. 1988. *Untersuchungen zur Arbeitswelt der Frau in der römischen Antike*. Frankfurt.
Einheitsübersetzung. 1981. *Die Heilige Schrift*. Stuttgart.
Elias, Norbert. 1986. "Wandlungen der Machtbalance zwischen den Geschlechtern. Eine prozesssoziologische Untersuchung am Beispiel des antiken Römerstaates." *Kölner Zeitschrift für Soziologie und Sozialpsychologie* 38:425–49.
Erman, Adolf. [1923] 1971. *Die Literatur der Ägypter*. Reprint, Hildesheim.
Farbstein, David. 1896. *Das Recht der unfreien und der freien Arbeiter nach jüdisch-talmudischem Recht*. Frankfurt.
Felder, Cain Hope. 1991. "Race, Racism, and the Biblical Narratives." In idem, ed., *Stony the Road We Trod: African American Biblical Interpretation*. Minneapolis: Fortress Press.
Frauenwiderstand im Hunsrück. Frauengeschichte(n) 1983–1985. 1985. Selbstverlag frauenwiderstand. Frankfurt.
Friedländer, Ludwig. 1964. *Darstellungen aus der Sittengeschichte Roms in der Zeit von Augustus bis zum Ausgang der Antonine*. Vols. 1–4. 10th ed. Aalen. [Leipzig, 1921–1923.]
Funk, Robert W. 1971. "Beyond Criticism in Quest of Literacy: The Parable of the Leaven." *Interpretation* 25:149–70.
Gebara, Ivone. 1987. "Option für die Armen als Option für die Frau." *Concilium* 23:517–23.
Gebara, Ivone/Maria C. Lucchetti Bingemer. 1988. *Maria, Mutter Gottes und Mutter der Armen*. Düsseldorf.
Gnilka, Joachim. 1978, 1979. *Das Evangelium nach Markus*. 2 vols. Zurich.
———. 1988. *Das Matthäusevangelium*. 2 vols. Freiburg.
Godel, Erika. 1992. *Gegenreden. Bibelarbeiten von Frauen auf Deutschen Evangelischen Kirchentagen*. Munich.

Goldfeld, Anne. 1976. "Women as Sources of Torah in the Rabbinic Tradition." Pp. 257–71 in *The Jewish Woman,* ed. Elizabeth Koltun. New York.

Goodblatt, David. 1975/76. "The Beruriah Traditions." *Journal of Jewish Studies.* 26/27:68–85.

Gössmann, Elisabeth. 1989. "Haec mulier est divinitas. Das Gleichnis von der Frau mit der verlorenen Drachme in seiner Auslegungsgeschichte bei den Kirchenvätern und Hildegard von Bingen." Pp. 607–15 in *Weite des Herzens—Weite des Lebens,* ed. Michael Langer and Anselm Bilgri. Regensburg.

Gössmann, Elisabeth, et al., eds. 1991. *Wörterbuch der feministischen Theologie.* Gütersloh.

Grässer, Erich. 1960. *Das Problem der Parusieverzögerung in den synoptischen Evangelien und der Apostelgeschichte.* 2d ed. Berlin.

Grundmann, Walter. [1969]. *Das Evangelium nach Lukas.* Berlin, n.d.

Gülzow, Henneke. 1969. *Christentum und Sklaverei in den ersten drei Jahrhunderten.* Bonn.

———. 1974. "Soziale Gegebenheiten der altkirchlichen Mission." Pp. 189–226 in *Kirchengeschichte als Missionsgeschichte.* Vol. 1: *Die Alte Kirche,* ed. Heinzgünter Frohnes and Uwe W. Knorr. Munich.

Günther, Rosmarie. 1987. *Frauenarbeit—Frauenbindung. Untersuchungen zu unfreien und freigelassenen Frauen in den stadtrömischen Inschriften.* Munich.

Gutiérrez, Gustavo. 1973. *A Theology of Liberation.* Edited and translated by Sr. Caridad Inda and John Eagleson. Maryknoll, N.Y.: Orbis Books.

Gutmann, Joseph. 1981. *Ancient Synagogues: The State of Research.* Chico, Calif.: Scholars Press.

Haas, Peter J., ed. 1992. *Recovering the Role of Women: Power and Authority in Rabbinic Jewish Society.* Atlanta: Scholars Press.

Harnack, Adolf von. 1900a. "Probabilia über die Adresse und den Verfasser des Hebräerbriefs." *ZNW* 1:16–41.

——— 1900b. "Über die beiden Recensionen der Geschichte der Prisca und des Aquila in Act. Apost. 18,1–7." In: *SBA Berlin.* Vol. 1. Berlin.

———. 1904. *The Expansion of Christianity in the First Three Centuries.* 2 vols. Translated by James Moffatt. New York: G.P. Putnam's Sons.

Harnisch, Wolfgang. 1972. "Die Ironie als Stilmittel in Gleichnissen Jesu." *Ev. Theol.* 32:421–36.

———. 1983. "Die Ironie der Offenbarung. Exegetische Erwägungen zur Zionvision im 4. Buch Esra." *ZAW* 95:75–95.

———. 1985. *Die Gleichniserzählungen Jesu.* Göttingen.

Harrington, Daniel J./Anthony J. Saldarini. 1987. *Targum Jonathan of the Former Prophets.* Edinburgh: T. & T. Clark.

Harrison, Beverly W. 1985. *Making the Connections: Essays in Feminist Social Ethics.* Edited by Carol S. Robb. Boston: Beacon Press.

Hatebur, Norbert. 1987. *Antikes Patriarchat und Frauenfeindlichkeit.* Münster.

Hausen, Karin. 1978. "Die Polarisierung der 'Geschlechtscharaktere.'" Pp. 161–90 in *Familie und Gesellschaftsstruktur,* ed. Heidi Rosenbaum. Frankfurt.

———. 1986. "Patriarchat. Vom Nutzen und Nachteil eines Konzeptes für Frauengeschichte und Frauenpolitik." *Journal für Geschichte* 5:12–58.

Heine, Susanne. 1990. "Brille der Parteilichkeit. Zu einer feministischen Hermeneutik." *Evangelische Kommentare* 23:354–357.

Herfst, Pieter. 1922. *Le Travail de la femme dans la Grèce ancienne.* Utrecht.

Heszer, Catherine. 1990. *Lohnmetaphorik und Arbeitswelt in Mt 20,1–16*. Fribourg and Göttingen.

Heyward, Carter. 1982. *The Redemption of God: A Theology of Mutual Relation*. Lanham, Md.: University Press of America.

Hillers, Delbert R. 1964. *Treaty-Curses and the Old Testament Prophets*. Rome: Pontifical Biblical Institute.

Hock, Ronald F. 1978. "Paul's Tentmaking and the Problem of His Social Class." *JBL* 97:555–64.

————. 1979. "The Workshop as a Social Setting for Paul's Missionary Preaching." *Catholic Biblical Quarterly* 41:438–50.

Hoffmann, Paul. 1981. "Eschatologie und Friedenshandeln in der Jesusüberlieferung." Pp. 115–52 in *Eschatologie und Friedenshandeln,* ed. Ulrich Luz et al. Stuttgart.

Holtz, Gottfried. 1986. *Die Pastoralbriefe.* 4th ed. Berlin.

Holtzmann, O. 1911. "Die täglichen Gebetsstunden im Judentum und Urchristentum." *ZNW* 12:90–107.

Horsley, Richard A. 1989. *Sociology and the Jesus Movement*. New York: Crossroad.

Jensen, Anne. 1988. "Thekla. Vergessene Verkündigerin." In *Zwischen Ohnmacht und Befreiung,* ed. Karin Walter. Freiburg.

————. 1992. *Gottes selbstbewusste Töchter. Frauenemanzipation im frühen Christentum.* Freiburg, Basel, and Vienna.

Jeremias, Joachim. 1963. *The Parables of Jesus*. Translated by S. H. Hooke. London: SCM Press.

Jeremias, Joachim/August Strobel. 1975. *Die Briefe an Timotheus und Titus. Der Brief an die Hebräer.* Göttingen.

Josephus, Flavius. 1981. *The Complete Works of Josephus.* Translated by William Whiston. Grand Rapids: Kregel Publications.

Judge, E. A. 1964. *Christliche Gruppen in nichtchristlicher Gesellschaft*. Wuppertal.

Jülicher, Adolf. [1910] 1963. *Die Gleichnisreden Jesu*. Tübingen. Reprint, Darmstadt.

Kahl, Brigitte. 1987. *Armenevangelium und Heidenevangelium*. Berlin.

KAIROS Document. 1986. *Challenge to the Churches: A Theological Comment on the Political Crisis in South Africa*. Grand Rapids: Wm. B. Eerdmans Publishing Co.

Kampen, Natalie. 1981. *Roman Working Women in Ostia*. Berlin.

————.1985. "Römische Strassenhändlerinnen." *Antike Welt. Zeitschrift für Archäologie und Kulturgeschichte* 16:23–42.

Käsemann, Ernst. 1960, 1964. *Exegetische Versuche und Besinnungen*. Vols. 1 and 2. Göttingen.

————. 1980. *Commentary on Romans*. Edited and translated by Geoffrey W. Bromiley. Grand Rapids: Wm. B. Eerdmans Publishing Co.

Kaser, Max. 1962. *Römisches Privatrecht. Ein Studienbuch.* 2d ed. Munich and Berlin.

Kautsky, Karl. 1953. *Foundations of Christianity*. Translated by Henry F. Mins. New York: S. A. Russell.

Kautzsch, Emil. 1900. *Die Apokryphen und Pseudepigraphen des Alten Testaments,* vol. 2. Tübingen: J.C.B. Mohr. Reprint, 1975, Darmstadt: Wiss. Buchgesellschaft.

Kegler, Jürgen/Debora Kegler. 1980. "Erwägungen zur politischen Funktion einer Frau in einer patriarchalischen Gesellschaft." Pp. 37–59 in *Traditionen der Befreiung*. Vol. 2: *Frauen in der Bibel,* ed. W. Schottroff and W. Stegemann. Munich.

Kiefer, Otto. 1933. *Kulturgeschichte Roms.* Berlin.

Klassen, William. 1984. *Love of Enemies.* Philadelphia: Fortress Press.

Klauck, Hans-Josef. 1978. *Allegorie und Allegorese in synoptischen Gleichnistexten.* Münster.

———. 1981. *Hausgemeinde und Hauskirche im frühen Christentum.* Stuttgart.

———. 1986. *2. Korintherbrief.* Würzburg.

———. 1987. *1. Korintherbrief.* 2d ed. Würzburg.

Klein, Charlotte. 1978. *Anti-Judaism in Christian Theology.* Translated by Edward Quinn. Philadelphia: Fortress Press.

Klein, Günter. 1982. "Eschatologie IV. Neues Testament." *TRE* 10:270–99.

Kloppenborg, John S. 1987. *The Formation of Q: Trajectories in Ancient Wisdom Collections.* Philadelphia: Fortress Press.

Klostermann, Erich. 1929. *Das Lukasevangelium.* Tübingen.

Krauss, Samuel. [1910; 1911; 1912] 1966. *Talmudische Archäologie.* 3 vols. Leipzig. Reprint, Hildesheim.

Kremer, Jakob. 1988. *Lukasevangelium.* Würzburg.

Kreissig, Heinz. 1967. "Zur sozialen Zusammensetzung der frühchristlichen Gemeinden im ersten Jahrhundert uZ." Pp. 91–100 in *Eirene. Studia Graeca et Latina.* Prague.

Küchler, Max. 1986. *Schweigen, Schmuck und Schleier. Drei neutestamentliche Vorschriften zur Verdrängung der Frauen auf dem Hintergrund einer frauenfeindlichen Exegese des Alten Testamentes im antiken Judentum.* Fribourg and Göttingen.

Lamb, Regene. 1986. "Aufbruchsversuche von Frauen in Kirche und Theologie in Brasilien." Pp. 72–78. in *Handbuch Feministische Theologie,* ed. Christine Schaumberger and Monika Maassen. Münster.

Lampe, Peter. 1989. *Die stadtrömischen Christen in den ersten beiden Jahrhunderten.* 2d ed. Tübingen.

Langford, Sally O. 1992. "On Being a Religious Woman: Women Proselytes in the Greco-Roman World." In *Recovering the Role of Women: Power and Authority in Rabbinic Jewish Society,* ed. Peter J. Haas. Atlanta: Scholars Press.

Lauffer, Siegfried. 1971. *Diocletians Preisedikt.* Berlin.

Libanio, Joao B./Maria C. Lucchetti Bingemer. 1987. *Christliche Eschatologie.* Düsseldorf.

Liddell, H. G./R. Scott. 1961. *A Greek English Lexicon.* Oxford: Clarendon Press.

Lietzmann, Hans. 1928. *Einführung in die Textgeschichte der Paulusbriefe. An die Römer.* 3d ed. Tübingen.

Lissner, Anneliese, et al., eds. 1988. *Frauenlexikon.* Freiburg.

List, Elisabeth/Herlinde Studer, eds. 1989. *Denkverhältnisse. Feminismus und Kritik.* Frankfurt.

Lloyd, G.E.R. [1983] 1986. *Science, Folklore and Ideology: Studies in the Life Sciences in Ancient Greece.* Reprint, Cambridge: Cambridge University Press.

Lucchetti Bingemer, Maria Clara. 1988. "Die Theologien der Dritten Welt: Die Bekehrung zum anderen. Überlegungen zur Versammlung von Oaxtepec/Mexiko 1988." *Concilium* 24:417–22.

Lührmann, Dieter. 1969. *Die Redaktion der Logienquelle.* Neukirchen.

Luxemburg, Rosa. 1970. *Rosa Luxemburg Speaks.* Edited by Mary-Alice Waters. New York: Pathfinder Press.

Luz, Ulrich. 1985; 1990. *Das Evangelium nach Matthäus.* Vols. 1 and 2. Zurich and Neukirchen. (ET of vol. 1: *Matthew 1—7.* Translated by Wilhelm C. Linss. Continental Commentaries. Minneapolis: Fortress Press, 1989.)

MacDonald, Dennis Ronald. 1983. *The Legend and the Apostle: The Battle for Paul in Story and Canon.* Philadelphia: Westminster Press.

MacMullen, Ramsay. 1966. *Enemies of the Roman Order.* Cambridge, Mass. Harvard University Press.

————. 1974. *Roman Social Relations 50 B.C. to A.D. 284.* London and New Haven: Yale University Press.

Malherbe, Abraham J. 1977. *Social Aspects of Early Christianity.* London and Baton Rouge: Louisiana State University Press.

Marquardt, Joachim. [1886] 1975. *Das Privatleben der Römer.* 2 vols. Reprint, Darmstadt.

Martin, Clarice J. 1990. "Womanist Interpretations of the New Testament: The Quest of Holistic and Inclusive Translation and Interpretation." *Journal of Feminist Studies* 6:41–61.

Maxey, Mima. 1938. *Occupations of the Lower Classes in Roman Society.* Chicago: University of Chicago Press.

Meeks, Wayne A. 1983. *The First Urban Christians: The Social World of the Apostle Paul.* London and New Haven: Yale University Press.

Mesters, Carlos. 1983. *Vom Leben zur Bibel, von der Bibel zum Leben.* 2 vols. Mainz and Munich.

————. 1991. "Bibellektüre durch das Volk." *Ev. Theol.* 51:3–7.

Meyer, Klaus. 1975. *Xenophons "Oikonomikos." Übersetzung und Kommentar.* Marburg.

Meyer, Rudolf. [1940] 1970. *Der Prophet aus Galiläa.* Leipzig. Reprint, Darmstadt.

Mies, Maria. 1984. "Frauenforschung oder feministische Forschung." *Beiträge zur feministischen theorie und praxis* 11:40–60.

————. 1988. *Patriarchat und Kapital. Frauen in der internationalen Arbeitsteilung.* Zurich.

Moltmann-Wendel, Elisabeth. 1982. *The Women Around Jesus.* Translated by John Bowden. New York: Crossroad.

Mosala, Itumeleng J. 1989. *Biblical Hermeneutics and Black Theology in South Africa.* Grand Rapids: Wm. B. Eerdmans Publishing Co..

Musurillo, H. 1954. *The Acts of the Pagan Martyrs.* Oxford: Clarendon Press.

The Nag Hammadi Library in English. 1977. Translated by members of the Coptic Gnostic Library Project of the Institute for Antiquity and Christianity. San Francisco: Harper & Row.

Newsom, Carol A./Sharon H. Ringe, eds. 1992. *The Women's Bible Commentary.* Louisville, Ky: Westminster John Knox Press.

Nickelsburg, George W. 1983. "Social Aspects of Palestinian Jewish Apocalypticism." Pp. 641–54 in *Apocalypticism in the Mediterranean World and the Near East,* ed. David Hellholm. Tübingen: J.C.B. Mohr.

Niditch, Susan. 1979. "The Wronged Woman Righted: An Analysis of Genesis 38." *Harvard Theological Review* 72:143–49.

Nissen, Andreas. 1974. *Gott und der Nächste im antiken Judentum.* Tübingen.

Pasquier, Anne. 1988. "*Prouneikos.* A Colorful Expression to Designate Wisdom in Gnostic Texts." Pp. 47–66 in *Images of the Feminine in Gnosticism,* ed. Karen L. King. Philadelphia: Fortress Press.

Patai, Raphael. 1959. *Sex and Family in the Bible and Middle East.* Garden City, N.J.: Doubleday.

Paulsen, Henning. 1980. "Einheit und Freiheit der Söhne Gottes—Gal 3,26–29." *ZNW* 71:74–95.

Peterson, Erik. 1959. "1. Korinther 1,18f. und die Thematik des jüdischen Busstages." Pp. 43–50 in idem, *Frühkirche, Judentum, Gnosis.* Rome, Freiburg, and Vienna.

Pesch, Rudolf. 1986. *Die Apostelgeschichte,* vol. 1. Zurich-Einsiedeln-Neukirchen-Vluyn-Köln: Benziger/Neukirchener Verlag.

Pithan, Annebelle/Elsa Tamez. 1992. "Hat die Befreiungstheologie nichts Neues mehr zu sagen?" *Junge Kirche* 53:11–18.

Plöger, Otto. 1973 "Zusätze zu Daniel." In Hans Bardtke and Otto Plöger, *Zusätze zu Esther. Zusätze zu Daniel.* Gütersloh.

Pomeroy, Sarah B. 1975. *Goddesses, Whores, Wives, and Slaves: Women in Classical Antiquity.* New York: Schocken Books.

Preuschen, Erwin. 1912. *Die Apostelgeschichte.* Tübingen: J.C.B. Mohr.

Preuss, Julius. 1905. "Die Pathologie der Geburt nach Bibel und Talmud." Pp. 448–81 in *Zeitschrift für Geburtshilfe und Gynäkologie* 54. Stuttgart.

Pusch, Luise F. 1984. *Das Deutsche als Männersprache.* Frankfurt.

Quesnell, Quentin. 1983. "The Women at Luke's Supper." Pp. 59–79 in *Political Issues in Luke-Acts,* ed. R. J. Cassidy and P. J. Scharper. Maryknoll, N.Y.: Orbis Books.

Radnoti-Alföldy, Maria. 1978. *Antike Numismatik.* Part 1: *Theorie und Praxis.* Mainz.

Ragaz, Leonard. 1948. Appendix: "Falsche Übersetzungen der Bibel von welt- und reichsgeschichtlicher Bedeutung." In idem, *Sollen und können wir die Bibel lesen und wie?* 2d ed. Zurich.

Reinsberg, Carola. 1989. *Ehe, Hetärentum und Knabenliebe im antiken Griechenland.* Munich.

Richter Reimer, Ivoni. 1990. "Aufbruch und Erinnerung. Eine sozialgeschichtliche Rekonstruktion der Lebenswirklichkeit von Frauen in der Apostelgeschichte des Lukas in feministisch-befreiungstheologischer Perspektive." Diss., Kassel.

———. 1992. *Frauen in der Apostelgeschichte des Lukas. Eine feministisch-theologische Exegese.* Gütersloh.

Ricoeur, Paul. 1970. *Freud and Philosophy: An Essay on Interpretation.* Translated by Denis Savage. New Haven: Yale University Press.

———. 1974. "Stellung und Funktion der Metapher in der biblischen Sprache." In Paul Ricoeur and Eberhard Jüngel, *Methapher. Zur Hermeneutik religiöser Sprache/Ev. Theol.,* special no.: 45–70.

Ringe, Sharon H. 1988. "Matthäus 13,33: Das Brot geht auf." In *Feministisch gelesen,* vol. 1, ed. Eva Renate Schmidt, Mieke Korenhof, and Renate Jost. Stuttgart.

Roloff, Jürgen. 1981. *Die Apostelgeschichte.* Göttingen.

———. 1985. *Neues Testament.* 4th ed. Neukirchen.

———. 1988. *Der erste Brief an Timotheus.* Zurich and Neukirchen.

Ruether, Rosemary Radford. 1977. *Mary, the Feminine Face of the Church.* Philadelphia: Westminster Press.

———. 1979. "Mothers of the Church: Ascetic Women in Late Patristic Age." In Rosemary Ruether and Eleanor McLaughlin, *Women of Spirit.* New York: Simon & Schuster.

———. 1983. *Sexism and God-Talk: Toward a Feminist Theology.* Boston: Beacon Press.

———. 1992. *Gaia and God: An Ecofeminist Theology of Earth Healing.* San Francisco: Harper & Row.

Sahebjam, Freidoune. 1992. *Die gesteinigte Frau. Geschichte der Soraya Manoutchehri.* Reinbek.

Sampley, J. Paul. 1980. *Partnership in Christ: Christian Community in Light of Roman Law*. Philadelphia: Fortress Press.

Sato, Migaku. 1988. *Q und Prophetie*. Tübingen.

Schaberg, Jane. 1987. *The Illegitimacy of Jesus: A Feminist Theological Interpretation of the Infancy Narratives*. New York: Crossroad.

———. 1989. "The Foremothers and the Mother of Jesus." Pp. 112–19 in *Motherhood: Experience, Institution, Theology*, ed. Anne Carr and Elisabeth Schüssler Fiorenza. Edinburgh: T. & T. Clark.

Schäfke, Werner. 1979. "Frühchristlicher Widerstand." *ANRW II* Principat vol. 23, 1:460–723.

Schaumberger, Christine. 1981. "Radikal in kleinen Schritten? Die Ökumenische Initiative EINE WELT und ihr Versuch eines alternativen Lebens." Pp. 71–93 in *Theologisch-politische Protokolle*, ed. Tiemo Rainer Peters. Munich and Mainz.

———. 1987. "Den Hunger nach Brot und Rosen nähren. Auf dem Weg zu einer kritisch-feministischen Theologie der Frauenarbeit." *Concilium* 23:511–17.

———. 1991. "'Es geht um jede Minute unseres Lebens'! Auf dem Weg zu einer kontextuellen feministischen Befreiungstheologie." Pp. 15–33 in *Befreiung hat viele Farben. Feministische Theologie als kontextuelle Befreiungstheologie*, ed. Renate Jost and Ursula Kubera. Gütersloh.

Schaumberger, Christine/Monika Maassen, eds. 1986. *Handbuch Feministische Theologie*. Münster: Morgana Frauenbuchverlag.

Schaumberger, Christine/Luise Schottroff. 1988. *Schuld und Macht. Studien zu einer feministischen Befreiungstheologie*. Munich.

Scheidel, Walter. 1990. "Feldarbeit von Frauen in der antiken Landwirtschaft." *Gymnasium* 97:405–31.

Schenk, Wolfgang. 1981. *Synopse zur Redenquelle der Evangelien*. Düsseldorf.

Schille, Gottfried. 1984. *Die Apostelgeschichte des Lukas*. 2d ed. Berlin.

Schlatter, Adolf. 1931. *Das Evangelium nach Lukas*. Stuttgart.

Schmidt, Eva Renate/Mieke Korenhof/Renate Jost, eds. 1988;1989. *Feministisch gelesen*. 2 vols. Stuttgart.

Schmithals, Walter. [1979] 1985. *Das Evangelium nach Markus*. 2d ed. Gütersloh.

Schnackenburg, Rudolf. 1965; 1971; 1976. *Das Johannesevangelium*. Parts 1–3. 2d ed. Freiburg, Basel, and Vienna..

Schneemelcher, Wilhelm, ed. 1991. *New Testament Apocrypha*. 2 vols. Translated by R. McL. Wilson. Louisville, Ky.: Westminster John Knox Press.

Schneider, Gerhard. 1984. *Das Evangelium nach Lukas*. 2 vols. 2d ed. Gütersloh.

Schneider, Helmuth. 1980. "Die antike Sklavenwirtschaft: Das Imperium Romanum." Pp. 95–154 in *Geschichte der Arbeit*, ed. Axel Eggebrecht et al. Cologne.

Schottroff, Luise. 1970. *Der Glaubende und die feindliche Welt. Beobachtungen zum gnostischen Dualismus und seiner Bedeutung für Paulus und das Johannesevangelium*. Neukirchen.

———. 1978. "Non-Violence and the Love of One's Enemies." Pp. 9–39 in *Essays on the Love Commandment*, ed. L. Schottroff, R. H. Fuller, C. Burchard, M. J. Suggs. Philadelphia: Fortress Press.

———. 1978. "Das Magnificat und die älteste Tradition über Jesus von Nazareth." *Ev. Theol.* 38:298–313.

———. 1982. *Der Sieg des Lebens*. Munich.

———. 1983. "Das geschundene Volk und die Arbeiter in der Ernte Gottes nach dem Matthäusevangelium." Pp. 149–206 in *Mitarbeiter der Schöpfung. Bibel und Arbeitswelt,* ed. L. Schottroff and W. Schottroff. Munich. 149–206.

———. 1986. *Sucht mich bei meinen Kindern. Bibelauslegung im Alltag einer bedrohten Welt.* Munich.

———. 1987. "Das Gleichnis vom grossen Gastmahl in der Logienquelle." *Ev. Theol.* 47:192–211.

———. 1988a. "How My Mind Has Changed oder: Neutestamentliche Wissenschaft im Dienste von Befreiung." *Ev. Theol.* 48:247–61.

———. 1988b. "Die befreite Eva." In Christine Schaumberger and Luise Schottroff, *Schuld und Macht. Studien zu einer feministischen Befreiungstheologie.* Munich.

———. 1988c. "Invokavit—Lukas 22,31–34." *Göttinger Predigt-Meditationen* 43, 1 (4th quarter):114–20.

———. 1989. "Schöpfung im Neuen Testament." Pp. 130–48 in *Ökologische Theologie. Perspektiven zur Orientierung,* ed. Günther Altner. Stuttgart.

———. 1990a. *Befreiungserfahrungen. Studien zur Sozialgeschichte des Neuen Testaments.* Munich. (ET selections: *Let the Oppressed Go Free.* Translated by Annemarie S. Kidder. Louisville, Ky.: Westminster John Knox Press, 1993.)

———. 1990b. "BotschafterInnen an Christi Statt." Pp. 271–92 in *Vernünftiger Gottesdienst, Festschrift für Hans Gernot Jung,* ed. F. Scholz and H. Dickel. Göttingen.

———. 1990c. "DienerInnen der Heiligen. Der Diakonat der Frauen im Neuen Testament." Pp. 222–42 in *Diakonie—biblische Grundlagen und Orientierungen,* ed. Gerhard K. Schäfer and Theodor Strohm. Heidelberg.

———. 1990d. " 'Was sie tun konnte, hat sie getan'. Die Salbung in Bethanien (Mk 14,3–9)." Pp. 142–54 in Luise Schottroff and Dorothee Sölle, *Hannas Aufbruch.* Gütersloh.

———. 1991. "Wanderprophetinnen. Eine feministische Analyse der Logienquelle." *Ev. Theol.* 51:332–44.

———. 1992a. "Die Samaritanerin am Brunnen (Joh 4)." Pp. 115–32 in *Auf Israel hören. Sozialgeschichtliche Bibelauslegung,* ed. Renate Jost, Rainer Kessler, and Christoph M. Raisig. Lucerne.

———. 1992b. "Frauenwiderstand im frühen Christentum." Pp. 129–59 in *Querdenken. Beiträge zur feministisch-befreiungstheologischen Diskussion,* ed. Frauenforschungsprojekt zur Geschichte der Theologinnen Göttingen. Pfaffenweiler.

———.1993. " 'Freue dich, du Unfruchtbare'. Zion als Mutter in 4. Esra 9–10 und Gal 4,21–31." In *Zwischen Zeiten und Kontinenten, Festschrift Elisabeth Gössmann,* ed. Helen Schüngel-Straumann and Theodor Schneider. Freiburg.

———. 1994. "The Sayings Source Q: A Commentary from the Perspective of a Feminist Theology of Liberation." In *Searching the Scriptures: A Feminist-Ecumenical Commentary,* vol. 2, ed. Elisabeth Schüssler Fiorenza. New York.

Schottroff, Luise/Willy Schottroff. 1984. *Die Parteilichkeit Gottes. Biblische Orientierungen auf der Suche nach Frieden und Gerechtigkeit.* Munich.

———. 1986. *Wer ist unser Gott? Beiträge zu einer Befreiungstheologie im Kontext der "ersten" Welt.* Munich.

———. 1988. *Die Macht der Auferstehung. Sozialgeschichtliche Bibelauslegungen.* Munich.

———. 1991b. *Die kostbare Liebe zum Leben. Biblische Inspirationen.* Munich.

————, eds. 1983. *Mitarbeiter der Schöpfung. Bibel und Arbeitswelt.* Munich.

Schottroff, Luise/Wolfgang Stegemann. 1978. *Jesus von Nazareth—Hoffnung der Armen.* Stuttgart. (ET: *Jesus and the Hope of the Poor.* Translated by Matthew J. O'Connell. Maryknoll, N.Y.: Orbis Books, 1986.)

Schottroff, Willy. 1980. "Psalm 23. Zur Methode sozialgeschichtlicher Bibelauslegung." Pp. 78–113 in *Traditionen der Befreiung,* vol. 1., ed. Willy Schottroff and Wolfgang Stegemann. Munich.

————. 1989. "Der Lobgesang der Hanna." Pp. 24–35 in *Gotteslehrerinnen,* ed. Luise Schottroff and Johannes Thiele. Stuttgart.

————. 1992a. "Die Armut der Witwen." In *Schuld und Schulden,* ed. Marlene Crüsemann and Willy Schottroff. Munich.

————. 1992b. "Ordal." In *EKL^3* III, pp. 891f.

————. 1993. "Kriegsgefangene." In *Neues Bibellexikon.*

————. 1994. "Conclamatio und Profectio. Zur Veranschaulichung neutestamentlicher Wundergeschichten." In *Quid ergo Athenis et Hierosolymis? Religious Propaganda and Missionary Competition in the New Testament and Its Environment (Festschrift Dieter Georgi).* Leiden.

Schottroff, Willy/Wolfgang Stegemann, eds. 1979. *Der Gott der kleinen Leute. Sozialgeschichtliche Auslegungen.* 2 vols. Munich and Gelnhausen. (ET selections in *God of the Lowly: Socio-Historical Interpretations of the Bible.* Translated by Matthew J. O'Connell. Maryknoll, N.Y.: Orbis Books, 1984.)

————. 1980. *Traditionen der Befreiung.* 2 vols. Munich and Gelnhausen.

Schrage, Wolfgang. 1991. *Der erste Brief an die Korinther.* Part 1. Zurich, Braunschweig, and Neukirchen.

Schramm, Hilde, ed. 1981. *Frauensprache—Männersprache. Ein Arbeitsbuch zur geschlechtsspezifischen Sprachverwendung.* Frankfurt.

Schreiner, Klaus. 1974. "Zur biblischen Legitimation des Adels. Auslegungsgeschichtliche Studien zu 1. Kor. 1,26–29." *Zeitschrift für Kirchengeschichte* 85:317–57.

Schroer, Silvia. 1992. "Wir sollten mit der Wirklichkeit beginnen. Gedanken zur Bibelarbeit im deutschsprachigen Raum." *Katechetische Blätter* 6:440–43.

————. 1993. "Feministische Bibelforschung. Anliegen, Methoden und Inhalte." In *Feministische Perspektiven in der Wissenschaft,* ed. L. Blattmann et al. *Zürcher Hochschulforum* 21:41–52.

Schulz, Siegfried. 1972a. *Gott ist kein Sklavenhalter.* Zurich and Hamburg.

————. 1972b. *Q. Die Spruchquelle der Evangelien.* Zurich.

Schüngel-Straumann, Helen. 1989. *Die Frau am Anfang. Eva und die Folgen.* Freiburg.

Schürmann, Heinz. 1969. *Das Lukasevangelium.* Part 1. Freiburg, Basel, and Vienna.

Schüssler Fiorenza, Elisabeth. 1983. *In Memory of Her: A Feminist Theological Reconstruction of Christian Origins.* New York: Crossroad.

————. 1984. *Bread Not Stone: The Challenge of Feminist Biblical Interpretation.* Boston: Beacon Press.

————. 1985. "Das Schweigen brechen—sichtbar werden." *Concilium* 21:387–98.

————. 1987. "Rhetorical Situation and Historical Reconstruction in 1 Corinthians." *NTS* 33:386–403.

————. 1988. "Biblische Grundlegung." Pp. 13–44 in *Feministische Theologie. Perspektive zur Orientierung,* ed. Maria Kassel. Stuttgart.

————. 1989. "The Politics of Otherness: Biblical Interpretation as a Critical Praxis for

Liberation." Pp. 311–25 in *The Future of Liberation Theology,* ed. Marc H. Ellis and Otto Maduro. Maryknoll, N.Y.: Orbis Books.

———. 1992. *But She Said: Feminist Practices of Biblical Interpretation.* Boston: Beacon Press.

Schwantes, Milton. 1991. "Wege der biblischen Theologie in Lateinamerika." *Ev. Theol.* 51:8–19.

Schweitzer, Albert. 1910. *The Quest of the Historical Jesus.* Translated by W. Montgomery. London: A. & C. Black, 1954.

———. 1967. *The Mysticism of Paul the Apostle.* Translated by William Montgomery. London: A. & C. Black.

Schweizer, Eduard. 1975. *The Good News according to Matthew.* Translated by David E. Green. Atlanta: John Knox Press.

———. 1984. *The Good News according to Luke.* Translated by David E. Green. Atlanta: John Knox Press.

Smallwood, E. Mary. 1981. *The Jews under Roman Rule.* Leiden: Brill.

Smith, Richard. 1988. "Sex Education in Gnostic Schools." Pp. 345–60 in *Images of the Feminine in Gnosticism,* ed. Karen L. King. Philadelphia: Fortress Press.

Söder, Rosa. [1932] 1969. *Die apokryphen Apostelgeschichten und die romanhafte Literatur der Antike.* Reprint, Darmstadt.

Soelle, Dorothee. 1990. *Thinking about God.* Translated by John Bowden. Philadelphia: Trinity Press International.

———. 1993a. *Stations of the Cross: A Latin American Pilgrimage.* Translated by Joyce Irwin. Minneapolis: Fortress Press.

———. 1993b. *On Earth as in Heaven: A Liberation Spirituality of Sharing.* Translated by Marc Batko. Louisville, Ky.: Westminster John Knox Press.

Stählin, Gustav. 1974. "Das Bild der Witwe. Ein Beitrag zur Bildersprache der Bibel und zum Phänomen der Personifikation in der Antike." *JAC* 17:5–20.

Stegemann, Wolfgang. 1984. "Vagabond Radicalism in Early Christianity? A Historical and Theological Discussion of a Thesis Proposed by Gerd Theissen." In *God of the Lowly: Socio-Historical Interpretations of the Bible,* ed. Willy Schottroff and Wolfgang Stegemann. Maryknoll, N.Y.: Orbis Books.

Stegemann, Wolfgang 1978, cf. Schottroff, Luise/Wolfgang Stegemann 1978 (1986); cf. Schottroff, Willy/Wolfgang Stegemann 1979 (1984), 1980.

Stellungnahme des Prüfungsausschusses der Evangelisch-theologischen Fakultät Tübingen anlässlich der Bitte der Evangelischen Landeskirche in Württemberg um eine gutachtliche Äusserung zu Fragen der Feministischen Theologie (= epd-Dokumentation 52). 1990.

Stier, Fridolin. 1989. *Das Neue Testament übersetzt.* Munich and Düsseldorf.

Stolle, Franz. 1914. *Der römische Legionär und sein Gepäck.* Strassburg.

Strack, Hermann L./Günter Stemberger. 1982. *Einleitung in Talmud und Midrasch.* 7th ed. Munich.

Strahm, Doris/Regula Strobel, eds., 1991 *Vom Verlangen nach Heilwerden. Christologie in feministisch-theologischer Sicht.* Fribourg and Lucerne.

Stuhlmacher, Peter. 1981. *Der Brief an Philemon.* 2d ed. Zurich and Neukirchen.

Sutter Rehmann, Luzia. 1993. " 'Geh, frage die Gebärerin . . .'—Feministischbefreiungstheologische Untersuchungen zum Gebärmotiv in der Apokalyptik." Diss., Kassel.

Tamez, Elsa. 1993. *Gegen die Verurteilung zum Tod. Paulus oder die Rechtfertigung durch den Glauben aus der Perspektive der Unterdrückten und Ausgeschlossenen.* Fribourg.

Taubenschlag, Raphael. 1930. "Das Sklavenrecht im Rechte der Papyri." *Zeitschrift der Savigny-Stiftung für Rechtsgeschichte,* rom. Abt. vol. 50:140–69.

Tellenbach, Hubertus, ed. 1978. *Das Vaterbild im Abendland.* Vol. 1. Stuttgart.

Theissen, Gerd. 1977. *Soziologie der Jesusbewegung* (= *Theologische Existenz heute,* no. 194). Munich. (ET: *Sociology of Early Palestinian Christianity.* Translated by John Bowden. Philadelphia: Fortress Press, 1978.)

———. 1979. *Studien zur Soziologie des Urchristentums.* Tübingen. (ET selections: *Social Reality and the Early Christians: Theology, Ethics and the World of the New Testament.* Translated by Margaret Kohl. Minneapolis: Fortress Press, 1992.)

———. 1987. *The Shadow of the Galilean: The Quest of the Historical Jesus in Narrative Form.* Translated by John Bowden. London: SCM Press.

———. 1989. *Lokalkolorit und Zeitgeschichte in den Evangelien.* Fribourg and Göttingen.

Thierfelder, Helmut. 1963. *Unbekannte antike Welt.* Gütersloh.

Thraede, Klaus. 1977. "Ärger mit der Freiheit. Die Bedeutung der Frauen in Theorie und Praxis der alten Kirche." Pp. 31–182 in Gerta Scharffenorth and Klaus Thraede, *"Freunde in Christus werden . . . ".* Gelnhausen and Berlin.

———. 1980. "Zum historischen Hintergrund der 'Haustafeln' des NT." In *Pietas. Festschrift für Bernhard Költing* (JAC.E 8), ed. Ernst Dassmann and K. Suso Frank.

———. 1987. "Der Mündigen Zähmung: Frauen im Urchristentum." *Humanistische Bildung,* no. 11:93–119.

Thürmer-Rohr, Christina. 1991. *Vagabonding: Feminist Thinking Cut Loose.* Translated by Lise Weil. Boston: Beacon Press.

Thyen, Hartwig. 1978. " ' . . . nicht mehr männlich und weiblich . . . '. Eine Studie zu Galater 3,28." Pp. 107–201 in Frank Crüsemann and Hartwig Thyen, *Als Mann und Frau geschaffen.* Gelnhausen and Berlin.

Tödt, Heinz Eduard. 1959. *Der Menschensohn in der synoptischen Überlieferung.* Gütersloh.

Treggiari, Susan. 1975a. "Family Life among the Staff of Volusii." Pp. 393–401 in *American Philological Association Transactions* 105, ed. Douglas E. Gerber. New York.

———. 1975b. "Jobs in the Household of Lis(v?)ia." *Papers of the British School at Rome* 43:48–77.

———. 1979. "Lower Class Women in the Roman Economy." *Florilegium* 1:65–86. Ottawa.

Troeltsch, Ernst. 1931. *The Social Teaching of the Christian Churches.* Vol. 1. Translated by Olive Wyon. New York: Macmillan Co.

Victor, Ulrich. 1983. *Aristoteles* OIKONOMIKOS. Königstein Ts.

Vogt, Joseph. 1975. "Der Vorwurf der sozialen Niedrigkeit des frühen Christentums." *Gymnasium* 82:401–11.

Wacker, Marie-Theres. 1988. "Gefährliche Erinnerungen. Feministische Blicke auf die hebräische Bibel." Pp. 14–58. in idem, ed., *Theologie feministisch.* Düsseldorf.

Wagener, Ulrike. 1993. "Fusswaschung als Frauen-Dienst im frühen Christentum?" *Schlangenbrut,* no. 40:29–35.

Wahlberg, Rachel. 1957. *Jesus According to a Woman.* New York: Paulist Press.

Wainwright, Elaine Mary. 1991. "Towards a Feminist Critical Reading of the Gospel according to Matthew" (= BZNW 60). Berlin and New York.

Waller, Elizabeth. 1979–1980. "The Parable of the Leaven: A Sectarian Teaching and the Inclusion of Women." *Union Theological Seminary Quarterly Review* 35:99–109.

Walter, Karin. 1988. *Zwischen Ohnmacht und Befreiung. Biblische Frauengestalten.* Freiburg, Basel, and Vienna.

———, ed. 1986. *Frauen entdecken die Bibel.* Freiburg, Basel, and Vienna.

Wartenberg, Bärbel von. 1981. "Kauft keine Früchte der Apartheid. Lernen im Widerstand und im Handeln." Pp. 262–66 in *Eigener Haushalt und bewohnter Erdkreis,* ed. Heinrich Dauber and Werner Simpfendörfer. Wuppertal.

Weder, Hans. 1978. *Die Gleichnisse Jesu als Metaphern* (= FRLANT 120).

Wegener, Hildburg/Hanne Köhler/Cordelia Kopsch, eds. 1990. *Frauen fordern eine gerechte Sprache.* Gütersloh.

Wegner, Judith Romney. 1988. *Chattel or Person? The Status of Women in the Mishnah.* New York and Oxford: Oxford University Press.

Weiss, Johannes. [1910] 1970. *Der erste Korintherbrief.* Reprint, Göttingen.

Welskopf, Elisabeth Charlotte, ed. 1981. *Soziale Typenbegriffe im alten Griechenland und ihr Fortleben in den Sprachen der Welt.* Vols. 3 and 4. Berlin.

Wengst, Klaus. 1987. *Pax Romana and the Peace of Jesus Christ.* Translated by John Bowden. Philadelphia: Fortress Press.

Wiefel, Wolfgang. 1988. *Das Evangelium nach Lukas.* Berlin.

Wikenhäuser, Alfred. 1961. *Die Apostelgeschichte.* 4th ed. Regensburg.

Wilckens, Ulrich. 1978; 1980; 1982. *Der Brief an die Römer.* Parts 1, 2, and 3. Zurich and Neukirchen.

Wilhelm, Friedrich. 1915. "Die oeconomica der neupythagoreer Bryson, Kallikratidas, Periktione, Phintys." *Rhein. Museum* 70:161–223.

Wilken, Robert L. 1986. *Die frühen Christen Wie die Römer sie sahen.* Graz, Vienna, and Cologne..

Windisch, Hans. 1951. *Die katholischen Briefe.* Tübingen.

Wink, Walter. 1987. *Violence and Nonviolence in South Africa: Jesus' Third Way.* Philadelphia: New Society Publishers.

Wire, Antoinette Clark. 1990. *The Corinthian Women Prophets: A Reconstruction through Paul's Rhetoric.* Minneapolis: Fortress Press.

Witzenhauser, Alfred. 1961. *Die Apostelgeschichte.* 4th ed. Regensburg.

Zanker, Paul. 1989. *Die trunkene Alte. Das Lachen der Verhöhnten.* Frankfurt.

Zeller, Dieter. 1984. *Kommentar zur Logienquelle.* Stuttgart.

Zimmer, Gerhard. 1982. *Römische Berufsdarstellungen.* Berlin.

Zscharnack, Leopold. 1902. *Der Dienst der Frau in den ersten Jahrhunderten der christlichen Kirche.* Göttingen.

Index of Scripture
and Other Ancient Writings